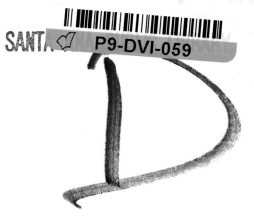

© 2012 by Sally Roth

Rodale books may be purchased for business or promotional use or for special sales. For information, please write to:

Special Markets Department, Rodale Inc., 733 Third Avenue, New York, NY 10017

Printed in the United States of America

Rodale Inc. makes every effort to use acid-free ♾, recycled paper ♻.

Illustrations by Christina Gaugler

Photo credits can be found on page 332.

Book design by Christina Gaugler

Library of Congress Cataloging-in-Publication Data

Roth, Sally.
    Attracting songbirds to your backyard : hundreds of easy ways to bring the music and beauty of songbirds to your yard / Sally Roth.
        p.   cm.
    Includes bibliographical references and index.
    ISBN 978–1–60961–753–0 direct hardcover
    ISBN 978–1–60961–754–7 trade paperback
    1. Bird attracting.   2. Songbirds.   3. Songbirds—Identification.   4. Gardening to attract birds.   5. Birds—Feeding and feeds.   6. Bird watching.   7. Songbirds—Vocalization.   I. Title.
QL676.5.R66827   2012
639.9'78—dc23   2012002302

Distributed to the trade by Macmillan

2   4   6   8   10   9   7   5   3   1   direct hardcover

2   4   6   8   10   9   7   5   3   1   trade paperback

We inspire and enable people to improve their lives and the world around them.
www.rodalebooks.com

To my friends—
wild, feathered, and furred—
of the Buckhorn Canyon

Contents

Part III: Songbird Sanctuary

Introduction

With a Song in My Heart

I was glued to the window on a snowy, bone-chilling day, watching the crowd of birds at the feeder just a few feet away, when the friend with whom I'd been staying offered some sage advice.

"You'd better get your book finished before it's spring."

"Why?"

"Because as soon as it warms up, you're going to want to be outside."

I laughed, because he was right. But what he didn't know was that I wasn't only enjoying watching the birds—I was researching. And from what I was seeing and hearing through the glass, I could tell the season had already turned the corner.

I was new to the Rockies, but I was learning fast. Winter weather lasted forever at 8,000 feet, from what I could tell. Yet no matter how much snow was piling up outside, or how much peanut butter we'd gone through to help our little friends get through the bitterly cold nights—or how much firewood we'd burned to help ourselves do the same—the signs of spring were all around us. A little bird had told me.

"Listen," I urged my friend, putting my ear closer to the glass. "Hear that? The chickadees have started singing."

Pursing my chapped lips, I whistled a feeble imitation of the simple *Fee-bee* song of the black-capped chickadee. The little guy outside paused in the midst of hammering a peanut and cocked his head, wondering if there was a competitor nearby.

"And look—the goldfinches are starting to turn yellow. See that guy that looks sort of blotchy? He's molting. It's spring!"

We both laughed, because it was snowing like crazy out there. But it was true.

And I guess spring fever is contagious. "Robins in another month," my friend said.

Oh boy, robins! I didn't know robins even came up this far into the mountains. Now I had something else to look forward to.

CYCLE OF THE SEASONS

Anticipation may well be my favorite thing in life, and spring is full of it. I stroll the yard with head down, looking for the first green shoots of daffodils and pointy, red-tinged tulips pushing up through the earth. The first new growth on the perennials. The fattening buds of any plant you can name. Every day, there's something new to get excited about. I keep my ears open, too, while I'm puttering around, because the soundtrack changes in spring.

The birds are singing!

It doesn't matter whether we know who those voices belong to. The singing makes us happy. Even folks who don't pay much attention to what's going on outside notice the difference.

"Got up too early this morning," said a friend who lives in town, trying to sound peeved. "Some bird singing right outside the window."

"Oh, nice!"

"Wonder who it was? And why it picked that spot to sing? Kinda made me feel special."

Nope, there's no need to know the name of a singing bird. But knowing who it is that's serenading us sure increases our connection—it's an introduction to a new friend that we can then call by name.

I took a guess. "Little brown bird with reddish purple coloring? Kept singing and singing and singing?"

"How'd you know?!"

"House finches just started singing last week down in town. Heard 'em when I went to the grocery store. And yep, he'll be back—he's claiming his territory and he likes your place."

"Cool!"

You bet it is. Getting to know songbirds is just like learning to garden. We feel a deeper, satisfying connection to nature that makes it more fun to be outdoors in our own backyard. And we learn the rhythms of the seasons, so that we know what to look forward to, what to revel in, and when to say goodbye.

Springtime Treat, Year-Round Pleasure

Birds sing only during breeding season, so their music is a seasonal treat. But what a season it is. Whether it's the simple notes of that first singing chickadee, or the bubbling cascade of a house wren, or the ecstatic carol of an oriole, songbird voices announce that winter is gone and spring is really here. They're a symbol of all the things we love about the season—the time of new beginnings, the warming sun on our shoulders while we putter around the garden, the thrill of finding a bird nest or watching our chubby baby cardinals try their wings.

But singing isn't all there is to songbirds.

Many singers are drop-dead beautiful, as well as talented. Red cardinals and tanagers, orange orioles, yellow goldfinches, green vireos, blue buntings, purple finches—they cover every color of the rainbow and then some.

The best thing about songbirds, though, is that most of them happily share our yards with us. They're around every day, making use of our birdbaths, our feeders, our plants, and raising their families in our birdhouses, bushes, and trees.

In Part I of this book, "The Joy of Songbirds," you'll meet the singers and learn when and why they use their wonderful voices. You'll discover which songbirds are likely to stay year-round, which ones will

most likely move on, and what the miracle of migration is all about. And you'll learn music appreciation—the repertoires of the birds and the best times to book a seat for their concerts at dawn, dusk, and even midnight. You'll find plenty of tips for understanding the behavior of your songbirds, too, so you can make them happy right in your own yard.

THE WAY TO A BIRD'S HEART

Attracting songbirds is different than bringing in other birds, because many songbird species depend heavily on natural foods instead of feeders.

Still, it's food that's the way to their hearts, as many songbirds are changing their habits and learning that feeders mean food. Seeds take a backseat to soft foods, though, as far as many songbirds are concerned. Suet and other fat-based foods mimic their natural diet, which relies on insects, and fruity treats at the feeder supply another favorite part of their menu.

In Part II, "Eat, Drink, and Be Merry," you'll find lots of suggestions for catering to the tastes and to the feeding habits of songbirds of every kind. You'll learn who eats what; what's tried-and-true; and what kinds of foods to experiment with to attract your friends. You'll discover the whole range of commercially made foods and feeders that are tailored to songbirds, and how you can make your own versions of both to save some, ahem, "dough," as well as to enjoy the fun of doing it yourself.

Water is just as big an attraction to songbirds as feeders, and it can attract songbirds that won't even look at the offerings in your feeder (at least, not yet). In Part II, you'll also find out how to put water to work and bring in even more birds, including lovely little wood warblers of a dozen different kinds or more.

SAFE AT HOME

When it comes to coaxing songbirds to stop in, what's in our yards is just as important as what's in our feeders. Cardinals, robins, wrens, and some other species have already adopted backyards as part of their natural habitat, but others are birds of the forest, treetops, or brushy edges, and they're still learning.

Plants, especially trees and shrubs, are absolutely vital for making songbirds feel at home. They provide cover, which is a must for every one of these birds, and plants supply all sorts of natural food, from buds to insects to fruit and berries—foods that can be tricky to duplicate at a feeder, even if we could coax the birds into landing at the tray.

Besides, why would we want to limit ourselves to a feeder when we can enjoy watching a tanager slink among the leaves for caterpillars or a kinglet flutter at the tip of a branch to snatch a bite? Providing the food as nature intended is part of getting to know our songbird friends. And nurturing is just as much of a pleasure when a bluebird family arrives to feed on the fruit of the serviceberry tree we planted, or a band of migrating tanagers and thrushes settles in the dogwood in our yard to choff down berries as fast as they can.

In Part III, "Songbird Sanctuary," you'll find out how to look at your yard from a songbird's point of view, assessing its potential as a nesting place as well as a resting place. Easy tricks in this section (and elsewhere throughout the book) will help you transform your backyard into a place that songbirds can call home.

No need to call in the landscapers, either. You can make these changes with very little money (or none at all) and only a bit of time.

From the simple act of putting up a birdhouse, to shifts in yard care habits such as letting fall leaves stay in place under shrubs, to more ambitious projects like moving foundation shrubs away from the house, this section of the book is jam-packed with ideas that can make a big difference to songbirds seeking sanctuary.

Oh, and let's not forget about pests—Part III will also tell you how to minimize the dangers of predators in your backyard, so that birds can safely raise their young or come for breakfast without fearing they'll be part of the menu. We can't eliminate all dangers, because some are just a natural part of bird life. But we can take steps to help tip the scale in favor of our songbirds.

MAKING A DIFFERENCE

Sometimes it seems like we get the better end of the deal when our yard is filled with songbirds. All year-round, we're given the gift of endless entertainment—the life that these lovely creatures bring to our backyard.

In spring and early summer, we get the pleasure of their music, the thrill of welcoming back the migrants, and the wonder of feeling like part of the family as they raise their young.

When nesting's over, we get to watch the next phase of the cycle, the feasting on berries and fruit in the ripe days of summer, the fueling up for migration, the change in colors as bright breeding plumage gives way to winter outfits.

In fall and winter, we're gratified when our feeders once again take center stage as the insect boom dies down and a handout is eagerly welcomed. We get to feel all warm and fuzzy, knowing that the crowd of birds outside our window is well fed.

Yep, the pleasure is all ours, it sometimes seems. But the fun of attracting and watching songbirds hides a deeper benefit—the difference between their life and death.

Generous food in winter can help birds survive a cold night or an ice storm. But even bigger issues are at stake: habitat destruction and climate change. As wild habitat gets more limited, with destruction at both ends of the journey for migrating songbirds, our backyards become real havens to our little friends. We're filling the gap, supplying food and nesting places.

Climate change is forcing songbirds to adapt, too, because the cycles of the insects they depend on are shifting in response to changing weather patterns. Some songbird species are moving northward in their ranges to try to keep in tune with that vital natural food, while others are moving to higher elevations where the insects' speeded-up schedule is still in sync with their nesting needs.

Bird feeding is a booming pastime with millions of us happily filling feeders, so backyards have now become a reliable food source. With the advent of soft bird foods—such as suet mixtures and doughs that are reasonable facsimiles of nutrition from insects—and with the growing popularity of mealworm feeders, many songbirds are beginning to look to backyards for sustenance.

Let's get ready to welcome them!

PART I

The Joy of Songbirds

CHAPTER 1

Meet the Singers

Whether we're listening to Bach's Brandenburg Concertos or listening to a robin singing in the backyard, music touches us in a place that words alone can't reach. Birdsong tickles our emotions in a way that simply watching a bird at the feeder can never do.

Music is magic that way—it creates a connection that feels personal to every one of us who's listening. And that connection isn't only about the music itself. Just as the smell of cinnamon can make us remember Mom's apple pie, and Mom's kitchen, and Mom herself, everything else connected with the moment we heard the music comes back, too.

Same thing with birdsong: It's uplifting, inspiring, and just as connected to our emotions. And it adds a deeper level of enjoyment of our birds. Their music tells us they're nearby, and it feels like they're talking to us. Whether or not we know who's singing, we can listen to and appreciate the music of our backyard birds.

And when we do learn a few distinctive songs, like the bubbling, joyful waterfall of notes from our house wren, we can greet our little friend personally every time we hear him, as well as when he stops by for a bite of suet.

It may sound corny, but we all know it's true: Listening to a singing bird makes us happy. That is, if we take the time to stop a minute, tilt our heads, and actually listen.

I'm always saying, "Listen! Hear that bird?" to my young friends—and to my not-so-young friends. Often I'll name the bird, the way my own mother used to do when she taught me to pay attention to the little wonders all around us.

The reaction is always the same. No matter how busy our day is, no matter how many tasks are still on that to-do list, we can't help but smile when we stop and listen to a singing bird.

Songbirds are especially beloved among our avian friends, and the better we get to know them, the more we can provide for their needs and encourage them to make their homes in our neighborhoods where we can enjoy their beautiful music. In this chapter, we'll explore some songbird basics. We'll take a look at our own emotional connection with music, and how ornithologists—as well as we backyard bird lovers—decide which birds qualify as singers. We'll examine the reasons behind birdsong, too, and we'll talk about which birds you can expect to hear and when. You'll also find practical tips for bringing more songbird music into your own backyard.

IT'S ALL ABOUT CONNECTION

Many years ago, back when playing vinyl LPs was the way we listened to music, a friend who was cleaning out her record collection gave me an album of birdsongs. "I never play it," she explained. "I'd rather just listen to the birds without trying to figure out who's who."

I happily accepted the gift, took it home to our cabin in the flat Indiana farmland, and put it on top of the three or four LPs already waiting to play on my stereo. Turning the volume low so it

wouldn't interfere with family conversation, I hit the start switch and went to tidying up and cooking dinner.

The music on the stereo was just a pleasant background sound as I worked. Although occasionally I hummed along to a song or two, most of it barely entered my consciousness as I chatted with my family and stirred my pots and pans. Then my friend's album dropped onto the turntable and started to play. The weird, quavering call I heard was soft but unmistakable. And I'd forgotten all about the record.

"Oh my gosh, it's a loon! Listen!" I cried, dropping my spoon and hurrying to open the door so I could get a better listen. "What in the world is a loon doing *here*?"

Duh.

Even after I had finished laughing at myself for being fooled by the recording, my head was still filled with memories of an evening on a lonely lake in the Far North, sunset streaking the still water,

A Matter of Timing
A SINGING VALENTINE

Browse through a box of old greeting cards in an antique shop and you'll notice that doves are a popular theme on valentines, anniversary cards, and other messages of love. Maybe it's because these songbirds are so prone to public displays of affection. "Billing and cooing" is exactly what doves do: avian beak-to-beak kissing, plus plenty of *"Cooo-cooo-coo."*

Mourning doves, and the larger, paler Inca doves that are replacing them in some regions, are early nesters. They begin cooing right around Valentine's Day in many areas; in warmer places, they may breed year-round.

It's easy to attract your own pair of lovebirds. Just pour some cracked corn and millet in a low feeder and add a sturdy, low-level basin of water alongside it.

the white bones of birches against near-black spruces. And the haunting voices of loons.

Loons are hardly backyard songbirds (well, maybe if you live on a lake in the North Woods). But the connection of music and memory works the same way with even a humble robin. Just hearing the first notes of that familiar song evokes the scents, the sounds, the sights of spring, and most of all, the happy feelings of other spring-times in which a singing robin played a part. Music: It's magic.

SONGBIRDS ARE SPECIAL

Songbirds are our nearest and dearest backyard friends. We quickly forge a personal connection with the singers in our backyards: That's our robin singing, our house finch holding forth, our cardinal feeding his mate a sunflower seed, our oriole pausing between bites of a fresh orange to whistle a few notes.

Sure, we love the downy woodpeckers at our suet, too, and all of the other birds who squawk or chirp instead of bursting into lyrical song. But songbirds add something special—the beauty of their music, to be sure, but also because their voices let us know when they're around. Who can resist looking up into the branches when a Baltimore oriole starts to sing? And once a pair of orioles or other songbirds chooses our yard as their home, the daily songfests just strengthen our connection with the happy couple. We're as territorial as birds are, which is why it feels so special when a robin makes its nest in the wreath on our front door, or a family of bluebirds comes to our feeder. Now we can really claim them as our own special backyard friends.

And these delightful birds happily share our yards with us. They're around every day, making

Decorative wreaths on our doors and walls have become prized nest sites for our most familiar and common songbird, the sweet-voiced American robin.

use of our birdbaths, our feeders, our plants, and raising their families in our birdhouses, bushes, and trees.

Even when the season of singing finally comes to an end, songbirds keep their friendship with us. Thanks to new foods on the market or made at home, those songbirds who don't migrate may become year-round neighbors, spending at least part of their day in our yards. Those who do move along to warmer climes will visit our yards to say farewell in fall—and gladden our hearts when they return in spring.

MEET THE GLEE CLUB

The earliest singers are birds we already know. They're year-round residents of our backyards and neighborhoods, part of the crowd that comes to our feeders in every season. In winter, they sample our suet, scratch in our winter gardens, and visit our hollies, hawthorns, and crabapples for berries.

Other singers—including the most musical as well as the most beautiful of our backyard birds, such as thrushes and orioles—arrive later in spring. They're our part-time friends who raise their families with us, but spend winter in warmer places. Some of them winter in our own American South, so, depending on where you live, you may get to enjoy these species even in winter—or all year, in the case of brown thrashers, house wrens, and some other species that roam the South year-round. Other songbirds fly to Mexico or Central or South America, and their return is a welcome part of spring. During migration, songbirds may stop off en route, even if your region isn't part of their nesting or wintering grounds.

The spring migration of the sprightly little birds called wood warblers, for instance, is a yearly late-spring thrill in many regions, even though many of these tiny songbirds are only passing through on their way to nesting grounds in the Far North. Surprise visitors are part of the fun of songbirds, too—individuals may get blown off course by storms on their long journey, or otherwise go far afield, showing up unexpectedly in your backyard.

Not all of our backyard birds are songbirds, though. Some of our year-round birds, as well as some migrant species, hardly sing more than a note or two, let alone a whole melody.

Those who belong to the glee club are something special.

As Thrilling as the First Daffodil

Anticipation is a big part of the joy of songbirds. Their songs are seasonal efforts, not year-round, so hearing those first notes makes our hearts sing, too.

When our black-capped chickadees shift into their two-note love songs—hey, spring is coming! Not only can we look forward to a chickadee family in the birdhouse and fuzzy-headed babies at the feeder, we can also start dreaming about daffodils and all the other glories of spring. That's pretty good for a two-note song.

Trick or Treat

Next time you make a batch of oatmeal cookies—with or without raisins or nuts—pop a few into a zip-top plastic bag for the freezer. When wrens, bluebirds, robins, or thrushes show up in your backyard, crumble the cookies into bits in a feeder for a tempting songbird treat. Native sparrows and juncos like cookies, too.

What Is a Songbird?

Songbird seems like an easy word to define. A bird that sings a pretty song, right?

Not so fast.

The first question to ask is: What is a song?

Music is a matter of taste. What's music to my ears may not be pleasing to yours.

Bach or blues? Yes, please!

Modern jazz or that amazing double-toned Tibetan throat singing? Uh, maybe in small doses.

Hip-hop? Better ask someone younger than me.

It's easy to agree on the super singers among the songbirds. None of us would argue that a wood thrush, say, isn't definitely a songbird. Its voice even resembles the sound of one of our own instruments—the beautiful, breathy sound of a flute.

But what about a killdeer? Its call—crying its own name over and over—is distinctive, all right. But is it music?

Depends on who's listening. To most of us, the answer is no, in the killdeer's case. It's an ear-catching call, to be sure. But it's not a song in the traditional sense of music.

In our own backyards, though, each of us gets to be the music critic, and the judge of who's a songbird and who's not. Who knows? Maybe listening to our birds can even help us gain an appreciation for discordant jazz or Tibetan throat singing, as well as the Baroque beauty of Bach.

Whistle, Warble, Trill, or Buzz?

Music is a matter of taste, so I've used a fairly broad definition of music when deciding which birds to include in this book. You'll find birds with warbling, melodic songs, such as our beloved house wren and American robin. But

A black-headed grosbeak makes a pit stop high in the Rockies during springtime migration, joining a fellow migrant, the gray-headed junco, and a year-round pine siskin.

you'll also find chickadees, phoebes, and other birds whose songs are very simple, as well as some birds with near-monotone trills, like the dark-eyed junco and the chipping sparrow.

Here's how I'd describe the voices of the birds that you will or won't find in this book:

Super singers. These birds are the standouts, with long, complicated, melodic songs. Thrushes and robins, natch; brown thrashers, welcome to the club; indigo buntings, house wrens, finches, rose-breasted grosbeaks, not a doubt.

Subdued singers. You may have to stand just five feet from a brown creeper to hear its sweet little song, but its voice is most definitely melodic. Bluebirds don't sing loudly or long, either, but their lilting voices are simply beautiful.

Two- or three-note singers. If the bird only gives this call in breeding season, it's a song. Chickadees, phoebes, wood peewees—they're all welcome in the songbird circle, even though they're not hugely musical.

Trillers. If a bird makes only a single-note call—think of a downy or hairy woodpecker—sorry, it's not a songbird. But if it rapidly repeats that note, with slight variation in pitch, that turns it into a trill. Now we've got a singer, like a chipping sparrow or junco with its near-monotone trill, or a prairie warbler or hermit warbler with a slightly more musical trill.

Sorry, shriekers and squawkers. Tone of voice matters, too. Birds with nonmusical voices, those that chatter, rattle, scream, or shriek, aren't included in this book unless they also have a musical song up their sleeve. So, yes, you'll find the Carolina wren, because it has a musical song in addition to its rattlesnake-like *chirr*. But, no,

The melodic wood thrush and other songbirds are becoming big fans of feeders.

even though I wanted to stretch it, I just couldn't see calling nuthatches "songbirds."

And, of course, only birds of the backyard. There are no loons in this book, no matter how much I love them. Nor other waterfowl, nor birds of the marshes, deep forests, and other natural places—unless they visit backyards, too.

Science versus Common Sense

Use the word *songbird* around ornithologists, especially taxonomists whose work is classifying birds, and you're likely to see them roll their eyes. They don't define birds that way.

To us bird lovers, the word simply means a bird with a pretty song. But musical talent isn't how birds are classified. Scientists identify them by physical characteristics first—the structure of their body parts—not by the sound of their voices.

Still, voice does enter into it, because the structure of a bird's vocalizing equipment (its syrinx, tongue, and related parts) is one of the factors that taxonomists use to decide which bird belongs in which classification.

But first come the feet.

Check Those Tootsies

In layman's terms, we can think of birds in just two categories: passerines (or perching birds) and nonpasserines.

Members of the order Passeriformes, the passerine birds, have four toes, three pointing forward and one pointing back. That means their legs and feet are adapted to grasp a branch. They're birds that perch. And that category includes a huge majority of our backyard birds, everybody from robins to chickadees to starlings—nearly all of our songbirds, plus a handful of nonmusical types, such as jays and crows.

So who's not a percher? Picture how your backyard birds move about at your feeders or on your trees, and you'll quickly realize that nuthatches and woodpeckers have a much different way of hanging on: They cling. Sorry, fellas—you just don't have the right kind of feet to be passerines, which means you can't scientifically be called songbirds.

Hummingbirds, swallows, martins, and swifts aren't passerines, either. Neither are hawks, owls, ducks, herons, and other birds who are distinctly different from our songbirds in body structure. Even though their toes may be arranged in passerine fashion, they get put in their own orders because of other, bigger differences. But for our purposes we can lump them all together as *nonpasserines*. And, according to ornithologists, nonpasserines aren't songbirds.

Suborder: Singers

Taxonomists, who are way more orderly than I'll ever be, divided the perching passerines into two suborders: One they dubbed the Oscines; the

Listen and Learn
Singing = Songbird

We backyard bird lovers can take a more casual approach to deciding which species is a songbird and which isn't: If it sings, it's a songbird. We can simply use our ears, instead of being sticklers about scientific classification.

Even though taxonomists don't classify them as songbirds, some nonpasserine birds are wonderful singers. Listen to the warble of a purple martin, tree swallow, or brown creeper. Tilt your head and cup your ears to catch the ethereal tinkling notes of a horned lark or woodcock performing its courtship flight high overhead.

And some of the official songbirds, the Oscine passerine "singing birds," are no great shakes at making music, such as:

- Jays, who mostly employ a harsh shriek rather than a soothing song.
- Cedar waxwings, whose voices are soft, high, single-note whistles. Elegant birds, yes; singers, uh, not exactly.
- Crows and ravens may sound musical to Edgar Allan Poe, but to us? *Squawrk!* Not so much.
- Flycatchers, who typically repeat a simple phrase that is more declarative than melodic. (A few flycatchers, though, have lovely, albeit simple, songs.)

Songbird or Not?

I started with this rule of thumb when deciding which birds are true songbirds: Does the bird have a different song in breeding season than it does the rest of the year? If the answer was yes, then I became judgmental: Could that breeding-season song, no matter how simple, be called musical? Yes? Yay, we've got a songbird! Here's who made the cut, and why.

STYLE OF VOCALIZING	BACKYARD BIRDS WITH THAT STYLE	IS IT A SONGBIRD?
Long, melodic song	American robin, black-headed grosbeak, blue grosbeak, brown creeper, brown thrasher, buntings, canyon wren, finches, gray catbird, horned lark, house wren, kinglets, northern mockingbird, pine grosbeak, rock wren, rose-breasted grosbeak, song sparrow, tanagers, most thrushes, vesper sparrow, winter wren, woodcock	YES
Short, often repeated songs made up of melodic notes	Bluebirds, Carolina and Bewick's wrens, northern cardinal, white-throated and other native sparrows, some thrushes, vireos, some wood warblers (including the black-throated green warbler, yellow warbler, and others)	YES
Two- or three-note phrase, repeated; breeding season only	Chickadees, cuckoos, doves, phoebes, titmice, towhees	YES
Trills; breeding season only	Chipping sparrow, grasshopper sparrow, juncos, many wood warblers	YES
Same song (or call) year-round; no musical song at breeding season	Cedar waxwing, downy and other woodpeckers, flickers, hummingbirds, killdeer, nuthatches, swallows, swifts	NO
Nonmusical chatter	Many flycatchers, magpies, tyrant kingbirds	NO
Shrieks and squawks	Crows, jays, ravens	NO

other, the Suboscines (now called Tyranni). And now we're talking voice. Or—sorry!—to be scientifically precise, not the voice itself, but the structure of the vocal apparatus.

Oscine comes from the Latin *oscen,* meaning "singing bird." Songbirds, according to scientists, are those birds with perching feet and the right vocal structure to be able to sing. And the Oscines suborder includes every passerine—hundreds of species—except for the handful of birds known as tyrant flycatchers (the non-Oscines, or suborder Tyranni), which have a different vocalizing structure.

Okay, I'll give the classifiers that. Because even though the scientists were looking, not listening, birds' vocal structures sure seem to make a difference in the quality of the sound. Tyrant flycatchers—think of a loudmouth kingbird or great crested flycatcher—are shriekers, not singers. But just because Oscine birds have the right equipment to be able to sing, making them "songbirds" by scientific classification, it doesn't mean they're equally talented musically. A lot of those Oscine birds would never get far on *American Idol.* Some sing sweetly, some squawk, some barely make a peep. I can hear the judges turning them down now: "You may have the right equipment, but your song choice is all wrong."

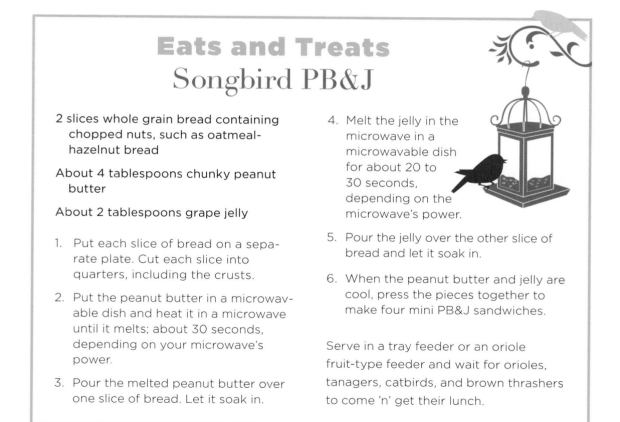

Eats and Treats
Songbird PB&J

2 slices whole grain bread containing chopped nuts, such as oatmeal-hazelnut bread

About 4 tablespoons chunky peanut butter

About 2 tablespoons grape jelly

1. Put each slice of bread on a separate plate. Cut each slice into quarters, including the crusts.

2. Put the peanut butter in a microwavable dish and heat it in a microwave until it melts; about 30 seconds, depending on your microwave's power.

3. Pour the melted peanut butter over one slice of bread. Let it soak in.

4. Melt the jelly in the microwave in a microwavable dish for about 20 to 30 seconds, depending on the microwave's power.

5. Pour the jelly over the other slice of bread and let it soak in.

6. When the peanut butter and jelly are cool, press the pieces together to make four mini PB&J sandwiches.

Serve in a tray feeder or an oriole fruit-type feeder and wait for orioles, tanagers, catbirds, and brown thrashers to come 'n' get their lunch.

Listen and Learn
An Extraordinary Effort

It's hard to tell where a robin's long song begins and ends, because there's barely a heartbeat's pause between the musical phrases. Other songbirds' melodies are easier to quantify, because their songs are distinctly self-contained.

Take the red-eyed vireo, for example, a small, greenish bird that mostly goes overlooked—except when he's singing.

One of the most abundant vireos, even though its population has declined dramatically in the past half-century, this little bird's song still rings out from seemingly everywhere in spring. It's easy to count the repetitions because of the pauses between his high, warbling phrases—if you have the patience. Which I do not.

Luckily, scientists at Cornell University's Lab of Ornithology have done the job.

How many times a day does the red-eyed vireo sing?

Twenty thousand, says Cornell.

No wonder our yards resound with birdsong in spring. Even a half-dozen singers will make the air come alive with the soundtrack of spring.

Come to think of it, you and I have the same vocal structure as Maria Callas or Pavarotti. I don't know about you, but I don't plan on stepping onto the concert stage anytime soon. But the point is, we can appreciate fine singers—of any species, order, or suborder—whether scientists consider them technically songbirds or not.

THE POWER OF SONG

Once the urge to sing sets in, songbirds can't stop. It's as if the switch that's been thrown in response to the sun simply has no off position.

Look up into a tree in late spring, when birds are moving through on migration, and you'll see songbirds checking leaves, topside and bottom, foraging for insects after a long night of flight, fueling up for the next leg of the journey. Does that slow down their singing? Not a bit.

From sinuous, slow-moving tanagers to hyperactive wood warblers and vireos, the birds barely pause between bites of bugs, but they still manage to burst into song every few seconds. That spells hours and hours of endless performance.

Ever have laryngitis, when your voice comes out as a squeak or a croak or maybe even nothing at all? That disconcerting affliction occurs when the larynx—the sound-making organ that sits at the top of your windpipe, or trachea—gets irritated and inflamed, so air can't pass through it. All mammals share our own structure of sound-making machinery, no matter whether they talk, moo, bark, or meow.

But birds are different. Their sound-making organ is called the *syrinx*, and it sits at the bottom of their trachea, not the top. As the bird breathes, membranes on each side of the syrinx move, causing the organ to vibrate and make a sound. What kind of sound? That depends on how fast and hard the bird exhales. What's more, some of our talented songbirds can work each side of the trachea independently—so the bird can sing two notes at once. Try that sometime!

Just listen to that favorite spring harbinger, your own backyard robin. He's already holding forth in the pre-dawn dimness, before we lift our heads from our pillows, and he keeps going strong all day, taking only short breaks during the concert. Next day, and day after and day after, he's back at it before sunrise. Hmm, maybe we should add soothing throat lozenges to our feeder treats?

Why Do Birds Sing?

No matter which bird is singing, the lyrics are the same. "Here I am," the male cardinal or finch or bunting proclaims, over and over. Singing attracts attention, and not only from us. A potential mate may be listening to that solo. So might a competitor. That kind of audience is just what the songster wants. He's hoping his vocalizing will sound better than that of all others of his kind, at least to the ears of one female. And he's warning away the other male birds of his species, by announcing that he's bigger, stronger, smarter, handsomer, has a better home to offer, and is in all other ways superior to them. After all, his indefatigable song proves it.

Listen and Learn
Diminishing Returns

Birdsong is at its peak when birds are establishing territories and pairing with mates. Migrants come in singing almost constantly, all day long.

If you have nesting birds in your backyard, you'll notice that their songs take a sudden dip in frequency once the eggs are laid. The male doesn't need to worry about another male stealing his mate, because she's now sitting pretty. He still greets the morning with song, but during the day, he stays closer to her to guard the nest, instead of reinforcing the perimeters of his territory by singing. Once the babies hatch, there's even less time for frequent songfests—the parents are consumed with collecting food.

The more plants you add to your yard, the more inviting it becomes to songbirds in all seasons. More plants mean more insects, more seeds and berries, more cover—and more nesting birds. Vary the heights of the plants to attract more species.

Persistence Pays

Repetition hammers home the "I'm a great catch!" message in birdsong. Females pay more attention to males that sing most frequently, so these guys win a mate faster than others of their kind. Singing is also a clue to the male's health and fitness as a provider. Birds who are in fine fettle sing better and more often—another big plus when a female is deciding which partner to choose.

In most species of songbirds, it's the male who selects a breeding territory, even before he has a partner. He chooses it by one simple guideline: Will it generously support a family? That means food, and plenty of it. Studies show that males who sing most persistently hold the prime real estate. Their extra fervor announces that they've nabbed a prime spot with superabundant food (which powers their singing). Females respond quickly to these braggarts because the extra food boosts their chances of a successful nest.

Hey, That's Mine!

Claiming a territory is just as big a reason for singing as claiming a mate. Without a suitable place to call home, the next generation won't succeed. It takes a few weeks, though, before courtship moves along to the commitment phase and the happy couple chooses its homesite. Meanwhile, our songbirds are singing away, even if they're only traveling through our backyards on their way to farther homes.

Once a male songbird selects its territory, it makes sure every other bird of its kind knows where the boundaries are. That sweetly singing rose-breasted grosbeak? Once he's chosen a territory with his partner, he's actually posting big, mean, NO TRESPASSING signs with his lovely melody.

First Line of Defense

Physical fighting takes a lot of precious energy, and a sharp beak can inflict wounds that may even be fatal. That's another reason for birdsong: It's the male's first line of defense, intended to deter actual combat.

Often, a skirmish erupts when a male bird blunders into an area that's already been claimed. That's when you'll hear a snatch of song accompanied by a quick rush of flight meant to

(continued on page 18)

Wren Window Feeder

Materials

Nail, ice pick, or awl

Plastic soda bottle, 20-ounce, rinsed, no cap

Sharp knife

2 strong magnets, such as those sold for hobbyist builders, capable of supporting about 6 ounces of weight or more; you'll find magnets at hobby shops or from suppliers in the Resources section of this book

Raw peanuts or pecans, chopped

Method

1. Using the nail, ice pick, or awl, poke several holes in the bottom of the soda bottle for drainage holes. If your bottle has rounded "feet," poke the holes into the lowest point of them.

2. Cut off the bottom of the soda bottle with a sharp knife, to make a saucer about 1½ inches deep. That's all there's to it!

3. Now, call a helper to mount the feeder; it's a simple operation, but one that's much easier with two people. Each person takes a magnet. With one person standing outside the window holding the feeder against the glass, and the other person inside, carefully match up your magnets. Hang onto your magnets tightly, as they're powerful—don't let them hit the window with a bang that may break the glass.

4. Fill the feeder with chopped nuts, and enjoy the Carolina or Bewick's wrens that will soon be investigating.

Get to Know Your Songbirds
Northern Cardinal

Most of the songbirds at our feeder are looking a little tired and worn by the time late winter rolls around. Their feathers may show frayed edges or faded colors, or the muted plumage they wear outside of breeding season.

Not so with cardinals. These spectacular redbird males seem to get brighter day by day. Could it be only our imaginations? Maybe it's the contrast of red feathers against a snowy landscape that makes these songbirds look so vivid?

Nope, our eyes aren't deceiving us. Cardinals do indeed get redder as winter moves along. But it's not because they're growing fresh feathers, as we might suspect. It's because their old feathers are wearing out.

When male cardinals molt at the end of breeding season—a process that takes several weeks—their new feathers come in tinged with gray on top and around the edges. Take a close look at a cardinal around Halloween, and you'll see what I mean. As the bird moves among branches and does other birdy stuff, the gray on its feathers gradually wears away. The subtle color change generally escapes our notice until one day in late winter, when we finally notice that our redbird suddenly looks very, very red.

Other color changes are happening, too, but you'll have to look even harder. Juvenile birds, which first resemble females in feather color, change the color of their bills as well as the color of their feathers. Their gray-black bills brighten to orange their first winter, and then to the same

By late winter, the cardinal is so red, he almost glows.

bright red-orange as their parents' beaks in spring.

Cardinals have a couple of idiosyncrasies: one physical, and one, shall we say, psychological. First, they're prone to bald heads. This is a lot weirder looking than it sounds, because the exposed skin is often blue. Plus, that distinctive pointy crest and black mask are part of what makes a cardinal a cardinal.

When its head feathers fall out, we've got a bird like we never saw at our feeder before. It eats like a cardinal, it eats what cardinals like to eat, it has a beak like a cardinal, but it sure doesn't look like a cardinal. Is it a cardinal that somehow crossed with a bluebird? Some sort of parrot? It's hard to tell, but we know it's gotta be a rare bird, indeed.

Many folks believe that a bald-headed cardinal is simply going through a natural molt. That may be, but more often, the loss of all head feathers at once indicates a parasite problem. Usually, it clears up quickly, and the bird soon starts to sprout pinfeathers (which look an awful lot like hair plugs) that soon lengthen to cover its bald pate.

As for the personality quirk, male cardinals are notorious for fixating on imaginary adversaries. All it takes is a glimpse of their own reflections in a window, a car mirror, or any other shiny surface, and they seem to slide into instant obsession. A bird may return frequently to that spot to do battle, even if the light is different and he can no longer see his "opponent."

After nesting season ends, the hormones die down, and that behavior usually subsides. But a few individuals carry it to extremes, continuing their attacks long past breeding season. Cardinals have been known to take up the battle again the following spring, too, after a winter of détente.

When to see them: Year-round

What to feed them: Black sunflower seed is the staple, but to really win their loyalty, offer them safflower seed and shelled raw peanuts, too.

Other ways to attract them: A pedestal birdbath will attract thirsty cardinals looking for a safe place to sip and splash. Plant a patch of safflowers and sunflowers for fall and winter foraging.

What they sound like: Loud, clear, whistled song, with a refrain of *What cheer! Cheer! Cheer!*

What to watch for: Cardinals are one of the most common backyard nesters, building their sturdy cupped nests in twiggy shrubs such as lilac, barberry, and burning bush, or in climbing roses, dense vines, and hedges. Watch for the birds carrying slim sticks at nest-building time, so you can pinpoint the location of their nests.

Cowbirds often parasitize cardinal nests; if that baby looks like a big gray blob instead of a young cardinal and has a loud, demanding voice, it's an impostor.

Singing helps a male rose-breasted grosbeak avoid physical confrontations.

A perceived challenge can drive a male songbird into a frenzy. Here, a yellow warbler attacks his own reflection in a car mirror.

scare away the intruder. When the competitor has been driven off, usually in a matter of seconds, the territorial bird will reinforce the message by singing from his boundary line, as if to say, "And stay out!"

Sometimes, bird fights are more serious. If a determined interloper doesn't get the hint by song alone or by a surprise rush, the birds may tangle in fisticuffs, pecking viciously at each other. Science suggests that such fights may occur because the defender's song is perceived as weaker than normal, which the competitor will take as an opening to show his own strength. The prize? The vanquished bird's mate and territory.

'Roid Rage

Hormone levels are low in birds outside of the breeding season. But when spring nears, the surge of hormones hits male birds like a tidal wave. All of a sudden, our mild-mannered cardinal or quiet catbird turns into a crazed warrior, attacking not only other males of his kind, but also his own image.

In male humans who pump up their bodies with testosterone-like steroids, the side effect of heightened aggression is called 'roid rage. Similar hormones fuel the fever in birds, and some behave just as irrationally as the amped-up human males. Any reflective surface may become a potential foe, if the bird catches a glimpse of himself in it. And once he thinks an enemy lurks in that object, he'll continue the attack, even when his reflection isn't visible.

Windows are a popular target, but I've also seen birds fixated on the side mirrors of cars, the shiny wheels of vehicles, and even the brass kick plate at the bottom of a front door. They fly at the offending object over and over, battering it with their wings, pecking and attacking.

Save your birds from battering themselves silly with their obsession by hiding the reflection with a cover of some kind, such as an old sheet or curtain tacked on the outside of a window, or use a washable paint on smaller reflective objects. If it's your car they've declared the enemy, simply park it elsewhere for a while.

Pure Joy

I'm a romantic at heart, which is why my favorite interpretation of birdsong is that some of it is simply pure joy. How else to explain singing that doesn't seem to be related to defense or to attracting a female?

Some scientists spurn any description of animal behavior that seems *anthropomorphic*—related to our own emotions. Birds don't "love" or "adore" a certain food: They eat it avidly, perhaps. Since we all know that "love" or "adore" simply indicates a strong preference, I see nothing wrong with that kind of language.

But when it comes to guessing what a bird is "feeling," I look to the birds themselves for help in figuring out an interpretation of their behavior. And birdsong is a toughie. Oh, sure, I can see that singing is used for courtship and for defense of a mate and territory. But some of that serenading—well, to me, it seems like some of it must be for joy alone.

In 2000, clarinetist David Rothenberg of the New Jersey Institute of Technology and author of *Why Birds Sing*, began making music with the birds at the National Aviary in Pittsburgh. They responded to his clarinet, even singing duets with him as he played. Rothenberg surmised it was the shared beauty of music that inspired the

Listen and Learn
He Said, She Said

It's a man's world for most songbird species—only males do the singing. But there are some exceptions in which both sexes sing. One of them is a common and abundant songbird that may be nesting in your backyard right now: the house finch. Another, researchers recently announced, is the American robin.

You won't find female songbirds using their voices to aggressively define boundaries or defend a territory. Instead, they sing endearingly to their mates—or to themselves. And they don't vocalize nearly as often, or as loudly, as their partners.

If you want to hear the sweet little concert of the streaky brown female house finch, just put up a hanging basket or two of annual flowers on your porch. Sheltered under the roof to ward off rain, these baskets are often a favorite site for this happy singer to tuck her nest.

birds, although it's practically impossible to measure motivation, of course.

Biologists are beginning to jump on the bandwagon of joy, too. Researchers at the RIKEN Brain Science Institute in Japan discovered that singing causes a release of dopamine in male bird brains. Dopamine stimulates the reward centers in the brain, the pleasure receptors—in essence, making the birds happy.

I, too, like to think that sometimes songbirds are simply singing with the joy of the morning. "Life is good," they warble. And we, feeling our hearts lift at their song, feel the same.

QUALITY, NOT QUANTITY

Every year, from about Valentine's Day until nearly Mother's Day, I thrill to the sight of an ever-growing group of goldfinches at my feeders. And I brag about it. "Twenty goldfinches," I announce proudly when the first of the flock shows up to spend hours cracking through niger seed.

When someone asks me who's at my feeder a few weeks later, I can practically feel my chest puff with pride as I run down the list, finishing with a casual, "Oh, and about a hundred goldfinches now."

By the time the lilacs are blooming, the finch flock may number 200 or even 300 birds, as long as I don't run out of seeds. Sign of success? Well, sort of.

Watching your feeders attract more and more birds feels like a real pat on the back, and it is. Their presence says you've got the right foods, the right feeders, and the right surroundings to attract their attention. But when it comes to songbirds, the real sign of success is not necessarily a multitude of birds in your backyard.

Special Birds

Most songbirds don't congregate in big groups, like goldfinches do when it's not nesting season. Instead, orioles, tanagers, wrens, and other friends visit our yards singly or as a pair. Bluebirds may stop by as a couple, but often they're part of a small family group.

With songbirds, it's quality, not quantity, that counts the most. A hundred goldfinches or a single indigo bunting? Why, I'll take both, thank you!

We want a variety of birds in our yards—an oriole or two, a few rose-breasted grosbeaks passing through, a sleek brown thrasher, a pair of perky wrens, and anybody else that we can manage to attract. And we want at least a few pairs who decide to call our place home when it's time to raise a family.

As for my giant gang of goldfinches? While these small songbirds are happy to gorge on my niger seed, they depart without a fare-thee-well when it's time for the flock to break up and go their separate ways to their nesting territories.

Even though goldfinches usually shun my yard as a nest site—probably because I don't have any thistle patches near my in-town house—I'm happy to report that those who live nearby still come to eat, drink, and be merry in my backyard, even in nesting season.

YEAR-ROUND REGULARS

American goldfinches and house finches are two of the most common feeder species, wherever we may live. They range across the entire country, from sea to shining sea, sharing feeder space with other year-round backyard birds, such as downy woodpeckers, jays, cardinals, mourning doves, and nuthatches.

It's All Connected

THANK A DANDELION

Even though dandelions have only been in America for about 300 years, our native songbirds depend on them as a source of abundant seeds. Those sunny yellow blooms turn to round puffs of parachute seeds right in time to nourish the boom of migrating goldfinches in spring, and boy oh boy, do the finches flock to them. Indigo buntings and white-crowned sparrows, which are on the move about the same time as goldfinches, seek out the seeds, too, as do other native sparrows.

The "perfect lawn" idea didn't take root in America until about the 1950s. Before that, dandelions were just part of the picture, adding beauty and character to the green sweep of grass. Personally, I'd like to see dandelion puffs in every yard, but I know I'm a weirdo that way.

If the thought of attracting a bevy of beautiful singers isn't enough for you to let a scattering of dandelions grow in your lawn, try planting a patch of dandelions as a container garden or in a window box. Just cover a few seed puffs with a sprinkling of soil, and by next spring you'll have a crop of sunny yellow—first of flowers and then of goldfinches.

Come spring, some of those common friends at the feeder begin to show another side of their personality. Almost overnight, they transform into songbirds. One by one, the goldfinches and house finches, as well as other year-round feeder regulars, respond to the lengthening days by breaking into song. At first, their opening notes are tentative. But as the season moves along, their songs grow stronger, and we get to enjoy a different aspect of our "ordinary" birds.

You won't hear those musical tones from your woodpeckers, nuthatches, or jays, though. Although their vocalizations may intensify or change somewhat in spring, melodic singing isn't their strong point.

Lend an ear to your feeder scene, and you'll notice the following familiar songbirds—among the most common and abundant feeder species across the country—begin to break into song as breeding season approaches:

Cardinal	Finches
Chickadees	Song sparrow
Doves	Titmice

THE CHANGING SCENE

I guess it's true for birds as well as men: The way to their hearts is through their stomachs. Millions of us have taken up feeding birds, and store shelves are brimming with all sorts of new bird foods. As songbirds discover those goodies and embrace using feeders, the cast of characters in our backyards is changing.

Bluebirds, for instance, were once pretty much

Mealworms are the magic feeder offering that may tempt bluebirds into calling your backyard home.

anymore. Nowadays, bluebirds recognize feeders as the source of yummy mealworms, soft doughs, and other foods they adore. They no longer wait for a wintry blast to become regular visitors. And they travel much farther afield than they once did, to include our feeding stations in their daily foraging trips. Bluebirds have become feeder regulars. And if we live within their nesting range, they often visit our backyards year-round, so we get to enjoy their singing as well as their beauty.

It's not only bluebirds that are looking to us for sustenance. Wrens, wood warblers, and other songbirds are changing their habits, too.

Welcome, newcomers! New birds are here. They've learned—or are learning fast—that feeders mean a reliable and tempting source of sustenance. And some of them are staying through the winter, instead of moving southward. But the best news of all? These newcomers are songbirds.

That's all the more reason to expand our feeder offerings in every season, with foods that will tickle the fancy of our new friends. You'll find plenty of recommendations and recipes, as well as tips and tricks for making your yard

a rarity at feeders, visiting only in snow or ice storms. In milder seasons, they happily feasted on natural foods. And even in winter, they limited their forays to backyards that were very near their wild habitat, so most of us never got a glimpse of those blue feathers at our feeders. Not

Trick or Treat

A dish of dried mealworms is one of the best ways to grab the attention of songbirds in any season. Mealworms cost more than birdseed, but they're worth it, because they draw in birds that might otherwise not visit your feeder.

Dole them out—about a tablespoon each morning—until your target birds become accustomed to looking in that feeder for their treat. Then increase the serving, if you like. Even in modest amounts, mealworms (or wax- and wireworms; see Chapter 10 for more about insect foods) will keep songbirds hooked.

more appealing to them, in later chapters. Meanwhile, keep an eye out for newcomers in your yard at any time of year, but especially in winter, when natural food is scarcer in the wild. And listen for the lovely voices of these songbirds, which winter in the U.S., to join your backyard chorus as spring draws near: American robin, bluebirds, brown thrasher, common yellowthroat, gray catbird, wrens, and the yellow-rumped warbler.

SEASONAL TREATS

I always feel a little disloyal to my year-round songbird friends when the super singers arrive back on the scene. That doesn't mean I don't love my regulars, though. In the winter doldrums, when February seems like it's going to last five years, the first sweet, soft song of a chickadee is as welcome as a dose of sunshine. I love hearing the robins begin singing all over the neighborhood, too, a few weeks later, and I'll give myself a stiff neck looking up at a male house finch pouring his heart out and posturing to catch his mate's eye on a branch above my head.

But as soon as I catch the first notes of a Baltimore oriole on a morning in May—well, I'm as helpless to resist as a roomful of men are when a blonde in a red dress walks in. My head swivels

The springtime arrival of Baltimore orioles, usually around apple-blossom time, is cause for celebration. Dish out the grape jelly!

toward the sound, my eyes strain to catch sight of the soloist, and I hurry to grab the oranges and grape jelly to lure the oriole from the treetops. Welcome to the glories of spring migration, when the super singers come in.

Just like our year-round friends, seasonal songbirds are also learning that backyards are a fine place to settle, whether it's only for a rest stop or—fingers crossed—for the entire season.

Meet the Migrants

Look and listen for these master singers in your yard during migration, which generally peaks from April through May. Some of them are bound to become regulars. With luck, they may even become nesting residents for the spring-to-summer season.

Buntings	Tanagers
Grosbeaks	Thrushes
Kinglets	Vireos
Orioles	Wood warblers

Ready and Waiting

Attracting migrant songbirds is a little different from garnering the attention of our usual backyard birds, but food is still the first place to start. You'll also want to make sure that other attrac-

Insects on foliage and flowers are the main attraction for many migrant songbirds, including the ruby-crowned kinglet, whose big voice belies his diminutive size. Soft-food and nectar feeders may keep him around.

tions, including water and sheltering plants, are ready and waiting.

- Be sure your bird food larder is well stocked with their favorite treats—soft foods, mealworms, fruits, and sweets.

- Water is as much of a temptation as food is to birds that have been traveling for hundreds, even thousands, of miles.

- The plantings in your yard are important to these guys, too, because you'll want them to feel safe enough to approach your feeder and birdbath, as well as to linger in your yard, and maybe even make a nest.

In later chapters of this book, you'll find all the details you'll need to draw in every migrant that comes your way.

A Bouquet of Bugs

Flowering crabapples and Bradford pears bloom at the perfect time to greet returning migrant songbirds. But it's not the pretty, fragrant cloud of bloom that the birds appreciate: They flock to the flowers for the zillions of tiny insects at the blossoms. At bloom time, you may see more than a dozen species of wood warblers, vireos, and orioles snatching insects as fast as they can.

For about $20, you can buy a tree that will bloom—with at least a few clusters of flowers—the first year you plant it. Plant it in an existing flowerbed of perennials, where it will soon provide nest sites and perching places as well as a feast—first of insects, and later of fruit—for your favorite songbirds.

CHAPTER 2

Here Comes the Sun

The birthday of one of my longtime friends—a pessimist by nature—falls on December 21. "Born on the shortest, darkest day of the year," he always says, feeling sorry for himself.

"You've got the best birthday of all!" I retorted last year, when we met to celebrate. "Hey, it's the day the sun comes back! After this, the days get longer instead of shorter. Who isn't happy to see that?" I wasn't trying to give him a pep talk; I was just telling the truth.

The winter solstice, which falls either on December 21 or December 22 from year to year, is a terrific cause for celebration. Our hemisphere of this good old planet now starts tilting toward the sun, instead of turning its back on it. Oh boy! Spring is coming! Any day now—okay, in a few weeks, that is—the birds will start singing.

SEX AND REAL ESTATE

"In the Spring a livelier iris changes on the burnish'd dove; In the Spring a young man's fancy lightly turns to thoughts of love," wrote Alfred Lord Tennyson in his poem "Locksley Hall."

That's putting it delicately.

In the spring, the burnish'd dove, the crimson-breasted robin, and all the other birds Tennyson put in his poem, as well as a young man or two, go

Listen for your chickadees to add a sweet, short song to their *dee-dee-dees*, and you'll know that spring is coming. This singer is a mountain chickadee.

a little nuts. We may have a veneer of civilization, but we're still animals at heart. And spring brings out the beast.

Blame it on the light. Little by little, as the days start getting longer, our winter-dulled spirits begin to lift. We start to feel happier and more energetic, less crabby and blue. And soon, young men—and young women, and not-so-young men and women—start showing signs of the boost in hormones that comes with the season. Sex hormones. The change in light sets off a signal that reverberates throughout the animal world: Breeding season is on the horizon.

Because we humans can breed all year 'round, the chemical signal isn't as strong in us as it is in birds, which have to cram family life into just a few months. Birds begin responding in a big way almost as soon as their part of the world turns toward the sun. Their brains start producing the hormones that set off all the behavior of the coming season—the breakup of companionable winter flocks, the male aggression, the tender wooing. It's all about sex.

But right along with it goes real estate. Male birds have to choose and establish a nesting territory, a place where there's plenty of food and appropriate homesites. And they have to defend that area from competitors—fighting to the death, if necessary. Yep, fierce urges, for sure. And it all starts with singing.

WARMUP ACT

It's a joy to listen to orioles, thrushes, tanagers, and all of the other migrants who return once spring is on firm footing. But even more precious are the brave songbirds who start tuning up when we're still struggling through the last dregs of winter. They may not be the super singers that will come later. But their simple efforts are as big a thrill as the first crocus—and they blossom forth even earlier.

Remember our winter solstice celebration? Here's another reason to make merry: Soon after that auspicious date, you'll hear the first tentative phrases of birdsong. No matter where you live and no matter what species of chickadees are nibbling at your feeder, you'll find that they are usually the earliest singers.

Their songs aren't much compared to the super singers that are still on winter vacation in the tropics. But, like the very first crocus, those few simple notes are even more welcome than the later full-throated chorus. After a fall and winter filled with *Chick-a-dee-dee-dee,* or whatever variation the species in your neighborhood says, you'll start hearing a different sound—the chickadee's song. *Fee-bee,* whistles the black-capped; its Carolina and mountain relatives chime in with similar versions of the song, but with more syllables.

Titmice start singing early, too, as if not to be outdone by their chickadee cousins. They too have a very simple song, but it's much louder: a clear, whistled *Peter!* from the tufted titmouse, and variations of that from the bridled, oak, and plain titmice.

Other year-round birds soon join in with their own brand of music-making, so keep your ears open. Even though it still feels like winter, these

First Seven Singers

Listen for the songs of these common backyard birds as a welcome signal that winter is drawing to an end. The birds usually begin singing in about this order, although your individuals may make their own adjustments to the schedule.

BIRD	SONG
Chickadees	Two or a few clear, simple, whistled notes, interspersed with typical chickadee calls and quick, gurgled phrases
Titmice	Loud, clear, high whistle, usually two notes; repeated after a moderately long pause
European starling	Long, complicated, musical song, often punctuated with skreeks and other nonmusical notes
Doves	Low, quiet cooing; the mourning dove sings *Ah-coo-coo-cooo;* the Inca dove, *Uh-COO-coo*
Song sparrow	Sweet, high *Seet seet seet* and then a trilled *Zeeeee*
House finch	Long, high, warbling, musical song
Northern cardinal	Loud, clear, whistled phrases, *What cheer cheer cheer cheer,* at first limited to perhaps a single *Cheer,* and then continuing at length as hormone levels increase

early birds let us know that the season is changing. And that means that, before we know it, the flood of migrants will begin. First it's a trickle, as our friendly house wrens, skulking thrashers, and other early birds return. And then it becomes a deluge, as migrant songbirds from the Tropics, such as rose-breasted grosbeaks, scarlet tanagers, and red-eyed vireos, move in.

Cure for Winter Blahs

About the time that it begins to feel as if Old Man Winter will never give up his grip, when you can't bear to hear the news that another snowstorm is on its way, try some songbird therapy. Just step outside in the morning and listen to the birds in your backyard. Ten minutes or so may do the trick, although an hour is even better. The earliest birds sing sporadically instead of continually, so the longer you can spend listening, the better.

Listen to your chickadees, for instance, those active little guys that have livened up your feeder scene for months. Although we don't usually think of them as songbirds, they are indeed, and late winter is when they start singing. Just when we need it most!

I CAN SEE THE LIGHT

It's no secret that birds start singing as the days grow longer. Poets have written about it, farmers have planted by it, cityfolk and countryfolk alike have thrilled to it. But exactly how and why it happens has remained a matter of mystery until just the past few years.

Now, thanks to the wonders of gene analyzing techniques, we know exactly what takes place in those little bird brains. A bird's fancy "lightly turns to thoughts of love"? Not hardly. Birds are at the mercy of a chemical process that's unstoppable. Ordained by evolution, and initiated by the lengthening light, the bath of chemicals in their brains gives birds a swift kick into gear so they can raise their next generation.

Chain Reaction

Scientists like to figure out exactly how things work, down to the smallest detail. But until a 2008 study published in the journal *Nature*, the mechanism that causes birds to start singing in spring hadn't been known for sure.

Japanese quail were the subjects in that study, a joint venture of British and Japanese

Listen and Learn
You Talkin' to Me?

The tufted titmouse's song is easy to imitate. Just whistle back to the bird and you may be able to draw him in closer to get a look at you, his "rival."

Even if you're no great shakes at whistling, mimicking the titmouse's song may do the trick. Male birds aren't too particular about a less-than-perfect imitation when hormones are on the rise. Want to practice before trying it out? Listen to the recording from Cornell University: www.allaboutbirds.org/guide/tufted_titmouse/id.

researchers. Thanks to the wonder of computer technology, the researchers were able to scan some 38,000 genes in birds' brain-tissue samples and examine the genes on the surface of the hypothalamus (an organ in the brain that produces hormones) and in other avian organs. What the scientists discovered is that the impetus to sing happens because of a chain reaction process:

1. After being exposed to 14 hours of daylight, certain hypothalamus genes began producing a hormone that stimulated the quails' thyroid gland.

2. That caused the thyroid to begin producing another hormone, which stimulated the pituitary gland.

3. The pituitary gland produced yet another hormone, which caused the males' testes to grow—and that's what made the birds sing.

Exactly when this process kicks into gear depends on the species of bird. How long must that "longer day" be? That depends on each songbird species' internal time clock.

In Japanese quail, it's 14 hours of daylight that pulls the trigger, reported the researchers. When the days reach 14 hours long, Japanese quail begin to sing. Earlier-season singers, like our little brown friend the song sparrow, who starts vocalizing as early as January, have their alarm clocks set differently. They get the signal weeks before other species.

Feeling SAD?

Seasonal affective disorder, or SAD, is an unfortunate fact of life for many folks who get the blues after a string of short, cloudy days. The Japanese quail research project, although it was targeted to birds, may hold the key to a cure that turns SAD into happy. The hormone secreted by the quails' pituitary glands was previously thought to be a metabolism regulator; turns out, it has more than one purpose.

Next project, suggest the researchers, may be to find out exactly how exposure to light causes those hypothalamus genes to kick into gear. By gaining more of an understanding of how the genes in the hypothalamus are activated by light, scientists may be able to figure out what causes the problem in SAD people.

FROM FLOCK TO PAIRS

When it's not breeding time, many songbirds hang around in groups to forage in the off season. The flocks may include just a dozen or so individuals of the same species, as with bluebirds or doves, or groups may swell to super size with hundreds of birds, such as finches, or monster size, as with blackbirds.

Some flocks include several species. Flocks of various native sparrows and juncos band together outside of nesting season, rustling in the brush or in our flowerbeds as they seek seeds.

Winter-foraging groups of chickadees, nuthatches, and titmice travel their feeding territory together, usually joined by a hard-to-see brown creeper, a downy woodpecker or two, and maybe a hermit thrush, a yellow-rumped warbler, or a couple of kinglets. Each bird has its own food-hunting niche—the creeper scours the bark while the chickadees search the twigs, for instance—so they complement rather than compete with each other.

There's safety in numbers, because the birds

in a flock can help each other keep watch for hawks and other dangers.

Birds of a feather that flock together tend to form pair-bonds earlier than singletons or migrants. When their breeding hormones kick in, in response to the lengthening days of late winter, a potential mate is near at hand. That's why most of these species are among the earliest singers. By late winter, they're already sweetly chirping and courting, and by very early spring, the deal is sealed. Listen for these wintertime flockers to begin switching to love songs as they start to get interested in courtship.

American goldfinch	Juncos
Cassin's finch	Kinglets
Chickadees	Native sparrows
Doves	Pine siskin
House finch	Titmice

CHOOSE YOUR PARTNER

Good-looking clothes, a fine voice, a nice home—female birds aren't much different than female humans when it comes to choosing a mate. They look for signs of success, and the

How Much Light Do Birds Need to Start Singing?

Since I haven't seen any Japanese quail scurrying about my yard lately (maybe they're all over at your house?), I decided to do my own experiment to figure out how many hours of daylight my backyard birds required to nudge their hypothalamuses into gear.

Unfortunately, I'm pretty lackadaisical about keeping daily notes. My research effort fell apart after just three songbird species: chickadees, January 6; house finches, January 28; and starlings . . . hmm, can't read my scribble through the coffee stain.

I'm sure you'll do better at this project than me. But even though my effort was minimal, the results were fascinating. The black-capped chickadees swung into their *Fee-bee* song when the days were 9 hours and 24 minutes long. House finches waited until their brains got almost exactly 10 hours of sunlight.

After the winter solstice, days lengthen by about 2 minutes every day, so that half-hour difference between the chickadees and finches adds up to about 3 weeks' difference between the start of their singing times.

As for those slowpokes, the Japanese quail in the original experiment, they wouldn't see 14 hours of daylight at my latitude until the first days of May. Late birds, indeed!

males that prove they have what it takes are the first to get snapped up.

Whether it's a suave Armani suit or a red suit of feathers on a cardinal, external symbols are important in the animal kingdom at mating time. They're clues to a male's ability to provide for his family, and that's the bottom line for females, whether they realize it consciously or not. At least female birds don't have to wonder whether those fancy duds were bought with a pushing-the-limit credit card. In the bird world, it's WYSIWYG— "What you see is what you get."

What makes a male songbird a prime pros-pect in the mating game? Three major symbols of power include:

Healthy plumage with strong color. Good nutrition is what's needed for a fine suit of feathers, and that means the snazzy male bird is a strong, well-nourished specimen. He'll take good care of his family, so he's a prime catch.

Loud, persistent singing. It pays to advertise, and male songbirds do it in a big way. Those that sing the most attract a mate more quickly than those that aren't so vocal. Biology is at work here, too, because a bird that sings well is a healthy bird—another clue that he'll do

Here's the method, so you can try it for yourself. Length of day depends on latitude: Song sparrows in Georgia may start singing in January; weeks later, in Wisconsin. Of course, since we're not working in laboratory conditions, it's possible we might get the exact start date wrong if we happen to miss the birds' first few tentative songs. But I'm betting that our ears will pick up the new sounds of the season mighty quick. After all, we're looking forward to spring as much as the birds are.

1. Use your year-round songbirds as research subjects, because there's no way to tell when migrants begin humming a tune. They could be hundreds or thousands of miles away when that happens, and they're already singing when they arrive.

2. When you hear the first song, jot down the bird's species and the date.

3. To find the number of hours of daylight for those dates, check the website aa.usno. navy.mil/data/docs/Dur_OneYear.php, which lists the length of daylight for every day of the year for many U.S. cities.

4. Go to the date for your bird, and choose the city nearest to you. Even though the latitude may not be exactly the same as your location, the total hours of daylight will only be off by a few minutes.

5. Jot down the day length next to the songbird's species, and there you have it: A somewhat scientific answer to the question of how many hours of light your birds need to start singing.

Get to Know Your Songbirds
House Finch

"You're going to Hollywood!" would be an entirely appropriate thing to say to your house finches, because that's where the birds originally came from. Nowadays, house finches are among the most common birds in backyards across the country. "California linnets," they were called, or "Hollywood finches," which gives you an idea of their natural range.

The birds have great voices—a cheerful, complicated song that goes on and on, full of melody and variations. What's more, the birds keep on singing, even if they're nabbed and stuck into bird-cages. Which of course *we* would never do. But back in the 1940s and '50s, when canaries and other caged birds were all the rage, some enterprising pet-shop owners smelled money. Even though it was totally illegal to trade in American birds, they bought some of those pretty raspberry-red finches and their streaky brown mates from unscrupulous folks who netted the birds in the wild. It was easy money dealing in such good singers. And easy for the pet shop owner to get rid of the hot goods before he got into hot water—he'd just open the cage and let 'em fly away.

Oops. House finches happily set up new homes on the East Coast, where they were released. And from there, it was just a matter of time until they spread, and spread, and spread.

"California linnets" aren't just in California anymore. Now they're making their nests in our front door wreaths or hanging baskets, or in our blue spruces, firs, or other backyard trees, from sea to shining sea.

"Bringing home the bacon" is a big part of a male songbird's job—first, to bond with his mate, and later, to help feed the family.

When to see them: Year-round

What to feed them: Black sunflower seed is the standby for feeding a crowd; they'll avidly eat hulled sunflower seed, "finch mix," and niger seed, too, when available. May also drink from nectar feeders.

Other ways to attract them: House finches visit birdbaths and other water sources many times a day, in all seasons. Plant sunflowers (*Helianthus annuus*), bachelor's-buttons (*Centaurea cyanus*), cosmos, and zinnias for fall and winter seeds. A dwarf peach or nectarine tree (*Prunus* spp.) or a mulberry (*Morus* spp.) will be a prime target for house finches.

What they sound like: Long-lasting high, sweet, warbling songs; the female often sings softly while on the nest.

What to watch for: An occasional male house finch may sport orange or even golden feathers instead of the usual strawberry color.

Exchanging gifts of choice food morsels is part of courtship behavior, strengthening the pair-bond of these northern cardinals.

a good job of defending and providing for his family.

A tempting territory. The best and brightest males lay claim to the most desirable territories—those that have abundant food and good nest sites. By snagging a male who's a good singer and a handsome bird to boot, a female can safely bet that his nesting territory will also be top-notch: prime real estate with plenty of food, and sure to support the family.

DON WE NOW OUR GAY APPAREL

One particularly gloomy winter day, when the world outside seemed devoid of color, I popped one of those little squares of yummy chocolate into my mouth and straightened out the wrapper to read the message printed inside. "You look good in red!" it enthused.

Red? Really? Me?

I glanced down at my usual wintertime outfit of long-sleeved gray T-shirt, charcoal wool vest, gray sweater, and well-worn jeans.

Red! Of course! I could feel my spirits lift just imagining the bright color.

Funny how much a dash of color can do for us in a winter landscape. Unless we're lucky enough to live in a mild region, flowers are still sleeping. And most of our feeder friends are dressed in feathers as somber as their surroundings—

browns, grays, muddy olive. But let a cardinal fly into view, and suddenly we perk up, just getting a glimpse of that red. It's no accident. Color has an effect on our emotions. Just ask anyone with a warm red kitchen.

For birds, of course, color isn't emotional. It's usually the males who carry the brightest feathers, and a good, strong hue indicates that that bird is healthy and well fed—a real plus when it comes time to catch the eye of a potential mate. That's why birds wear their brightest colors at breeding season. Like me and my drab winter outfit—practical but not exactly eye-catching—some songbirds, such as goldfinches and tanagers, switch to subdued colors in fall and winter, when looking good isn't essential.

A Sharp-Dressed Bird

The rock band ZZ Top got it right when they sang that every girl is crazy about a sharp-dressed man. Once again, songbirds parallel our own lives. A fine suit—of feathers, natch—is one of the main attractions of a male songbird to potential mates. Behind those pretty feathers is something practical, and vital to the females' interests. It takes a lot of energy to grow feathers, and the birds that get the best nourishment—plenty of food, and the right kinds—sport the most handsome plumage. To a female, that bright suit translates into a good provider. A male in fine fettle is likely to be holding a prime nesting territory, with exactly what his offspring need.

FORM FOLLOWS FUNCTION

"How'd I get that scratch?" I often wonder after a walk in the woods. I don't usually stick to a path when I'm out exploring, and brush or tree branches leave their marks on me without my realizing it. Usually, it's only the parts that aren't covered by my clothes that get battle-scarred on my bushwhacking excursions. In winter, the scratches are usually on my hands or wrists; in summer, they may be on my arms, shoulders, legs—you name it.

Clothing is our protection from all kinds of potential skin injuries. My jeans shield my legs from scratches and also protect my skin from a hot car seat, say, or the roughness of the rock I decide to sit on. Feathers are a bird's clothes, and just like that outfit you're wearing right now, they do more than make the bird look good.

Just imagine if you had to fly through dense branches, snuggle up in a prickly spruce for the night, or scratch about on the ground among dead weeds in your bare skin. Like our own clothing, feathers serve as protection against physical damage. They also shield a bird's body from rain,

Strong color, indicative of ample food, makes this male pine grosbeak a good catch in the eyes of a female.

wind, snow, heat, cold—all the vagaries of weather, which can change from balmy to breezy in an instant.

There's a third reason birds need feathers—for flight. They need wing feathers to get airborne and guide their trajectory, and tails to steer and brake.

Bird feathers take even more abuse than my favorite pair of jeans. And they're exposed to strong sunlight, too, which further weakens the feathers. To keep that vital feathery barrier between their skin and the cruel world, birds have to renew their feathers at least once a year. During their annual molt, they shed worn-out feathers and grow new ones in their place. When we see our songbirds looking spiffier than usual, or blotchier as new feathers replace old, we know it's time to start watching for them to pair off and begin the job of raising their families.

The vivid feather colors of the western tanager and his relatives are a result of eating foods rich in carotenoids, which produce the pigments.

Look on the Bright Side

Color changes in our songbirds are a big clue to what's going on at that time in the birds' world. The bird may be getting ready for a long flight south, brightening up to woo a partner, or simply showing the signs of age on its feathers. Nutrition can be a factor, too, which is when a change in the menu at our feeders may help, by supplying the nutrients that songbirds need to grow healthy, colorful feathers. Changes in feather color are a result of these three main factors:

- **Molt,** in which old feathers are shed and replaced by new ones

- **Feather wear,** in which tips or other outside parts of feathers wear off, resulting in a different overall look

- **Nutrition,** a factor in cardinals, orioles, tanagers, goldfinches, and other red, orange, and yellow birds, whose new feathers get their colorful glow in part from the carotene in the foods they eat

Perfect Timing

Feathers grow fast, but not fast enough to cover a big bare patch in a day or two. So songbirds shed them only a few at a time, ensuring that their suit of clothes stays functional. To preserve that precious flying ability, wing feathers are shed symmetrically: one feather on the left wing and the same feather on the right. The process goes on for weeks, until all of the worn-out feathers are gone, and new ones have grown in their place.

Changing en Route
THE PAINTED BUNTING'S METHOD

On family trips to the beach when I was a kid, we used to pull off the road as soon as we saw sand along its edges—oh boy, getting close!—and squirm and wriggle into our swimming suits. That way, we could head straight for the water when we arrived, without wasting time (or a precious 25 cents) at a changing room.

I wonder if painted buntings might have a similar motivation for their unusual method of molt? The western population of these beautiful birds are real oddballs among songbirds, when it comes to molting—they change their feathers along the migration route. Instead of molting after breeding season, before fall migration, they start the journey south with worn feathers. Then they stop partway, in staging areas in southern Arizona and northern Mexico, to change their clothes. When their feathers are freshened, they resume the journey to southern Mexico and Central America.

The shedding or molting process happens at least once a year for songbirds. Many species also go through a second molt, in which they renew only part of their feathers. Here's how it works:

Complete molt. All of the feathers on the bird's head and body, as well as the wing and tail feathers, are replaced.

Partial molt. Many songbirds, such as American goldfinches and native sparrows, also go through a partial molt, in which only the feathers on the head and body are shed, leaving the vital feathers of wings and tail intact. These birds have already gone through a full molt about 6 months earlier, so their biggest, strongest feathers are still in decent shape.

Energy Conservation

Feathers are made of protein, just like our own hair and fingernails. It takes a lot of energy to grow a whole new suit of clothes, so songbird molt happens when there aren't a lot of demands on the birds otherwise. The complete molt is tucked between the end of nesting season and the start of fall migration. It's called the *postnuptial molt*, because it takes place after breeding is finished. Natural food is still abundant in late summer when the complete molt begins, so songbirds have the fuel they need to grow those feathers.

The timing works perfectly for other reasons, too. After the molt, birds that travel long distances start the journey with strong new feathers. Meanwhile, birds that stay put in winter have the best possible protection from the elements.

The partial molt takes place in late winter to early spring, before breeding season. That's when head and body feathers are shed to show off bright new markings for spring.

A very few species of birds—those whose feathers are subject to extreme wear and tear—have two complete molts every year. They're not usually birds of our backyards: They're species who live in wild places that are extra tough on feathers. The marsh wren, for instance, stays deep in cattails, rushes, and other boggy vegetation, which often carry abrasive edges. As this little brown bird slips between the close-spaced grassy blades, its feathers become rapidly worn. Thanks to the rigors of its daily life, two suits of clothes are *de rigueur*.

Colors and Seasons

Silver maples and red maples sport some of the earliest blossoms of spring. Wait—scratch "spring." These trees burst into bloom in late winter, as soon as they get a few days of mild weather. Spring is still weeks away by the calendar when their fuzzy red flowers first appear, even before those of pussywillows. Hybrids of these two trees are known as Freeman maples. Their fast-growing cultivars, including 'Autumn Blaze', 'October Glory', and many others, are among the most popular backyard trees and street trees around.

Keep an eye on the swelling buds of these types of maples in your neighborhood, and you'll see that their reddish blossoms are linked to reddish songbirds. House finches, Cassin's finches, and other red finches begin singing at about the same time the maples bloom.

This molting male summer tanager looks blotchy now, but he'll be beautiful when it's time to impress a potential mate.

It's All Black and White
PLUMAGE AFFECTS PECKING ORDER

Beauty is in the eye of the beholder, and even birds that lack red, yellow, or other bright colors show off for their mates. In 2002, researchers from the University of Windsor, Ontario, banded more than 170 wild black-capped chickadees and figured out their pecking order by watching how they behaved at feeders. (Or, as the research paper puts it, they "assessed winter flock dominance hierarchies by tabulating pairwise interactions at feeders.") Later, the scientists recaptured more than 70 of the same birds and got a little more personal, figuring out their gender and examining their feathers.

Although we backyard bird watchers think of male and female chickadees as looking pretty much alike, the scientists learned that males are distinguishable after all. Their whites are brighter, their black patches bigger, and the contrast between the two is more sharply defined.

Those subtle differences matter when it comes to mate selection and to the position each male holds in a wintering flock. Males with "darker black" plumage not only stand out as superior to others of their kind, they also grow their feathers faster than inferior males.

Yellow Is "In" for Spring

The most dramatic color change in songbird plumage that we can watch as it happens occurs in the American goldfinch. Male birds, in particular, undergo an astounding shift from drab olive winter feathers to sunny yellow spring outfits. The feather color of females warms up, too, although it's not nearly as striking a switch.

When to watch for the color change? Just look for yellow in your yard, as well as at your feeder. Blooming pussywillows laden with yellow pollen, daffodils, forsythia, and the first burst of dandelions are all great clues that you'll soon be seeing golden finches, too.

Free Flower Seeds

To help nourish your colorful songbirds, you can supplement their diet by planting flowers that produce seeds they like. Pick white, pointed safflower seeds out of your birdseed mix to start a patch of these easy-to-grow annual flowers. The fluffy, bright orange daisies begin blooming in summer on the branching plants. Let the blossoms mature into seeds right on the plants, and enjoy cardinals, grosbeaks, and all sorts of finches foraging in the cover of the stems all through fall and winter.

BOYS WILL BE BOYS

It's a real treat to have a dozen cardinals at a feeder in winter, when it's not uncommon to see a bunch of redbirds calmly feeding side by side on a cold, snowy day. In March? Different story.

By then, the hormones that fuel the urge to sing have had another major effect—they've made the males start to feel competitive toward each other. Those same hormones that turn on the love light also fuel the fierceness that makes a male fight beak and claw for his family. (Or batter himself against our windows when he gets a little confused.) And that's where things really get interesting in our little backyard kingdom.

It's all about the women, of course. They're the object of the desire every male is feeling, and winning their attention becomes an all-consuming quest. Male birds aren't any different from any other male animal, including us humans. Although we have a veneer of civilized behavior to keep us from fisticuffs most of the time, competition for a female can be a flash-point for men of a certain temperament, who may in fact come to blows. Just as with human

Trick or Treat
Wheatgrass Wonder

Wheatgrass is touted for its health benefits to humans, but it also allegedly works wonders on birds. Well, on chickens anyway, according to American agricultural chemist Charles Schnabel (1895–1974), who said wheatgrass improved their health and egg laying. His chemical analysis of the nutritional properties of the wheat plant showed that nutrients were at their highest before the wheat stem had formed joints—when it was still just grassy blades, or "wheatgrass."

No one knows what effects wheatgrass may have on songbirds, but goldfinches, house finches, song sparrows, and other songbirds do love to nibble on the tender green shoots when I offer them at my feeder, especially in late winter and early spring, when fresh grass is scarce on the lawn.

It's a cinch to grow your own for the birds. Here's how.

1. Poke a few drainage holes in the bottom of a yogurt or cottage cheese container and fill the cup with moistened potting soil.

2. Sprinkle a handful of wheat seeds on top, sowing them thickly, as you would grass seed on a lawn. Set the cup on a sunny windowsill.

3. Keep the soil moist, and the seeds will soon sprout. They'll grow fast, quickly lengthening into wheatgrass shoots in just a few days.

4. When the grass reaches about 3 inches tall, set the cup in a feeder, so the birds can pluck at the shoots.

You may also find pots of wheatgrass, sold for cats to nibble on, in garden centers or pet stores.

males, avian aggression usually starts with a much milder display of superiority. But the main order of business is the same: Drive off the competition, whatever it takes.

Reading the Signs

Birds can't growl and lay back their ears like dogs, but they sure show unmistakable signs when they're ready to attack. It happens super quick, though, and the signs of aggression in birds are

Eats and Treats
String of Hearts

Seems like there are never enough perches at the tube feeders when finch numbers start to build in late winter to early spring. That's when I hang an auxiliary feeder to celebrate the season: a string of homemade niger seed hearts for my much-loved songbirds. Here's how I make them.

Cookie sheet

Wax paper

White cotton string or jute twine, 3 feet long, with triple knots at about 6- to 9-inch intervals

1 envelope unflavored gelatin

1 cup water

Deep saucepan

6 cups niger seed

Vegetable oil to grease hands

1. Cover a cookie sheet with wax paper and have your string at the ready.

2. Stir the gelatin into the water in the saucepan over low heat. Warning: This will smell awful, so be sure to run your stove's exhaust fan.

3. When the gelatin crystals have dissolved, stir in the niger seed until it's evenly coated.

4. Scoop the coated seed down the center of the cookie sheet and lay the string loosely over it. Working quickly with heavily greased hands (to prevent the hot gelatin from sticking to them), mold the seed into heart shapes around the knots on the string. You should have enough seed mix for about six hearts of about 3-inch width.

5. Let the hearts remain on the tray in a cool, dry place, such as your kitchen counter, until they dry and harden, which can take a day or two.

6. Tie one end of the string to a tree branch or other support, clip off the extra length of string below the bottom heart, and watch your finches flock to their new feeder.

much more subtle than in that Rottweiler next door—or in the guy who's had a few too many down at the corner bar.

At first, you'll only notice the end result, not the warning signs that lead up to the actual attack. But keep watching your birds as spring hormones are on the rise, and you'll soon be able to tell when they're starting to feel feisty. Here's how the progression usually goes.

1. First thing you'll notice at your feeder is one male bird looking at another, as the bird takes the measure of his opponent and tries to intimidate him without needing to come to blows. Birds who aren't being aggressive rarely look at each other; they merely move aside without making eye contact if another bird comes too close, just as we do in a crowded theater or in the aisle of a store.

2. If the other male doesn't respond, next comes a lowered body posture, with the bird crouching rather than standing erect. He's getting ready to get physical.

3. In a flash comes the follow-up: The wings are dropped, the neck snakes out, and a swift jab with the beak is employed—usually not making actual contact—to convince the opponent to retreat.

4. If that doesn't do the trick, the male quickly escalates to actual attack. He'll pursue his opponent, pecking and beating with his wings to force the other bird into the air, all the time cussing at him vociferously. Then comes a quick chase.

5. The victor returns to cracking seeds as if nothing has happened. Don't be fooled, though—should the opponent dare to

A pair of Cassin's finches perch atop a pine, where the ever-alert male can keep an eye out for potential invaders of their territory.

approach the feeder again, it's right back to the attack, skipping the preliminaries.

THE PAIR BOND

Pair bonds, as biologists call the dedicated couplings among birds (and other animals), are for real. In spring, a female songbird chooses the best male she can find, and they become a real couple, working together to raise their family (even if, as in some species, the female does the largest share of the actual work). They're dedicated to each other, all right, as far as doing everything they can to ensure that the next generation survives to leave their nest.

But that bond isn't quite like Cinderella and Prince Charming. In fact, mounting evidence shows that it's a lot more like *The Jerry Springer Show.*

'Til Death Us Do Part

Once upon a time, I had a wonderfully romantic view of the love life of birds—and of people, too, come to think of it. Songbirds mate for life, my mother told me way back when, and I believed it. Of course: Prince Charming and Cinderella would be the case in the bird world as well as in our own world.

Being older now, and if not exactly wiser, at least more educated, I've become much more cynical about the love lives of birds. My thoughts of forever were wrong. It should've dawned on me years ago, I suppose, because as much as I wanted to cling to the Cinderella story, evidence to the contrary was right in front of my nose.

What evidence? Well, the most obvious is the behavior of male birds. Most songbird guys seem to have a split personality: Sometimes they behave like Prince Charming, tenderly attending their partners, but other times they behave more like Attila the Hun, fervently trying to claim other females, even after they've already committed to one special girl.

A Fling on the Side

Orioles do it, cardinals do it, robins do it, and so does just about every songbird in our backyards. And in recent years, a variety of researchers have proved that what we see with our own eyes is decidedly true: The partnerships of birds are as complicated as those of any other species in the animal kingdom, including, ahem, our own.

Famed sex researcher Alfred Kinsey—whose groundbreaking research into human sexuality and infidelity in the 1950s showed that our species isn't nearly as monogamous as we'd like to believe—would've had a field day with songbirds.

First, the good news: More than 90 percent of bird species (not only songbirds) fall into the monogamous category. But wait, there's bad news, too, at least for the romantics among us: Even though songbirds do form a solid pair bond, that doesn't mean they stay true-blue all the time. "Monogamous," in biologist language, has some wiggle room.

- Some species of birds are indeed monogamous in the traditional sense—one partner and one partner only for life, for both sex and raising a family. Experts group these birds, such as swans, into the *sexually monogamous* category.

- Most songbirds, though, are *socially monogamous*: One or the other partner—or both— engages in sex with others, even though they've formed a primary bond with their main mate. As studies continue, it may turn out that all songbirds follow this model.

- And some songbird species are definitely polygamous, or to be more correct, *polygynous,* which means the male has more than one partner and helps care for more than one female's nests. Less than 5 percent of all bird species (not only songbirds) are polygynous, although the count seems to be going up as research continues. So far, most of the male songbirds with a harem seem to be mainly those who live in marshes or grasslands, not backyards, including yellow-headed and red-winged blackbirds, the marsh wren, and the bobolink.

You'll find more gossip—excuse me, I mean more details—about the love lives of songbirds in Chapter 15. You'll also learn how to interpret the behavior you see in your own yard and how to help the birds succeed in raising their families— no matter who Daddy might be.

They're a Couple

Male and female birds are joined at the hip, so to speak, from the time they accept each other as a pair until egg laying begins. Like a human couple that's just fallen in love, they go everywhere together, spending every possible moment with their chosen one. Once a pair of songbirds chooses each other as partners, you'll rarely see one without the other. The pair bond is so strong that the birds eat together, drink together, sleep together, and travel together to feeders and perches.

Researchers have learned that neither gender dictates these movements. Should the female decide to visit the feeder, the male goes along. Bath time? You guessed it—it's a double deal. Unlike some humans I know, neither bird seems to mind such "clinginess," or protest that it "needs some space." The songbirds are simply acting naturally—like a couple.

Feathered Butterflies

Watch your house finches after they begin singing, and you may spot what ornithologists call the *butterfly flight*. That's when the usually earthbound male takes to the air, fluttering up nearly 100 feet above the ground before gliding back to his perch. All the while, the handsome red-headed guy is singing his heart out, loud and long. This special display occurs early in the season, when pairs are still forming. So listen up, and when you hear a house finch warbling from overhead, see if you can catch the butterfly.

A Matter of Timing
SWEETHEARTS

Usually around Valentine's Day, you'll notice that finch numbers start to rise at your feeder as migrants begin joining the winter-long regulars. Now's the time to start watching for songbirds that may not winter in your area but are beginning to pass through on migration. Depending on where you live, you may spy rosy finches, purple finches, or Cassin's finches among the burgeoning crowd of goldfinches, house finches, and perhaps pine siskins at your place.

CHAPTER 3

A Room with a View

"Come see the bird feeder," a new acquaintance urged when I visited her house for the first time. "A robin's been coming! And my finches are back!" She was new to feeding birds and wonderfully enthusiastic, and I couldn't wait to share her excitement about them.

Quickly scanning the windows while I waited for my new friend to give me a clue, I saw no sign of a feeding station.

"Oh, we'll have to step outside," she said matter-of-factly. "You can't see it from inside the house."

Uh-oh. That rang a bell. I learned the hard way, too.

Attracting orioles, rose-breasted grosbeaks, and other songbirds to a feeder is easy enough when you choose the right foods. But remembering to mount that feeder in easy view from the house? Ah, now there's the part that's all too easy to forget!

We want to see the songbirds we attract, no matter what the weather. In this chapter, we'll talk about how to choose the best place for your feeder and how to choose and use smaller feeders that are attached directly to your window. You'll also learn how to increase the temptations of feeder goodies by planting natural foods, too—easy-to-grow flowers that will bloom right outside your window—to bring even more songbirds into easy view.

THE CARDINAL RULE

My first official bird feeder—after I'd graduated from scattering seed and crusts on the ground to hammering a few boards together—was mounted on a post at the far end of a concrete sidewalk in the backyard of my rented house. The pavement, which I soon lined with a jumble of flowers, led to a couple of outbuildings.

It seemed like a good location. My bird food

was stored in a galvanized pail in one of the sheds, so it was handy for refilling the feeder, and I often strolled along the walk, visiting my flowers. It worked like a charm, too. A couple of cardinals, a perky little wren, and even a couldn't-believe-my-eyes pair of bluebirds soon arrived to check out the offerings. Which is not to say that it was ideal. Far from it, in fact.

My feeder setup had a couple of major flaws. First and foremost, I couldn't see it from inside the house. The window on that side of the kitchen looked into a cluttered porch that had been closed in for storage. And second, when I did manage to crane my neck enough to get a glimpse of the feeder from another window, I could hardly tell which bird was which—they were simply too far away. Back to the drawing board.

I left that feeder in place, since the birds already knew where to find it, and whacked together another tray to put up elsewhere. This time, I actually put some thought into it. Which window did I spend a lot of time at? That answer was easy: the window over the kitchen sink. I often glanced out as I did dishes, cooked, and puttered around the kitchen. This time, I mounted the feeder just inches from that kitchen window. The birds soon found it, and we all lived happily ever after.

The cardinal (heh-heh) rule of bird feeding: Put your feeder where you can see it. And I mean, *really* see it. Within about 5 feet from the window is best for you and fine for the birds. Of course, like most of us who feed birds, I don't have just a single feeder. Others are farther away, and some are invisible from the house, because I put them near places where I sit and contemplate when I'm in the yard.

Feeder Conversion

Got a favorite feeder you'd like to attach right to your window, except that it's too heavy for standard suction cups to hold it in place? Explore the world of super-strong suction cups to give it a secure grip. Industrial models cost a little more than general-purpose products—about $2.99 for a suction cup that supports 3 pounds—but they'll keep your feeders from falling, for sure. Ask for them at hardware stores or check the Resources section at the back of this book.

Front-Row Seat

It's easy to spend a half-hour at a stretch watching songbirds at the feeder. Okay, better make that an hour. Or two. Or all morning, if there are no other pressing matters to attend to.

Since I'm not good at standing still for long periods of time, I make sure my feeder window has a comfy seat nearby. And by "nearby," I mean just inside the window. No sense putting the feeder right up close and then sitting on the sofa at the far side of the room.

Spend a little time thinking about your own seating arrangements before you set up a feeder. Here are some possibilities for front-row seats.

- Kitchen tables are a natural gathering place and comfortable for lingering. Got a window by your table? Perfect!

- Does your kitchen have an island or bar where you and others gather? Maybe there's a window with a good line of sight from that space.

- A desk window is another great choice, because you can mix work and play—er, I mean, observational research.

- Where's your favorite easy chair or recliner? Turned toward the TV, most likely. Perhaps a little furniture rearranging can give you a view of the big wide world as well as of *As the World Turns* reruns.

MAKE THE MOST OF YOUR WINDOWS

We want those songbirds where we can see them. Not at the end of the walk, not back beside that garden bench we never sit on, but right up close, as near to our noses as we can get them. That means making the most of our windows.

The better the view, the more fun it is to watch songbirds and the more you'll see. Not only will you see the fine points of their feathers, but you'll also notice the subtleties of their behavior. Like how a rose-breasted grosbeak adroitly nibbles the shell off a safflower seed, never dropping an iota of the meaty seed. Or how a Carolina wren sorts through the feeder, scything with his dagger bill, until he finds just the right kernel of walnut for breakfast.

Behavior includes a lot more than eating habits. When you really bring in the birds, getting them in close viewing range, you'll see how they interact with one another. At courtship time, you'll see males gently feeding their mates . . . and turning combative in a heartbeat, should another male get too close.

Danger Deterrent

It may take your birds a little while to get used to your presence on the other side of that window, but they'll soon overcome their fear. Try to avoid sudden movements while you watch, until your

Hard to say who'll win in this squabble of cardinal and rose-breasted grosbeak. Next round, the loser often comes out on top.

friends learn to accept you as a nonthreatening part of the scenery.

Most songbirds are quick to sense danger, and some other birds are even swifter to react to a perceived threat. Wary and intelligent feeder visitors, such as jays, crows, and grackles, are likely to be less comfortable about coming to a feeder that's so close to the house. That's why I keep more than one feeding station in my yard. The warier birds, which are usually the most aggressive when it comes to food, happily turn their attention to other handouts that are farther from the house, instead of competing at the close-range feeder.

Even starlings may be deterred, or at least become less-frequent guests. If a horde of these hogs takes over your feeder, you can scare them off easily by hollering, thumping the glass, and waving your arms wildly on the other side of the window. They'll get the message fast, and they'll be wary about coming back.

Hawks will also steer clear of your setup, since they keep their distance from human habitation. They may perch or patrol nearby, though, hoping to nab songbirds going to and fro, so be sure you have shrubs and trees around the area to give your songbirds vital cover.

Create a Mini Spa

It's just as much fun—maybe more!—to watch songbirds at water as it is to see them at a feeder. So I often add a miniature spa setup outside my

---

Eats and Treats
Fledgling Food

Add some nutritious, high-protein soft foods to your menu when bird parents begin bringing the family to visit. This rich mix easily slides down the hatch, whether the fledgling is sampling it himself or being fed by an adult. Young bluebirds, orioles, tanagers, grosbeaks, wrens, catbirds, and other fledgling friends will avidly gobble up this treat. Don't forget to put the feeder outside your favorite window, so you can get to know your youngest customers!

2 tablespoons raw hamburger

2 tablespoons canned high-quality beef dog food

1 scrambled egg, in small pieces

1 tablespoon roasted waxworms, a plumper, more expensive mealworm alternative; if you can't find them, use roasted mealworms

1. Break apart the hamburger and dog food with a fork.

2. Add the other ingredients and toss the mixture so that it's a loose collection of small bits, not a packed mass.

3. Serve in a mealworm feeder, a domed plastic feeder, or the jelly dish of an oriole feeder. You'll find more information on these various styles of feeders and which songbirds are best suited to them in Part II of this book. Parent birds may also take the food back to their babies, before they leave the nest.

---

window, in addition to the feeder tubes, dishes, and trays.

The spa can be as rudimentary as a 10-inch clay pot saucer of water sitting on a rustic bench or a traditional pedestal-type birdbath. If you want to upgrade your spa services to the deluxe version, hook up a misting device above the basin to give your songbirds a refreshing spray.

Keep your mini spa at least 4 feet away from your bird-watching window: Songbirds are vigorous splashers. And plant a pussywillow or other tall, branching shrub near the bath, so that you can have the pleasure of watching your songbirds preen their nice clean feathers. The shrub will also provide a safe place to perch when the birds are vulnerable because of their wet feathers.

All songbirds adore water, but some seem to be especially partial to it. You can expect to see finches of all descriptions, catbirds, cardinals, orioles, robins, bluebirds, and thrashers at your bath. Dozens of other species, from tiny wood warblers, kinglets, and vireos to quiet thrushes and large, flashy grosbeaks, are also a strong possibility. You'll find more ideas for using water in Chapter 13.

Have Fun with Fledglings

I can't think of anything cuter than a fuzzy-headed baby bird—well, unless it's a puppy or a kitten or a lamb or just about any other kind of baby. We don't usually get a good look at our youngest songbirds, because their parents teach them to crouch in dense shrubs or flowerbeds where they're hidden from view. "Out of sight, out of mind" is the watchword when it comes to evading predators, and fledglings do a fine job of laying low.

When you have your feeder in close view,

Set up a mister by connecting it to a garden hose, aim it to spray at a low-level basin, and a fox sparrow may come to enjoy a shower.

however, you have a good chance of getting a look at those youngsters soon after they leave the nest. Parent birds, which have no doubt been snitching bits of suet and other feeder foods to stuff down those gaping beaks, will soon shepherd their brood to your setup and teach them how to get the goodies themselves.

Getting the fledglings to the feeder may call for some tough love from bird parents. I've seen my Baltimore oriole pair gulping down mealworms while their two youngsters, lacking the courage to test their wings, cried plaintively from a nearby branch. Orioles typically hide their babies low to the ground when they first leave the nest; I figured these two were several days old, since they were already using their wings to flutter from branch to branch in my sycamore. Eventually, the first fledgling screwed up his courage and made an awkward plunge to the feeder. As he teetered on the edge, his mama rewarded him with a mealworm and what I'm sure were chirps of high praise. Minutes later, the second youngster joined the family there.

Getting to Know You

It's easy to get to know our backyard songbirds personally when they're only one or two of a kind.

The gray catbird pair, yep, that's them. (Though which is he and which is she may still be a mystery in these look-alike birds.)

The single fox sparrow stopping in on his way north? We'd know this big, rusty brown sparrow with his heavily streaked breast anywhere. Or at least we do when he's the only foxy scratching under our feeder.

But what about that bunch of white-throated sparrows that's kept us company all winter? To most of us, they're not individuals. Neither are the half-dozen bright blue indigo buntings that came in last week when the dandelion heads went to puffs. Nor the four male bluebirds that finally found our mealworms in the snowstorm.

It's tricky to tell one bird from another of the same species, because at first glance, they all look alike.

Which of the Seven Dwarfs Are You?

When a small flock of unpaired male and female pine grosbeaks arrived at the feeder outside my winter retreat in the Rockies, I had no idea which bird I was looking at. Until, that is, I watched them closely enough and long enough to get to know them. It only took a few days to realize that one of the females was much more aggressive than the other birds. She was first at the feeder every morning, last in the evening. And she ruled the roost, threatening any bird that came near, grosbeak or otherwise. Even the raucous Steller's

---

Trick or Treat
One-Way Glass

Just like a suspect being interrogated on one of those TV detective shows, your songbirds will have no idea that they're being watched when you use a window feeder equipped with one-way glass. Well, not actual glass—these feeders generally employ a film over plastic that does the same trick.

That's great except for one small problem: The film blocks your birds' view only from the feeder itself. Your birds will still be able to see you through other areas of the window, so they may panic and fly away if you move suddenly—or if Kitty or Pooch decides to take up bird-watching, too.

It's an easy trick to shield everything inside your window from the birds' view. Just buy one-way film at a hardware or craft store and apply it to the inside of your whole windowpane. It'll preserve your own view and solve your birds' panic problem.

---

jays stood no chance; they wisely waited until she departed before they ventured in.

When they start a study, researchers rely on leg bands in different colors to tell birds apart. Interestingly, though, they soon learn to recognize individuals by their particular traits, just as do biologists studying other animals. Sometimes it's a slight difference in coloration that's the clue. In spring, for instance, you'll soon be able to discern individuals among your flock of molting goldfinches. Oh, there's the really yellow one!

But it's personality—that is, behavior—that usually gives away a bird's identity. Individual birds are just as different in their basic natures as we are. They don't quite cover the entire gamut of the Seven Dwarfs, but some are definitely happy, some dopey, and some grumpy.

The personalities of songbirds really become clear when you watch the birds up close so that you can clearly see the nuances of their behavior. That's another good reason to make the most of your windows and put your feeder in easy view!

WINDOW FEEDERS

Feeders that attach directly to your windows are a wonderful way to get to know your songbirds. You'll find windowsill models; feeders that extend, through your window; and clever contraptions that attach directly to the glass.

Most feeders that attach directly to the windowpane are made of plastic so that the additional weight of the food and the bird doesn't pull them askew or onto the ground. Clear plastic window feeders are my first choice because I can see the birds inside them. Of course, they may see me, too, so I'm careful to not make any sudden moves that might scare them away.

You can also mount a regular feeder directly on your windowsill, if you don't mind drilling a few holes into the wood. If the feeder is too large to fit your sill securely, attach a bracket underneath to give it extra support.

You Get What You Pay For

High-quality see-through window feeders seem unusually expensive for just a little piece of plastic. For years, I was reluctant to pay the price—$25 for a bent piece of plastic and three suction cups?!—and tried to make do with cheaper models that soon cracked or fell off the window, never to stick again. Finally, I bit the bullet and paid the price. That was more than 10 years ago, and my original feeder is still going strong. So are the other models I added, after I fell in love with that Expensive Feeder #1. Yep, I'm sold. Even though I still love making my own feeders for practically nothing, I wouldn't be without plastic stalwarts.

Read the fine print of the label or catalog description to see what kind of plastic the feeder is made from. If it's the Lexan brand, you're in luck. This polycarbonate is so strong that it's used for motorcycle windshields. It resists clouding, scratching, and ultraviolet light from the sun that can cause lesser plastics to deteriorate.

Out of Harm's Way

On a windy day, a feeder hanging near the window may swing wildly, whack the windowpane, and leave you with an expensive repair job. To head off this problem, I use a hinged, movable bracket mounted on the side of the window frame. On calm days, I swing the bracket so that the feeder hangs in front of the window. When storms blow in, I simply swing the bracket away from the window so that the feeder knocks harmlessly against the siding of my house, should it catch the wind.

You can buy hinged brackets in a wide array of styles and prices at wild bird supply places, garden centers, or hardware stores. Be sure to choose a bracket whose mounting will fit onto your window frame. Check the package to see whether the screws or other hardware you'll need to mount the

Tennis, Anyone?

If your dogs are anything like my canine friends, you probably have a stray tennis ball or three lying around in the yard. If you can manage to snitch one of the used balls without Fido noticing, you can make a window feeder (actually *two* window feeders) in about 5 minutes.

You won't have to worry about this hanging feeder cracking your window. Should the breezes give it a whirl, it'll bounce harmlessly against the glass.

Materials

Tennis ball

Sharp knife

Ice pick or long, skinny nail

Florists' wire, 9 feet

Wire cutter

Bracket or nail for hanging

Method

1. Slice a tennis ball in half with a sharp knife and poke three equidistant holes around the rim of each half. An ice pick or nail works well for puncturing a tennis ball.

2. Cut three pieces of florists' wire for each feeder, each about 3 feet long. Twist one end of each wire in tight circles, to make a knot.

3. Thread the unknotted ends of the wires into the tennis ball holes, leaving the knots on the inside.

4. Grasp the wires at their base and run your hand up to their ends, checking their length and straightening them so that each half of the ball will be suspended evenly. Twist the free ends of the wires together to make the hangers for your feeders.

5. Hang the feeders from nails or brackets at the top of your window frame. Fill them with bird dough crumbles (see recipe for Millionaire's Mix in Chapter 8) or a dozen mealworms each to attract house wrens, Carolina wrens, Bewick's wrens, yellow-rumped warblers, vireos, gnatcatchers, and other small, agile songbirds.

bracket are included; if not, save yourself a second trip and pick them up before you leave the store.

Staying Stuck

Suction cups are the usual method of attachment for window feeders. They work well as long as you prepare the window surface first and secure them properly. It's a good idea to check them often, because if the feeder does give way when a songbird lands on it, the bird will be as shaken as we would be if a rickety chair collapsed beneath us—and just as reluctant to risk it again.

1. Grab some window cleaner and scrub every bit of dirt off the glass. Rinse thoroughly, so that the glass is free of any residue. The slightest bit of dirt, soap, or grease can cause your feeder to fall off.

2. Follow the directions that came with your feeder to attach it. In some cases, the suction cups are an integral part of the feeder. In others, you'll mount the suction cups first, then attach the feeder to them.

3. Test the feeder to make sure it's firmly attached by giving it a gentle tug, then a firmer one. If it holds fast, fill the feeder, and test again.

4. Check your feeder every week or so. Give it a tug, and examine the suction cups to make sure they're still holding securely. Chances are that the attachment will still be firm. Those suction cups work surprisingly well— I've had them hold for more than a year with no adjustment!

Trick or Treat
Grow a Crop of Caterpillars

Ornamental kale and cabbage are popular for late fall window boxes and containers, but most folks yank them out when spring rolls around. If yours are still showing signs of life in early spring and haven't disintegrated into a smelly mess, leave them alone so they can do what comes naturally—shift back into growth again, eventually sending up stems of small yellow flowers.

If your window box or container cabbages have definitely kicked the bucket over winter, replace your planting with broccoli starts, spaced about 4 inches apart. They'll quickly grow into pretty gray-green bushy plants. All these cabbage-family plants are a beacon to the cabbage white butterfly, who lays its eggs on the plants.

"Oh boy, caterpillars!" That's what our wrens, bluebirds, catbirds, cardinals, rose-breasted grosbeaks, thrashers, song sparrows, and a host of other songbirds will be saying as they quickly strip the little green 'pillars from the plants. No worries—there'll be another crop as soon as another egg-laying butterfly visits.

WINDOW GARDENS

Not all songbirds readily visit feeders, whether they're near a window or far from one. Perhaps the birds haven't yet learned that those feeders hold something mighty tasty, or maybe they simply like natural food better.

You can still coax these standoffish types into view by planting a garden for them—at your window, of course. Other songbirds may also come close to investigate the insects, seeds, and flowers. And you'll have a wonderful view of both the birds *and* your garden.

Garden in a Box

Most plants harbor insects on their leaves, stems, or flowers, and songbirds are quick to investigate the possibilities. Even when your garden is in a window box, kinglets, vireos, and wood warblers, especially on migration, may drop down to the box to see what's good to eat. Songbirds who take up residence in your yard, such as the sweet-voiced hermit thrush and the cheerful American robin, may also visit the box to grab a bite. If your plantings attract butterflies, why, that's even more food for the taking. Bluebirds,

Weeds for the Window Box
FREE SEED FOR THE PICKING

After a hard frost, the annuals in your window box will be looking mighty . . . well, dead. Let them stay if they've had time to set seed that songbirds can find, but take the focus off the sad stragglers with an additional lovely bouquet of weeds for fall and winter.

Yes, I said "weeds." Finches, buntings, native sparrows, and other seed-eating songbirds avidly seek the nutritious seedheads of lamb's-quarters, ragweed, mullein, curly dock, and lots of other weeds. Just take a field trip to the nearest roadside or overgrown meadow, and snap the stems of anything that strikes your fancy. Don't forget wild grasses, too, such as fuzzy, arching foxtail. Add a few sprigs of small wild rosehips (multiflora roses make great ones for bird food), bittersweet, or other berries to add color and further bird appeal for northern mockingbirds, catbirds, wrens, and bluebirds.

You can stick the strong stems directly into the soil in the window box. Or make a graceful arrangement of your weeds, bind the bouquet with twine, and anchor it to a sturdy stick shoved deep into the soil.

Swamp sparrow on foxtail grass.

cardinals, flycatchers, phoebes, and other song-birds that like a snack on the wing may arrive at a nearby perch to snatch insects as they come and go from your window box.

The following plants are easy care, so you won't have to do a lot of fussing, and they thrive in the often hot and dry conditions of a window box. All attract a myriad of insects, including butterflies.

Agastache or anise hyssop (*Agastache* cvs.), in warm colors and shorter heights

Bidens (*Bidens ferulifolia*)

Dwarf Asiatic lilies (*Lilium* cvs.), such as the 'Pixie' series

Lantana (*Lantana* cvs.)

Love-in-a-mist (*Nigella damascena*)

Marigolds, dwarf or low-growing varieties (*Tagetes* spp.)

Petunias (*Petunia* cvs.)

Sedums (*Sedum* spp.), including early bloomers like goldmoss stonecrop (*Sedum acre*) and later bloomers like *Sedum spathulifolium* 'Cape Blanco' and *Sedum* 'Autumn Joy'

Verbenas (*Verbena* cvs.)

Zinnias, dwarf and 'Profusion' types (*Zinnia* hybrids)

Outside-the-Window Garden

What better place to plant a garden than right outside your window? The flowers of the following perennials, self-sowing annuals, and shrubs—and even a trio of vegetables—will gladden your heart every time you glance out the glass. They'll also bring in insect-seeking birds. And that includes every songbird in your backyard, especially at nesting time. For the best view

Flowers provide insects for eastern phoebes.

Goldfinches can't resist anise hyssop seeds.

Safe Haven
LOVE THAT LETTUCE

Lettuce plays a way different role when we're vegetable gardening than it does when we're seeking songbirds. Sow lettuce early, we veggie gardeners know, because once the weather warms up, it bolts fast, switching from tender leafy growth to a flower head and bitter leaves.

Ah, but that's the beauty of growing lettuce for birds: There's no need to worry about timing, because the plants are assets at all stages of growth.

A bed of lettuce, nothin' but lettuce.

- Tender leaves attract slugs for thrushes and robins, and finches and sparrows may nibble the greenery themselves.

- When your lettuce bolts, so much the better: Those tall stems of small flowers bring in tiny insects, putting them at just the right height for the vireos and warblers that eat them.

- And when the flowers mature to seeds, look out—here come the finches! Goldfinches and house finches (and their relatives, the buntings) all adore lettuce seeds, whether they're wild types or garden variety.

- Sow lettuce seeds thickly in a patch instead of in tidy rows, or intermingle them in your flower gardens. The tall dead stems will supply cover in fall and winter, and come spring, seeds that escaped the birds will sprout to renew the planting.

and a graceful design, arrange the plants in a semicircle arcing out from the window.

Try these easy growers to give your room a view of songbirds as they snatch insects, including butterflies, and later search for seeds from spring right through winter.

Agastache or anise hyssop (*Agastache foeniculum*)

Blue spirea, or blue mist shrub (*Caryopteris clandonensis*)

Broccoli, superb at attracting butterflies and insects!

Butterfly bush (*Buddleia davidii*)

Cherry or pear tomato, colorful fruits and a bounty of bugs—what could be better?

Hollyhocks (*Alcea rosea*)

Leaf lettuce, any kind

Purple coneflower (*Echinacea purpurea*; not the new warm-colored hybrids)

Spider flower (*Cleome hassleriana*)

SOUND SYSTEM

"Open-windows season" is a short-lived opportunity in my region of southern Indiana, where mosquitoes and biting buffalo gnats (close kin of the notorious blackflies of the Far North) hatch long before sultry summer sets in. But what a window of opportunity it is. It falls between the last cold snap and the start of 'skeeter season—right at the peak of spring bird migration.

There's no sleeping in when open windows bring birdsong right into the bedroom. It's always a robin who wakes me first, because they start singing at the dimmest crack of dawn. I love lying in bed enjoying lazy reverie as the light gradually brightens, listening to robins and wrens and—who's that!?

Yeah, who am I kidding? Morning reverie

Listen and Learn
Listening In

If you really want to hear the best version of amplified birdsong, you'll need to shell out a thousand bucks or more for a parabolic microphone. These devices collect the sound and record it on an attached tape recorder; you'll find sources in the Resources section at the back of this book.

You can also use the mike to just listen to birds—and it's a revelation. Aim the wide cone toward the bird, don your headphones, switch on the mike, and *whoa!* You'll hear songbirds louder and clearer than you've ever imagined, because the mike catches the sounds of the singing bird, not the background noise our own feeble ears have to try to filter out.

Don't have a spare grand handy? Then try these low-tech versions:

- Find a singing bird, turn toward it, and cup your hands behind your ears, thumbs inward. Free, quick, portable—and they give you a surprising boost in volume. Well, a small boost . . . but enough to make a difference.

- Make your own parabolic ears! I use a clear plastic "clamshell" take-out container, cut at the hinge into two halves. Hold one cupped around the back of each ear, aimed toward the singing bird. Crude, uncomfortable, with plenty of room for improvement in design—for sure. But several notches above your bare hands in listening power.

Get to Know Your Songbirds
Indigo Bunting

An absolute jewel, the iridescent male indigo bunting sure stands out in a crowd. And when male buntings gather by the dozen at a feeder during migration, it's enough to take your breath away.

These small neotropical songbirds are only temporary treats in the backyard for most of us. Unless our yard is very large or borders the wild fields and brushy places where they prefer to nest, the buntings will stay for only a few weeks at best in spring, before moving on to nesting grounds. Still, what a few weeks it is! The bright blue birds join goldfinches and other finch family cousins at the tube feeder or a tray, or settle on the ground to find spilled seeds.

Buntings are low-level birds that usually nest and forage within about 5 or 6 feet of the ground, but they often fly to much greater heights to

Male indigo bunting.

sing—or to seek the mulberries they adore.

Indigo buntings are unusual among the songbirds—they not only sing during the heat of the day, long after the dawn chorus has petered out, but they also keep singing all summer long. Look around and you'll spot the bird holding forth from a high perch on a utility pole or wire or the tippy-top of a tree.

When to see them: Spring, throughout migration range; spring through fall in nesting range

What to feed them: White proso millet is tops; they also eat niger, black sunflower, hulled sunflower, and "finch mix" seed.

Other ways to attract them: Provide a birdbath. If you have a big yard, plant a red mulberry (*Morus rubra*) to draw them in from wild places in summer. But keep the tree well away from sidewalks, driveways, and patios—the fruit is messy and leaves stains. If you have a large yard that borders a field or woods, attract a nesting pair by letting the edge go wild with tall grasses, weeds, wild roses, and whatever shrubs or seedling trees happen to sprout. If you find a deep little cupped nest in your meadow garden with trash lovingly woven in, it's likely to be a bunting's home. Indigos often include candy bar wrappers, strips of chip bags, and the like in their nests, perhaps to mimic the crinkly effect of the shed snakeskins they also use.

What they sound like: A long, rapid song of high, paired phrases, *Sweet, sweet; where, where; here, here; see it, see it,* repeated about five times a minute for an hour or more.

What to watch for: Identifying the female indigo bunting is a humbling experience for many birdwatchers (yep, it fooled me, too). While the male is a cinch to peg at first glance, the female looks like a plain, dowdy brown sparrow—all the better to remain unnoticed when she's sitting on the nest.

never lasts, not during migration. There's always some bird or other who'll sing or chirp or chip from the yard, yanking me out of bed with a start. Gotta hurry and go see who's arrived overnight, before they move off down the block!

I like to think I spend a lot of time outside, but when it comes right down to it, it's only a very few days that I'm out from dawn to dusk. The rest of the time, like anyone else, I'm indoors, doing the usual stuff we all do in our houses.

A couple of decades ago, some bird supply places offered a bird feeder with a built-in microphone designed to let us listen in on bird voices at the feeder. Apparently, the "Wind Song" feeder wasn't the big seller they'd hoped, because it's no longer on the market. Birds don't do much singing at feeders, anyway, and I guess the sound of beaks cracking sunflower seeds didn't draw a crowd of buyers.

COLOR CHANGERS

Songbirds that typically have patches of red or are entirely red sometimes show up wearing plumage that can fool us. Their red may lean toward orange, as happens occasionally in cardinals, house finches, and tanagers, or even to gold. In the case of rose-breasted grosbeaks, that dramatic crimson V on the breast can be bright yellow on rare occasions.

These pigment aberrations are known as *morphs,* like the varying dark or light plumage of a red-tailed hawk. They may be genetic or seasonal; after breeding season, adult male rose-breasted grosbeaks switch from their boldly graphic red-black-and-white plumage to brown with brown-streaked golden breasts.

Color morphs may also be related to diet. Carotenoids are necessary to create the red pigment in bird feathers, and if the crop of carotene-rich berries or insects is scanty when new feathers are forming during postnuptial molt, or the right combination of color-changing chemicals isn't present, the bird may not acquire its usual coloration.

You Are What You Eat

Ever wonder what makes a goldfinch yellow? Dandelion seeds, for one. All parts of dandelions, including the parachute seeds, a big favorite of goldfinches, are rich in carotenoids—the pigments responsible for yellow feathers.

Carotenoids are like a living paint palette—different ones create red, orange, yellow, and even green colors. Mix them together in varying amounts, and you get everything from flamingo pink to dandelion yellow to lobster red (all, the results of carotenoids).

So why are goldfinches yellow, orioles orange, and cardinals red? Because of both genetic factors

Look up to spot tiny wood warblers in spring, gleaning insects from oak catkins and leaves.

(like the genes that determine our own hair color) and because "they are what they eat."

Each songbird species has its favored diet of particular seeds, insects, and fruits. Even though there's often overlap among various species' menus, the balance is probably tipped toward foods that contain the carotenoids for their color. While goldfinches go for the gold (carotenoids called xanthophylls), for instance, cardinals relish the red (lycopene and other red carotenoids).

Nature's Balance

It's easy to recognize carotene-rich foods like apricots, papaya, mango, and good old carrots: Their color is an obvious clue. But carotenoids are also present in red berries, including those of

Can You Hear Me Now?
SONGBIRDS ADJUST THE VOLUME

When I arrived at a friend's place in the Rockies to spend the winter, the first thing I noticed—after I got done oohing and aahing at the mountains—was the silence. No cars, no trucks, not even barking dogs, except for our own. Every soft bird voice was clear and easily audible from a much longer distance than in my backyard or the neighboring woods in small-town New Harmony, Indiana.

"I love how quiet your birds are," I commented. "They sing like they're giving a private concert, but I can hear every one of them. Even the chickadees aren't as loud."

Like us, birds raise their voices when they have to compete with background noise. Several recent studies have shown that urban birds sing higher and sometimes longer than rural birds of the same species.

A study by David Luther and Luis Baptista of white-crowned sparrows (published in *Proceedings of the Royal Society, Biological Sciences*, in October 2009), reporting 30 years' of recordings and analysis, proved that their voices had shifted to higher frequency levels over the years. Why? Low-frequency urban noise, like the rumble of traffic, had increased, and generations of the songbirds had adjusted their tone so they could still be heard.

Another study (published in *Biology Letters* in February 2011), a short-term look at house finches, showed similar results. The urban finches also sang longer songs.

Can you hear me now? Sure can!

White-crowned sparrow.

Inspiration from Birdsong
COMPOSERS COPY THE BIRDS

Birdsong has universal appeal, which may be why musicians as far apart in style as Vivaldi and Pink Floyd have been inspired by it. Some musicians use their own musical interpretation of bird voices. Just listen to the soaring, sprightly "Spring" from Vivaldi's *Four Seasons*—it's easy to imagine the singing birds he intended for us to hear. Other composers incorporate actual recordings of birdsong, as in Pink Floyd's "Grantchester Meadows." Come to think of it, maybe Vivaldi would have done the same if he'd had a handy tape recorder.

One of the earliest creative efforts, way back in the 1500s, came from Renaissance composer Clément Janequin. Inspired by birds singing, he composed "Le Chant des Oiseaux" ("Birdsong"). The song is a long, complicated antiphonal *chanson,* in which voices alternate like a tree of singing birds. And it's still performed nearly 500 years later. The choir of De La Salle University of Manila included its fluttery phrases in the repertoire of its world tour in 2004.

As for which songbirds Janequin was trying to evoke? You've got me. I've never been to France, but I'm sure its songbirds are beautiful.

dogwoods, roses, and honeysuckles. Red fruits, such as tomatoes and hot peppers? You guessed it—carotenoids. Even green leaves contain the stuff. We just don't see the colors until the green chlorophyll disappears in fall, revealing those beautiful carotenoids.

Research on wild bird nutrition is way back in the Dark Ages when compared with studies of human nutrition. And we still have a long, long way to go before we understand exactly how our own bodies work. What's the "good-for-you" food this week? And the "bad" one? Or is anything-and-everything okay in moderation? We're still learning, but good nutrition seems to be a matter of balance and common sense. But common sense isn't always easy for us to exercise. Not with chips and dip on the table, another

helping of mac-and-cheese there in the dish, and constant bombardment from commercials for less-than-wholesome foods.

Wild songbirds, though, seem to have no trouble getting it right with natural foods. Tanagers and cardinals manage to find foods with enough carotenoids to keep their intense colors. On the other hand, when wild cardinals and American goldfinches were trapped, kept captive, and fed a carotenoid-deficient diet in a study by biologists Dr. Geoffrey Hill of Alabama's Auburn University and Dr. Kevin McGraw of Arizona State University (published in *Functional Ecology* in 2001), they clearly showed the inadequacy: Although the birds were healthy, their feathers grew paler and paler every time they molted.

TALK TO THE ANIMALS

I know that vampire books are all the rage today with young readers, and Harry Potter is still holding strong, but back in the old days, it was Doctor Dolittle that every child knew.

The good doctor was invented by Hugh Lofting, who began a series of illustrated letters to his children when he was in the trenches during World War I. He wanted to give his kids something to make them happy, so he came up with the empathetic doctor who had learned to communicate with animals by learning their languages.

And not only that: Lofting also assured his readers that they could do it, too. How? By learning to notice things.

Getting to Be a Good "Noticer"

"Don't sweat the small stuff?" Maybe not, but definitely take notice of it! Getting to know your backyard songbirds—or any animal—depends on noticing their small details. Every action and pos-

Cactus spines protect a mourning dove's nest from climbing predators—but not from peeping bird-lovers. Do not disturb: Use binoculars to get a closer view.

5-Second Bird Blind
HIDE UNDER A THROW

Birds behave differently when we're not around. Even though our backyard birds may seem to accept our presence, they act more naturally when they can't see us.

Here's a cheap and easy way to be a sneaky bird-watcher: Just use a fleece blanket in a camouflage pattern as an instant throw-over-your-head bird blind. Sit in a comfy spot outdoors, cover yourself in the camo, and you'll soon see birds in a whole new way. No need to cover your face, as long as the camo is over the top of your head.

You'll find camo fleece throws in the outdoors department at discount stores or at sporting goods shops, often for $20 or less. You can even buy a Snuggie version with sleeves (add a camo hoodie from your favorite outfitter), so you can take photos easily without disturbing the birds.

It's All Connected

EARLY START

A dusting of spring snow often falls at onion planting time in early spring. The inch or two of white stuff on top of the buried onion sets does them no harm, and even gives them a drink of water when it melts, to hasten their sprouting. Known by countryfolk as "the onion snow," that harmless dusting of white signals another start—the beginning of bluebird nesting season. Like onions, bluebirds don't need to wait until the weather is warm to get going.

ture and sound is a clue, a communication that you can read clearly once you get some practice.

As Polynesia, the parrot, asks young Tommy Stubbins in *The Voyages of Doctor Dolittle*:

"But listen: Are you a good noticer?—Do you notice things well? I mean, for instance, supposing you saw two cock-starlings on an apple-tree, and you only took one good look at them—would you be able to tell one from the other if you saw them again the next day?"

Tommy says he's never tried to do that. And neither have most of us. He also says it sounds pretty hard.

Polynesia offers more wisdom. All it takes is patience, she says. But noticing is the key:

"[T]he way they walk and move their heads and flip their wings. You have to notice all those little things if you want to learn animal language. For you see, lots of the animals hardly talk at all with their tongues. . . .

"But that is the first thing to remember: being a good noticer is terribly important in learning animal language."

I'm still not sure I could ever tell my starlings apart, unless one of the birds had some special characteristic, like, say, a white feather. But learning to notice things will definitely tell us which songbirds are nesting in our yards, and where; when predators are on the prowl; when baby birds have left the nest; and lots of other interesting details about the lives of our backyard birds.

CHAPTER 4

Joy in the Morning

Early birds may get the worm, but early risers get the very best of the songbird concert. The performance reaches a crescendo as the sun peeps over the eastern horizon in May and June, when the singers are at full throttle, the days are at their longest, and that sun is rising mighty early. Is it worth crawling out of bed at 5:00 a.m. or earlier to lend an ear? You better believe it.

In this chapter, you'll discover how to make the most out of that concert, by simple appreciation as well as by learning to recognize the singers' voices. You'll find out how to interpret the messages they're trying to get across in their singing, and you'll discover handy catchphrases, like the *Pleased, pleased, pleased to meetcha* of the chestnut-sided warbler, that will help you sort out the singers. And who knows: If you've got an ear for music (songbird music, that is), you may even want to take part in birding competitions, tallying up all the birds you can see—and hear!—on a given day. You'll find all the details in this chapter.

WORTH A WAKE-UP CALL

"I hope I don't oversleep," I said to a friend one evening in mid-March. With an early deadline facing me the next day, I wanted to be up-and-at-'em early. "That bedroom is mighty dark. No windows facing east."

He laughed. "The robins start singing at 5:30 a.m. No way you can sleep through that."

No kidding.

As soon as the notes of the first robin filtered in through the window in the gray predawn light, I was awake. Almost instantly, as if they'd been waiting for someone to be brave enough to go first, every robin in the neighborhood joined in. The chorus went from 0-to-60 in just seconds, as if a switch had been thrown.

It had. Songbirds begin their morning songs according to their alarm clock—the sun. Even though the bedroom was still so dim I could barely find my clothes, the light outside was gradually increasing. As soon as it hit a certain intensity, albeit well before sunrise, the songbirds started their performance.

Light Just One Candle

Our eyes need a good amount of light to be able to see. Sunlight is great, of course, but when we work in the house, we want the brightest bulb we can find. Candlelight may have been fine for Honest Abe. But we're so keen on seeing clearly that we gripe about the relative dimness of fluorescent lightbulbs, even when we know that incandescents are energy hogs. When we use a 100-watt lightbulb to read by, we're using the equivalent of 120 candles. That's a lot of candlepower—or *candelas* or *foot-candles*. All of these units of measurement describe the same thing: the amount of light a single candle emits at a distance of 1 foot.

That's not much, as young Abe Lincoln and anyone else who's ever tried to read by candlelight can tell you. One foot-candle of light is pretty darn feeble. It'd be even dimmer than a 1-watt lightbulb, if they made such a thing, which they don't.

The indefatigable house wren starts singing even before the sun rises, and his bubbling voice rings out all day long.

Songbird eyes, though, are so sensitive to light that the birds wake up and start singing long before we're even thinking about coffee. "[I]t is completely predictable that the robin will give voice when the light intensity reaches 0.01 candlepower, and that the bedlam of other singers will follow in predictable sequence," wrote Aldo Leopold in *A Sand County Almanac* in 1949.

No wonder I was still snoring when the first robin began to sing that March morning. It was at least a solid hour before dawn. My sleepy human eyes could barely discern anything in the dim light, let alone a single candle somewhere in the distance. Oh well, the robins were singing—up and at 'em!

Each in Turn

The dawn chorus may sound like a grand symphony, but it's actually a progression of soloists. Their performances are on a tight schedule, with each species chiming in, in turn, as the light grows gradually brighter. Jumping the gun? These singers wouldn't dream of it. Or maybe they would, if birds do in fact dream. Our feathered friends sleep until the increasing light wakes them up and inspires them to join the choir.

The exact time that birdsong begins each morning moves earlier day by day during the singing season. The time of sunrise changes as the seasons progress, and our singing friends wake up earlier in May than they do in April.

A CHORUS OF SOLOISTS

I'm not much for getting up at the crack of dawn, but I hate to miss the opening strains of a concert. So at least once or twice a season, I make sure I'm outside before dawn, ready and waiting in my lawn chair when the songbirds start up. It's well worth finding some extra time on an April, May, or early June morning, so you, too, can hear the full concert.

Robins are usually the earliest of the early birds, and you'll hear a lot of them. They're our most common and most abundant songbirds, and they generally have the stage all to themselves for the start of the concert. Soon after they get things going, you'll hear other voices join in: the liquid burble of a house wren, the lyrical repetitions of a brown thrasher, the clear whistle of a cardinal, and the voice of every other songbird that's in your neighborhood.

This isn't exactly a chorus. Symphony? Forget it. Morning birdsong is a conglomeration of soloists, busily singing as loud and as often as they can, with no regard for the overall effect. Aldo Leopold's description of "bedlam" wasn't far off the mark: It's a free-for-all, with each bird adding his voice to the ever-swelling sound.

Not long after sunrise, when the day has reached full light, the singing begins to slow down. Songbirds drop out of the grand chorale to begin going about their daily business of feeding themselves and their families. It's breakfast time—for the birds and for their audience.

What Time Shall I Meet You?

The first hour of birdsong is the best. It takes a while for everybody to join in, and it's a real pleasure to be in on it from the start . . . even if we're barely awake at the beginning.

Here's how to make the most of your morning date with the birds:

- Plan on taking your seat outside about an hour in advance of sunrise.

Like other migrants, the white-eyed vireo is already singing when he travels in spring.

- Dress warmly, because even a dewy May morning can be mighty chilly before the sun comes up.
- Grab the insect repellent, too; a mosquito whining about your ears can be quite the distraction, and those pesky critters can be bloodthirsty in the early morning.
- Pack a thermos of coffee or orange juice and a snack, too, if you like—there's no intermission until the show is over, and you won't want to miss a note.

LEND ME YOUR EARS

Morning music, and the singing that goes on throughout the day, reveal a lot more than just a bunch of lovely voices. It lets us know which birds are in our backyard and in our neighborhood. We find out who doesn't yet have a mate and who's already nesting. We can even learn who's just passing through.

How in the world can we figure all this out when many of us don't even know which birds we're listening to? Easy! Just follow our ears. Here are some tips in the box below.

This Land Is My Land

Songbirds are like miners heading for a gold rush when it comes to claiming a nesting territory. Spring migration is one big land grab. It's first come, first served, and you better get your claim staked out fast, before others try to horn in on your find.

It's amazing that male birds manage to stake a claim mainly with voice. But that's their major way of advertising "This land is my land." In songbird language, though, the next line is a little different from Woody Guthrie's lyrics: It's "This land's not your land" instead.

"On Territory" or Traveling Through?

Migrants that are still on the move sometimes adopt some of the same behaviors as birds "on territory"—meaning those that have claimed a nesting area to settle down in. So we need to do a little detective work before we get too excited about having a pair of orioles or hermit thrushes sharing our homeplace. Listen to and watch individual songbirds in your backyard, and you'll soon be able to quickly discern whether your singers are temporary visitors or true homesteaders.

BEHAVIOR	INTERPRETATION
Sings from random places while constantly moving, generally in a northward direction	Still on the move
Sings from the same perches day after day	Homesteader, for sure
Sings for more than a day from an elevated, visible perch, such as the top of a tree	Good possibility he's a homesteader
Male and female seen together	Maybe, just maybe . . .
Male tenderly feeds a morsel to the female	They're engaged; start watching for nesting behavior.
Investigates nest boxes between bouts of singing	Might settle down and raise a family
Sings from roof of nest box	Welcome home!

Nesting territories vary in size from one songbird species to another and from one family to another. The homestead has to be big enough to include enough food, water, and other resources to sustain the family without skimping.

As you might expect, these avian properties are usually pretty irregular in shape, not like the neatly geometric plots in a human subdivision. The boundaries, though, are just as clear as those privacy fences we put up—except that the property line markers are audible, not visible.

Follow the sound of a particular singing bird as he moves around your yard or neighborhood, and you'll be able to "see" the extent of his territory. Until the female is actually laying eggs, the male mostly sings from the plot's perimeter. Keep an eye out for a nest somewhere within that boundary.

DO YOU HEAR WHAT I HEAR?

One of the most poignant scenes in film takes place in a movie called *Strangers in Good Company*. Two elderly women, caught by circumstances in a rural area, are standing in the midst of singing birds. "You never hear white-throated sparrows anymore," says one, pursing her lips and whistling the *Old Sam Peabiddy-Peabiddy-Peabiddy* song with a gentle quaver very much like the bird's itself. The sparrows used to be common, she tells her companion, and she would hear them everywhere.

Her friend is silent for a bit, and it doesn't take long for us to realize that real live white-throats are singing softly all around them, perfectly echoing that quavery whistle. The reason the elderly woman can't hear them is because she's going deaf.

One of the most beloved songbird voices belongs to the white-throated sparrow.

Ample food, such as these serviceberries, can tip the balance for eastern bluebirds and other songbirds seeking a home.

Get to Know Your Songbirds
Rose-Breasted Grosbeak

Want to win the loyalty of these dashing birds on their spring travels? Two words: safflower seeds.

Once a rarity at feeders, rose-breasted grosbeaks (and their western counterpart, the black-headed grosbeak) are now backyard regulars.

Sunflower seeds run a close second to safflower, but the songbirds rarely bother with tiny millet. I serve safflower at the feeder in spring to hook any passing rose-breast on its way to breeding grounds in the northern quarter of the country and Canada.

I also grow the plants in my flower gardens. Just like sunflowers, safflowers (*Carthamus tinctorius*) sprout wherever birds happen to drop them. And like sunflowers, they grow fast, zooming up into somewhat prickly-leaved annual plants. But the flowers and form of safflowers are way different than those of tall, slim sunflowers: They form a branching, bushy plant studded with big, bright orange, pincushion flowers in summer.

I like the serendipity of letting them grow

Male rose-breasted grosbeak.

where they will. That color is extra bright, but it works well with the other orange and apricot flowers in my yard. A patch of pure safflower is gorgeous next to a swath of blue bachelor's-buttons (*Centaurea cyanus*).

Rose-breasted grosbeaks, cardinals, and other strong-billed songbirds will find the safflower seeds when they ripen.

That happens to be right at fall migration time, when rosies visit our backyards on their way to the Tropics.

When to see them: Spring and fall migration; spring through fall in nesting range

What to feed them: Safflower or sunflower seed, fruit, and jelly

Other ways to attract them: Small fruits right on the tree are a big draw. Serviceberry (*Amelanchier* spp.) and sweet cherries or pie cherries have big appeal in early summer; elderberries are a favorite in summer; and dogwoods (*Cornus* spp.) and hollies

(*Ilex* spp.) catch their attention in fall. Rosies also love water, so be sure to keep that birdbath freshly filled.

What they sound like: A rich, musical warble, and a sharp *"Pink!"* call note.

What to watch for: Like other red and orange songbirds, this grosbeak depends on carotene-rich foods to achieve its vivid crimson breast. Some individuals' breasts may be orange or even yellow instead of rosy red.

Finally, the companion—who can hear the sparrows perfectly well—slips her arm around her friend's shoulders and says gently, "No, you don't. I wonder where they've gone." It's an act of such kindness that it makes me cry every time.

We all hear things differently. Acuity is part of it, for sure. But just taking the time to notice what's going on around us is an even bigger factor when it comes to birdsong.

Birding by Ear

I love to "read" the world around me with both my eyes and my ears. Everything is laid out in it, so it's just like reading a book. Even a short stroll around the yard holds countless clues. That *Chip* means a song sparrow is defending its nest in my garden. That sudden squall of house finches means somebody's trying to steal a partner. That hoarse warble—hang on, I think it may be a scarlet tanager!

Birding by ear comes in even handier when I'm out exploring. I don't have to slog through the swamp to know that northern parulas are guarding their nests in the buttonbushes. No need to trudge through the brier patch to find the brown thrasher; I can hear him from the path. And why disturb the wood thrush when I can listen to his haunting flute without brushing through the poison ivy?

It may seem impossible to learn the voices of our songbirds, but in fact it's fun. All it requires is noticing things—and getting to know our backyard friends a little better.

Noble Prize

It's not quite time to award us backyard bird-watchers the Nobel Prize, but "noble," well, that description definitely fits. Many of us have become scientists, dedicating hours every year to furthering knowledge about birds.

Citizen scientists, that's what we are. Everyday observations in our backyards—who's at the feeder, what they're eating, who's nesting, and other things we notice—are providing reams of data that ornithologists and other researchers are

No Ears Needed!
WATCH YOUR FEEDER FOR SCIENCE

There's plenty of room for citizen scientists who aren't, shall we say, aurally astute.

Project FeederWatch is exactly what its name says. Although the tally also includes birds that come to sources of water or other features we've provided in our backyards, as well as to feeders, no song recognition is needed.

Since its start in the mid-1970s, Project FeederWatch has grown to thousands of backyard participants, each one of them committed to keeping track of who comes to visit from November through April. That's a big commitment and an important one.

You'll find all the details for joining the effort at www.birds.cornell.edu/pfw/. A $15 annual fee from participants funds the massive project.

putting to use. Without us, real scientists wouldn't have nearly as good a picture of birdlife as they now do. Inventorying birds is a big part of that science, whether the counting is centered on the feeder, the backyard, or the wider world.

Birding by ear is vital to these inventory efforts, because birds are heard way more often than they're seen. Plus, you can cover a lot more ground without having to stop to find birds in your binoculars, and covering ground is the basis of many bird counts.

Bet I Can Find More Birds Than You Can

Helping gather data is tremendously satisfying, but there's another element to citizen science that's even more fun. Competition.

The Christmas Bird Count (CBC), begun in 1900 by Frank Chapman of the just-hatched Audubon Society, is the granddaddy of them all. It began back when the popular method of competing at "bird watching" was to shoot them. (My, what a pretty oriole! BAM!) With the CBC, counting birds by sight and sound quickly became an even more popular alternative. (Duh.) If you record the only gray catbird in your region's CBC, you're gonna feel mighty proud. Heck, my chest even puffed up when I discovered that the giant flock of starlings I'd spotted (a shape-shifting smudge that I'd estimated at 30,000) was added to the tabulations.

Competitions are fun and they're spreading like, um, starlings. Here are just a few of the bigger, more established events, all of which raise much-needed funds for conservation:

Bird counts are a great way to boost your knowledge—experts love to help beginners get to know the birds.

- **World Series of Birding.** Form a team, roam New Jersey, and see how many species you can find in a 24-hour birdathon in May that's organized by New Jersey Audubon (www.birds.cornell.edu/wsb/what-is-wsb).

- **Big Day.** Corral your bird-loving friends into a team and see how many birds you can find in a single day in any geographic area of any size. This contest is organized by the American Birding Association (ABA), which publishes its results at www.aba.org/bigday/.

- **Big Sit!** This one's for individuals who count how many birds they can see in 24 hours from any circular plot of land of a certain diameter anywhere in the world. Not a mile-wide circle—the circle must be only 17 feet in diameter. Held in October and hosted by *Bird Watcher's Digest,* this free event was founded by the New Haven, Connecticut, Bird Club (www.birdwatchersdigest.com/bwdsite/connect/bigsit/index.php).

- **Great Texas Birding Classic.** Scour the Texas coast with a team during spring migration in late April. This fund-raising event is sponsored by Gulf Coast Bird Observatory and Texas Parks and Wildlife Department (www.tpwd.state.tx.us/huntwild/wild/birding/gtbc/).

- **Youth Birding Competition.** This 24-hour team competition just for kids is held in Georgia in mid-April and is sponsored by the Georgia Department of Natural Resources (www.georgiawildlife.com/node/951).

Check with your local chapter of the Audubon Society for events in your area, or Google "birding competitions" or "birding competitions [your state's name]." Birding magazines, such as *Bird*

Quick-moving and well-camouflaged wood warblers, such as this black-throated green, are always a prize on bird counts. Use your ears to find them.

Watcher's Digest (www.birdwatchersdigest.com), *BirdWatching* magazine, formerly *Birder's World* (www.birdwatchingdaily.com), and others, both in print and online versions, often include announcements of birding contests. If there aren't any in your area, why not create one? Just don't forget to send me an invitation. I love a good competition.

Stalking the Singer

The thought of fame and glory can be terrific motivation for learning bird songs. But the real pleasure, as I'll bet even Roger Tory Peterson knew, is simply the personal connection between singer and listener. Whether or not that songbird even knows we're standing there listening, we still feel like we know him. And being able to call him by name even when we can only hear his song—well, that's as rewarding as recognizing the voice of Ol' Blue Eyes on the radio. Or perhaps of Lady Gaga, if your taste happens to run in another direction.

So what are you waiting for? Put down this book, perk up your ears, and let's go find some birds.

Pleased, Pleased, Pleased to Meetcha!

Often I feel like the last of the dinosaurs, trying to get along in a world that isn't mine anymore. Or as I've griped to friends ever since I was a kid, "Wish I'd been born 100 years ago." (By now, I suppose, I should change that to 150 years, but who's counting birthdays?)

Back in those old days, when I would've fit right in, the school curriculum was a little different than it is now. Here's part of a list of goals for 6-year-old students that was devised by Charlotte Mason, a British educator of the late 1800s:

- To recite, beautifully, six easy poems and hymns

- To add and subtract numbers up to 10, with dominoes or counters

- To read

- To know the points of the compass with relation to their own homes, where the sun rises and sets, and the way the wind blows

- To mount in a scrapbook a dozen common wildflowers, with leaves (one every week); to name these, describe them in their own words, and say where they found them

- To do the same with leaves and flowers of six forest trees

- To know six birds by song, color, and shape

Not only did schoolkids know their birds back then, but most other folks did, too. People spent way more time outside than they do now, and without electronic entertainment, nature was a bigger part of their lives. Living on small farms and walking the countryside were a way of life for

Hit a Home Run
TEAMING UP TO COUNT BIRDS

If you have a good memory for bird songs and calls, you might be ready to start training for the World Series of Birding, organized by New Jersey Audubon and held each May within the boundaries of New Jersey.

The first winning team, in 1984, included some real luminaries: Roger Tory Peterson, naturalist, ornithologist, and inventor of the modern field guide; David Sibley, author of my favorite field guide (*The Sibley Guide to Birds*); and Pete Dunne, director of the Cape May Bird Observatory and the fellow who started the competition, among others.

In 24 hours, the five-man team found 201 species of birds—many of them by ear. Yep, time to start brushing up on those birdcalls. At, where else, spring training. And where's home field for this training? Why, the best place to start practicing is right in your own backyard, when singing season starts in spring! In the upcoming sections of this chapter, you'll find tips for decoding who's singing, beginning with *Pleased, pleased, pleased to meetcha!*

Can You Find Orion?
START WITH AN EASY ONE

Okay, maybe that's too tough. How about the Big Dipper? Once you know one constellation in the night sky, it's much easier to make sense of the rest of that vast universe. Your next constellation will be a lot easier to distinguish, and eventually you'll know a handful of star patterns at a glance. No need to learn them all, of course, unless you're passionate about star study. But even knowing a few will make looking up at the night sky a more rewarding experience. Call it the process of elimination: As you learn to pick out the patterns you know, the other stars are simpler to pinpoint, because there are fewer of them.

The American robin is the Big Dipper of backyard songbirds: always around in singing season and easy to find with your ears. And because they're so plentiful, robins make up a big part of the birdsong chorus. Learn a robin's warbling *Cheerily, cheer up*, and you can eliminate every robin song from the confusing cacophony you're trying to sort out early on a spring morning.

"Oh, that's a robin, hi, Robin! But who's that . . . ?"

many, too, and knowing about songbirds came with the territory.

Go ahead, call me a dinosaur. But I'm *pleased, pleased, pleased to meetcha,* Schoolteacher Charlotte—as a chestnut-sided warbler would say.

Putting It into Words

Maybe it's my word-loving brain, but I've always found English translations of bird songs much easier to get a grip on than listening to their music on recordings meant to aid identification. The cardinal sings *What cheer!* Black-throated green warblers glorify their landing spots by caroling, *Trees, trees, beautiful trees!* And my personal favorite, the olive-sided flycatcher, who's not really a songbird, huskily demands, *Quick! Three beers!* Way easier than trying to remember the notes, in my opinion. But then, I'm not very musically inclined.

Memory Records

Now there's a phrase that still strikes fear in my heart, four decades down the road: memory records. That's what my music teacher in junior high called the selections she would play to us in class. We would have to identify the songs—after only two listenings, days apart—as part of our letter grade. These weren't songs with lyrics, and they weren't songs I ever heard at home. They were classics, like Aaron Copland and Beethoven; my parents listened to Tommy Dorsey and Elvis.

Mostly, I flunked the memory records tests. I just couldn't retain the music without the words. Which may indicate why, so many years later, I still have trouble learning birdsong from recordings. Still, plenty of people find birdsong CDs, bird identification cards with built-in computer chips of songs, and other types of recordings to be an enormous aid to figuring out who's singing.

Me, I've never had much luck hearing a bird, running inside, fumbling for the recording, and matching them up. It's way easier for me to simply track down the singer myself and take a gander. I do, however, turn to recordings when I'm trying to pinpoint a bird I already have a pretty good idea about. Was that a Harris's sparrow or a vesper sparrow singing on top of that brush pile?

A quick check of recordings makes it all clear.

Whether I'd recognize him the next time . . . uh, just ask my old music teacher. I think I know just what she'd say.

Online Aids

My very first computer was a secondhand Texas Instruments TI-99/4A, and I thought it was

Don't Forget the Lyrics

Just in case you, too, find songs easier to remember when you know the lyrics, here's another blast from the past. Mnemonics like these helped schoolkids learn bird songs way back in the dinosaur days. They were passed on by word of mouth; included in some old schoolbooks; and incorporated into field guides and other bird books over the years. As for whomever first thought them up—kudos to those sharp-eared bird lovers, whose names are lost in the mists of time.

SONGBIRD	TRANSLATION OF SONG
Eastern bluebird	*Cheer, cheerful charmer*
Indigo bunting	*Fire, fire; where, where; here, here; see it? see it?*
Northern cardinal	*Cheer cheer cheer purty purty purty*
American goldfinch	*Potato chip*
Baltimore oriole	*Here, here, come right here, dear*
American robin	*Cheerily, cheer up*
Savannah sparrow	*Take, take, take it easy*
Song sparrow	*Maids, maids, maids, put on your tea kettle-ettle-ettle*
Vesper sparrow	*Here, here, where, where, all together down the hill*
White-crowned sparrow	*More more more cheesies, please pink*
White-throated sparrow	*Old Sam Peabiddy-Peabiddy-Peabiddy* or *O sweet Canada Canada Canada*
Scarlet tanager	*Cheer up, cheerily, cheerio*

miraculous. Why, I could type in some lines of gobbledygook code, and in just an hour or two (okay, maybe four), I had the thing chirping like a bird. Literally—because birdcalls were what I first tried to create.

What did we ever do before computers? And tiny electronic chips that can put a song inside a plush toy (and yes, I love those chubby, funny-looking stuffed songbirds) or inside the pages of a book.

Countless websites nowadays include recordings, too, and everybody and his brother, it seems, is out there poking a microphone or a video camera at their birds.

You gotta love it. Sharing birds with far-flung folks around the world is the real miracle. It's easy to spend hours every day looking at others' songbird

SONGBIRD	TRANSLATION OF SONG
Brown thrasher	*Drop it, drop it, pick it up, pick it up*
Hermit thrush	*Why don't you come to me?*
Swainson's thrush	*Run to your home hear me*
Wood thrush	*Ra-vi-o-li*
Tufted titmouse	*Peter peter peter*
Eastern towhee	*Drink your tea*
Blue-headed vireo	*See you, be seein' ya, so long*
Red-eyed vireo	*Here I am, over here, vireo*
Solitary vireo	*Come here Jimmy quickly*
Warbling vireo	*When I sees you I will seize you and I'll squeeze you till you squirt*
White-eyed vireo	*Quick give me a rain check*
Black-throated warbler	*Trees, trees, beautiful trees*
Chestnut-sided warbler	*Pleased, pleased, pleased to meetcha*
Magnolia warbler	*I'm, I'm, I'm so sweet*
Northern parula warbler	*Da-da-da-da-that's all folks!*

When I seize you, I will squeeze you, begins the warbling vireo's song.

photos and videos, or talking to folks by typing. We can even peek into a songbird's nest in real time, if it has a tiny camera set up to watch it, no matter where in the world that songbird is sitting.

It's all about connection, and the online community is warm and welcoming. I check in about once a week on birding forums, like those on www.davesgarden.com and other websites, to see what others are seeing.

Mutual Altruism

Songbirds are quick to come to another bird's aid when it issues a distress call. Even a squirrel's chattering alarm can bring birds flocking. When the "Help!" signal goes out, other nesting birds in the neighborhood—no matter what species— will band together to fight off snakes and drive away cats or crows. Sure, the neighbors may have been fighting among themselves a few minutes earlier, but as soon as one needs aid, the fight is forgotten and they fly to the rescue.

This response isn't entirely altruistic, because there's some self-interest at work. Fending off a predator helps keep other nests safe, too. Besides, those helpers may need aid themselves sometime in the future. Although their response is swift and instinctive, not calculated, the result of doing a good deed has a payoff for them: It means they can count on their neighbors to come flocking to them in turn.

Five-Alarm Warning

Whenever you notice an unusual commotion of songbirds, pay attention: Your help might be needed, too. Those alarmed chirps and squawks say: There's trouble, right here in River City. And we big scary humans can scare away a cat or hawk much faster than our little feathered friends can.

Don't forget to take a look-see at the birds that have joined forces to fight off the predator. It's a great way to get an instant census of who's nesting in your neighborhood, because they all join in the attack. Some fly fearlessly at the snake or other danger, while others hang back, their only role to add their voices and their cautious presence to the mob.

Among the most aggressive combatants are northern mockingbirds, brown thrashers, cardinals, red-winged blackbirds, starlings, and non-songbird jays and crows. These brave troops dive at and harass the intruder, even pecking at it if they can get their jabs in safely.

Chickadees, robins, vireos, wood warblers, thrushes, orioles, and many other songbirds make up the second rank: the backup forces that stay to the rear and rarely make direct contact with the predator.

Native sparrows, juncos, and wrens usually perch nervously near their own nests instead of joining the chase, but they do add their alarm calls to the fracas.

COME OUT, COME OUT, WHEREVER YOU ARE

Songbirds don't always want to be seen. They're too busy finding food, fighting with others of their kind, or tending to their families to put themselves in plain sight for our viewing pleasure.

What's a bird lover to do? Cheat, say some folks. Imitating the bird or making a noise it's curious enough about to investigate—called *pishing*—are tried-and-true tricks for coaxing songbirds into view. Here's how to do it—and some reasons why I don't. Instead, I use another tried-and-true trick: good old-fashioned patience. I sit still and wait until the bird recognizes that I'm not a threat and then comes into full view.

Psst! Over Here!

Human ears respond instantly to a *"Psst!"* Even when we're not the target, we swivel our heads instantly to see who's trying to get our attention. Similar sounds work for some birds, too, and birders commonly use them to draw skulking birds out into the open.

The simplest method of *pishing* is just using your mouth to make a series of quick *"Psst! Psst! Psst!"* or *"Pish! Pish! Pish!"* noises, following up with a rapid *"Chit-chit-chit-chit."* Or you can try a variation, known as squeaking, by noisily kissing the back of your hand. Experienced pishers have their favorite sounds, and there's even been an entire book, with accompanying CD, written on the subject.

Squeaking can sound like a distress call, and birds in hiding quickly come to investigate. They may also come to check out the source of what seems like an innocuous *"Psst,"* because any unusual sound can spell trouble to birds.

The Ethics of Pishing

I've never been a fan of pishing, although even the most passionate birders of my acquaintance have no problem with it. The technique seems harmless at first—but is it? My own experience

"Pease Porridge" Works, Too
TRANSLATING BIRDSONG

The biggest names in bird history are often pretty funny when they're talking birds. Here's a bit of a letter that Aretas Saunders, author of a little masterpiece called *A Guide to Bird Songs* (1951), once wrote to Arthur Cleveland Bent, another famous bird guy.

Bent was in the process of finishing up his 20-plus volume series of books on American birds when Saunders offered this observation on the indigo bunting:

"One remarkable song that can give an idea of the rhythm was *zay-zay zreet zay-zay zeah zay-zay seeteeteet zit-zit zeah*. The remarkable thing about this is that the rhythm is exactly that of a well-known human jingle, 'Bean porridge hot, bean porridge cold. Bean porridge in the pot, nine days old.'"

plus common sense have always made me wonder. And in recent years, the trick is causing quite a debate in the birding community.

When I tried pishing, a vireo cautiously moved out from the shadowy interior of a patch of blackberries. And a gray-cheeked thrush paused in mid-gulp of some spicebush berries to fly to a higher branch for a better view. I got a better look at the birds, all right. But I felt mighty selfish. The only reason I used pishing to lure them out was for my own benefit, not for theirs. Instead of patiently waiting and watching, observing the bird as it did whatever it was doing, I caused it to stop in its tracks and see what I was up to.

Pishing may seem like a small thing to us, but to birds, it can be cause for concern.

- Many pishing sounds—there's a whole book, remember—imitate distress calls or alarm notes. If the pisher is good at it, the sound will quickly draw the target bird out in the open. Great, now we can see him! But what about the physiological cost to the bird? Like us, birds respond with racing heart, quickened breath, and other responses to perceived threats.

- The energy the bird spends to come and see what's going on may have been put to better use in ways that benefit it—collecting food, cleaning its feathers, or chasing off that peeping tom from down the block.

- Luring songbirds into the open can put them or their families at risk. If a predator is lurking—where's that neighbor's cat?—the sight or motion of the bird, or the sound of the pishing, can make the bird-eater curious enough to investigate, too. That could spell certain death if there's a nest nearby. And when a songbird is laying low, its nearby family or mate may be the reason. That vireo that came to see what I was doing? Turned out she had a nest right there at waist level.

With millions of us bird-watchers out there, the combined effects of the agitation we cause by pishing are much greater than if there were only a few of us trying this trick. And the issue is big-

Whistle a Happy Tune
TALKING BACK TO BIRDS

Even though I eschew pishing and recordings to lure songbirds, I do still attempt to talk back to them. Not with distress calls, though (I don't want to scare anybody), but by replying to their own songs. I'll still whistle back to a cardinal or anybody else I can reasonably imitate. Not to try to bring the bird into view—because all I have to do is follow my ears to be able to see it—but because I can't resist trying to communicate.

Although it's possible that the birds might think I'm a competitor, they seem to know I'm faking it. Instead of getting agitated, they exhibit mild curiosity at most. So there's no harm done, and I feel as if we've just exchanged a greeting.

ger than pishing alone. Often our imitations are too crude to get the attention of the birds we want to see. That's why many birders, including research scientists, instead use recordings to really bring out the birds.

The Boy Who Cried Wolf

The first—and only—time I went "owling" with some birder friends, I was horrified and enchanted, all at the same time. One of the fellows took along a small pocket tape recorder, and when we were well into the dark forest, he pushed the "Play" button. The deep hoots of a great horned owl sounded while our little group stood silently.

I'd thought we were looking for tiny saw-whet owls, not giant eared owls. And we were. The great horned is a predator of birds on the nest, including the smaller-than-a-robin saw-whet, and when the small owls heard its call, they became so perturbed, they responded. So did songbirds in the forest. The recorded owl calls, which kept going, woke everybody up. I could hear rustlings and *chips* from all sides, where thrushes were nesting near the forest floor and other birds were in the bushes or branches overhead.

"Stop it!" I demanded in a normal speaking voice, ruining my credibility with the other birders. "We're disturbing them!"

They shushed me instantly, pointing to the tiny saw-whet that had flown in to keep an eye on what it thought was a killer on the prowl. The little owl looked like a toy on the branch, blinking its wide eyes, and I was charmed. But the poor thing was scared, and I wanted no further part of that.

Researchers and recreational birders use other recordings, too, to bring their subjects out of hiding. Distress calls are the most common, but recordings of adult males—competitors—are often used, too.

Messing with Mother Nature

With the rise in ecotourism, the ethics of bird-watching have become a hot topic. While no one would throw a stone to flush out a secretive bird, pishing is generally allowed and recordings are often used.

In research, recordings are the rule of thumb. And researchers themselves notice that the subjects of their experiments are affected by their methods. That seems counterproductive to me, but I suppose the goal is the study results, not the effects of the experiment on the birds.

An "interactive playback experiment" on black-capped chickadees, conducted in 2000 by researchers at Queen's University in Ontario, tried to see whether female chickadees were swayed in their mating choice by superior singing ability among males. The scientists used recordings to fool both males and females, and not in a nice way.

Female songbirds, including chickadees, seek out superior singers for mates and for extra couplings on the side (for more on songbirds' love lives, see Chapter 15). The males' songs are the females' primary clue as to which birds would make top partners.

"I engaged some males in singing contests by mimicking a very aggressive territorial intruder, to create the impression that these males 'lost' a song contest," reported Daniel J. Mennill of Queen's University in a 2002 issue of *Science*. He continued: "I engaged other males in singing contests by mimicking a very submissive territorial intruder, to create the impression that these males 'won' a song contest."

And, sure enough, he got results: "In the weeks following playback experiments, I collected blood samples from the playback subjects' offspring. I found that high-ranking males who lost song contests [against the songs played by his computer] also lost paternity in their nests."

The pairs stayed together, but the females had flings with better singers. Those birds' genes were in the eggs raised by the straying female and her still-loyal spouse.

Under natural conditions, a superior singer usually has superior genes—healthy and good at finding food—so some diversification probably improves the survival of the species.

Under these conditions, I just feel sorry for the poor birds that got fooled by the computer.

Eats and Treats
Raspberry Parfait

Mimic thrushes—our friends the thrashers, gray catbird, and northern mockingbird—are huge fans of bite-size bramble fruits, like red and black raspberries and blackberries. Tickle their fancy with this treat, served in a feeder near their favorite bramble hideout. If any of these songbirds already visit your feeding station, you can simply set the saucer in a tray feeder there; they'll soon find it. Or place the saucer beneath a bush where the birds hang out. This treat is especially popular in spring, before garden raspberries begin to ripen.

1 or 2 slices whole-grain bread

½ cup chopped suet

Clay pot saucer

1 cup fresh or frozen red raspberries

1. Cut or tear the bread into small bits, about ½ inch in diameter.

2. Mix the chopped suet and bread pieces together until they're evenly distributed.

3. Scoop the bread/suet mixture into a clay pot saucer or other shallow,

rough-surfaced dish on which songbirds can get a secure grip and see the food easily.

4. Smush the raspberries (thaw first, if frozen) with the back of a spoon or fork until juicy.

5. Spoon the raspberries over the bread/suet mixture, plopping them on by separated tablespoonfuls. Don't cover the surface evenly: Allow some of the bread and suet to remain visible.

Unfortunately, all's fair in love, war, and science, I suppose.

SNEAKY SINGERS

A bird in the bush is mighty easy to overlook, and that's what secretive songbirds are counting on. Staying out of sight is a great insurance policy against hawks, cats, and other problematic parts of life—including people who can't resist the urge to take a daily peek at the progress of a nest.

Brambles are a popular hideout for thrashers, as well as for the gray catbird, another skulker. Native sparrows seek weedy areas or naturalistic garden beds; Carolina wrens hide out in brush piles; and hedges harbor thrushes, towhees, and other privacy-seeking songbirds. These undercover agents spend much of their time within dense shrubs or hedges or laying low in the most overgrown parts of our yards.

In spring, though, the urge to sing reveals the presence of even our most secretive songbirds. Most venture out to a high branch or perch on the tip of a weed or flower for their performance. Their nests are likely to be nearby, and you may never find them until winter strips the vegetation bare. But if you pay attention to the singers, you'll soon be able to figure out which skulkers are calling your backyard home.

CHAPTER 5

Grandmasters of Song

I've always loved Hans Christian Andersen's story of "The Nightingale," a cautionary tale about preferring a fancy appearance over a good soul. The emperor in the story preferred a bejeweled, mechanical version of the dowdy, real live bird—until he was near death, when the plain-Jane singer's melodious song saved his life.

But it wasn't until just lately that I heard the fabled songbird for the first time.

Nope, I haven't taken a trip to Europe yet—I listened to a recording online. What a revelation! The nightingale is certainly a skilled songster. But he doesn't compare to our own American avian musicians, at least not in my book. You can hear for yourself at ibc.lynxeds.com/species/common-nightingale-luscinia-megarhynchos?only=sounds #sounds.

The nightingale's song is lovely, yes. But is it haunting, like the fluting song of our wood thrush or veery? Nope. It's sprightly, sure. But our wrens have him beat, hands down. Complex? Of course. But I'll take an oriole or robin any day.

Perhaps it's my cultural bias showing here, but the nightingale's song just doesn't connect with me on an emotional level. It's the birds in my own backyard and in wild places that have provided the soundtrack of my outdoor life. Like the Top 40 records I listened to in my formative teenage years, they may have shaped my tastes.

Sorry, Emperor—you can keep your nightingale. I have my own favorites, just as near and dear to my heart. In this chapter, you'll meet the cream of the crop—the best singers in our own backyards.

MAKING THE GRADE

Judging the quality of a bird's song is certainly subjective, but bird lovers have tried to nail it down for centuries. Some have written gushing praise, using words like "lyrical" or "melodious," or depending on simile or metaphor: a waterfall of notes, a flute, a trumpet, a ballad.

I'm just as guilty as the rest, because it's hard to describe birdsong in words. Listening is the only way to really get it—and to find out which songs you like best. Still, we all love to see things laid out in black and white. Therefore, the songbird with the best voice is . . . drumroll, please . . . well, it's not quite so simple.

Englishman Daines Barrington, a lawyer and bird lover of the 1700s, may have tried harder than anyone else, then or now, to break down birdsong. Like the judges of Olympic events, he came up with a scoring system that he based on these five attributes of birdsong:

1. Mellowness of tone
2. Sprightly notes
3. Plaintive notes
4. Compass (the interval between the lowest and highest notes)
5. Execution

Who ranks first on Barrington's "Table of Comparative Merit of British Singing-Birds"? The nightingale, of course, who earns a score of 19 in four of the five categories, but only a 14 in sprightly notes. (A "20 is perfection," Barrington tight-lippedly notes.) The skylark comes in at second, but his score isn't even close. Poor guy gets graded only a 4 in mellowness of tone and plaintive notes, although he aces the other categories. As for the wren, whatever species it was in his neck of the woods, Barrington puts it near the bottom. Proverbial goose eggs in mellowness and plaintive notes. A minimal 4 in compass and execution. But a 12 in sprightliness, yay!

As for our American birds, I wouldn't dream of imposing such a regimented system on their singing. But since I do love the idea of a competition, I'll go out on a limb here and list the birds I consider the best singers.

1. Wood thrush
2. Other thrushes
3. House wren
4. Winter wren
5. Grosbeaks (rose-breasted, pine, and black-headed)
6. American robin
7. Orioles
8. Northern mockingbird
9. White-throated sparrow
10. Vesper sparrow

Oh, never mind. This is as impossible as trying to list the best flowers. So many birds, so many songs, so many reasons to love them and their music. It doesn't seem right to put one above the other. But when it comes to naming favorites, that's easy: My favorite songbird is the one I happen to be listening to right now.

SINGING LESSONS

Songbirds fall into two categories: those who continue learning songs throughout their lives, and those who stop learning once they have it down.

Mockingbirds, thrashers, and catbirds (and starlings, too) are the big learners—they keep adding new elements to their songs throughout their lifetimes.

Most of these fillips are mimicry. Any repeated sound may catch their attention as something that would sound good in the repertoire. Could be that your special whistle for your dog catches their ear. Before you know it, you may hear your mockingbird repeating the summons at 3 a.m. on a summer night.

As for song sparrows, finches, tanagers, thrushes, bluebirds, and all the rest—well, I guess they haven't heard about the memory enhancement effects of *Ginkgo biloba* extract yet. They learn their songs by listening to their daddies, then fine-tune their vocals on their own. But after a few months, their learning stops: They've got it, and they'll stick to that same song forever.

Daddy's Genes?

How songbirds learn to sing has been a subject of curiosity for ages. Today's scientists are still experimenting to try to figure out the fine points, but all evidence does appear to point to Daddy as the major influence.

(continued on page 92)

Fearless but wary, the northern mockingbird flashes its wings to drive off snakes.

Wood "Warblers"
WHAT'S IN A NAME?

Not much, when it comes to wood warblers. That romantic name sure makes it seem like these birds must be fabulous singers. They're not. Well, not unless you're partial to notes that often run so high up the scale that they pierce your eardrums, rhythms so fast that they make you dizzy, and repetitive phrases that make you want to yell "Quiet!"

Or maybe that's just me. You may adore their sprightly voices and indefatigable singing, most of which sounds something like *Zhee-zhee-zhee-zhee-zhee*. And, lest you get the wrong idea, I do love wood warblers. Several have songs that are quite lovely, and all of them are welcome songbirds whose vocalizations are absolutely charming, even if they are in the same key as my teakettle.

Wood warblers are beautiful, active little birds. Their colors and markings are gorgeous, and there are so many species that spotting them is as much fun as collecting buttons or baseball cards.

Get to Know Your Songbirds
Brown Thrushes

Some members of the thrush family are already familiar backyard birds: the American robin and bluebirds. Now their wilder neotropical brown cousins are beginning to investigate our backyards as sources of food, water, and shelter, as well.

Subtle differences in markings separate the wood thrush, Swainson's thrush, gray-cheeked thrush, Bicknell's thrush, hermit thrush, and veery. All are brown with varying numbers of speckles or streaks on their breasts—perfect clothing for blending in on the leafy forest floor. All we have to do to win the favor of thrushes is to mimic their natural habitat—and lure them from nearby wild places with foods they can't resist.

The five species of brown thrushes look very much alike. Learn the subtle differences—this wood thrush sports bold spots—or just listen for their songs to set them apart.

It's easy to create your own mini-woods beneath shade trees by planting bit by bit. Add a few shrubs and groundcovers the first year—and maybe some ferns—beneath or near an existing shade tree. Then build on that planting year after year. Be sure to let fall leaves lay in place to nurture insects, snails, slugs, and other thrush foods. And haul in the biggest log you can find, because thrushes use logs as perches and travel routes, as well as singing platforms.

If you ever needed a compelling reason to try native plants, here it is: Thrushes are familiar with the insects and berries these plants offer, and the timing of these foods is right on target for the birds' nesting and migration needs.

Include native small trees, shrubs, groundcovers, ferns, and shade-loving perennial wildflowers, such as Jack-in-the-pulpit (*Arisaema triphyllum*) and Solomon's seal (*Polygonatum* spp.), in your mini-woods, and thrushes will soon come to see what's for dinner. After they do, it's just one small leap to your feeder.

When to see them: Spring through fall for all but the hermit thrush; these species are neotropical migrants.

What to feed them: Suet and other soft foods; fresh and dried fruit, especially blueberries and cherries; mealworms.

Other ways to attract them: The sound of moving water is irresistible to thrushes; consider putting in a naturalistic creek or waterfall or try a ground-level birdbath with a dripper or fountain. Lipid-rich berries are vital as a source of fat for thrushes that are bulking up before and during fall migration. Red berries are one of the main signals of such foods, so choose native shrubs and small trees that offer that attraction. Flowering dogwood (*Cornus florida*) is always reliable, but there are a plethora of other choices for every area of the country. Just peruse a catalog from a native plant nursery, such as those listed in the Resources, page 329.

What they sound like: There's a physical reason why the brown thrushes are such fabled singers: The muscles around their voice box can create multiple notes simultaneously. The resonant, flutelike tones carry well through the forest, so that the singer can easily be heard by a potential mate—or by a songbird appreciator. All of the brown thrushes have an ethereal, haunting quality to their music that inspires poets into flights of praise and stops nature lovers in their tracks. Listen to recordings of thrush music to see what all the fuss is about, or just go for a walk in the woods at dawn or dusk and listen for the most beautiful and mellifluous voices—they almost certainly belong to the brown thrushes.

What to watch for: The brown thrushes are the last singers of the day—they keep singing as the dusk deepens and other songbird voices drop out of the evening vespers.

Wood Warblers Made Easy

More than 50 species of wood warblers roam the country, but most of them are only temporary delights. Many species nest far to the north in Canada; others head for homesites in very specific sorts of habitat, such as cypress swamps or near mountain streams. Several species are indeed backyard birds, however, even in nesting season. And many others stop off to grab a bite to eat or get a drink during migration. Warblers were once rarities at feeders, but a number of species are quickly becoming regulars, and more seem to be joining the ranks as we serve up the soft foods they seek. Suet, bird doughs, mealworms, and nectar feeders tend to get the most attention. Look for these pretty little singers at your place.

WARBLER	COMMENTS
Black-and-white	May sample suet and other soft foods
Common yellowthroat	May nest in backyards with brushy areas or meadows
Orange-crowned	Fond of sugar water; visits hummingbird feeders
Pine	May investigate suet and soft foods
Prothonotary	May stop by for suet and soft foods, and may even take up residence in a birdhouse
Townsend's	Visits feeders for suet, soft foods, and mealworms
Yellow	Often adapts to living in backyards, especially if there's a pond or willows
Yellow-breasted chat	A skulker that may nest in backyard hedges or thickets
Yellow-rumped	Summer or winter backyard friend, depending on region; eats suet, soft foods, fruity treats, mealworms; loves bayberries

Genes no doubt play a part, even though an early experiment appears to prove otherwise. In that effort, a linnet (*Linnet acanthis cannabina,* a sweet-singing European finch) was taken from the nest and fostered by a totally different species, the skylark (the even sweeter-singing *Alauda arvensis*). Lo and behold, the misplaced baby learned the song of its adoptive parents. Or so it's said, anyhow. No similar "successes" have ever been reported. And every baby bird I've raised sang its species' own song, even though Daddy was nowhere to be heard.

You from New Joisey?

When my daughter moved to Boston years ago, she spoke in a Pennsylvania style. After a decade or so, though, I noticed that she had begun sounding like the Kennedys—dropping her r's and broadening her pronunciation of o's to an *"ah"* sound. *"Bahst'n,"* not Boston. *"Hahvahd,"* not Harvard.

"You're talking different," I helpfully pointed out.

"I am? No, I'm not," she insisted. To her own ears, she sounded just like everyone else around her.

Regional variations of songs, or "dialects," are common among songbirds. The prize performer is the mockingbird, who really lives up to his name—a mocker in Massachusetts imitates an entirely different bunch of birds than a mocker in Texas.

But even songbirds that we think sound alike have tiny variations in their songs. The white-crowned sparrow, for instance, is famed (among ornithologists, at any rate) for its regional dialects.

Those vocal differences are a matter of learning from birds around them, say researchers. It takes white-crowned sparrows and most other songbirds nearly a full year to begin singing. They take it all in as nestlings and fledglings, but they don't begin singing themselves until the following spring. When white-crowned sparrows were removed from their singing tutors soon after hatching and kept in a soundproof room, they sang only the most basic song, with none of the regional or individual variations that set one bird apart from its fellows.

The research didn't follow up on the birds years later, so there's no way to say whether they picked up the accent later. For all I know, they may be singing in "Valley Girl" dialect now, like, you know?

Practice Makes Perfect

In one of my favorite episodes of *The Simpsons*, Bart gets a guitar, but doesn't want to practice. Worried that dad Homer will be mad, Bart finally confesses.

Despite modifications made by a gnawing squirrel, a prothonotary warbler chose this nest box as home.

"Of course I'm not mad," Homer reassures him. "If something's hard to do, then it's not worth doing. You just stick that guitar in the closet next to your shortwave radio, your karate outfit, and your unicycle, and we'll go inside and watch TV."

"What's on?" asks Bart eagerly.

"It doesn't matter," says Homer.

After I stop laughing at that scene, I always get the impulse to pick up a guitar and play. Except that I never learned—it was too hard. As every musician knows, it takes hours of practice and then some more practice to get any good at it. When my fingertips were sore with grooves from the strings, I gave up before I grew calluses or learned to play more than the G major chord. Which, if memory serves, involved pressing down on just three strings. That lack of stick-to-itive-ness only gives me a greater appreciation for any guitar hero, from Eric Clapton to Spain's Andrés Segovia. I simply don't have the passion for making music that these virtuosos do.

But like musicians with a passion, birds are born to sing. For the first few months of their lives, they listen to the masters—their parents and other birds around them. Then when it's finally time to try out their own voices, they practice, practice, practice.

Learning by Listening

Scientific experiments—some of them too dreadful to detail—have shown that a certain area of a songbird's brain responds best to the bird's own voice. Apparently our backyard friends can evaluate their own singing by hearing themselves.

When this capacity is removed (and, no, you don't want to know how; let's just say brain surgery is involved), the bird can't give itself the necessary feedback to fine-tune its song to become a virtuoso. Although its song may still be identifiable—as, say, that of a white-crowned sparrow—it becomes more like a bad karaoke version of the original or a pale imitation of the real thing.

"Stop Copying Me!"

Playing copycat—by repeating whatever is said—is incredibly aggravating, as any child knows. Eventually the subject of the copycatting gets so frustrated that he gets angry or simply shuts up.

Works with birds, too. When researchers used a computer to play copycat with a songbird, it soon got aggravated. The subject bird was an adult whose song had already "crystallized," as biologists say. But when the computer began playing copycat, repeating the singing bird's phrases, the songbird got confused. It soon reverted to the basic unadorned song it had learned as a youngster, eliminating any individuality it had developed over its years of practice. Worse yet, the bird not only lost the creative parts it had developed: It also began stuttering, dropping notes, and distorting its song.

Scientists weren't too surprised by this. (Who knows, maybe they'd had some experience as grade-schoolers who'd hollered, "Stop copying me!") The finding that did surprise them? After the copycat experiment ended, the bird slowly regained its adult song. "Great plasticity of aural memory," said the researchers. "Thank goodness that's over," sang the bird.

TROPICAL TREATS

Early-season singers, as we talked about in Chapter 2, are the birds that we see in our backyards year-round—the goldfinches, house finches, chickadees, and other friends that help winter days pass quickly with their presence at our feeders. They're fine songsters, to be sure. But—forgive me if I sound a little like scorekeeping Daines Barrington here—they're not the best of the bunch.

It's the migrants that really set the season on fire. With spectacular plumage in vivid reds, oranges, yellows, greens, and blues, they come winging home from tropical climes where they've spent winter. Neotropics, to be exact—the hot, humid regions of the New World near the equator. *Neo* simply means "new," and it's

One of the few birds that sport a significant amount of orange feathers, the Blackburnian warbler was once known as the firethroat. This is a male; the female is duller, to blend in on the nest.

She doesn't look much like a world-class athlete, but this female blackpoll warbler, snapped in late September in New York's Central Park, is about to take off on a 2,000-mile nonstop flight over the Atlantic.

used to distinguish these birds from those of Old World tropics.

Not all of the 200 species of neotropical migrants are songbirds. The majority are indeed those beautiful singers we look forward to, such as thrushes, tanagers, vireos, and warblers. But many neotropical migrants are birds of other kinds: shorebirds (such as sandpipers), hawks, and waterfowl.

Pack Your Bags

About 23 degrees north of the equator is an imaginary line called the Tropic of Cancer. It circles the globe, running through the Bahamas and across Mexico to Baja and beyond.

Bird species of the Western Hemisphere that breed above this line, but winter below it, are neotropical migrants. They winter in places like Brazil, Ecuador, and other spots in South America, as well as Central America, Mexico, and islands off the coasts.

Everything south of this line is called the

Tropics, and it's a hot, steamy place, lush with insects, fruit, and other yummy stuff. That's why our neotropical migrants head that way in fall—they have food on their minds.

Not all individual birds of a neotropical species go that far south, though. Some members of a species may never get any farther than Florida or South Texas.

Join the Gang

Neotropical migrants aren't flocking birds like finches or chickadees are. When we see neotropicals in our backyards, we see only one or two at a time—and we feel honored. But when they're traveling, they go in groups. When you step outside to find a number of tanagers or other usually solitary birds singing from your trees, you've been honored by a stopover of a migrating flock.

Eventually the birds will drop out one by one from the flock as they reach their destinations, or peel off to go their separate ways. But for a few days, the batch of birds in your backyard is likely

Brand-New Box of Crayons

Bright colors are one of the best things about songbirds. Once the neotropicals return, our backyard singers run the full gamut of ROY G. BIV—that's every color of the spectrum. In fact, these birds even show a few extra colors, so they're more like a box of crayons than the colors of light split through a prism. Let's put them in order and see how they look.

COLOR	SONGBIRD
Red	Cassin's finch, hepatic tanager, house finch, northern cardinal, scarlet tanager, summer tanager
Orange	American redstart, Baltimore oriole, Blackburnian warbler, Bullock's oriole
Yellow	Goldfinch, prothonotary warbler, yellow-breasted chat, yellow warbler
Green	Female tanagers and warblers, many vireos, many male warblers
Blue	Bluebirds, blue grosbeak, indigo bunting, lazuli bunting
Indigo	Indigo bunting, with iridescent shades from turquoise through indigo
Violet	Interestingly, purple birds are a rarity in North America. Only the purple finch, which is more magenta than purple, sneaks into this category.
Brown	Native sparrows, pine siskins, thrushes
Black	Rose-breasted grosbeak, starlings, towhees
Gray	Chickadees, doves, gray catbird, juncos, titmice
White	There are no white American songbirds, except for the rare albinistic bird.

to keep growing as others join in at the abundant source of food. Today, it's one indigo bunting at the tube feeder; tomorrow, it may be six; the next day, a dozen. Better stock up!

When thinking about treats for these travelers, remember that insects in the wild are still the food of choice for most neotropical migrants. But these spectacular singers are learning to use our feeders, too. Up the ante at your place by providing extra suet blocks, putting out cut-up fruit, offering live mealworms and other insect foods, and serving homemade treats like those in recipes you'll find in Chapters 8 and 9. Whether they're just passing through or at the end of the route, the host of springtime birds in your backyard—tanagers, thrushes, vireos, wood warblers, and other migrants—may be tempted to try a sample.

Seasonal Shortage

The songbirds that migrate long distances have a big thing in common: They eat mostly insects, fruit, or nectar. In contrast, songbirds that stick around in winter rely mainly on seeds. Their preferences make sense, and so does their timing:

- At the end of summer, neotropical migrants depart before the bugs disappear around the time of the first frost. The birds aren't taking any chances.
- Those that depend on flying insects, such as flycatchers, swallows, and purple martins, are gone even earlier.
- In spring, the reverse is true. Look for migrants to start filtering in a month before your last spring frost date, when warm days bring the bugs out of hiding.

- Those birds that eat flying insects wait until the weather stays warm, because flying insects go aloft later; these neotropicals will be back about the time of your last spring frost.

Heard but Not Seen

Got a shade tree in your backyard? Then you'll be honored by the sights and sounds of the migrant songbirds known as vireos and wood warblers.

Lots of luck spotting the birds, though. The word *vireo* comes from the Latin word *virere*, meaning "to be green." Warblers seem to be extra fond of the color, too, hiding among green leaves. And wait, there's more bad news: These songbirds are small and highly active, constantly flitting from one twig to another.

Greenish feathers, plus small size, plus

Eats and Treats
Trail Mix

1 cup dried cherries, chopped

1 cup hulled sunflower chips

½ cup raisins, chopped

½ cup raw peanuts, chopped fine

½ cup raw shelled pumpkin seeds, chopped

Stir up a batch of this super mix and dole it out one small handful at a time. Use a feeder that's protected from starlings and other gobblers, such as a plastic feeder with an adjustable dome that can be lowered to block

bigger birds. All sorts of songbirds will avidly eat this mix—seed eaters, soft-food lovers, and fruit eaters alike—because the "seeds" are soft enough to swallow. You may see wrens, warblers, grosbeaks, catbirds, and any other songbird under the sun coming to your dish to snatch a bite. Keep in mind that the type of feeder you use and where you place it will influence which birds find it.

Trick or Treat
Seeds for Songbirds

Some of the most beautiful songbirds of springtime are easy to attract, because they eat seeds as eagerly as our year-round friends. Be sure to offer the seed in feeders that accommodate their various eating styles. Most of these birds nibble a variety of seeds, but the following are highly favored:

Fancy feathers, simple tastes: Lazuli buntings love white proso millet.

- Serve *white proso millet* in tubes or trays to indigo buntings, painted buntings, and lazuli buntings. They'll happily eat niger seed, too, but millet is their top choice in most regions—and a lot cheaper, to boot.

- Fill a tube feeder or tray with a mix of *millet* and *niger* seeds to satisfy blue grosbeaks. Closer relatives of the smaller buntings than of their larger grosbeak cousins, these birds are suited to small seeds, although they will eat sunflower seeds, too.

- Provide *millet* in tray or hopper feeders to attract scarlet tanagers, summer tanagers, western tanagers, and hepatic tanagers.

- Give rose-breasted grosbeaks, black-headed grosbeaks, and blue grosbeaks *black sunflower* seed and *safflower* seed in a tray or hopper feeder.

- Offer *millet* in tray feeders, low feeders, or on the ground to white-throated sparrows, white-crowned sparrows, fox sparrows, chipping sparrows, and any other native sparrows. Because they number more than 30 species, you're bound to bring in a variety of these pretty brown songbirds.

hyperactivity . . . Well, let's just say you're gonna need those binoculars. The good news is that you can use your ears to pinpoint these pretty little migrants. Then all you have to do is zero in on them, adjust the focus, and—whoops! He's gone!

Not to worry, though. With a little practice, you'll quickly improve your spying skills. These pretty little singers are worth the extra effort.

Albinism

We depend on color clues to recognize our songbirds, way more than we realize. If a white songbird shows up in your yard, it's a safe bet that you already know who it is. It just happens to be wearing a different outfit, that's all. And that makes it darn hard to identify.

Albinism can affect any bird of any species, but brown or black birds seem to be more susceptible, judging from reported species. It rarely occurs in birds with red, orange, or yellow plumage.

To identify your albinistic songbird, look at

Built to blend in, red-eyed vireos forage in treetops but mostly nest at lower levels.

its shape and behavior, not its color or lack thereof. First guess? Robin. Along with the house sparrow, it's the most common albinistic backyard bird.

Nice Bracelet!
LEG-BANDED BUNTINGS

If you happen to see a gorgeous painted bunting wearing a pretty ankle bracelet, PBOT wants to hear from you. Since 2005, the Painted Bunting Observer Team, a group of citizen scientists, has netted and marked nearly 4,000 painted buntings, using a combination of silver and colored leg bands.

Snap a photo of the bird, using high resolution and zooming in on the band if you can. For more info on the group's efforts and how you can become part of them, go to www.painted buntings.org/.

WHAT A LONG, STRANGE TRIP IT'S BEEN

Migration is no easy feat. Neotropical migrants cover a lot of miles, in all kinds of weather, with all sorts of dangers on every side. Wind turbines, tall buildings, windows, cars—all can deal death and destruction to flocks of songbirds moving through.

Even when they reach their wintering grounds, there's no guarantee that a welcome rest awaits. With habitat destruction continuing at an alarming rate, the rainforests they usually find respite in just might not be there anymore.

Weather's a huge peril, too. Storms can blow them off course. Sudden cold snaps can kill the insects they depend on or the birds themselves. Climate change has thrown them a curve, too. As weather patterns change, birds may not be able to adapt their traveling schedules to make the necessary shifts.

Some migrants still manage to make it through, though fewer and fewer of certain species every year, unfortunately. These species are among the ones of most concern, because their numbers are dropping fast. The Audubon Society has collected data on bird populations for more than 40 years, through the Christmas Bird Count and Breeding Bird Survey, and analysis of that data is alarming (check out birds.audubon.org/common-birds-decline, as well as the Audubon WatchList, updated every few years, at birds.audubon.org/species-by-program/watchlist). More than 200 species of American birds are on a downward slide. In 2000, eastern painted buntings and California thrashers were down in number by more than 50 percent from the previous three decades. Cerulean warblers are down 80 percent since 1967, and lark sparrows are down 63 percent in that time. Migrants like these face challenges on both their nesting range in North America and on their wintering range south of the border, and also must undertake the long and grueling journey between them twice a year.

Conservation efforts are under way by many groups and institutions, but we can make a big difference ourselves, too. A bird-friendly backyard is an oasis in this changing world. For a much more detailed look at the problem and possible solutions, you may want to pick up another of my books, *The Backyard Bird Lover's Ultimate How-To Guide*.

Mother Nature's Meals

The majority of neotropical migrants aren't interested in seeds. In fact, most haven't even learned yet that feeders mean food. Natural food is the way to win them over. That means plants, and plenty of them. It's the best inducement you can offer to migrating songbirds—food, shelter, and safety all rolled into one.

Talk about timing: Redbud (*Cercis canadensis*) blooms when gray catbirds arrive, proffering plenty of bugs.

Caterpillars are prime food for songbirds.

Add shade trees, conifers, fruit trees, small flowering trees, shrubs, you name it: The more the merrier when it comes to these birds. They'll scour the foliage and branches for insects and find the fruits and flowers, while feeling right at home in the safety of all that cover. You'll find lots of great bird plants in Chapter 14, "Home Is Where the Heart Is," and in Chapter 9, "Fruits and Sweets," as well as other bird-tempting plant suggestions scattered throughout this book.

Back Away from That Bottle

If you ever needed extra incentive to forgo pesticides, just take a look at a flaming tanager or a gentle green vireo. So-called insect pests are vital food for neotropical migrants, and a good balance of bugs is an excellent incentive to draw in these beautiful songbirds.

So tolerate those caterpillars on your oak, ignore the aphids dropping their "honeydew" from the maple, think of tent caterpillars as bird

Coffee Break
REDUCE HABITAT LOSS WITH THAT CUP OF JOE

Our own habits have played an indefensible part in putting neotropical migrants at risk. Yet all is not lost: Little changes in the way we live now can help the songbirds recover.

One of the easiest ways is to switch to drinking shade-grown organic coffee. Your wallet may complain, because these coffee beans are more expensive than the bargain brands. But you'll be doing songbirds a great big favor.

Coffees that don't carry the seal of approval label are grown on huge monoculture farms in the very epicenter of wintering songbird habitat. These farms destroy the natural, nurturing habitat and expose the birds that do try to scratch out a living there to frequent doses of dangerous pesticides.

So make the switch: Guilt-free coffee is great to savor.

treats, and thank the spiders crawling about your yews and boxwood—they're all food for our songbird friends.

Are We There Yet?

Songbirds take it slow when they're migrating in fall. The pace is generally leisurely, with plenty of stops for rest and refueling, compared to the headlong dash of spring.

Even in spring, though, many neotropical migrants start out slowly at first, picking up the pace as they near their destination. They may cover as few as 30 miles a day in fall or at the start of spring migration, stopping at a welcoming place for a while—like your yard or mine—before moving along.

In spring, the situation changes while the birds are en route. Hormones kick in and hurry the migrants home, so that they can claim a breeding territory or a mate. By the end of the trip, they may be covering 200 miles a day.

Superhuman Effort

Any bird that migrates has a tough road to follow, but the blackpoll warbler's migration is simply mind-boggling. This tiny bird, roughly chickadee size, has the longest migration trip of any wood warbler, with some individuals going from Alaska to Brazil. Part of that trip—and here's where the staggering part comes in—is directly over open water. The Atlantic Ocean, to be exact. Nearly 2,000 miles of it. Not many places to sit and rest a spell on those open waves. Not any, in fact. So the warblers fly nonstop,

Trick or Treat
The Grass Is Always Greener

Seeds of wild grasses in a meadow garden attract finches and native sparrows.

Add a bag of lawn grass seed to your feeder repertoire, and you'll attract songbirds that eagerly seek the seeds of both cultivated and wild grasses. Any kind of grass seed will do, but be sure the seed isn't treated with herbicides or other chemicals. A long list of songbirds, including blue grosbeaks, many native sparrows, and all sorts of finches, avidly eat grass seed. Serve it in a tube feeder for finches and buntings and in a low tray for native sparrows, grosbeaks, and towhees.

Bird Migration by the Numbers

How many birds?	Long-distance migration is the exception rather than the rule among the birds of the world. Of the roughly 10,000 species found worldwide, only 1,800 make a long, twice-a-year trip. Of those, 200 are North American breeding birds.
How far do they go?	It varies greatly, from about 300 to 5,000 miles, depending on species and takeoff point. Some scarlet tanagers and wood thrushes go only 600 miles; others of their species travel 4,000 miles.
How long do their trips last?	Several weeks for most species
How fast do they fly?	15 to 45 mph, on average, for 95 percent of songbirds; larger birds fly faster than smaller species.
How many miles per day?	20 to 100 miles, on average
How high up?	Between 500 and 2,000 feet, for 75 percent of songbirds

making the crossing in about 72 to 88 hours. That's about 660 miles a day.

Care to join that little songbird? Maybe you'd better think twice. Scientists have calculated that the blackpoll expends the same energy as a human running at 15 miles an hour (a 4-minute mile, for you marathoner types) . . . for 80 consecutive hours.

Next time a blackpoll warbler stops in your backyard on its way north or south—the species crosses the eastern half of the United States on its trip—just imagine where it's come from and what's still ahead of it. *Bon voyage,* little guy or gal!

Which Way Did They Go?

South, of course, if it's fall. Or north, if it's springtime. That directional pull is so strong that even captive birds turn to face the right direction at migration time.

Navigation, though, is still mostly a mystery to us. Songbirds travel at night, so they can't depend on landmarks to guide their route, like day-flying hawks and other birds can. Tons of research has been done on the subject, and while we still don't know the answers for sure, we do know that various birds follow the cues below to one extent or another:

- The stars
- The earth's magnetic field
- The direction of the setting sun
- Geographic features, such as coastlines, rivers, and mountain ranges, that are still visible at night
- The direction of prevailing winds

Get 'Em When They're Young

"Ladies first"? Not when it comes to songbirds. When it's time to depart on migration in either direction, it's adult males that go first, then females, and finally Junior brings up the rear.

Since young birds wait until last to travel, they can't follow a more experienced bird to the right place. Luckily, the urge for migration is in their genes, and so are the direction and the general length of the flight. "Fly in this direction, for this long," say their bodies, and the birds obey. Their first flight is completely on automatic pilot, so to speak. But the places the young bird chooses to rest, refuel, and ultimately stop to winter or nest are under its own control.

That's why it's so important to have your backyard ready and waiting before the birds return. With safe surroundings, plenty of natural and feeder foods, and a refreshing source of water, the young birds may just decide to stay. Once they do, they'll return in following years, just like we revisit our favorite bed-and-breakfasts on repeated road trips.

A NEW SUIT FOR SPRING

Migrant neotropical songbirds—the gorgeous rose-breasted grosbeaks, orioles, and other bright spots of our summer backyards—change into their spring finery beyond our view, on wintering grounds in Central and South America and elsewhere.

Songbirds who winter in the South, such as the friendly little chipping sparrow, do the same thing. By the time they return to their nesting

---

Color Changes

Here's what to watch for in the all-year friends that most of us share across the country.

SONGBIRD	PLUMAGE CHANGE
American goldfinch	Males and females molt into drab olive-colored feathers in fall after breeding season. In early spring, they molt again, with males turning first blotchy, then sunny yellow; females molt to warm yellow-green.
Doves and pigeons	Iridescent feathers on the male's head and neck begin to shine, or as Tennyson put it, "a livelier iris changes on the burnish'd dove."
European starling	The creamy feather tips that give the starling its name are very noticeable when the bird molts in fall after breeding season. Over winter, those pale tips wear off, so that the bird looks black, not starry, and its iridescence becomes evident.
Northern cardinal	The gray edges of that new fall suit wear off over winter, leaving the male bird its best and brightest for spring.

grounds or pause en route to sample the goodies in our backyards, they're already looking mighty spiffy. If you live in the wintering range of chipping sparrows or other songbirds who stick around in the South, you can see these changes happening right outside your window.

As for our year-round songbirds, the ones that keep us company all winter, they start switching their duds right in front of our eyes. The change is so gradual that we may not notice it day by day. In some species, the color change is because the bird is molting; in others, it's because the feathers are wearing down. But whatever the reason, eventually it'll hit us—that cardinal is practically glowing, the goldfinches are getting yellow, and even the starlings we might want to shoo away are looking different.

High Calorie Needs All Year Round

We're used to thinking that high-fat foods are best for birds in fall and winter to help them stay warm. But these foods are also just the ticket for songbirds in spring and summer.

What with all that springtime fussin' and fightin' over territories and partners, and later feeding the young 'uns, songbird bodies are demanding extra energy. Offer birds high-fat treats in summer, too, especially those with a high dose of vitamin E, to nourish the new plumage they'll grow when nesting is finished.

Even better, give your songbirds both at once! Wheat germ oil, made from the tiny germ inside grains of wheat, is one of the best sources of vitamin E around and has a high fat content, too.

You'll usually find it in the health food aisle at supermarkets.

For the simplest serving suggestion, just pour about ¼ cup of oil into about 2 cups of hulled sunflower seeds, stir well to coat the seeds lightly with oil, and put the nourishing treat in a tray or domed feeder.

Southern Living

The songbirds of each season vary, depending on where we live. That means that the plumage we see may vary, too, depending on who's spending the summer or winter with us, and whether or not they change their colors for different seasons.

The difference is most dramatic in migrating species, because we don't get to see it happening. Molting occurs on wintering grounds, before songbirds begin the long flight back home. In summer, molt occurs after nesting is finished, before the birds take to the air to head south.

In some regions, especially the Southeast, the cast of characters in winter includes quite a few species that many of us think of as our spring and summer friends.

Some of these birds look the same, no matter what the season—the brown thrasher, gray catbird, and house wren, for example—while others, especially native sparrows, add brighter feathers for breeding season.

In spring, southern-wintering songbirds go their separate ways. Many individuals of these species head north to delight the rest of us, while the rest stay near where they wintered in the South to raise their families.

CHAPTER 6

Lullaby and Good Night

A few songbirds may still come to the feeder in late afternoon to stuff a last bedtime snack down the mouths of their nestlings, but by the time the sun starts to sink, they have other priorities in mind. It's time to sing the day to sleep.

In this chapter, we'll follow our songbirds as the sun goes down. You'll learn how the evening concert differs from the exultation of morning, as birds settle down to sleep instead of getting charged up for the new day. You'll meet the nighttime singers, too, who sing a little or a lot in the still of the night, including the indefatigable northern mockingbird with its unique repertoire. You'll learn how to listen for the voices of birds on the wing at night—migrants flying under the cover of darkness. And since helping birds is what we all love to do, we'll talk about how and where birds spend the night and how we can help keep them safe when they're at their most vulnerable.

EVENSONG

The serenade at sunset in spring is a poignant one. Not all songbirds join in, and it has a whole different mood than the uninhibited joy of the morning. Like a Vespers service in a cathedral, the voices sound more like a soothing hymn than a stirring celebration.

It's a lullaby.

The singers seem to slow down, with their voices grown sweeter in the glow of sunset. The silvery notes of thrushes are solos now, their musical voices almost unearthly in the shadowy woods. The brown thrasher in the hedge holds a private concert, a whisper song for his partner that's so soft and tender it's almost inaudible from just a few feet away. The last white-throated sparrows, not yet moved on to northern homes, gather in the bushes or honeysuckle vine and sing an evensong of simple, plaintive notes. Robins near and far join in the vespers, singing a benediction on the day.

They're just ordinary backyard birds doing what comes naturally. But the gathering dusk lends an emotional magic to their music, as the cares of the day fall away. The sweetness of the lullaby is enough to make a listener cry. And I sometimes do.

Then I get jerked back to reality as a ticked-off robin breaks the mood by bursting into loud *yeep*s. Oh, well, the peace of evening was nice while it lasted.

RESTING PLACE

Your work is done, family fed, and household chores can wait 'til tomorrow. When the sun goes down, it's time to kick off your shoes and get comfortable.

Out in the backyard, songbirds are doing the same thing. Their bellies are full, their quarrels with neighbors are forgotten, and they've been finding snug spots to sleep since an hour or so before sunset. Mama birds with nests settle themselves over their precious eggs or nestlings, tucking everybody in under their wings to keep them safe and warm. Their partners find a sleeping spot nearby, where they can be ready to spring into action at a moment's notice, in case of nighttime prowlers.

If it's not breeding season, songbirds often gather together to roost for the night. Several species may join the group, sharing the benefit of extra warmth. There's safety in numbers, too, because the likelihood of being picked off by a predator is lessened.

Under Cover

Dense branches are the bedroom of choice for nearly all of our backyard songbirds. A tangle of vines, a hedge, a big thorny bush, an evergreen, and the thick, leafy canopy of a shade tree are all inviting spots to spend the night. The dense vegetation helps deter owls and other predators from sneaking up on the sleeping birds, and it shields the songbirds from wind, rain, and snow.

Birds sleep at different levels, depending on their daytime habits:

- Songbirds that spend most of their daylight hours on or near the ground, such as native sparrows and towhees, choose nighttime roosts nearby in brush piles or in low, dense branches of shrubs.

- Birds of the treetops, including red-eyed vireos, Townsend's warblers, and orioles, among others, sleep in the treetops.

- And birds of the bush, such as brown thrashers, cardinals, catbirds, buntings, and the common yellowthroat warbler, which range from the trees to the ground and back again during the course of the day, sleep at medium heights in the plants in our yards. A hedge or dense shrub may suit them perfectly.

Green-tailed towhees, like other towhee species, stay in or near dense cover.

A large, "unmanicured" planting of taller perennials and shrub roses is the kind of habitat that attracts the common yellowthroat, a bird of the brush.

Songbirds sleep with their feet locked onto a perch. A flexor tendon runs down the back of each of the bird's legs to its toes. As soon as the bird lands on a perch, whether it's going to sleep or just briefly stop, its tendons instantly and automatically lock those tootsies into place. That reinforced grip stays secure until the bird moves its feet; then the tendon swiftly locks the toes again into their new position. Pretty nifty trick when you sleep upright, as songbirds do.

Once they've settled on a sleeping spot, songbirds lower their bodies to rest and curl their heads to the side, often tucked under a wing. Final touch: They fluff up the "covers," their feathers, to keep out the cold or to let circulating air cool their bodies on a steamy summer night.

Going Green

Conifers are a favorite nighttime roost for house finches, grosbeaks, cardinals, and other backyard singers, thanks to their dense, prickly branches. Add a spruce (*Picea* spp.), a fir (*Abies* spp.), or an upright juniper (*Juniperus* spp.) to your yard—or better yet, a group of three, if you have enough room—to give these birds a sleeping place.

Varieties of the eastern redcedar, which is actually a juniper (*Juniperus virginiana*), are a great choice, because they're fast-growing and beautiful. The sharp tips of the short needles go a long way in deterring prowling cats and other nighttime predators. You'll find these junipers in all sorts of ornamental foliage colors, including cool blue-grays and golden varieties that seem to glow on a snowy day. Bonus: Fruit-eating songbirds, including bluebirds and yellow-rumped warblers, ardently seek their ripe berries.

Snug as a Bug

"Think I might sleep outside tonight," a friend commented on a mild spring day. "It's so clear. The stars will be beautiful. Maybe I'll just bring a blanket out on the porch."

That bright idea didn't last long. As soon as the sun went down, the air turned chilly. And with no blanket of clouds to hold the day's heat close to the earth, my shivering friend soon retreated indoors. "Colder than I thought," she said through chattering teeth.

Yep, a roof overhead is a nice idea, and some songbirds second the motion. They sleep in houses—birdhouses, that is, or roosting boxes or natural holes in trees. You won't find a robin in a roost box, though. Nor most of our other backyard singers. Only a few songbirds use cavities for nesting, and they're the same ones that seek such shelters for sleeping, especially on cold nights.

Still, it's worth adding a roost box to your repertoire, because these species are among our favorites: bluebirds, chickadees, titmice, and wrens, to name the main takers. My Carolina wrens have taken the shelter idea one step further. Instead of using that nice snug roost box I mounted, they squeeze under the crack of the door of my old wooden garage and make themselves at home inside.

BY THE LIGHT OF THE SILVERY MOON

Morning birdsong is a delight, but a few of our musical friends entertain us during the dark hours, too. While the robins are fast asleep, no doubt dreaming of nice juicy worms, a brown

Trick or Treat
Bedtime Snack

Sharing a child's company over cookies and milk before bed is more about connection than it is about food. The time of day, the special treat, and the close companionship send a message of love to whoever's eating those cookies.

Maybe that's why I like to give my birds a special treat before they retire in the evening—it's a way of connecting as well as nurturing. Give it a try and see how good it feels. While there are still a few birds at the feeder, set out a dozen or so mealworms or a small handful of chopped nuts. Because the remaining feeding time is short, scatter the food in a tray feeder for easy access by a number of birds.

Keep your nest boxes up all winter to serve as nighttime shelter for tufted titmice, chickadees, wrens, and bluebirds.

thrasher, gray catbird, or northern mockingbird may be stirring in the bushes. These mimic thrushes have a penchant for making music after hours. Thrashers and the gray catbird are cousins of the mockingbird, but their night singing is more an occasional treat than a regular, full-fledged concert. On a full-moon night, these birds may rise to the occasion and perch at the tip of a branch to sing for half an hour or more. Usually, though, they carol briefly from the bushes.

A few other songbirds are also noted for occasionally singing at night. If your yard is woodsy, listen for the sweet voices of thrushes, especially the hermit thrush and veery. Song sparrows, one of the most common backyard songbirds, often hold forth at night, too.

Sleep with an open window, and you may hear the sweet voice of a veery during the night.

Get to Know Your Songbirds
American Robin

If you have a yard with even a little bit of lawn or a flowerbed, you've got robins. Robins' songs are the predominant part of the daily chorus, and no wonder: This is one of the most abundant birds, ranging across the entire country, and females often sing, too.

Robins have been our longtime backyard friends. But until recently, they showed little or no interest in feeders.

Then new bird foods hit the market: Fruity and soft foods, premium seed mixes with the dried berries that robins love, and mealworms all have turned the tide, and all of a sudden, robins are showing up at feeders in many areas.

It still looks plain weird to see a robin on a feeder, eating alongside chickadees. Better get used to it. Feeder visits are a new behavior for robins, but they've taken to them with gusto.

The female American robin has a paler breast than this male.

When to see them: Robins are present in warmer months in many areas, but usually retreat to milder places in winter. Some individuals are changing their habits and visiting backyards year-round to feed on soft foods, fruit, and mealworms; this behavior seems likely to increase.

What to feed them: Raisins, apples, dried fruit bits served à la carte or in premium seed mixes; mealworms; soft foods in small bits on a low tray; soft cat or dog food.

Other ways to attract them: Robins love a daily bath. Small fruits on a tree are a huge draw, too: Sweet cherries, sour pie cherries ('Montmorency' is quick to bear a big crop), and native cherries (*Prunus* spp.), including pin cherry, black cherry, choke-cherry, and others will draw them in. Serviceberry (*Amelanchier arborea*), dogwoods (*Cornus* spp.), elderberries, mulberries, and holly (*Ilex* spp.) are irresistible. In spring, offer lengths of string or twine and a patch of very wet mud to help robins in nest building. Robins don't nest in birdhouses, but they may quickly accept a roofed nesting shelf mounted on a tree or on an outside wall. A large, sturdy grapevine wreath on the door often serves as a nesting place, too.

What they sound like: Long, lively, melodic song; usually the first to greet the day and the last to sing it to sleep.

What to watch for: Watch for robins at mud puddles or wet places in the garden, collecting beakfuls of mud for nest building.

When the moon is bright, other songbirds may be inspired to hold a nighttime concert. Step outside and listen.

Artificial Sunrise

Late one April night, in the midst of burning the midnight oil, I took a break to step outside and clear my head in the fresh air. It was 2:30 a.m., and my small town was asleep. I enjoyed the silence as I stood on the porch.

But I didn't enjoy the light. The view down the block should've been velvety black in the shadows under the big old sugar maples that line the street. Instead, bright yellowish sodium-vapor streetlights made it possible to see just about everything going on.

Those lights are a good idea, I suppose, in high-crime urban areas. In a sleepy little town, they're overkill. And they interfere with the natural rhythms of some songbirds—robins, to be exact. Which, unbelievably, were already waking up. First one, then another and another robin began their morning songs. Sunrise wasn't until 6:00 a.m. or so, but by 3:00 a.m., when I turned in for the night, the birds were singing from all parts of town, everywhere that the light reached.

The robins don't seem to suffer any ill effects from their extra-long day. But I often wonder whether, like me, they'd feel better if they got a full night's sleep.

I also wonder why they don't sing all night. After all, the streetlights don't get any stronger in the wee hours. Maybe songbirds simply need a certain amount of sleep before they respond to that irresistible level of light.

Not-So-Sweet Dreams

Once in a while, you may hear a sudden snatch of song in your backyard at night that's not the usual mockingbird, thrasher, or catbird. That's usually a sign of bad tidings: Sleeping birds that are startled during the night often let loose with a bit of song instead of an alarm call.

We could think positive and suggest that the singer was only jostled by a companion in the roost. It happens. But sometimes that snatch of

---

Trick or Treat
Open Wide

"Sleeping porches" used to be a standard part of houses in the steamy South. In the days before air conditioning, they were a great solution to getting a comfortable night's rest. Many folks still make use of these appealing enclosed porches. Screens keep the mosquitoes at bay but welcome the slightest breeze.

If you don't have a sleeping porch, try the next best thing: Sleep with your windows open. A cross breeze is heavenly on a summer night, and you won't miss a trick when nighttime singers in your backyard add melody to the moonlight.

song means a nighttime skulker has nabbed the bird. If the panicked burst of song stops abruptly, it's probably not a happy ending. In breeding season, nighttime predators often grab a parent bird right off the nest.

DANGER IN DARKNESS

Like all animals, including us, songbirds are at their most vulnerable when they're sleeping. And like all animals, they do everything they can to try to stay safe.

Birds are at the bottom of the totem pole when it comes to vulnerability. Even though they have wings, they can still get taken by surprise—and plenty of critters want to surprise them. No wonder nighttime is the most dangerous time for songbirds. Cats, opossums, raccoons, snakes, and owls all stalk our singing friends when they're sleeping.

Man the Barricades!

Barriers have long been used to discourage trespassers, including those who try to sneak up

Safe Haven
BIRD VINEYARD

No complicated pruning needed to grow 'Concord' grapes for birds!

For a fast and easy way to attract a pair of night-singing gray catbirds, get some grapevines growing. We're not talking about the how-the-heck-do-I-prune-these-things style of vines. These are for the birds, so the wilder, the better.

An arbor will work, but planting a grapevine to clamber up a fence, into the trees, or over a natural hedge is even better, because there will be less human traffic, which is just what these privacy-seeking birds like best. Don't try this growing trick over prized plant specimens, though, because these vines exert a constrictor grip as they grow, and their foliage may block the light, resulting in bare spots on your hundred-dollar boxwood. Instead, add the grapevine to a wilder area, where plants can sort things out for themselves.

Good old 'Concord' is a reliable, trouble-free variety, and it grows like lightning. No need to worry about pruning, unless the vines block your own path; then just snip off the offending branches.

Catbirds will appreciate the jungle, as well as the privacy, of your untended "vineyard." And when the vine bears fruit, you can expect to see a bevy of beautiful songbirds—rose-breasted grosbeaks, orioles, and bluebirds, to name just a few—arriving for the feast.

Listen and Learn
Night Flight

Birds in flight are vulnerable to attack from hawks, but hawks fly by day, even on migration. That's probably a big reason why all songbirds migrate under cover of darkness. It makes safe travels, except for those obstacles that we've added to the landscape, like high-rise buildings and satellite towers.

It's hard to spot songbirds on their journey in the dark, but it's easy to hear them. Just step outside on a spring night from March to May, depending on where you live, and listen up. I really mean "up": Tilt your head toward the sky, cup your ears for extra amplification, and listen for the soft twitters and *chips* filtering down from our friends in flight.

It's the best kind of traffic noise you'll ever hear. And it's a nifty reminder to have your feeders and water ready to welcome the birds when they drop down from the sky just before dawn.

One of the first feeders a returning oriole will visit in springtime? The hummingbirds' nectar feeder.

at night. A moat works wonders, or at least it used to for those who lived in castles. Many of us have fences or driveway gates to keep out interlopers.

Birds don't have these options, but they do have their own versions of them. Some songbirds place their nests on branches over water, an effective way to make climbing predators think twice about crossing the swaying "suspension bridge" to get at the nests.

But as a low-tech and less labor-intensive solution, thorns and spines are a much more common way of discouraging trespassers. And

they're effective, for us and for birds. Just ask the villagers in Africa who pile thorny brush around their animals and their own huts; the barricades deter even lions from getting at the goats—or the humans—at night. Birds choose thorny plants for nighttime roosts or nest sites for the same reason: The spines help deter hungry cats, raccoons, snakes, and other predators, so the songbirds can sleep in safety.

If a plant makes you say "Ouch!" it's probably a great choice for your songbird-friendly yard. Many of our singers seek thorny plants as resting places at night, and some, such as cardinals and catbirds, seek out roses, blackberry bushes, or other prickly plants as homesites.

One of the best plants for both bird uses—as a nighttime roost and as a nest site—is the evergreen holly (*Ilex* spp.), because it protects birds year-round from danger and from weather. Choose a tree-type holly for maximum versatility; it'll appeal to birds of the trees as well as birds of the bush that usually stay low. Varieties of holly with small leaves, such as the Foster holly (*Ilex × attenuata* 'Fosteri'), work just as well as those with normal-size leaves. Just make sure your pick has plenty of prickles on its beautiful glossy foliage. Remember to plant it well away from walks and your usual strolling areas, so you're not the one being poked.

Add other prickly plants to your backyard sanctuary, too, to accommodate more birds. Choose plants with dense branches that make it tricky for predators to enter, such as junipers (*Juniperus* spp.), barberries (*Berberis* spp.), brambles (*Rubus* spp.), and shrub roses (*Rosa* spp.). Native sparrows, thrashers, robins, and many other songster friends will be quick to take advantage of them—and all offer a bonus of berries, too, to attract even more birds.

You'll find more details about the habits of songbird-eating predators, as well as lots of ideas for helping birds stay safe and secure from them, in Chapter 16, "Plain Talk about Pests."

The Startle Reflex

I'm a sound sleeper, but I wake with a start whenever I hear an odd noise. A smell can do it, too. And as for touch, well, just let a stray tick from my last walk in the woods start crawling on my skin, and I'm vertical in a flash. Anything that's out of the ordinary and that reaches any of our five senses can yank us animals from our slumber. It's part of how we protect ourselves from danger when we're sleeping.

It's also why I don't ride horses anymore. Equines have a strong startle reflex, and my last horse was way too quick on the trigger. When I landed on my head—again—after she spooked at a shadow, I packed up my saddle for the last time.

Songbirds have an even sharper startle reflex. They can be snoring away one moment—okay, they don't really snore, but you get the idea—and ready to do battle to the death the next. In the daytime, you can see their hair-trigger reflexes at work right in your backyard. One songbird spooks, often for no apparent reason, and instantly the yard is bare of birds. Only when they're convinced that the danger is past will they come out of hiding.

PART II

Eat, Drink,
and
Be Merry

CHAPTER 7

Singing for Their Supper
(and Breakfast, Lunch, and Snacks)

I'm a dyed-in-the-wool country girl. Give me those wide open spaces and big stretches of woods to walk, with uncrowded paths where the only footprints are those of deer or elk or my own hiking boots. Can't see a neighbor's house? Perfect!

And yet, I've spent a large part of my life living in town. I've managed to adapt, because the benefits of living in civilization have balanced out my craving for isolation.

Take restaurants, for instance. I love to eat. And socializing. I may be a hermit at heart, but I love the company of others. A helping hand when needed is another reason I've chosen a place in town, instead of way out in the middle of nowhere. It's reassuring to know that if I have a mishap—and I have them regularly—there's help next door.

Still, I leaped at the chance to spend time high in the Rockies, far off the beaten path. It wasn't exactly solitude, since I was sharing the place with my best friend who had invited me. But the peace and quiet was wonderful. Finally, I felt like myself. Days of nothing but nature and the undemanding companionship of my friend . . . with a weekly visit to town to enjoy the fruits of civilization. Somebody say pizza?

Restaurants lure plenty of us into town, even when we're stay-at-homes at heart. That concept works for birds as well as for people, so stock up on goodies that'll bring that oriole down from the treetops or that towhee in from the woods nearby. In this chapter, we'll cover the basics of how to turn our yards into bird bistros that draw in customers aplenty. You'll find lots of tips for stocking your larder and arranging for the kind of ambience that lures songbirds into easy view.

DIFFERENT DRUMMER

Coaxing songbirds to our yards isn't quite as simple as attracting the usual bunch of feeder birds. Although tempting feeder foods go a long way, not all songbirds take naturally to our backyards, especially if our backyards are in the heart of a town or city, far from wild places.

Many species are, like me, hermits at heart. Some songbirds—including, of course, the ones we want most, like bluebirds, thrushes, and tanagers—are at home only in very specific kinds of wild habitat: forests, thickets, grasslands, and at the edge of water.

If your backyard happens to be near wild places, you're in luck. It'll be a cinch to get every songbird nearby into your yard year-round. We'll soon talk about how.

If you're not near wild places, though, you're still in luck. Many songbirds are already using backyards as habitat.

As for those birds that prefer life on the wilder side, they'll be more of a challenge. But how does that old saying go, about appreciating things more when you have to work for them? Every songbird that shows up will feel like a personal victory for you—and that's what it is. You've attracted the songbirds by providing what they need: food, water, and a place to rest.

Orange You Pretty!
GAUDY FEEDERS NOT NEEDED

I like my bird feeders to blend in with their surroundings, not stick out like sore thumbs. So I generally eschew those made of bright plastic and instead go for natural-looking wood or at least something in a dull color.

That's the only reason I've resisted every orange plastic oriole feeder on the market. Although

Orange plastic isn't needed to attract Baltimore and other orioles to a feeder.

the feeders may be functional, to me they look like, well, orange plastic. Besides, my orioles have no problem finding the food I put out for them, no matter what color the feeder is. These songbirds adore halved oranges, and the fruit is a constant at their feeder. But so are lemons, limes, tangerines, and whatever citrus I can get my hands on. They're all high in carotenoids that contribute to the pretty hues of our oriole friends. And the birds peck avidly at them, no matter what color they are.

Trick or Treat
Extra E-zy

Birds can't use special shampoos and conditioners to make their feathers shine. That healthy glow has to come from inside them. To keep your songbirds looking their best, give them treats that are high in vitamin E.

This essential nutrient, sometimes called the fertility vitamin, is an ideal feather booster and helps with reproductive health, too. To aid your songbirds in growing their best plumage, serve them treats made with wheat germ oil, safflower oil, and sunflower oil, all rich in vitamin E.

Make sure the oils are mixed well with other foods, so your songbirds don't get that "greasy kid stuff" look to their feathers. Oily feathers can be dangerous, because the oil reduces the insulating capability of the plumage. Birds are usually very careful not to get into oil, except with their beaks, but a little cornmeal, oatmeal, flour, or crumbled crackers or cereal will reduce their risk.

The Traveling Kind

The songbirds that are most standoffish, those that haven't yet adapted to backyard life, are also the travelin' kind. Twice a year, they migrate across long stretches of the country. By turning our yards into mini oases that are visible from the air, we can tempt nearly every one of these species into stopping off for a spell. And once a songbird finds a favorite restaurant, you can bet it'll be back—even if it's six months later, when it's time to travel in the other direction.

Those of us who live near wild places (and by "near," I mean within a mile or so) have it easier. Songbirds may visit in any season, and if your place happens to be right beside a wild area, you'll be able to attract nesting pairs, too.

No matter where we live, our backyards will be prime targets when the birds return from migration, as well as when they're beefing up for their return trip. Songbirds explore far outside their usual haunts when they need a helping hand. Our backyard handouts and habitats will attract them in winter, too, if they happen to be around.

The Urge for Going

For years, the common thinking was that birds leave on fall migration according to an internal time clock that is impossible to counteract. Lately, though, we've been finding out that that's not always the case.

Spring migration is definitely hormone driven, and routes to familiar breeding grounds seem to be hardwired into songbirds. So the birds make a beeline when they head for summer homes.

In fall, though, the migration appears to take place because of dwindling food supplies, not because of the irresistible urge to reproduce. Timing for that migration may indeed be part of a songbird's heritage, an internal time clock instilled over the eons, but it seems that the urge for going can be overridden.

In recent years, insect- and fruit-eating songbirds, including thrashers, catbirds, wrens, bluebirds, and even orioles, are staying later in summer and fall. Some are even wintering in areas they formerly fled when the weather turned cold.

Is It Us?

The changes in fall migration habits may be because of bird feeders and backyard plantings, suggest some scientists. With millions of us providing a reliable source of nutrition, what used to be the lean season is now full of suet, soft food, berries, and other easily available foods.

Is that why some songbirds are sticking around? We still don't know. Climate change has caused shifts in insect populations and their timing and in other sources of songbird foods as well. Some songbirds still get the urge for going, even when food is abundant. Indigo buntings, for instance, which avidly eat seeds, still disappear right on schedule, heading south.

It's also possible that nothing has changed at all—that with more of us watching birds, we're only now noticing something that's been going on forever. What we do know is that some migrant songbirds linger long past their usual departure dates. So keep an eye out for unseasonable songbirds in your yard. And keep the suet, soft foods, and those ever-popular mealworms coming.

THE WAY TO A SONGBIRD'S HEART

Even the songbirds that are hermits at heart sometimes need our support. We may not entice them to nest with us, but we can lure them to our backyards to eat. Just like us, they love a good meal.

In that sense, attracting songbirds is as simple as attracting other birds that already call our yards home. Food, the key to their heart.

The only difference? The menu—and the ambience.

A Different Diet

A well-stocked feeder setup goes a long way toward attracting birds. For those species who already are accustomed to visiting feeders, it's the primary attraction.

But when it comes to songbirds, even the most well-stocked feeders won't necessarily bring us all the birds we want to see. Despite all those oriole foods and bluebird foods on the market, not to mention the photos of wood warblers on

Suet or meat fat is a magnet for songbirds, including the beautiful varied thrush.

some bird food products, some songbirds simply don't recognize feeders as a food source.

Natural foods are still number one for songbirds. And these food sources go hand in hand with habitat—the plants we add to our yards and the way we arrange them. Insects are a huge incentive. So are fruits and berries, on the bush or tree. Earthworms, slugs, and snails appeal to some songbirds, including thrushes, of which our friend the worm-eating robin is one. Flowers are a draw to some species, too, both for the insects they attract and for the nectar and pollen that orioles seek.

You'll find lots of ideas for increasing the natural food supply in your yard in the following chapters, as well as throughout this book. The plants and the way we arrange them pay off in another big way, too, when it comes to songbirds: They supply the cover and nesting possibilities that help attract these birds. Chapters 14 and 15 focus on these homemaking aspects.

And, of course, our songbird friends need something to wash down all these goodies with, as well as to freshen their pretty feathers. Water is a huge draw, and you'll find plenty of ideas for using it to tempt songbirds in Chapter 13, "The Allure of Water."

Let's start, though, by taking a look at natural foods and how we can put them to use.

Insects

Crawling insects, hopping insects, flying insects—songbirds nab 'em all. Each songbird species has its own niche in its environment, and these species cover every inch of our yards and wild places. In one tree alone, you may spot a dozen different songbird species foraging for insects. Wood warblers, vireos, and tanagers move through the foliage, snatching bugs from the leaves. Brown creepers scour the crevices of the bark as they spiral up the trunk. Kinglets and chickadees hang like parrots from the very tips of branches, while orioles move along the main limbs.

Meanwhile, down near the ground, thrushes, towhees, and some native sparrow species are busy among the leaf litter under shrubs and around plants, searching for ants, beetles, spiders, and anything else they can uncover.

Songbirds don't care whether a butterfly is beautiful or not; butterflies are part of their food supply and they're crazy 'bout cabbage whites. Ultra-common cabbage white butterflies originally came from Europe, but songbirds don't care: All they know is that these insects make a fine meal. Bluebirds catch the adult butterflies on the wing, while house wrens are particularly big fans of the caterpillars. Attracting cabbage whites to your yard couldn't be easier. Just plant

The ubiquitous cabbage white butterfly is a prize to songbirds.

anything in the cabbage family, even among the flowers in your beds or in bunches near your shrubs, and the butterflies will soon arrive to lay their eggs on it. Their small green caterpillars are well camouflaged, but wrens have sharp eyes—and sharp beaks.

Unless you, too, are hungry for a little creepy-crawly protein, you'll have to give up the idea of getting any of the cabbage-family crop for yourself. (To bar cabbage whites from your veggie garden, just shield your plants with a spun-polyester row cover.)

All insects are high in protein, whether they're eggs, larvae, pupae, or adults. They're a perfect food for birds, and that's what nature intended. You'll find tons of tips for adding insects to your yard, by way of plantings and gardening, throughout this book.

Fruit

Many tropical birds are *frugivores,* animals whose diets consist mainly of fruit. So are some of our neotropical songbirds—they adopt frugivore habits when they're at their winter quarters in tropical gardens of Eden, with all manner of

Brown thrashers, gray catbirds, and robins are big fans of strawberries of any sort.

fruits hanging heavy on all sides. Other songbirds, both neotropicals and all-year residents, include fruit in their more varied menus throughout the year.

Trick or Treat
Fool-'Em Fruit Feeders

The trick to using fruit to attract songbirds (songbirds that haven't learned to use feeders, that is) is twofold: arrangement and attachment.

Offer the fruit in a way that looks real, as if it were growing naturally instead of being a grocery-store leftover. And make sure it's securely attached and not likely to fall suddenly and scare off the bird when it tugs or pecks at the fruit.

Only a handful of songbirds aren't interested in eating fruit or berries: Native sparrows, juncos, and most finches usually don't bother with fruit. But that general trait seems to be changing these days, too. I've seen many of the seed-eating types try a sample of fruity foods offered at feeders. In the wild, they may not eat much fruit, but when it's right near their favorite seeds or mixed in with them, "Why not try a bite?" seems to be their attitude.

Apples on the tree are much more popular in winter than at autumn harvest time. Weeks of freezes and thaws soften apple skin and flesh, so that robins, bluebirds, finches, and other fruit eaters can easily peck out pieces. Get the same effect by storing your "bird apples" in the freezer to soften them. Let them thaw before serving, and to make access even easier, halve them or peel off a strip of skin to expose the flesh to encourage that first bite.

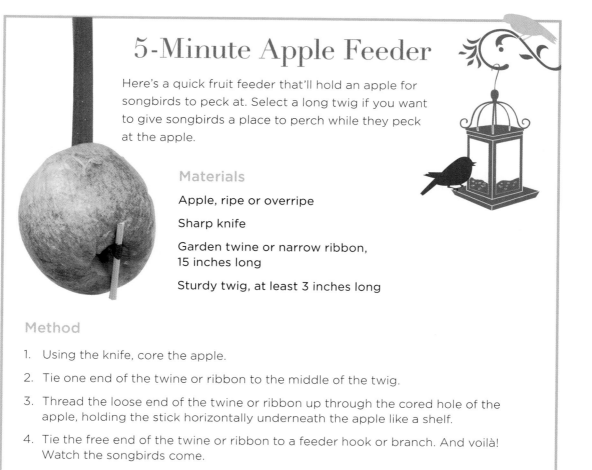

5-Minute Apple Feeder

Here's a quick fruit feeder that'll hold an apple for songbirds to peck at. Select a long twig if you want to give songbirds a place to perch while they peck at the apple.

Materials

Apple, ripe or overripe

Sharp knife

Garden twine or narrow ribbon, 15 inches long

Sturdy twig, at least 3 inches long

Method

1. Using the knife, core the apple.

2. Tie one end of the twine or ribbon to the middle of the twig.

3. Thread the loose end of the twine or ribbon up through the cored hole of the apple, holding the stick horizontally underneath the apple like a shelf.

4. Tie the free end of the twine or ribbon to a feeder hook or branch. And voilà! Watch the songbirds come.

Include a capacious tube feeder to serve a multitude of mixed finches in spring.

Seeds and Nuts

Goldfinches and other finches, juncos, and dozens of native sparrow species eat mainly seeds most of the year. Cardinals, grosbeaks, red-winged blackbirds, and towhees eat seeds, too. Oh, and let's not forget our friends the chickadees, titmice, and glorious buntings—seed eaters, all. Need any more reason to include seeds at your songbird restaurant? How about scarlet tanagers?

All of these birds, as well as wrens and other species, happily eat nuts, too, especially if they're chopped into small pieces.

It's simple to offer seeds at a feeder. But it's fun to grow your own, too, because you can watch the birds behaving naturally as they feast on your plants.

Let the Landscape Provide

Songbirds and trees—it's a match made in heaven, or wherever such matches are decided.

It's easy to see why Central Park in New York City attracts so many species—the oasis is readily visible to any songbird in the air.

Overflow Parking

When I hauled home a dead juniper bush that had weathered into a fan of gnarled bare branches, I was planning to use it on the wall, as a hanger for homemade pinecone birds after coating it with glitter, of course (oh boy! shiny!).

I never quite got around to that project. But my twiggy branch found an even better use: a natural perch for the flock of finches that regularly overflowed the feeder.

To make your own "parking lot," all you need is a bare, twiggy branch, a couple of screws, and a wooden post to support it. Fine twigs, such as those on the outer branches of hawthorn, hackberry, birch, maple, oak, and many other trees, are perfect for tiny lightweight finches, even if you're hosting a hundred. But larger birds will be reluctant to settle among the entangling, unreliable web of flimsy twigs, so your little singers can sit there undisturbed.

You'll need a sturdy post, such as a wooden fence post or a deck post, to attach the perch. Don't have either? A wooden feeder post will work well, too.

Materials

Twiggy branch, 3 to 4 feet long with a "trunk" 1 to 2 inches in diameter and side branches fanning out 2 to 4 feet, or a few smaller branches to bind together

Twine or silicone tape (optional)

Wooden fence, deck, or feeder post

Cordless drill

Screws, at least 3 inches long

Method

1. If your branch is shy of side stems, fasten two or three branches together with twine or silicone tape at the trunk end, so that they overlap to make a wide fan of slender twigs.

2. Enlist a helper to hold the perch alongside the post, at least 5 feet from the ground—the higher the better, to keep birds safe from predators. Check to be sure branches are right side up and in a visually appealing, natural-looking position.

3. Use the drill to insert the screws through the trunk of the branch into the post. Insert the screws about 2 to 3 inches apart for stability.

Trees offer food and plenty of it to grosbeaks, tanagers, wood warblers, vireos, kinglets, orioles, robins—you name it. The birds always find a bounty of insects, and often fruit, seeds, or nuts as well, depending on the tree.

But that's just the beginning.

These all-in-one songbird attractions also provide storm shelters, sleeping places, nest sites, hiding places, and travel "corridors." Even in cities, songbirds hop, skip, and jump from one backyard or street tree to another. In New York City's Central Park, more than 230 species of birds have been recorded. It's not the jogging paths or the concerts that attracted them—it's the trees.

Short but Sweet

No room for a stately oak or sky-scraping silver maple? The smaller-scale trees listed below are medium-size when mature, so they won't take up your entire yard. All are popular with a big variety of songbirds, who use their flowers, seeds, or fruit for food and scour their branches and foliage for insects.

Alder (*Alnus glutinosa*)

Aspen (*Populus tremuloides*)

Eats and Treats
Carb-Loading Travel Treat

Serve your migrant songbirds a meal before their marathon, and make it one that's high in carbs—with a good amount of fat and protein, as well.

1 cup cooked whole-grain spaghetti, drained

½ cup plain suet or beef fat, chopped or ground into pieces about ¼ inch in diameter

½ cup bread crumbs

½ cup dried cherries, chopped

½ cup raw peanuts, chopped

¼ cup pecans, ground

1. Cool the pasta and chop into very small pieces about ¼ inch long.

2. Toss the chopped suet with the bread crumbs in a bowl.

3. Add the rest of the ingredients and stir to combine.

Serve in small quantities of about ½ cup at a time in a domed feeder, tray feeder, suet feeder, or mealworm dish—whichever feeder your songbirds use most and which starlings use least. Catbirds, thrashers, bluebirds, orioles, wrens, wood warblers, and tanagers will all appreciate this treat. Scatter a handful beneath shrubs, too, for any thrushes that may be passing through.

Get to Know Your Songbirds
Blue Grosbeak

The blue grosbeak is both the smallest of the grosbeaks and the largest of the buntings—they're all in the same family. This lovely neotropical songbird nests across a huge stretch of the United States, yet we rarely see it. Although the population is widespread, the number of birds is scanty, so count yourself lucky if you have a pair of these birds in your neighborhood or a singleton at your feeder.

It's worth seeking out a blue grosbeak if you've never watched one in action. These neotropical migrants have some fascinating—or should we say "gross"?—eating habits. Praying mantises and

The blue grosbeak is easy to mistake for a sparrow when it's not lit by the sun.

other large insects are among their favorites. To find a mantis, the blue grosbeak flies low over weeds and brush, looking intently. When it spots its prey, it hovers and snatches up the bug, then rips off its nice meaty abdomen. Cicadas and grasshoppers are on this bird's most-desirable list, too.

Blue grosbeaks also eat seeds and grain and have finally discovered feeders. Some of them are becoming regulars in backyards that have plenty of the sheltering shrubs, weedy brushy areas, or in the South, the loblolly pine (*Pinus taeda*) and longleaf pine (*Pinus palustris*) that they seek in the wild.

When to see them: Spring through fall, across the entire southern half of the country and extending northward in the midsection to South Dakota and northern Illinois

What to feed them: This is one bird that happily eats seed mixes with cheap wheat, oats, and corn fillers. Millet, finch mix, grass seed, and mealworms are welcomed, too.

Other ways to attract them: Plant shrubs in groups for habitat and let fall leaves nestle under them to nurture snails and other critters that blue grosbeaks crave. Bolster your grasshopper population by letting grass grow tall and allowing weeds to fill in where they will along a split-rail fence or hedge; this kind of brushy strip is favored habitat.

What they sound like: A long, warbled song with a rich, mellifluous quality, somewhat similar to that of the house finch and purple finch.

What to watch for: Blue grosbeaks are big fans of escargot—in the raw, of course. The bird will capture the snail on the ground, and the dining process is much like you'd imagine, complete with plenty of vigorous bill-wiping. Watch for snail-seeking grosbeaks after a rain, when snails are out and about.

Birch (*Betula* spp.)

Chokecherry (*Prunus virginiana*), may grow as a large shrub or small tree

Crabapple (*Malus* spp.)

Flowering dogwood (*Cornus florida*)

Redbud (*Cercis canadensis*)

Serviceberry (*Amelanchier* spp.), shrub or small tree

SAVOR THE SEASON

"Seasonal food" is the motto for many of my favorite restaurants, and it applies to how I eat at home, too. In winter, I want slabs of meat, stick-to-the-ribs root vegetables, and cold, crisp apples.

Oh, and don't forget the bread—dense and chewy, please, and speckled with seeds and nuts. Slathered with butter, of course.

In summer, it's garden fare all the way. Tender lettuce, ripe tomatoes, sweet corn. And fruit, mmm, fruit. From the first strawberries to the prime of peach season to the last of the blueberries, I'm smacking my lips.

Insects aren't on my menu. But other than that, my tastes aren't much different than those of the birds.

Eating seasonally is a natural instinct. You'd never know it by looking at our supermarkets, though, where produce sections look pretty much the same in December as they do in May. Still, our cravings change with the seasons, just like

Trick or Treat
Trash Talk

When bulldozers started scraping away a hedgerow near my Indiana home, I was horrified. That border of trees that was mixed with shrubs and tall wildflowers (okay, "weeds" to most folks) was home to all kinds of songbirds and a favorite stopping-off place for wood warblers and vireos on spring migration.

"Why destroy it?" I wanted to know.

"Trash trees," the bulldozer operator replied scornfully, revving his engine for another go.

Trash trees. What a horrible human phrase. To birds and other wildlife, there is no such thing. That hedgerow of chokecherries, box elders, young catalpas, and river birches may not have been of any use for lumber. But making a buck is the furthest thing from a songbird's mind. It's thinking about making a living, in the most literal sense. And "trash trees" are perfect for that. They're loaded with insects, fruit, and seeds that support every songbird species that comes along. So before you reach for the loppers or the chain saw, consider how much treasure birds can find in your "trash tree."

the birds' do. Even though we're not living on the farm anymore, we still get hungry for heavier, fattier foods in fall and lighten up again in spring.

Songbirds don't have the option of eating cherries in midwinter—well, unless they're neotropical migrants, eating those cherries in Chile—so they make the most of what's at hand, just as they always have.

Nature's worked it out perfectly, too:

- The first burst of insects—flying, creeping, and crawling—appears just as birds are moving on migration.

- Protein-packed insects peak in early summer, when birds need extra nutrition for the demands of breeding season.

- Bumper crops of caterpillars coincide with the height of nesting season, ideal for filling a bunch of hungry young beaks.

- Sweet fruit develops for fast energy in summer.

- High-fat berries ripen when birds need to pack on weight for fall migration.

- Nutritious seeds mature for nourishment all fall and winter.

- Slow-ripening berries and fruits soften for non-seed-eaters in winter.

Moving to Match

Nature's timing on natural foods is perfect—or used to be, until climate change started throwing a monkey wrench into the works. In recent years, the timing has gotten a little skewed in some areas. Insects now hatch earlier, and berries and seeds may ripen earlier, too.

Songbirds are changing their own habits to match. Many are moving north from their usual ranges to find the foods they need. Nearly 60 per-

Flowering dogwood blossoms attract insects for chickadees and other small songbirds; berries nourish tanagers and thrushes in fall.

cent of the 305 bird species that winter in North America have moved northward since 1967, the Audubon Society reports. Their wintering range has shifted an average of 35 miles farther north (see birdsand climate.audubon.org/).

In 2009, researchers at the SUNY College of Environmental Science and Forestry confirmed a similar shift during breeding season, although their study dealt only with birds of New York. They found that many of the 83 breeding species, including Carolina wrens, pine siskins, and Nashville warblers, had shifted their northward boundary, some by as much as 40 miles, and forsaken the southerly parts of their former breeding range.

FEEDER FOODS

Ah, now we get to the instant gratification aspect of attracting songbirds. I love a fast payoff, too, which is why I pour time and money into my feeders. And as for convenience—well, it's way easier to buy a bag of birdseed labeled "Songbird Treat" than it is to get out the shovel and figure out where to plant another tree.

Besides, with feeder foods, I get to see songbirds up close. Not to mention that warm feeling of pride: They like me! They really like me!

Well, no, they don't. They like the fats, carbs, and proteins I put out for them.

A Varied Diet

Seeds are the first thing we think of as feeder food, and a good variety of songbirds definitely seek them out. But to attract the rest of the crew, we need a much wider menu. Many species of songbirds aren't seed eaters. If they can't find a reasonable facsimile of their natural diet in our backyards, they'll go elsewhere rather than settle for seeds.

Soft foods are the top choice for songbirds. That catchall term covers a wide range of menu options, but the idea is the same: They're easy to swallow and require no cracking of shells.

- Suet is a standby. Make sure you provide at least one suet feeder. More are even better, especially when you add a diversity of styles to suit the eating habits of various songbirds.
- Supplement the suet with soft doughs, store-bought or homemade.
- Add peanut butter and peanut-butter-based treats.
- Chopped tree nuts, such as pecans or walnuts, and chopped peanuts are avidly eaten, too—they can be swallowed in one gulp.
- Fruit and berries are a little trickier to coax birds into eating at a feeder. But many songbirds are finally getting the idea.

Eats and Treats
Power Bar

Here's a high-fat, high-protein, high-carb treat for songbird friends. Migrants and nonmigrants alike will enjoy it.

1 cup oatmeal, uncooked

½ cup chunky peanut butter

¼ cup whole-wheat flour

¼ cup hulled sunflower chips

Mix all ingredients together. Press into a flat bar about ½ inch thick. Serve in a tray feeder, so bluebirds, tanagers, orioles, titmice, grosbeaks, catbirds, mockingbirds, and thrashers can easily access the treat. If starlings are pesky at your place, stuff the mix into a log feeder for agile songbirds, including yellow-rumped warblers, gray catbirds, chickadees, titmice, brown creepers, and wrens.

Both male and female orioles are songsters. The male takes the principal seat, singing from an exposed perch. The female's songs are usually softer and delivered from a lower, more hidden perch among the leaves.

- Jelly, nectar, and other sweet treats appeal to some of the most beautiful songbirds, including orioles and tanagers.
- Mealworms may be icky, but once you see how much songbirds adore them, you won't want to be without them.

You'll find details on all these foods in the coming chapters, as well as suggestions for augmenting them with the real thing—natural foods supplied by the plants in your own backyard.

A MARATHON EFFORT

Migration is prime time for songbirds in our backyards. It's not hard to figure out why. The birds are making a marathon effort, and our one-stop "convenience store" offers a good meal with minimum effort, as well as a welcome respite from the road.

Fattening Up

Songbirds spend the weeks leading up to migration doing pretty much nothing other than chowing down. No worries about putting on weight—that's exactly what these birds are trying to do. From dawn to dusk, they scarf down the most nutritious foods they can find.

Road Food

Birds have a way different sense of taste than we and other mammals do. Birds lack taste receptors for spicy-hot foods, for instance, which is why we can sprinkle cayenne pepper on our birdseed to deter squirrels whose mouths do indeed taste that flavor.

Songbirds have sensitive receptors for *umami*. No, that word doesn't mean they're looking for a sushi bar, although I'm sure they'd find plenty of umami there. It's the name of a savory fifth sense of taste identified by Japanese researchers. Umami gives birds and us a feeling of satiation, and it's not a false one. The foods with this taste provide plenty of long-term fuel. Often, they're high in fat.

This new taste has led to some interesting research in recent years. Tests reported in the journal *Plant Ecology* in 1993 confirmed that the berries that migrant songbirds most avidly seek when they're fueling up for fall migration—dogwood (*Cornus florida*), spicebush (*Lindera benzoin*), and others, all red in color—are high in umami and high in fat.

Of course, we songbird lovers will want to add some of these plants to our backyards. And no need to stop there. We also can supply other high-fat, high-protein foods at our feeders to augment our natural foods. Carbohydrates are vital, too. They provide a dose of quick energy, and extra calories are converted to fat for long-term use.

CHAPTER 8

Be a Softie

Soft, fatty bird foods are about as close to serving insects as we can get—without serving our songbirds actual insects, that is. That's why these foods have big appeal, because bugs are the favorite dinner (and breakfast, lunch, and snacks) of many of our most beloved songbirds, from bluebirds and robins to tiny ruby-crowned kinglets and perky brown wrens.

Soft foods are convenient for us to serve and easy for birds to eat. Every bird on our planet has its own niche when it comes to the food it eats. Many songbirds lack the strong bill that's needed to crack seeds and nuts. Others have the right equipment, but have evolved to take advantage of different foods and still sample seeds as well.

To attract the widest range of songbird species, make it a habit to include soft foods on your feeder menu. We're not talking a squishy slice of white bread here. Although that may be enough to draw in a robin or catbird to sample your wares, the real trick is to focus on fat—suet, peanut butter, and other soft, easy-to-peck, high-fat foods.

In this chapter, you'll learn which soft foods work best for attracting your favorite songbirds. We'll look at soft bird foods we can buy at stores, and I'll share recipes that you can cook up your-

self to nurture your favorite friends. And when you're ready to serve up these goodies, you'll find out how to make quick and easy feeders by recycling household items. "Going green" is for the birds, too!

SOFT-FOOD AFICIONADOS

In winter, soft foods nourish chickadees, titmice, bluebirds, brown creepers, and other songbirds that may be staying with us in the cold months. But from spring through fall, and especially during migration, the cast of characters at soft-food feeders goes through the roof.

- Quick, agile wrens slip in and out like little brown mice.

- Big, long-tailed brown thrashers wangle their way onto feeders to help themselves to a hearty serving.

- Groups or pairs of breathtaking bluebirds settle in to fill their bills.

- Flashy orioles and tanagers stop for a second to snatch a bite, then come back for more.

- Tiny wood warblers quickly learn where the soft foods are, as do robins, catbirds, and others.

- Even vireos and kinglets—rarely seen at feeders until recently—may come to sample the softies.

Why such a surge in popularity? Because soft foods—those based on fat—are a fine facsimile of real live insects, as far as songbirds are concerned.

Getting Acquainted

Thrushes, robins, wood warblers, and many other songbirds are relatively new to feeders. That means they're still investigating our offerings and learning what they like best. As these birds travel from backyard to backyard or move many miles on migration, they take their newly acquired tastes with them. An apparent lack of interest in a certain feeder food, or a preference for one over another, may simply be because that particular songbird hasn't yet sampled an offering. Be patient. Our songbirds are still learning.

And don't be surprised if your birds take a liking to something that my birds aren't as fond of. Your robins may enjoy vegetable shortening more than suet, for instance, while for mine, it's vice versa. The birds are developing new habits, and it's a whole new world of feeder foods to them.

Excluding Soft-Food Hogs

Oh boy, do starlings love suet! And peanut butter. And any other soft foods you serve your songbirds. If they can get at the food, they will, and it'll be gone so fast you won't believe your eyes. Raccoons and other furry critters may come after your soft foods, too. Even the neighbor's cat might try to make the leap to your feeder.

A bluebird feeder, which allows access through entrance holes like a birdhouse, is your best bet for protecting your soft foods from unwanted guests. But many songbirds aren't comfortable entering the box, even if they can fit.

Luckily, there are other tricks we can try to outwit the unwanted birds, and you'll find these tips detailed in Chapter 16, "Plain Talk about Pests."

Trick or Treat
Opportunity Knocks

Birds are opportunists. They quickly learn where a reliable source of food is available, and our feeders become a regular stop. It's easier to snag a few bites of suet than it is to ferret out the 50 leafhoppers that would equal its nutritional value. Keep your feeders stocked with soft foods year-round, and songbirds will soon become regulars.

GREASE IS THE WORD

Unless you're way more adept than I am at rounding up beetles, aphids, and earthworms, there's no way we can provide a songbird's natural menu at our feeders. Sure, we'll want to serve mealworms for real live food, and you can read all about them in Chapter 10, "Getting Bugged." As for the insects, slugs, and other crawly critters of the natural world, they aren't so easy to herd into a feeder. But we can offer a reasonable facsimile: fat.

Soft fat-based foods appeal to bluebirds, orioles, thrashers, wrens, robins, and other songbirds nearly as much as nice fat caterpillars or a handful of not-so-cheap mealworms. You'll find plenty of info on feeding real mealworms and insects in Chapter 10. But for now, let's focus on the faux—the fats that satisfy a wide cast of insect-eating songbirds.

Following the Food

During songbirds' nesting season, insects are a mainstay for nearly all of them, even those who also eat seeds. When bugs are scarce, so are the songbirds that depend on them. In fall, those who rely on such soft morsels head southward, where the foods they need will still be available throughout winter. The only songbirds that stick around are those who switch to seeds or winter berries—or feeder foods.

Play with Proportions

You'll find various kinds of soft foods for birds in stores, garden centers, farm supply stores, and of course, wild-bird supply stores. The selection will vary and so will prices, so shop around. It's fun to experiment with various store-bought foods to see which ones your songbirds like best. My

Mountain bluebirds migrate when insects become scarce as the weather turns cold.

brown thrashers and catbirds were particularly fond of some nutty, suety, peanut-buttery balls I found, but although the balls were undeniably convenient, they were too pricey for me to use them regularly. The good news is that they're easy to replicate at home, using simple recipes that take just a few minutes to mix up—and only one bowl, so there's little cleanup.

There's plenty of leeway in measuring when it comes to making fat-based soft foods at home. Peanut butter, melted beef fat, and other ingredients vary in the amount of oil they contain, and suet blocks that contain seeds or other ingredients aren't as greasy as pure suet or lard.

Don't be afraid to adjust the ingredients, because there's room to play with proportions in every bird food recipe. If your mix isn't stiff enough to mold into blocks or plugs, simply add a little more dry stuff. Or add a little more fat or

Get to Know Your Songbirds
Yellow-Rumped Warbler

If wood warblers were in our yards every day, we'd eventually get to know them, no matter how fast they move. But for most of us, these little insect eaters are only transients at migration time. They flit through over the course of a few weeks, heading for nesting grounds in the North or to winter quarters. Backyards hold little temptation for them, except as a source of insects to be grabbed on the fly, or perhaps for a brief stop at a birdbath.

Yet one species—the yellow-rumped warbler—follows a different drummer. Instead of wintering in the Neotropics, many birds of this species stay in the United States as far north as New York. They pal around with mixed bands of winter-foraging chickadees, titmice, nuthatches, and brown creepers.

And now, the little gray, black, and bright yellow bird has become a confirmed feeder friend. Why? Soft foods is my guess.

As bird feeding has grown, millions of us have been offering suet and other soft foods instead of just seeds that most warblers don't eat. And the yellow-rumped warbler has followed his winter

The yellow-rumped warbler is becoming more common at feeders.

companions to the feeder and soon figured out that suet is a close match to his natural insect diet.

The yellow-rumped warbler was the pioneer of warblers at feeders, and it's still by far the most common. (The species includes the myrtle warbler of the East and Audubon's warbler of the West.) But other warblers have been jumping on the bandwagon in recent years, too. These species are usually migration visitors, but the same foods that satisfy yellow-rumpeds in winter will do the trick for them, too, in any season.

When to see them: Winter, in most areas; nesting season in New England and the Great Lakes region

What to feed them: Suet and soft foods; peanut butter; raisins and other small or chopped dried fruit; oranges; and mealworms. Some birds may visit nectar feeders. Look for premium seed mixes containing juniper berries, which these birds eat.

Other ways to attract them: Provide a low birdbath or naturalistic creek or waterfall. Plant an east-ern redcedar (*Juniperus virginiana*), bayberry or wax myrtle bushes (*Morella,* formerly *Myrica,* spp.), or Virginia creeper (*Parthenocissus quinquefolia*) for berries. Plant conifers for birds to forage in.

What they sound like: High, lispy songs and adamant *Chips.*

What to watch for: With its white tail patches and flashes of yellow, the yellow-rumped warbler looks like a butterfly when it flutters after flying insects.

Sleek, warbling purple martins aren't backyard songbirds for most of us, because they prefer catching their insect food on the wing, high in the air or over water, rather than visiting feeders. If you have appealing open space near water, try a martin house or gourds to tempt a colony into nesting.

oil, if it's too dry. Stir in extra goodies, too, if you like, including dried mealworms or other insect foods.

Your songbirds will be happy to sample all of your experiments, whether or not you follow the recipe to the letter.

START WITH SUET

Whether you buy it in blocks or cadge chunks of fat from a butcher, the white fat known as suet is at the top of the backyard food menu for songbirds. It's pure high-energy fat. It's easy to serve as is or add to recipes. And just about every songbird under the sun will eat it with relish.

Oh, and need we say, it's cheap—a real bargain compared to other bird foods. For just a couple of bucks a block, we get weeks of watch-

ing pleasure. Until, that is, the squirrels or starlings, jays, or other birds with big appetites move in. Then a suet block can disappear practically overnight. You'll find ideas for deterring these animals and birds from gobbling down your goodies in Chapter 16.

Straight Suet

When suet blocks first came on the market, there was only one kind: nothing but fat. No seeds, no flavors, no nothin' else: just melted fat, solidified into a plastic block-shaped mold.

Savvy manufacturers quickly wised up, or at least that's what I'm guessing, and realized that if they added seeds to the fat, they'd make a few more pennies a block. Seeds are cheaper than fat. Cracked corn, another common filler in suet

Black-headed grosbeaks aren't fond of suet, but they will pick out the seeds from a block.

blocks, is even cheaper. That way, less fat is needed to fill the mold. And besides, birds eat seeds, too, so it's not really a nefarious thing to do, is it? You'll find a detailed look at commercial suet blocks later in this chapter, so you can make up your own mind.

For now, let's just say that straight suet is the main attraction of those blocks. When it comes to suet-eating songbirds, it's all about the fat.

Ask and Ye Shall Receive

Unfortunately for us bird lovers, the in-store butcher is quickly going the way of the dodo. Today's supermarkets get their meat pre-trimmed, with the big chunks of fat already removed. The butchers in the back merely do a bit of fine-tuning before they slide those roasts and chops through the wrapping machine.

But there's a way to get around this fat-free situation. You can still find fat at the supermarket—just ask. Most stores will let you know

A Broader Definition
SUET OR SIMILAR FAT IS FINE

You know that "muffin top" that bulges above the waistband of a person's snug pair of jeans? Some of that is the human fat that protects our kidneys, which lie against our backs below our ribs. In other words, suet.

The official definition of *suet* is the layer of fat that covers the kidneys of animals. But to bird lovers, the definition of suet has become a lot broader, to include any sort of animal fat. The trimmings from a steak, for instance, are just as beloved by songbirds as the softer suet around the cow's kidneys.

In our common usage, those trimmings are lumped into the suet category, too. We use the word *suet* to describe what's more properly known as tallow: hard white fat, usually from beef, and a mainstay for backyard birds.

Waste Not, Want Not

Fat trimmings, whether from a butcher or from the meat department at your super-market, often include a bit of meat, tendons, or other trimmings, and sometimes the fat is tinged with blood. That's not a problem for birds, which devour those bits, too. But meat goes rancid much faster than pure fat.

That's not a problem in cold weather, when your scraps will stay frozen. But if you're planning to put out the scraps in warm weather, you'll need to do some further slicing yourself to remove the impurities. Cut them from the fat and store them in your freezer for winter use.

what day they trim the fat, so that you can stop in to buy a package of scraps. If you have an old-fashioned butcher shop in your neighborhood, your chances of getting bigger, purer chunks of fat are way better. All you have to do is ask.

Both kinds of stores usually charge a very reasonable price for fat. If you're a regular customer for their meat, or if you're holding a package of premium-priced steaks in your hand when you ask about scraps, you just might get your songbird fat for free.

OTHER WHITE FATS

Songbirds are quickly becoming accustomed to visiting our feeders for suet, and other soft white fats have high songbird appeal, too. Animal fats seem to attract them more than vegetable fats do, at least at my feeder, so investigate animal fats first.

These fats are easier to incorporate in bird food recipes than suet, which is a harder fat that requires melting to soften it or chopping to cut it down to size before mixing it into other foods.

Carolina wrens slip in and out quick as a mouse, so watch your soft food feeders.

Get the Lard Out

Lard is pig fat, pure and simple. The highest grade of lard, prized for baking flaky piecrusts, is *leaf lard,* from a layer of fat near the pig's kidneys. It's almost flavorless, with hardly a hint of pork. The next highest grade of lard is cut from *fatback,* a harder fat between the pig's skin and backbone.

Premium grades of lard, as well as lard cut from other less desirable parts of a pig's fat, are often sold as "rendered" lard, which means the fat has been heated, liquefied, and cooled. This process slows down spoilage and helps remove odors or strong flavors.

You can buy lard in plastic tubs or blocks at the grocery store, usually in the dairy department. Lard is reasonably priced, but it isn't nearly as cheap as suet or fat scraps from a butcher. For lower prices and bigger quantities, you may have better luck in the Mexican foods section or in a Mexican grocery store.

Use lard as you would suet or other fats: either all by itself, or in homemade soft-food recipes, such as the Mini Mince Pies mentioned below. Lard is too soft to fill a suet cage, so fill a log feeder instead, or simply smear it onto tree bark, where wrens, catbirds, wood warblers, and other songbirds can peck it off.

Eats and Treats
Mini Mince Pies

This is the songbird version of mincemeat pie, also known as suet pie in England, where it's a traditional dish. Salt, seasonings, and sugar are eliminated from this version, leaving only the meat, fat, and fruit for songbirds, plus the high-carb crust.

1 pound hamburger, high fat content

1 pound suet (a commercial pure suet block or fat scraps), chopped

Skillet

Saucepan

4 large apples, peeled but with cores, coarsely chopped

2 cups water

2 cups currants

1 cup raisins

Piecrust for two-crust pie, homemade or commercial

Muffin tin

Zip-top plastic freezer bags

1. Prepare the mincemeat: Combine the hamburger and suet in a skillet and cook over low heat, using a fork to break the hamburger into bits.

Crackling Rosies

Rendering pork fat is often done by frying it, as you would bacon, but on a grand scale. Bits of skin separate from the fat during the frying process and are packaged (or eaten on the spot, at country hog butcherings) as *cracklings*. Cracklings taste something like bacon, but they're not as dense and hard. Many songbirds quickly develop an appetite for these fatty treats.

When neighbors brought me a bowl of fresh fried cracklings, I took a taste, then froze the rest for my birds, figuring they could use the calories more than I could. I doled out the cracklings a few at a time, and sure enough, the birds snapped them up. When I served the last few handfuls in April that year, rose-breasted grosbeaks quickly took a liking to them. The striking black-and-white songbirds with the bold crimson chests carefully picked out every morsel of fried pigskin from their tray of sunflower and safflower seeds, before they started cracking the shells and gobbling down the seeds.

Mama's Little Baby Loves Short'nin', Short'nin'

Lard was once the cheapest fat on the market, but all that changed when vegetable shortening rolled onto the scene in the early years of the

---

2. When the meat is in separate small pieces of about $1/4$ to $1/3$ inch in diameter (it'll still be pink in places), transfer the mixture to a saucepan and add the remaining ingredients, except for the piecrust.

3. Simmer uncovered over low heat for about 45 minutes to an hour, stirring occasionally. Cook until most of the water has evaporated, leaving a thick, not watery, mixture. Remove from heat.

4. Cut the piecrust into circular pieces of about 4 to 5 inches in diameter, big enough to line the cups of the muffin tin and extend about $1/2$ inch above the rims.

5. Line each cup with a piecrust circle, covering the bottom and sides and extending it above the rim.

6. Crimp the piecrust around the edge by folding and squeezing it between your thumb and forefinger, to make a thicker rim.

7. Fill each cup to just below the rim with the meat mixture. If you have extra mincemeat left over, cool and freeze it in freezer bags.

8. Bake at 400°F for about 30 minutes, until the crust is golden brown.

9. Serve one at a time in a small feeder or in a mealworm dish. Freeze the extras.

All manner of songbirds enjoy these meaty, fruity, fatty treats. In my yard, bluebirds, Carolina wrens, and robins are particularly fond of them. You might also spot thrashers, mockingbirds, orioles, and other soft-food fans coming to celebrate your cooking.

20th century. Oils from plants are a lot cheaper to produce than oils from animals. Crisco shortening (a combination of cottonseed oil and soybean oil, hydrogenated to a semisolid consistency) and its kin were an instant hit with cooks, because they work nearly as well as lard in home cooking and are inexpensive and convenient.

Songbirds like shortening, too, in "short'nin' bread" (a fried dough of cornmeal, eggs, and shortening) as well as other treats made with the stuff.

Shortening needs no refrigeration. That means it's great for songbirds in another way, too: You won't have to worry about it turning rancid for a long, long time. And it's usually been eaten up long before it's in any danger of going bad.

Use shortening as you would use suet or lard. It's too soft for a suet cage, so serve it in a small plastic container, such as a cottage cheese cup or the cut-off bottom of a soda bottle. Or mix it with other ingredients in your homemade bird treats.

Trick or Treat
Lardy, Lardy

Despite its killer fat content, lard has gone from rural staple to hifalutin foodie must-have in the past few years. The demand for lard in England has been increasing, too, as foodies resurrect traditional British cuisine. It even caused a lard crisis in 2006, when the supply of pigs couldn't keep up with England's taste for lard.

One of those traditional British recipes is lardy cake, a time-honored treat made with a yeast dough. The dough is rolled out and then folded with lard, sugar, and raisins sandwiched between the layers. The final step? After baking, the cake is turned upside-down so that the grease can soak through all its layers.

I'm sure lardy cake is delicious. But if I ever happen to find myself with this zillion-calorie cake on hand, I'll spare my arteries and donate the treat to my bluebirds, thrashers, catbirds, and other songbirds.

In addition, lard sandwiches have been eaten for centuries in rural Europe and England, where the white fat is also used like butter. Topped with sliced onions and sprinkled with a dash of paprika, a thick slice of crusty bread smeared with lard is popular with beer in Poland and Slovakia.

Skip the onions and paprika, and give your songbirds that open-faced lard sandwich instead. Simply spread lard or vegetable shortening on a sturdy slice of bread and set it in a feeder, impale it on a nail, or slip it into a suet cage. Your bluebirds, wrens, robins, and other songbirds will love "chewing the fat" as they nibble at the greasy bread.

Oils

Oils aren't as convenient as suet for songbird food, because we can't simply put them out as is. But their high fat content makes them just as nutritious, so I often include oil when I'm mixing up many of my bird food recipes. Oil soaks into dry foods, such as bread crumbs or crushed breakfast cereal, making them more appealing to songbirds that eat soft foods. It can be messy, though, so use it sparingly and include a more solid fat in the recipe, such as suet, lard, shortening, or peanut butter, to bulk it up.

Seems like more and more kinds of oil show up on the grocery store shelf every year. When I'm mixing up soft foods for the birds, I experiment with just about any kind of oil that comes along: grapeseed, sesame seed, flaxseed, walnut, hazelnut, and other tree-nut oils. (I haven't had any luck getting my birds to eat treats made with olive oil, which is probably a good thing. I'm happy to keep that pricey bottle of cold-pressed oil for my own cooking.)

For basic songbird fare, I stick to the most reasonably priced, widely available oils—which just so happen to be made from foods that songbirds enjoy eating.

- Canola oil
- Corn oil
- Peanut oil
- Safflower oil
- Sunflower oil
- Vegetable oil, which can be made from a blend of any or all of these five, with or without soybean oil

Use feeders that allow the birds to access food that contains oil without getting smeared with it.

Not all songbirds are as agile as chickadees or wrens, so make sure your soft-food feeder has a perch of some sort where the birds can safely stand to eat these foods without getting messy.

Yummy, Rich Cream Cheese

Cream cheese is pretty much pure fat, and some soft-food eaters quickly develop a taste for it. It costs a pretty penny, though, so I check the discounted just-past-due-date section of my grocery store to buy cream cheese for birds. It keeps forever in the freezer, whether I buy solid blocks or the type in tubs—which work great as ready-to-go mini feeders for my catbirds, brown thrashers, wrens, and, yes, starlings. You can serve cream cheese in any season, but reduce the amount in warm weather so that it doesn't spoil before the birds eat it.

PEANUT BUTTER MAGIC

"You should be a millionaire," someone told me when I demonstrated my favorite peanut butter bird food recipe at an event a few years ago. "You invented that bluebird food that everybody's selling nowadays."

Invented? Me? Uh, thanks, but nope—I'd just used what I happened to have on the shelf during a blizzard one year when a flock of hungry bluebirds arrived in my yard. I knew I needed some kind of soft food for the poor guys, and lo and behold, that jar of peanut butter and bag of cornmeal turned out to be the magic recipe.

In other words, I just lucked out.

Besides, I'm sure the same idea must've occurred to lots of other bird lovers, long before I dumped the two ingredients together. So when someone with way more business sense than I'll ever have eventually realized they could package the stuff, give it a name, and make some bucks, I say, more power to 'em!

As for that millionaire status, I'm perfectly happy just sharing what works for me, in hopes that it will help other bird lovers see bluebirds, too. Which is why, no doubt, I still wait for grocery store sales so I can stock up on peanut butter and buy generic store brands to save a few pennies.

Both creamy and chunky peanut butter have high appeal to birds, as a spread and mixed into recipes. But chunky peanut butter is chock-full of tempting, bite-size bits of peanuts that can lure birds that are unfamiliar with the food to try a bite. The bits of nuts are just the right size for any songbird, big or small, to swallow. The pieces slow down the bird's consumption, too, and make the spread easier to eat than the creamy type.

Songbird Magnet

So what's the secret formula? Simple! Peanut butter and cornmeal are all you need.

Good ol' peanut butter is the magic ingredient that brings bluebirds to the feeder. Cornmeal is nutritious, too, but songbirds won't eat it all by itself. Mix it with peanut butter, though, and the birds will be fighting for a place at your table.

Bluebirds gulp down the magic mixture, which I stir to a crumbly cookie-dough consistency. House wrens, Carolina wrens, and Bewick's wrens love it, too. So do a whole long

Warnings against feeding peanut butter straight from the jar are completely unfounded. Songbirds, like this house finch, are perfectly capable of eating peanut butter without suffering any ill effects.

list of other songbirds—orioles, thrashers, gray catbirds, mockingbirds, titmice, and chickadees among them. Even the elusive brown creeper can't resist peanut butter and treats that are made with it.

Simplest Serving

It's not true that peanut butter will kill birds by clogging up their bills or throats unless you mix it with cornmeal or anything else. The only reason I mix it with fillers is to make the jar stretch further. Songbirds adore the treat with or without fillers, so if your budget is no obstacle, feel free to feed it straight from the jar. Often, I simply smear straight peanut butter onto a wooden post or onto bark, to give my songbirds a nourishing meal of concentrated fat.

Lots of songbird species ardently eat peanut

A long list of songbirds enjoys peanut butter, including the Altamira oriole of south Texas.

butter, from big brown thrashers to tiny brown creepers. The stuff is a guaranteed bird magnet in any season. In winter, I often go through a 16-ounce jar in a week, which is why I watch for sales and stock up. Even birds that don't usually seek out soft foods will visit the smear of peanut butter—wrens, wood warblers, finches, juncos, you name it. Only grosbeaks, thus far, seem to be completely uninterested.

To slow down starlings, I spread the peanut butter on the side of a post or tree, where there are no perches. Starlings are clever birds, though, and they soon figure out how to get their share.

SHOPPING FOR SOFT FOODS

Manufacturers have jumped on the soft-food bandwagon big-time. You'll find bird foods based on fats in every bird supply store and most discount stores. Many are shaped to fit specific feeders to make offering these foods even more convenient. All you do is unwrap the package, slip it in, and step back so your birds can eat.

Blocks, Plugs, and Balls

Suet blocks are the granddaddy of the soft-food products. Today, you can find them in dozens of flavors, each supposed to attract specific birds.

A smear of peanut butter is the first stop for many birds, including mountain chickadees.

Orange flavored for orioles, for instance, or berry flavored for bluebirds.

Similar ingredients go into the making of cylindrical plugs and billiard-size balls. Birds eagerly eat these products, no matter what their shape—and often with no respect for which ones they're supposed to be most attracted to. From my observations, it seems that the fat itself is the biggest draw. My robins and catbirds, for instance, will happily peck at the oriole block, which may or may not have orioles at it, since they seem to like the bluebird block just fine.

Red-Letter Day
TIME TO PUT ON A SPREAD

Mark your calendar for January 24—that's National Peanut Butter Day. For those of us who love songbirds, it's something to celebrate, because the spread is irresistible to bluebirds, titmice, and other favorite songbirds. Sounds like a great day to mix up a batch of peanut butter bird treats!

Eats and Treats
Grape-Orange Suet

Fruit-flavored soft foods are a great way to attract orioles, tanagers, and other songbirds that love sweet fruit. You can buy suet blocks and other foods already tailored to their preferences. Or you can mix up your own fruity suet with this simple recipe.

2 cups melted suet or beef fat

1 navel orange

1 small bunch red seedless grapes (about 10 to 12)

½ cup uncooked regular or quick-cooking oatmeal

¼ cup grape jelly

Small clean plastic container, such as from onion dip

1. Melt the fat and set it aside to cool.

2. Peel and chop the orange, keeping the juice. Chop the grapes and save their juice, too.

3. Mix the fruits, juice, and oatmeal; the oatmeal flakes will absorb the juice and soften. Stir in the jelly.

4. When the fat is thickened but still soft, mix in the other ingredients and stir thoroughly so that they are evenly distributed.

5. Scrape the mix into the container or other mold and place it in the freezer to harden.

6. Remove the suet from the container and serve it in a suet feeder or oriole feeder, where your songbirds can easily find their treat.

Wrens will visit any of them. Those with peanuts or other nuts in the mix are highly appealing, too, especially to chickadees and titmice.

Of course, those observations aren't exactly scientific, since I usually have only a couple of the products offered at any one time. It'd be fun to try a taste test by setting out every flavor that's sold. I wonder which one would win.

Check the expiration date on the label of your soft foods to make sure you're buying fresh products, not blocks or plugs that have sat on the shelf for a year or more. If there's no date, you may want to contact the manufacturer before you buy a large quantity, to find out how you can determine their freshness before you purchase them.

Whether you buy or make fat-based bird foods, be sure to store them in your freezer to prevent the fat from turning rancid. Slip the

Get to Know Your Songbirds
Summer Tanager

I keep my distance from a nectar or fruit feeder that's well attended by bees and wasps, just in case any of the stinging insects are feeling a little crabby when I come by. But summer tanagers seek out stinging insects to make a meal of them.

Bees and wasps are a big part of the diet of summer tanagers, and these beautiful neotropical migrants are adept at snatching the stinging guys right out of the air. Then the bird will beat its hapless victim against a branch, wipe off the stinger against the bark, and swallow its body.

Wasp and hornet nests are fair game, too. Summer tanagers will harass the buzzing adults until they back off, or they'll kill them outright. Then the bird will rip off pieces of the paper nest and eat the tender larvae inside.

Dragonflies, moths, and other insects are gobbled up, too. And as soon as fruit ripens—or when we put it in a feeder—summer tanagers will fill their bellies with mulberries, cherries, blueberries, and other goodies.

Tanagers usually forage in treetops, but the summer tanager spends a lot of time in shrubs and gardens and even on the ground. Don't bother to crane your neck to look way up high for the grassy cup of a nest—it's often placed at only about 10 to 12 feet on a branch above a road or driveway.

Male summer tanager.

When to see them: Spring through fall

What to feed them: Tanagers are rapidly becoming feeder regulars, at least in some backyards where individual birds have apparently gotten the word. The summer tanager likes citrus fruits, bananas, grape jelly, fruit juice, dried fruit, and other fruity treats; peanut butter; suet and other soft foods; and mealworms.

Other ways to attract them: Water is a big draw, and running water works even better. Provide a birdbath, a naturalistic waterfall, or a man-made creek to attract thirsty migrants. Plant a mulberry tree or fig tree. And let a stout pokeweed (*Phytolacca americana*) become part of your garden—summer tanagers (along with bluebirds, thrushes, and other songbirds) love the strings of berries.

What they sound like: A musical, rolling song of phrases and pauses, something like that of the American robin.

What to watch for: Summer tanagers catch many insects by "hawking," or flying out from a perch to grab a bug that's going by. Look for the bird at the tip of the tree, ready to fly at a moment's notice. A mated pair is very aggressive near its nest, chasing away birds of other species that venture too near.

packages inside a zip-top plastic freezer bag. You can thaw them before serving, or simply let them thaw in the feeder (or stay frozen, if it's cold out).

If your birds are ignoring your soft-food offerings, the fat may have gone rancid. Fat can spoil fast when it's exposed to sunlight and air, and heat makes it go bad even more swiftly. Replace your blocks, plugs, balls, or homemade foods with fresh ones, and your bluebirds, brown thrasher, and their friends will soon return.

HOMEMADE SOFT FOODS

Making your own soft foods is a great way to save money, because commercial plugs, balls, and doughs can cost a pretty penny. You can mix up your own for a fraction of the cost.

Songbirds are highly supportive of our efforts, no matter how uneven our first try at suet balls may be or how flat our bluebird breakfast muffins may turn out.

Collecting Ingredients

You can follow a recipe to the letter to make your own bird foods. But seeing what we can invent with foods we have on hand is a big part of the fun of making bird treats.

Ingredients for homemade soft-food treats fall into four basic categories:

- **Fats.** The foundation of every soft-food recipe.
- **Grain-based foods.** These foods help stretch the fat and bulk up the recipe, as well as supply protein, carbs, and vitamins.
- **Nuts and seeds.** Not a must, but very much appreciated by and irresistible to some songbirds, including wrens and titmice.
- **Fruit.** Extra enticement for fruit-loving songbirds, such as tanagers, bluebirds, and orioles.

Recipes for homemade soft foods are scattered throughout this book. You'll find ideas for using fruit in them in Chapter 9, suggestions for using seeds and nuts in Chapter 11, and all kinds of kitchen goodness in Chapter 12. Just remember to start with fat. It works as the "glue" in bird food recipes, and it flavors and moistens the dry ingredients so that they're appealing to songbirds. Fat also makes dough malleable, so that your treats can be shaped to fit wire cages and other feeders.

Molding Soft Foods

Soft-food plugs and balls are a cinch to mold to fit a feeder. Just put a lump of dough in your hands and roll it into a cylinder or a sphere. Be sure to check the size of your feeder, so that your plugs aren't too big for the holes. Or you can simply compare your foods to the size of a commercial product you've bought for your feeder.

If you plan to fill a square suet cage with your soft foods, save the stiff plastic shell from a purchased suet block. You can reuse the packaging to mold your soft foods to the right size.

SOFT FOOD AND SUET FEEDERS

A suet cage is by far the cheapest commercial bird feeder around. Costing just a few dollars, these wire baskets last for years. Their simple design is pretty much perfect: easy to use, easy to hang, and small enough to fit just about anywhere. Commercial suet blocks are inexpensive, too. And the cage is great for serving up homemade soft foods, as well.

Beyond the Basic

There's just one problem with a nice, cheap, easy suet cage. Well, make that two problems: The food is exposed to the weather and the sun, so it may deteriorate or spoil more quickly. And starlings are adept at using these feeders, which means your suet will disappear like lightning once the black birds find it.

Look for the following improved versions of the basic wire cage, to prevent or mitigate these problems:

Roofed suet cages will help protect the food from rain, snow, and sun.

Upside-down suet feeders, with the cage held horizontally under the feeder, will slow

---

5-Minute Window Feeder

This easy DIY feeder is simple to make for winter feeding. Just attach it with a strong magnet to a window to attract wrens and other small songbirds who eat soft foods.

Materials

Suet or bird dough, commercial or homemade

1 hard plastic lid, about ½ inch deep or deeper, with a ribbed rim, such as from a peanut butter jar

Florists' wire

Wire cutters

1 strong magnet

Small, sturdy twig for a perch

Tin punch or drill

Method

1. Press the soft food firmly into the lid with the back of a spoon, to fill the lid.

2. Wrap the lid and food tightly several times with florists' wire. Allow a bit of space in between the wires, so that your birds can get at the treat. Vary the direction of the wire so that the wires cross in a grid pattern. The ribbing on the lid will keep the wire from slipping. Cut the wire with wire cutters when you have covered the lid. Twist the loose ends of the wire together.

3. Have a helper hold the magnet on the inside of a window, while you hold the wire-wrapped lid in place against the outside of the pane. The magnet will keep a surprisingly strong grip on the metal wire.

4. Poke the twig into the soft food in the lid, to give your wrens, titmice, and wood warblers a place to perch while they eat. If the perch isn't secure enough, poke a hole through the lid with a tin punch or a drill and insert the twig into the hole.

down starlings. These models aren't foolproof, but they will help keep your soft foods from being gobbled up by a flock, because only one or two starlings at a time can snatch a bite.

Caged suet feeders keep the fat safe from larger birds and squirrels by enclosing it in a cage of metal bars.

Bluebird feeders are enclosed boxes that birds must enter in order to eat. The entrance holes block larger birds, including starlings.

Log feeders can hang horizontally or vertically. They may be sized to fit commercial suet plugs, for easy filling. Starlings will find them, too.

Basic Bird Dough

One part white fat to three parts grain-based ingredient is the basic recipe, but there's plenty of room for innovation. Use this handy chart to create your own mixes. Mix and match however you like; no need to use the ingredients as they appear in the rows below. Just choose one ingredient from each column.

FAT	GRAIN-BASED INGREDIENT	NUTTY EXTRA	FRUITY EXTRA
(use 1 cup)*	(use 3 cups)	(use ¼ to ½ cup)	(use ¼ to ½ cup)
Suet, chopped	Cornmeal	Raw peanuts, chopped	Currants
Beef fat, chopped	Half cornmeal, half whole-wheat flour	Walnuts, chopped	Raisins, chopped
Lard	Crushed crackers, any kind	Hulled sunflower seeds	Dried cherries, chopped
Half suet, half vegetable shortening	Crushed cornflakes	Hulled pumpkin seeds, chopped	Dried apple, chopped
Half vegetable shortening, half lard	Buckwheat flour	Raw almonds, ground	Dried coconut shreds
Peanut butter, chunky	Half cornmeal, half buckwheat flour	Hot pepper flakes with seeds	Dried blueberries, cut in half
Half peanut butter, half vegetable shortening	Amaranth flour	Sesame seeds	Dried apricots, papaya, or mango, chopped

*Substitute ¼ cup of peanut oil or other cooking oil (see page 145 for a list of those that songbirds enjoy) for ½ cup of the semisolid fat, if you prefer.

Chicken Dome

You can transform the container from a grocery store rotisserie chicken into a domed feeder for your songbirds' soft foods. The clear plastic lid acts like the dome on a "real" domed bird feeder, blocking access by starlings and other feeder greedies. Hang the feeder, keeping the lid a couple of inches from the tray, so that wrens, bluebirds, and other songbirds can get in at the goodies. For a smaller version, try a similar method using a sturdy plastic clamshell container, such as the kind used for take-out salads. Cut the lid and bottom apart before making the feeder. If you increase the gap between the lid and tray, larger songbirds, such as brown thrashers, will be able to access the food. Starlings are still likely to be deterred, at least for a while, because when they attempt to land on top of the feeder, as is their wont, they'll slide right off.

Materials

Center punch or hammer and nail

Plastic tray and lid from supermarket rotisserie chicken, washed

Scissors

Garden twine, 9 to 12 feet long, for hanging

Large-eyed plastic needle, sold with knitting supplies

Method

1. Using the punch or hammer and nail, poke three equidistant holes, about 2 inches apart, in the tray and in the lid, in a triangular pattern, lining up the holes in the tray and lid.

2. Cut three pieces of twine, each about 3 to 4 feet long.

3. Knot one end of each piece of twine with a triple knot, so it can't pull through the holes in the tray and lid.

4. Thread the pieces of twine through the holes in the bottom tray, so that the knots are on the underside of the tray.

5. Tie a triple knot in each piece of twine, about 6 to 8 inches above the bottom tray, to hold the lid level in an elevated position.

6. Thread the twine through the top lid. The knots will rest under the lid, to keep it raised about 2 to 3 inches above the bottom tray.

7. Tie the loose ends of the twine together evenly, and hang your new domed feeder from a shepherd's crook or branch.

Sandwich suet feeders keep the suet between two pieces of wood or plastic. Clinging birds peck into the edges to access the fat. These feeders aren't easy for starlings to use, but the pesky birds are clever—and determined. Even a sandwich feeder may not deter them for long.

Recycling Is for the Birds

Plastic containers make great bird feeders for the fat-based soft foods I like to experiment with. Which is why you may spot me at the recycling center, head down in a giant cardboard box and legs dangling in midair, as I reach for just the right piece of treasure. Those bins hold an incredible variety of plastic containers, and many of them make great bird feeders or molds for soft foods.

All you have to do is use your imagination. Yogurt cups, onion dip bowls, a sturdy tray from a rotisserie chicken, a clamshell box from a piece of cake—you name it, there's gold in them thar boxes of plastic trash. Before you take your recyclables to the curb or your local sorting station, take another look at them to gauge the possibilities. And next time you drop off your own wares, have a look-see at what others have left. You just may find your next bird feeder—for free.

And metal can be a treasure, too. Keep your soft foods safe from rain, snow, and sun by attaching a folded piece of scrap metal to the top of an inexpensive suet cage. Not handy with tools? Then recycle an aluminum casserole pan, turkey roaster, or pie pan into a feeder roof. Cut a rectangle of the sturdy pan large enough to overhang the cage, crease the center, and attach it to the top with a piece of florists' wire. Use a sharp nail to poke the holes for inserting the wire.

CHAPTER 9

Fruits, Berries, and Sweets

Mmm, fruit! Who doesn't love a juicy strawberry, a sun-warmed peach, the first 'Beefsteak' tomato, a bowl of hard-as-rocks dogwood berries?

Okay, maybe not so much the last one, unless we're talking to robins, bluebirds, and other berry-eating birds. And that tomato is iffy on a couple of counts, too: Some folks just can't stand the taste and texture. Plus, we think of them as vegetables, not as fruits.

But all of those foods, along with hundreds of others that hold their seeds within a fleshy, often juicy receptacle, are technically fruits. And fruits are manna to some of our favorite songbirds, especially the bright, beautiful neotropical migrants—many of whom eat fruits in their winter quarters.

In this chapter, we'll focus on both the foods we don't hesitate to call fruit as well as on the berries and other treats that botanists put in this category.

We'll add other sweets to the list, too, because some songbirds are as sweet on nectar as the hummingbirds and insects are that attend our feeders and flowers.

FEATHERED FRUGIVORES

Frugivores? Frugivorous? Where'd that word come from, anyhow? Well, if you studied Latin, which I didn't, you might know that it stems from the combination of the word for fruit, which is *frux,* plus *vorous,* which means "gaining sustenance from."

See? Easy! A "fruxvorous" critter gets its sustenance from fruit.

Hmm, guess we're not quite there yet. The problem is pronunciation—the g in frugivore is a soft g, pronounced as a j. So it's not *froog,* it's *frooj.* Which is very close to how the Latin *frux* rolls off the tongue. *FROO-jih-vors. Froo-JIV-or-us.* Got it? Fruit-eating birds are *frugivores.*

Can we just say "fruitarians" instead?

Whatever we call them, birds that earn this moniker are species that eat fruit. Some are totally frugivorous, or nearly so. But the vast majority of frugivorous American birds are only part-timers. They have a more varied diet, with plenty of room on their plates for insects, seeds, and other munchies, as well as fruit.

Hardly the Whole Enchilada

Most birds that are complete frugivores (*FROO-jih-vors, FROO-jih-vors*; we'll get this yet) are tropical species, and that makes sense. Down near the equator where they live, the fruit they need is available year-round. All they have to do is follow the season, moving from one exotic plant to another as the crop ripens.

Up here, it's a different story. One cold blast and most of our fruits go bye-bye. That's why hardly any North American birds are entirely frugivorous (yay, nice job on your pronunciation!). The cedar waxwing is our most fruit-eatin' bird, but since its high, lispy *tseee* isn't very musical, we're not considering it a singer in this book.

What about songbirds that depend heavily on fruit, with an occasional helping of insects but nary a bite of seeds? It's a very small list and it's seasonal, in most cases. Bluebirds, yellow-rumped warblers, and thrushes, for instance, depend mostly on fruit in fall and winter, but eat insects or similar critters in warmer months.

Fruit Appreciators

Songbirds that have a more varied diet, yet still love fruit—ah, now we're talking. Those part-time frugivores include dozens of our backyard friends, who will happily snatch a bite of blueberry in between nabbing insects or pecking at seeds. Take a look at the songbirds plucking mulberries from a tree in summer, for instance. You'll spot dozens of species gobbling up the berries—including indigo buntings, which usually eat seeds, and vireos, which lean heavily toward insects. Although full-fledged total frugivores are almost nonexistent among North American birds,

Robins love apples softened by winter cold, whether they are still on the tree, have already fallen to the ground, or are served at the feeder.

songbirds that enjoy a bite of fruit are more common than we might think.

So why haven't we been offering fruit at our feeders for decades? Because many of these bird species are only now adapting to our backyards and our feeding stations. Some of us have been serving fruit all along, although we haven't gotten much fancier than tossing out the occasional apple or putting some raisins in the bluebird mix.

Time to meet the fruit eaters among our backyard songbirds. None of them are completely frugivorous, but these birds readily eat fruit or berries when they're available. These birds also consume plenty of insects, and some species add seeds, nuts, or other foods to their menu, too.

Those wide tastes give us plenty of room for attracting these songbirds to our backyards. As usual, you'll have the highest chance of success by using the three-pronged approach of plants for natural food, cover, and nesting; feeder foods; and a welcome source of water.

Oh, and don't be fooled by what appears to be a fairly short list of fruit appreciators—each plural group of songbirds (thrushes, say) includes several species, so the total number of frugivorous backyard songbirds fills out to 30 or more possible customers:

American robin	Pine grosbeak
Bluebirds	Rose-breasted
Buntings	grosbeak
Cardinal	Orioles
Cassin's finch	Tanagers
House finch	Thrushes
Purple finch	Veery
Black-headed	Vireos
grosbeak	Wood warblers
Blue grosbeak	Wrens

KINDS OF FRUITS

Not all fruits and berries are created equal. Some are soft, some hard; some small, some big; some have big pits, others are full of tiny seeds. And, of course, every possible variation in between. All of those differences affect songbird preferences (as well as our own), but there's an even bigger factor—the nutritional content of the fruit.

Sweet as Sugar

Some fruits, including all those we love best ourselves, are high in sugar. They're sweet and usually juicy. Songbirds love the same sweet fruits that we do. They'll seek them out as au naturel on the tree or bush in our backyards, and many birds are learning to eat them at the feeder, as well. These fruits are in season throughout summer, when birds are actively raising families. The sugar content gives the songbirds a burst of quick carbohydrate energy, as well as important vitamins, minerals, and other substances (like carotenoids, which their bodies use to color their feathers).

Fruits fresh, frozen, or dried—songbirds will sample these delicious treats in any fashion. Fresh is best for birds that are still learning to use our backyards as a farmers' market, because they can recognize the fruit at first sight. On the tree

Safe Haven
"JUST PEACHY," SAY HOUSE FINCHES

House finches can become real pests in an orchard, especially if there are sweet, juicy peaches to be had. The small songbirds don't eat much, but they cause big problems, because they ruin the salability of the fruit. One peck, one sip of juice or bite of flesh, is often all they take, but that's enough to make orchardists fume at the thought of finches. In our backyards, though, it's easy to share the crop with pretty house finches, because we can quickly cut that beak mark out of the peach, or eat around it.

Choose a dwarf peach tree variety to save space and make picking a pleasure instead of a chore. Most grow best in USDA Plant Hardiness Zones 6 through 9; 'Reliance' is hardy to Zone 5. Your local garden center will have peach trees that are perfect for your area, or you can shop a wider selection in mail-order catalogs or online.

is even better, because the crop will draw in birds that might otherwise fly on by.

Favored Fruits

If we like it, they like it. That's pretty much how it works with sweet fruits and songbirds. They'll flock to any ripening crop on a backyard fruit tree or in an orchard, ready to take their share.

Among the "people fruits" they favor most are:

Apricots	Pears
Blackberries	Plums
Blueberries	Raspberries
Grapes	Sour (pie) cherries
Figs	Strawberries
Peaches	Sweet cherries

You may wonder why apples aren't on that list. Most songbirds wait until winter to help themselves to apples, perhaps because the fruit is too hard to puncture and eat before frost softens the skin. So add an apple tree to your yard, by all means, and include the fruit in your songbird treats, if you like. Other fruits may be more popular, just as they are with us, but songbirds will still appreciate an apple.

Want to make a wintering robin happy? Just slice an apple in half (or better yet, a few apples) and set the fruit in a low feeder or right on the ground, cut side up. In no time, your robin will hollow out every bit of flesh, leaving nothing but the cupped skin behind. The gray catbird and brown thrasher are also fond of apples in winter, when natural fruits are scarce.

Fruits for Fat

Other fruits, including nearly every one of the red berries that songbirds find so irresistible, are packed with fat. Fats, or lipids, are an enormous benefit when songbirds are piling on the calories for their long-distance flight during fall migration. The birds can store the fat and draw on those reserves as they travel.

And here's another one of Mother Nature's neat tricks—these lipid-rich berries ripen exactly at the right time. They nourish the birds before they take off, as well as along the way.

Best Bets for Berries

Want a list of berries for birds? That would be a book in itself, with almost every berry-producing native American plant on it, as well as scores of plants from other countries that we've added to our gardens.

Trick or Treat
What a Windfall!

The simplest way to serve apples, oranges, crabapples, pears, and any tree berries you may have collected (including dogwood, hawthorn, or holly berries) is right on the ground. Songbirds are accustomed to seeing and seeking fruit that has fallen naturally.

Get to Know Your Songbirds
Gray Catbird

When a swarm of starlings descended on my suet feeder, gobbling the entire block, I refilled the wire cage with a couple of chunks of cream cheese I happened to have on hand. It was white, it was high in fat, and it was soft enough for songbird beaks, so I figured it might make an acceptable substitute until I could go to the store to restock the suet.

"Acceptable" is putting it mildly—my pair of gray catbirds loved it! They'd been regular visitors at the suet, but they never stayed for long. Now they pecked away for half an hour at a time at the cream cheese, which was way easier for them to devour than hardened suet. And they returned several times a day to get more.

The catbird is one of my favorite backyard songbirds, even though I hear my pair much more often than I actually see them. These are birds of the bush, and dense shrubbery is where they hide out when they're not at the feeder or birdbath.

Catbirds are smart cookies. They quickly become accustomed to our presence as the feeder filler, and it's fun to experiment with foods you think they may enjoy. They're also one of only about a dozen bird species that can recognize in their own nests the parasitic cowbird's eggs and give them the heave-ho.

The gray catbird is an eager eater, and remarkably adventurous at trying new foods.

When to see them: Spring through fall across most of the country, except for the Far West, Southwest, and Gulf Coast; in winter along the Gulf and in Florida. Catbirds are year-round birds along the Atlantic Coast, and individual birds are pushing the envelope elsewhere, too, perhaps because of our welcoming feeders.

What to feed them: Suet and soft foods, peanut butter, fruit, chopped nuts, mealworms; try any homemade treat you can dream up.

Other ways to attract them: Water is a must; these birds love a daily bath. Shrubs or hedges are vital, too, for that all-important cover. Plant elderberries for summer fruit; dogwoods (*Cornus* spp.) and hollies (*Ilex* spp.) for fall and winter berries.

What they sound like: Not quite like Kitty, but close enough—that's the basic mewing call of the catbird.

Their songs, however, are rich and varied, with phrases often repeated three times and snatches of mimicry sometimes thrown in.

What to watch for: Tail-flicking is a typical trait. And beware: Parents are determined defenders of their nests and may even fly out at a person who comes too near.

Just take a look at the menu in "Make a Hermit Happy," on page 165, which lists the favorite berries of the hermit thrush, a species found across much of our country. The berries eaten by these lovely brown songbirds run a wide gamut, from peppervine (*Ampelopsis arborea*) in Texas, to toyon (*Heteromeles arbutifolia*) in California, to mountain holly (*Ilex mucronata*) in Maine, to blueberries anywhere they can find them.

To narrow down the list, think about the plants that *you* find appealing, too. Native berry shrubs and trees are always a great choice; only a very, very few aren't eagerly sought by songbirds. Try any native fall-fruiting shrub that catches your eye, especially those with red berries, which are likely to be high in lipids valuable to birds.

It's a snap to choose a good songbird berry, just by looking at the color of the fruit. Red berries, dark blue berries, and black berries are practically guaranteed to attract birds, whether the fruits grow on a vine, a shrub, or a tree. Very few plants with berries of these colors aren't instantly appealing to birds. The berries of nandina (*Nandina domestica*) and some nonnative viburnums (including the popular ornamental doublefile viburnum, *Viburnum plicatum*) often go begging. Bright purple beautyberry (*Callicarpa americana*), white snowberry (*Symphoricarpus albus*), and the related coralberry (*S. orbiculatus*) also have much lower appeal than most other berried shrubs.

Since we'd rather see our efforts embraced than scorned, go for a surefire winner: a shrub with red, blue, or black berries that's native to your region. You'll find suppliers for all geographic areas in the Resources section at the back of this book.

FRUIT HAS A ROLE TO PLAY

Everything in nature has a purpose. The same purpose.

Survival of the species.

Plants can't move around themselves, so they depend on all kinds of mechanisms to help them guarantee the next generation. Among the most important? Birds.

Fruits figured it out long ago. They have a *mutualistic* relationship with the birds and other animals that eat them. Just as the nectar in flowers is nothing less than a bribe for pollinators, so the

Safe Haven
INSTANT HEDGE FOR FRUGIVORES

Every fruit-eating songbird likes elderberries, so why not grow a whole hedge of these easy, fast-growing shrubs? The bushes will provide a corridor for safe travels, as well as a great hideout for the shyer songbirds, such as thrashers, catbirds, and perhaps thrushes.

Plant a garden cultivar such as 'York', 'Adams 1', 'Adams 2', or 'Wyldewood' for super-fast growth. It'll blossom and bear fruit the same year you plant it. By fruiting time in late summer, a spindly spring-planted starter will be shrub size.

Cardinals and pears? Why not? Offer any fruit you have on hand, especially in winter.

fleshy parts of fruits and berries beckon to songbirds and other fruit eaters, offering an incentive to eat them. In the process, the seeds in that fruit get dispersed. Birds, bats, even elephants, spread the seeds far and wide. So do we, whenever we spit a cherry pit out the car window or across the yard. New plants spring up from those seeds, and the cycle continues, with benefits to both eatee and eater. It's mutualistic—a win-win situation for both the fruiting plants and the fruit eaters.

For birds, it's all about food. For fruits and berries, the vital issue is the next generation.

Which Way Out?

I used to think that the seeds in fruits and berries were spread by birds by way of their main exit route for undigested food: out the hind end, shall we say.

One autumn, when my backyard spicebushes (*Lindera benzoin*) had a particularly prolific crop of berries, I spent hours watching the hermit thrushes, wood thrushes, gray-cheeked thrushes, and veeries that moved into my yard for a week or so to gobble them up. At first I couldn't believe what I was seeing. These birds weren't passing the seeds through their digestive tract onto the ground—instead, they were regurgitating them. Throwing them up, in other words. The convulsive action happened every 15 minutes or so for each bird. A few spasms of the throat, and up came a lump of the seeds.

What in the world was going on? Was there something wrong with the berries, something that was making my songbirds sick?

Nope. What I was seeing was perfectly normal. Seeds come out of a bird in two different

Grow Your Own

Here's a year's worth of fruits for our songbirds, all of them easy to grow in your backyard for hearty crops, good cover, and other bird benefits. All fruit-eating songbirds—and that's quite a flock, of at least 30 species—may come to harvest their share of any of these fruits. The birds listed in the column at right are those you're most likely to spot, because they're common backyard species. But be alert for any pretty singer, including some not listed here.

FRUIT	DESCRIPTION	SEASON	SONGBIRDS MOST LIKELY TO BE SEEN
Strawberry	Groundcover plants with white flowers and yummy berries	Late spring to early summer; ever-bearing varieties produce berries into fall.	American robin, gray catbird, song sparrows, thrashers, white- and golden-crowned sparrows, white-throated sparrows
Sour (pie) cherry	Dwarf cultivars are small trees, to about 15 ft.; fragrant white flowers followed by large crop of glossy red, tart cherries	Early to midsummer	American robin, bluebirds, gray catbird, grosbeaks, northern mockingbird, orioles, thrashers, thrushes
Serviceberry (*Amelanchier* spp.)	Small trees or shrubs, depending on species, with white flowers followed by deep blue-purple berries; birds love them all.	Midsummer	American robin, bluebirds, buntings, gray catbird, grosbeaks, northern mockingbird, orioles, thrashers, thrushes, vireos, wood warblers
Elderberry, cultivated varieties	Fast-growing bushes; huge clusters of tiny purple-black berries follow fragrant creamy flowers.	Mid- to late summer	American robin, bluebirds, gray catbird, grosbeaks, thrashers, thrushes, vireos
Apple	Small to large trees, from about 20 ft. for dwarf cultivars to about 30 ft. for standard varieties	Late summer to fall; fruit continues to attract songbirds into winter, whether on the ground or on branches.	American robin, gray catbird, house finches, thrashers, thrushes
Bayberry (*Morella pensylvanica*)	Evergreen shrub to small tree with glossy, aromatic foliage and small, waxy, whitish gray berries	Winter to very early spring	Bluebirds, yellow-rumped warblers

ways, depending on the species of bird and the species of seed. Some pass all the way through in the regular way. But many are regurgitated instead. Regurgitation saves the seed from going through the grinding of the digestive tract, and it does away with what I used to think was a good thing—the little dab of built-in fertilizer when the bird defecates. Recent studies show that bird feces can actually inhibit the germination of seeds. When seeds of juniper berries that were defecated by cedar waxwings were compared to juniper seeds regurgitated by robins, the robins' method won by a mile. Nearly 100 percent of the seeds germinated.

Many fruits and berries are eaten by both kinds of seed-dispersing birds, so the plants have

Make a Hermit Happy

Here's a list of some of the plants whose berries are eagerly sought by the hermit thrush. Other frugivorous birds eat many of these berries, too. Can you find any of your own native or garden plants here?

Blackberry

Blueberry

Dogwood, at least 5 species (*Cornus* spp.)

Elderberry, at least 3 species

Firethorn (*Pyracantha* spp.)

Greenbrier, at least 3 species (*Smilax* spp.)

Mountain holly (*Ilex mucronata*)

Japanese honeysuckle (*Lonicera japonica*)

Juniper, every species (*Juniperus* spp.)

Pacific Madrone (*Arbutus menziesii*)

Manzanita (*Arctostaphylos* spp.)

American mistletoe (*Phoradendron serotinum*)

Moonseed vine (*Menispermum* spp.)

Mulberry, 3 species

Nightshade (*Solanum* spp.)

Peppervine (*Ampelopsis arborea*)

Poison ivy (*Toxicodendron radicans*)

Poison oak (*Toxicodendron diversilobum*)

Pokeweed (*Phytolacca americana*)

Privet (*Ligustrum* spp.)

Sassafras (*Sassafras albidum*)

Serviceberry, at least 5 species (*Amelanchier* spp.)

Spicebush (*Lindera* spp.)

Sumac (*Rhus* spp.)

Summersweet (*Clethra* spp.)

Toyon (*Heteromeles arbutifolia*)

Virginia creeper (*Parthenocissus quinquefolia*)

to hedge their bets. Some seeds won't make it, but some always will.

Three Ways of Eating

Songbirds eat fruits in three ways, depending on various factors. The size of the fruit or berry, the size of the seed, and the bird's typical style of eating all have an influence.

- The bird may swallow a small fruit or berry whole, as thrushes, vireos, catbirds, and thrashers do.
- The bird may peck off the flesh and drop the seed, as tanagers often do.
- The bird may eat the fruit and also crack open the seed to eat it, too, as strong-billed cardinals do. Luckily for the plant, other fruits will be eaten by birds that don't crack open the seeds, so those seeds will survive.

In any case, the end result is the same: The plant that produced those fruits or berries is perpetuated. Of course, the birds' only concern is on the other side of the equation. Their goal? Removing the delicious flesh of the fruit or berry from the seed.

Taking the Bait

The tasty part of a fruit has no value to the plant. It's only a bribe for birds and other fruit-eating creatures. Seeds need moisture to sprout, which means they must be freed from that fruity covering—which withers and dries—so that rainwater or snow melt can soften them. If the dried fruity part remains in place, it actually inhibits the seed from germinating. It's a do-or-die gamble for the seeds. That's why fruit and berry plants have to count on their tasty flesh to deal them a winning hand.

The risk is biggest for plants that produce berries high in fats—the lipid-rich, fall-ripening ones, like dogwood berries, that attract birds like a magnet. The same fats that cause the birds to make a beeline to those berries can have a negative effect, as far as the seed is concerned: They prevent water from reaching the seed.

Good thing those high-fat berries do their job when it comes to bringing in the birds. Because any berries that birds or other creatures overlook, well, they're dead on the vine, so to speak. If no bird comes along to take the bait, the plant

It's All Connected
BECKON WITH RED

Red berries begin to ripen on bushes and trees just as birds are getting ready to migrate in fall. The color signals that the fruit is ripe and that it's usually high in fat, too. Bluebirds, robins, grosbeaks, thrushes, and other songbirds taste the *umami* (satisfying savory flavor) of the berries, which lets them know it's extra nutritious, and they settle in to chow down. By paying attention to when your dogwood or other red berries ripen, you'll know when songbirds are on the move.

It's All Connected

JACK BE NIMBLE

The unusual flower of Jack-in-the-pulpit (*Arisaema triphyllum*), with its hooded spathe covering a jaunty spadix, is a charming character in a shade garden or in the woods where it grows wild. But it's not the flower that enchants berry-eating songbirds—it's the spike of densely clustered, gleaming red berries that mature in early fall.

The timing is perfect, of course, because when Jack's berries go red, the thrushes that eat them are moving through on fall migration. Keep an eye on your wildflower garden or during your woods walks, and look for shy thrushes when Jack-in-the-pulpit berries are bright.

Not all plants have berries—only the female ones. But oddly enough, a Jack can change gender and become a Jill the following year, or vice versa, gathering its strength betweentimes before it produces another stem of berries.

embryo inside each seed may die before it ever has a chance to sprout.

Fruit for Love

A gift of fruit makes for a tender moment between songbirds. Who doesn't love to get presents? Even female songbirds seem to soften and smile when their mates present them with a little something. Cedar waxwings are the champs at this behavior, but songbirds of the frugivorous sort sometimes engage in this ritual, too.

Cherries are a popular target, because the fruit ripens at the height of courtship and nesting season. The action starts when a pair of gray catbirds, cardinals, rose-breasted or black-headed grosbeaks, or other fruit eaters settles on a branch of the cherry tree—or at your feeder, if cherries are on the menu.

The male bird plucks a plump ripe cherry and passes it to his partner, maneuvering carefully so that he doesn't drop it. Sometimes the pair will exchange the fruit several times, before one or the other eventually eats it.

Elderberries, blueberries, and other bite-size fruits may get the same treatment by pairs of songbirds. It's an endearing gesture no girl can resist.

Exotic Fruits

Like college kids on spring break, many of our neotropical migrants behave quite a bit differently when they head south on winter vacation. Temptations are everywhere they turn—not of the beer party variety, but of delectable exotic foods they never see when they're with us.

Fruit is plentiful, and what fruits they are! Mangoes, bananas, plantains, papayas, coffee berries, and a fantasyland of fruits that haven't even made it to our grocery stores yet.

Songbirds roam the rainforest, sampling all kinds of exotic treats. Exotic to us, that is. To the birds, it's simply what's for dinner. That's why

This Baltimore oriole may recognize bananas from its winter home in Central America.

there's no need for us to stick to common fruits like apples, peaches, and grapes for feeding songbirds.

Who knows what that summer tanager was eating just a month before it showed up in our backyards? Try anything at your feeder, and you just may hit on a fruit that your songbirds remember fondly from their last vacation.

Spring is the best time to offer fruit, especially tropical fruits like bananas, at your feeders. Long-distance migrants returning north, such as the Tennessee warbler, hepatic tanager, or Baltimore oriole, may stop off for a little reminder of the winter home they just left.

DUI? Make That FUI

"Flying Under the Influence," that is. Some fruits and berries are notorious for fermenting on the

Eats and Treats
Banana Mash

This treat couldn't be simpler. Well, unless you skip the cereal, which is used mostly as a filler to make the banana "stretch." But once your songbirds find this snack, you'll understand why the filler is a good idea. Orioles, tanagers, and other fruit-eating songbirds that winter in the Tropics can go through bananas in a hurry. "Oh boy," they'll sing, "a taste of home!" For an even simpler banana treat, partly peel the banana and set it in a feeder. Songbirds will find it, and the peel will hold the fruit together.

1 ripe banana

½ cup high-protein dry baby cereal

Using the back of a fork, coarsely mash the banana into the baby cereal in a small bowl. Leave it chunky; don't make it a smooth paste. Serve on a tray feeder, in a plastic domed feeder, or on an oriole feeder.

bush or tree, but that doesn't stop songbirds from seeking them out. In fact, it seems to add to their appeal. So, don't be surprised if you see your robins, bluebirds, or other fruit eaters acting a little intoxicated as they gorge themselves on fermented firethorn berries (*Pyracantha* spp.), pears, or other alcoholic fruit.

But do give them a hand by keeping your pets inside, because imbibing definitely dampens a bird's natural self-protective instincts. Intoxication can also lead to fatalities if there's a street nearby: Collisions with vehicles are a common aftermath of these kinds of parties.

FRUIT AT THE FEEDER

It seems like it should be a cinch to get songbirds to eat fruit at our feeders, but that's not the case. Bluebirds, robins, rose-breasted grosbeaks, finches, and others quickly descend on a cherry tree, elderberry bush, or other tempting fruits and berries, yet they don't seem very interested in gobbling down the same fruit when it's in a feeder.

Maybe it's just that our soft foods and mealworms are too tempting. Maybe it's because the birds are conditioned to their "Pick Your Own" style of eating. Maybe they're huge fans of the freshest goodies. Or maybe they simply haven't learned to accept feeders as a source of fruit yet.

Most Likely Feeder Fruit Eaters

These songbirds have already adapted to visiting our feeders for fruit and fruity treats, as well as for soft foods—or at least the birds have been spotted dropping in on occasion. Eventually, we hope, all of their friends will join them. Any fruit-eating songbird may show up as a pioneer, of course, so keep your eyes open. That's the fun of feeding songbirds—you never know who may drop in for your treats.

American robin	Northern mockingbird
Bewick's wren	Orioles
Black-headed grosbeak	Red-eyed vireo
Bluebirds	Rose-breasted grosbeak
Brown thrasher	Tanagers
Carolina wren	Townsend's warbler
Gray catbird	Varied thrush
Gray-cheeked thrush	Yellow-rumped warbler
Hermit thrush	
Northern cardinal	

High Potential

Luring songbirds to our feeders to eat fruits can be challenging, but the rewards are worth it. Just hanging a sprig of grapes on your hopper feeder won't do the trick. At least, not yet.

But there's hope, because songbirds are learning what feeders are for. As the birds become accustomed to looking to our backyards for food and shelter, and as we bolster our

Purple finches eat cherries off the tree, but eschew fruit at the feeder, in favor of seeds.

menus with soft foods and fruity goodness and especially mealworms, more and more songbird species are investigating feeders. But until the day comes when we're shooing away scarlet tanagers like starlings, capturing the attention of these finicky sorts will still depend heavily on providing them the natural foods and protective cover of plants.

Fruits and berries on bushes and trees go a long way toward capturing the attention of songbirds. But there's no need to wait until your first crop of fruits; start luring in these birds with feeder foods.

Fake It 'Til You Make It

Use your shrubs and the low branches of trees—whatever you can easily reach—as fruit "feeders," by attaching grocery-store fruit goodies to their limbs. Songbirds feel at home in trees, so vireos, tanagers, and other less adventurous types are likely to investigate these offerings before they venture to a feeder.

Sure, they may be taken aback to find a cluster of tiny champagne grapes hanging from a maple tree branch, or stray blueberries impaled here and there on a burning bush. But those birds that love fruit won't wait long to sidle up and try a bite.

Ties That Bind

Plastic zip ties are great for securing fruit or stems of berries to twigs or small branches. They create a really snug fit—better than twine, which often loosens up. And they're easy to use. You can quickly pull them tight with one hand while you hold the offering in place with the other. Drawbacks: They're pretty noticeable, being made of plastic, and they're not reusable, unless you can manage to wiggle a refill in under them.

Tried-and-True

The word about feeder fruit is spreading among songbirds. Orioles were the first to be attracted, with oranges as the lure. Grape jelly is another fast favorite of these beautiful birds. Now that they know what a feeder is, it's easy to entice them: Just put out their favorites, and they will come. Then you can expand your offerings by experimenting with other fruits.

To lure an oriole to your feeder, put out your fruity treats when these colorful songbirds are moving through on spring migration. They're hungry then, and they'll soon be staking out nesting territories. A feeder with oranges, jelly, and soft foods is a great incentive to them to include part of your yard as their home.

For other songbirds, the allure of fruit begins

Hooded and other orioles enjoy all sorts of citrus fruit. So do tanagers and thrushes.

Kiss Me Quick

THE MISTLETOE CONNECTION

Mistletoe was the plant of peace, according to old Scandinavian folktales, and if enemies met beneath a tree that hosted the plant, they would lay down their weapons and embrace. But it's not the chance to hug or smooch that draws songbirds to this parasitic plant—it's the berries. Thanks to thrushes and other frugivorous songbirds that dine on the white fruit, mistletoe spreads from one tree to another.

Bluebirds are such big fans of mistletoe that you're almost guaranteed to see one at the berries if you wait for a while. Next time you visit the horse country of Kentucky, look for balls of mistletoe in the pasture trees, bluebird boxes lining the roadsides, and flashes of blue feathers flying back and forth between home and food.

with raisins. Robins have become raisin fans and feeder friends in many backyards, and so have gray catbirds, thrashers, and others. Smaller fruit-eating songbirds, including wrens and yellow-rumped warblers, appreciate smaller pieces, so I chop raisins for those guys.

Dried blueberries are popular with songbirds, too. These berries have become much more reasonably priced lately, since they landed on the list of most-healthy foods because of their antioxidant content. It's a matter of familiarity, I think, as well as of tempting taste. Premium seed mixes often contain dried blueberries. And since birds play follow-the-leader at the feeder, all it takes is one robin to discover the goodness; other songbird species soon take the cue.

Small Is Better

Lingering over a meal isn't the style for many songbirds. When a bird remains in one place, it ups its chances of getting noticed by a predator.

So most of our backyard friends drop in for a few bites, fly away, then return. Oh, I still set out halved apples and oranges for the birds to work at, and some songbirds, including robins and orioles, will stick around to peck the tasty flesh from those fruits.

For my other friends, I take a different approach: I use bite-size fruit in my feeders. The boom in dried fruit for humans has boosted my feeder choices. Dried blueberries and dried cherries are my mainstays, but I experiment with anything I can get my hands on. Songbirds love exotic fruits, too, I've learned, like small pieces of mango and papaya.

Dried currants are a good choice, too. They're about half the size of raisins or smaller, and easy to mix into soft-food recipes to add a fruity boost. If you plan to serve them in the feeder alone, you may want to rinse, separate, and freeze them to break apart the sticky clumps and make it easier to pour out a small helping.

Get to Know Your Songbirds
Hooded Oriole

Hooded orioles and palm plants are a perfect match. These gorgeous songbirds are strongly inclined to weave their nests into palm trees as well as palms of shorter stature.

In fact, palms are the reason the hooded oriole expanded its range. As their favorite plants became common in backyards, the birds moved outward from parts of California and the Desert Southwest to take advantage of them. Today, the oriole's range is still spreading. Stray birds show up fairly often far from their usual haunts, ranging north to Washington and east to Louisiana.

Although the home base of these neotropicals is expanding, their numbers have dropped in the past century. Early visitors to the Rio Grande Valley remarked on the abundance of hooded orioles; today, those populations are way down.

Backyards and urban areas are a favorite homesite for hooded orioles, especially if they feature some palm plants. The birds also hang their nests in sycamores and other trees. Your guess as to their most popular nesting material? It's palm fibers, which orioles strip from the plant. In the Rio Grande Valley where trees are draped in Spanish moss, those gray fibers are the birds' material of choice.

As for the bird's "hood," it's not black as you might expect, but golden orange. "Bibbed orioles" might've been a better name. Then again, this bird already has another nickname. It was once known as the palm-leaf oriole.

Male hooded oriole

When to see them: Spring through fall

What to feed them: Nectar; oranges and other citrus fruits; bananas; grape jelly; suet and soft foods; mealworms

Other ways to attract them: Plant palms! Provide a birdbath. Add tubular, nectar-rich flowers on strong stalks, such as redhot poker (*Kniphofia* spp.) and agave (*Agave* spp.), to supply natural nectar.

What they sound like: The rapid, warbling song of hooded orioles doesn't carry very far, but you'll hear it just fine when the bird visits your backyard.

What to watch for: Like other orioles, hoodeds usually call a truce when it comes to choice feeding areas. You're likely to see more than one male visiting feeders or flowers at the same time, even in nesting season.

Dried Fruits Are Just as Popular

Dried fruit can be expensive, so I often buy it at natural food markets where blueberries, cherries, raisins, currants, chopped papaya, and other small dried fruit are sold in bulk. The fruit isn't as perfect as that sold in brand-name packages, but broken bits suit my birds just fine. Besides, I often come across an unusual offering to add to my menu—dried coconut, for instance, which I suppose is technically a fruit. My scarlet tanagers love it, and a little goes a long way.

Keep your stash of dried fruit (whether you dry it yourself or buy it) in a dry, dark place. Room temperature is fine for at least a month, so store your frequently used dried cherries, blueberries, raisins, and other goodies in tightly sealed bags in a cabinet. The freezer's a good choice for long-term storage; I've served dried fruits after a year in the freezer.

Free Harvest

If I pick and fill a bag with dogwood berries in fall, will I be shortchanging the migrating songbirds that depend on them? What about those arrowwood viburnums (*Viburnum dentatum*)? They're loaded with fruit this year. Surely the bluebirds won't miss a few of them, will they?

It's a balancing act, for sure, so I walk a fine line. If there's a bumper crop, I gather a share to freeze for later. If the berries are sparse, I leave them all there on the plants for the birds.

Many backyard plants with berries produce prolific harvests for songbirds. Here are some great choices.

American bittersweet (*Celastrus scandens*)

Flowering crabapple (*Malus* spp.)

Flowering dogwood (*Cornus florida*)

Hawthorn (*Crataegus* spp.)

Holly (*Ilex* spp.)

Juniper (*Juniperus* spp.)

Pyracantha (*Pyracantha* spp.)

Sumac (*Rhus* spp.)

Winterberry (*Ilex verticillata*)

Trick or Treat
Small and Soft

Bluebirds can be picky about raisins. Some folks find that their lovely friends avidly eat the dried fruit; others watch the raisins get ignored.

Some have theorized that the fruit is too big for bluebird beaks, but I suspect it's not the size, but the hardness of the raisins—they're tough to swallow whole and difficult to rip into pieces.

I find my bluebirds like them much better when I simmer the raisins in water for about 5 minutes, cool them, and chop them up. Bluebirds eagerly eat the softened pieces, whether I serve them alone or mix them into soft-food treats.

Freeze the berries in a single layer on a cookie sheet immediately after you pick them, and then pour them into a plastic freezer bag. Hollies and sumac need a spell of cold weather to become palatable, and they'll get that in your freezer.

Mix a handful of your harvest with the seeds in a tray feeder for cardinals, catbirds, and others, or serve them in small amounts in a domed or window feeder. You can also add the berries to soft-food recipes, but I generally reserve them for special stand-alone treats. The berries will attract songbirds most in winter and spring, when natu-

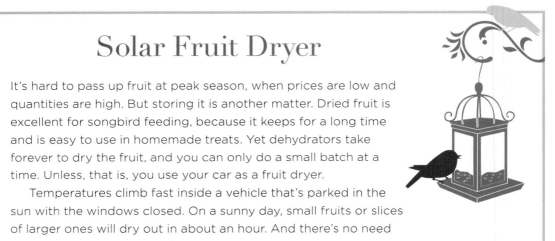

Solar Fruit Dryer

It's hard to pass up fruit at peak season, when prices are low and quantities are high. But storing it is another matter. Dried fruit is excellent for songbird feeding, because it keeps for a long time and is easy to use in homemade treats. Yet dehydrators take forever to dry the fruit, and you can only do a small batch at a time. Unless, that is, you use your car as a fruit dryer.

Temperatures climb fast inside a vehicle that's parked in the sun with the windows closed. On a sunny day, small fruits or slices of larger ones will dry out in about an hour. And there's no need to worry about insects or dew.

Here's how to do it:

1. On a sunny day, park your vehicle in full, all-day sun, or as close to those conditions as you can get. Close all the windows.

2. Prepare the fruit for drying. Blueberries, raspberries, and blackberries can be dried whole. Cut larger fruits, such as strawberries, apricots, and peaches, into thin slices or dice to save time later.

3. Arrange the fruit on metal cookie sheets in a single layer.

4. Set the trays on your dashboard, seats, or back window ledge—wherever you can find a flat space.

5. Check the trays in about an hour. Using a spatula, turn the fruit over to thoroughly dry the other side.

6. Store the dried fruit in zip-top bags or in canning jars with screwed-on lids (no need to process them). Slip an unsalted saltine cracker in with the fruit, to absorb any moisture that may still be in it.

Trick or Treat
Baby Your Songbirds

Next time you want to flavor your soft foods for frugivores, try a small jar of pureed fruit baby food. It's inexpensive, convenient, and comes in flavors that fruit-eating birds enjoy. Banana, pear, peach, apricot, and plum are popular with orioles, tanagers, house finches, and other fruit-eating songbirds. You can serve the food in small quantities all by itself, or mix it with uncooked regular or quick-cooking oatmeal or bread crumbs to give it more texture.

ral fruits are scarce, but you can serve them in any season to year-round songbirds such as robins, bluebirds, cardinals, and Carolina wrens.

Convenience Counts

Bird-food manufacturers have added lots of new products to their lineup to help us attract frugivorous songbirds. We can buy fruity suet blocks, fruity bird-food plugs and balls, or plain dried fruit at the same places we buy our birdseed.

These foods are super convenient to serve, and that's their biggest selling point. No fiddling with messy ingredients, no dirtying a mixing bowl, no muss, no fuss. And birds eagerly eat them. Still, there's no substitute for the warm, fuzzy feeling of making our own treats for songbirds. It's like the difference between buying a bag of chocolate chip cookies or baking your own for your kids. Making bird foods yourself saves money, too, and costs can really add up fast if you're feeding a lot of birds.

Combination Platter or à la Carte?

I experiment with new foods all the time, but I don't notice a big upswing in certain songbird species when I buy soft foods that supposedly bring them in. Those robins, bluebirds, brown thrashers, wrens, and other species are already at my feeders, happily eating soft foods.

It's the fat that's the main attraction in these foods, I'm convinced. No matter what it's flavored with, suet is a huge hit with songbirds. Until manufacturers up the ante by including more real fruit in their soft-food products, I'll stick to the bargain-priced suet blocks and soft foods and serve up my fruit à la carte. Or on a day when I don't mind mussing and fussing, I'll make my own offerings.

But the dried fruit that's now in birdseed mixes and sold by the pound is a different story. I wouldn't be without it, because it definitely draws in the birds I want most—and keeps them coming back, too. My Carolina wrens are so fond of the raisins, juniper berries, dried cherries, and blueberries in a certain brand of premium seed mix that they scold me if I don't have their breakfast ready and waiting. Of course, they don't bother with the seeds, no matter how high quality they are.

Now there's a niche that I hope some savvy

Eats and Treats
Fruity Breakfast

Tanagers, orioles, robins, and other fruit-loving songbirds will thank you for babying them with this mix.

1 jar pureed plums baby food

2 cups uncooked high-protein baby cereal, any grain

½ cup cottage cheese, not low-fat

¼ cup raisins

¼ cup dried mealworms

Mix all ingredients until evenly distributed. The mixture should be lumpy but not soggy. If it's too wet, add more cereal. Serve the breakfast in a mealworm feeder, an oriole feeder, or a domed feeder. Store leftovers in the fridge; they'll keep for several days.

---

manufacturer soon fills: fruit and berry mixes, sans seeds, for frugivorous birds. It'd be priced high, of course. But it'd be worth it to be able to fill a feeder just for tanagers, orioles, rose-breasted grosbeaks, bluebirds, and other fruit-loving friends. Can you imagine what the picture on that label would look like?

Until that mix comes along, the fruit-added seed mixes are a fine choice. They allow our songbirds to pluck out the foods they like best. And it's fun to see how they jockey for a seat at the table, whether they're after the safflower seeds or a bite of blueberry.

Fruit or Fruit Flavor?

A friend and I were picking up litter along a nearby road when he snagged a bright orange foil-lined pouch.

"Haven't had this since I was a kid!" he announced, reading the name of the fruit drink with nostalgic glee.

"Never tried it," I responded. "What's in it? Bet it's water and corn syrup right at the top of the list." We peered at the label and confirmed my hunch. Although the label promised orange juice, there was precious little in the mix.

I've been reading the fine print on "fruit" products for years. Most, I've discovered, rely on fruit flavorings or just a smidgen of the real thing. Even the maker of Fig Newtons, my favorite cookies, uses apples for filler, adding only enough figs to make them seem figgy.

The same tricks of the trade are often used in commercial bird foods. Here's the selling copy for a popular berry-flavored suet block that's widely available where bird products are sold: "These delicious cakes contain nutritious, rendered beef suet, millet, oats and corn along with sweet, berry flavor. Attracts catbirds, cardinals, wax-wings and more."

Real fruit or fruit flavored—does it matter when it comes to attracting birds?

That's a question we backyard bird feeders can answer for ourselves, or we can let our birds decide. I've used the fruity soft foods meant for songbirds, and my wrens, catbirds, and the occasional wood warblers seem to like them just fine. On the other hand, they also flock to suet blocks that supposedly appeal most to other species, like the peanutty blocks I buy for my woodpeckers. As always, experiment with whatever seems interesting to you—and then see what your birds decide they like best. I like the real thing myself, so that's what I usually choose.

Homemade Treats

It's easy to duplicate commercial bird foods in your kitchen and just as simple to improve upon them. As you can see from the ad copy for the suet block mentioned above, manufacturers sometimes use ingredients that aren't necessarily the best in order to pad out their products. Cardinals and cat-birds almost never eat millet or oats, and wax-wings don't eat seeds or grain of any kind—unless, that is, they're coated in fat. Then they slide right down with every bite, unnoticed by the birds.

That's not such a bad thing, because seeds and grain are nutritious. But when we're in charge of that mixing bowl, we can tailor our recipes to exactly what our songbirds prefer to eat, rather than what's cheapest to make wholesale.

It's the fat in soft foods that's the primary attractant. After that, everything else is just gravy, so to speak. But gravy can make a lump of mashed potatoes look mighty tempting to eat.

And extra added attractions in soft foods can have the same effect on songbirds.

To really bring in the birds, give them a five-star meal. Or three-star, that is, because these three foods have star power when you mix them together in a soft-food recipe:

- White fat (suet, fat scraps, or lard)
- Bite-size dried fruit
- Dried mealworms (for more details on meal-worms, see the next chapter: "Getting Bugged")

You can stop right there, and songbirds will come flocking. But if you want to make molded treats, like plugs or balls to refill your feeders, you'll need to bulk up this recipe with grain. Yep, then it's time to add the filler.

FRUIT AND SWEETS FEEDERS

It's easy to serve most kinds of fruit in any tray, hopper, or domed feeder, and soft foods made with fruit will work in any suet or soft-food feeder.

There's a big advantage to using a feeder that's dedicated only to fruit and fruity treats, though: Songbirds will soon learn where to check for their goodies, and they won't have to compete with seed eaters at the tray. Keeping a feeder solely for fruit makes refills fast and easy, too.

An oriole feeder is a great place to start. These feeders have holders for fresh oranges and other fresh fruits, and dishes for the grape jelly that ori-oles, tanagers, catbirds, and other sweet-eating songbirds crave. For individual fruits, such as apples, pears, and bananas, you can buy a feeder or make a similar one yourself. The apparatus is simple: a nail protruding from a board, on which you impale the fruit. Some models use a hook instead, and that's easy to replicate, too.

Here's how to make a simple feeder for your deck: Just pound a large nail into your deck railing. Hammer it in an inch or two, so it's solidly attached, but leave the head and shank extending about two inches from the rail. To use as a feeder, simply push a halved apple, a banana, or other fruit onto the nail; the head will help hold it in place.

Want another quick feeder that's perfect for offering a halved pear, apple, or banana to small songbirds? This one will give you a great view of your wrens, yellow-rumped warblers, and other diners. Just attach a stick-on hook to the outside of your windowpane.

Choose a sturdy plastic self-sticking model that can support about a pound of weight, which is usually too much for a suction-cup hook to hold. Attach the adhesive hook to the outside of your window fairly high up, so that the fruit that hangs from it will be near eye level.

If the hook is too stout to impale the fruit on, slip a metal S hook onto the plastic hanger, and use that to spear your fruit.

Inexpensive wire suet cages are perfect for feed-

The gray catbird adores sweet fruits—and sweet jelly. Grape works great, and it's cheap.

ing oranges to orioles and other songbirds, which can easily cling to the grid of sturdy wire. They're perfect for other larger fruits, too, including pears, apples, and bananas. Just slice your fruit in half and slide it in. One suet cage holds about three orange halves, depending on their size.

The best news of all is that songbirds have learned to recognize these cages as a source of reliable food. It won't take long for them to find the fruit.

SWEET, SWEETER, SWEETEST

"Sweet, sweet, sweeter than sweet," sings the yellow warbler, and he ain't kidding. Like many songbirds, this sunny yellow guy with a penchant for hanging out in willows has a serious sweet tooth. Insects are his food of choice, but nectar at feeders has joined the menu for this species. The yellow warbler is just one of 16 different wood warblers that have been spotted taking a sip of sugar water at hummingbird feeders.

Sixteen different wood warblers?! These tiny birds are among the most challenging to coax to a feeding station, because they're almost entirely insectivorous. My own feeder list includes only four species so far, and I thought I was doing good. Guess it's time to add more sugar water.

Nectar Feeders for Songbirds

Hummingbird feeders began to attract the attention of other species of birds a couple of decades ago when they zoomed in backyard popularity, and the list of species that visit them keeps growing. More than 60 different species have been observed sipping sugar water. Everyone from house finches to tanagers to downy woodpeckers has been spotted at the feeders. Although "sip-

A nectar feeder with perches accommodates bigger birds, like this black-headed grosbeak.

ping" isn't quite the right word. Many of these birds are guzzlers that park themselves at the feeder for many minutes and even hours at a time. That can't be good for them. We can only hope that they eat enough other foods to balance that sugar rush.

Even large birds can manage to maneuver into position at a hummingbird feeder. But you can also provide a larger oriole nectar feeder to make it easier for them to get a grip. The bigger reservoir will cut down on your refill duties, too. Hummingbird nectar is mixed at a 4:1 ratio, that is, 4 parts water to 1 part sugar. Or to put it another way, $\frac{1}{4}$ cup sugar to 1 cup water.

Songbirds don't need such a sweet treat, but they'll happily drink it if it's offered. With a songbird nectar feeder, or an auxiliary hummingbird model that they can use, you can wean them to a less sugary 6:1 mix, meaning 6 parts water to 1 part sugar, or $\frac{1}{3}$ cup sugar to every 2 cups water.

For fast preparation, measure the sugar and set it aside, and then zap the water in a microwave-

proof measuring cup for a couple of minutes. Carefully pour in the sugar and stir until it's dissolved. Let it cool before serving; adding a few ice cubes will do the job in a hurry and won't significantly change the dilution. Change the nectar every 3 to 4 days, so that it doesn't ferment, and scrub the feeder frequently, at least once a week, to prevent mold.

Jelly Belly

Sweet fruit spreads are a hit with orioles, tanagers, wood warblers, and other sweet-toothed songbirds. Grape jelly is the standard, because the birds absolutely love it. But it's fun to experiment with other flavors, too, to find out if your birds have connoisseur tastes.

So far, my best find was an odd spread I picked up at a fancy farmers' market—apricot-jalapeño. It was scrumptious, but I only got to enjoy it a few times. My wrens, orioles, and tanagers couldn't get enough of it, and I used up the little chunky jar in less than a week. Sorry, birds, but no refills—that stuff cost $8 for a few ounces, so it's back to giant economy-size Welch's instead.

Jams and preserves aren't as popular as jelly is with songbirds. Those sticky lumps of fruit make it a challenge to eat the stuff without getting messy. And birds are understandably finicky about keeping their feathers clean. Serving jelly doesn't need to involve an elaborate dish, although the store-bought ones are attractive. Nearly a dozen models of jelly feeders are on the market, with new ones popping up every year. While the designs vary, they're all simply systems for holding a small dish of the sweet treat in place. You can easily make your own jelly feeder by simply nailing a plastic lid to a post, or setting a shallow dish in a feeder or on a deck rail.

CHAPTER 10

Getting Bugged

Every songbird eats insects, and caterpillars (the larval stage of moths or butterflies) are right at the top of everybody's list. They're soft, they're packed with protein and fat, and they supply a much bigger meal than, say, a crunchy little beetle.

If it looks like a caterpillar and moves like a caterpillar and happens to be in the feeder . . . well, most likely it's a mealworm. It isn't a caterpillar, but it sure looks like one. It's no surprise that mealworms are tops in popularity at the feeder.

Popular with the birds, that is. Many of us are still squeamish about these creepy-looking critters, and their price can be prohibitive, too.

Get over that "ick factor," though, and you'll discover a whole new world of songbirds. Bluebirds, orioles, tanagers, vireos, warblers, native sparrows, you name it—songbirds simply can't resist these pale, writhing, disgusting . . . uh, never mind. But if you really want to make your songbirds happy, read on for a short course in mealworms.

MEET THE MENU

In the beginning, there were mealworms. In the end, there'll be mealworms. These critters are the alpha and omega of insect foods for songbirds:

They're easy to raise, easy to ship, easy to serve (well, pretty easy), and pure magic when it comes to bringing in the birds.

Thanks to the demand for mealworms, other insect goodies have entered the market, too. These days, we can stock up on waxworms as well as mealworms, or explore the wider world of store-bought bugs to see which birds they may bring in. (See "Other Insect Foods" later in this chapter for more info).

Soft foods bolstered with insects are beginning to show up on store shelves and in catalogs. Experiment with them to see which ones your birds like best, or try your hand at homemade. You'll find recipes in this chapter and in other places throughout this book.

MIGHTY "MEALIES"

Mealworms are the mainstay of my insect menu. These beetle larvae cost a lot more than sunflower seeds and suet, so for most of us, they won't be a staple at our bird feeders. But as a small daily treat or added to soft foods, they're a great way to induce songbirds to visit.

At first, mealworms were used mainly by folks going fishing. It was British bird lovers, who may be even more nuts about birds than we are, who spread the word about using them as bird food. Lo and behold, mealworms—"mealies" for short—work just as well at drawing songbirds down from the trees or out of the bushes as they do for bringing piscatorial skulkers out of the watery depths.

Mealworms look like skinny, creamy white caterpillars, but they're actually beetles. Beetles-to-be, that is. They're the larval form of the meal-

Come at Your Call
USE MEALWORMS TO TEACH THIS TRICK

Bluebirds are so enamored of mealworms that you can even train these songbirds to come at your call. The trick works for other birds, too—I've used it on my Carolina wrens. Just whistle or call them every time you fill the mealworm feeder.

It won't take long before the birds associate your call with feeding time. If you really want to show off for your friends and neighbors, ring a bell when you fill the mealworm dish. Songbirds can't salivate like Pavlov's dogs when they hear the dinner bell, but they'll come flying.

Put out mealworms at the same time every day, and even a yellow-rumped warbler may learn to come at your call.

Trick or Treat
Pitch and Catch

If you're the adventurous sort, you can buy some earthworms at a bait shop to reward your robins with a labor-free handout.

And "handout" is, literally, the word. It's nearly impossible to corral earthworms for long, let alone hefty night crawlers, so forget about putting them in a feeder. But it's surprisingly easy to train robins to play catch. Just toss a worm in a robin's direction and watch what happens.

worm beetle (*Tenebrio molitor*), a species of darkling beetle. Like all darkling beetles, the mealworm beetle is, you guessed it, dark. It's a blackish beetle with no iridescence, about half an inch long as an adult. The mealworm beetle is a common pest in barns and wherever grain is stored. Each female can lay 500 eggs at a time, and the voracious progeny chew through grain like little machines.

Waxworms

Waxworms are shorter and fatter than meal-worms, and many songbirds find them just as appealing as the skinny mealies. Sunfish are particularly fond of them, too, and the worms have been sold as fishing bait for years.

Waxworms are actually caterpillars. They're the larvae of a moth, not a beetle. Both the greater wax moth (*Galleria mellonella*) and the lesser wax moth (*Achroia grisella*) are raised for waxworms. Also called bee moths, these easy-to-overlook small brown moths originally came from Europe. It's believed that bee moths were introduced in North America at the same time as honeybees

were first brought over in the early 1800s. And here's where feeding birds gets complicated.

The bee moth gets its name from the eating habits of its waxworm larvae. They tunnel through the honeycomb inside honeybee hives, feeding on the wax and the cocoons. Worker bees try to kill off the egg-laying adult moths, but when the hive is in a weakened state, as so many seem to be now, the bees fail, and the larvae can quickly take over and decimate the colony.

With bees under attack from all quarters and beehives failing fast, I have to wonder whether putting more bee moth larvae into the world is a good thing. Their depredations are already costing American beekeepers an estimated $5 million a year.

Simple solution: Play it safe and serve our feathered friends only dehydrated waxworms, not live ones that might escape and breed.

Be Stingy

It's better to feed your birds too few mealworms rather than too many, because any leftovers will quickly spoil. Live worms will die in a couple of

Trick or Treat
Cube Cage

To make your own bluebird feeder, in which the birds can eat undisturbed by larger starlings or mockingbirds, try recycling a coated wire storage cube. Use the snap-together kind about 1 foot square, designed to organize kids' toys or closets. (Garage sales are great hunting grounds to pick up this prize on the cheap.)

Snap the panels together to form a cube, but use twist ties instead of the usual connectors to fasten one side like a hinged door. Staple your new feeder to the top of a wooden post, put about a cupful of your bluebird food inside on the middle of the floor, latch the door, and watch the bluebirds arrive for their treat.

days, since they can't escape the bird feeder, and dried worms will absorb humidity and become moldy. Start with a scant handful of about 12 to 15 worms in a small, shallow, straight-sided dish or plastic domed feeder, and see how long it takes your birds to clean them up. If it's more than 15 to 20 minutes, reduce the size of the handout.

The number of mealies a bird eats in a day varies hugely, depending on the size and appetite of the diner and whether or not it's feeding nestlings. During breeding season, a bluebird may take 25 to 50 worms a day; a single house wren without a family, only 3 or 4. You'll soon get a feel for how many mealies your birds will consume. Or you can consult your pocketbook and budget the mealworms to match. It's a good idea to mount your mealworm feeder at a good distance from your seed feeders, so that other birds don't get curious about what's in that special dish.

Mail-order mealworms are usually the best deal, price-wise. They cost about $9 or $10 per thousand (as I wrote this), which sounds like a lot

of worms, but it's really only about a cupful. Bigger quantities usually cost less; the going rate for 5,000 via mail order is about $20. Pet stores are the most expensive place to buy mealworms, charging about $2.50 per hundred. Bait shops can also be pricey. Bird supply stores generally fall somewhere in the middle between mail-order and pet stores.

Wanted, Dead or Alive

Dehydrated mealworms are easier to use than live mealies, because they can't make a getaway. They're easier to buy, easier to ship, easier to store, easier to serve—easier all around.

Only trouble is, birds like the live ones better.

Use live mealworms when you first start offering this treat. Their motion will catch the eye of wrens, bluebirds, and other potential customers more quickly. After songbirds are accustomed to visiting the feeder, you can switch to the dried type (also called dehydrated or roasted), if you like. Some birds can be particular, though, so if the traffic comes to a halt, add a few live ones to the dish. See "Mealie Feeders" later in this chapter for info on feeders to use.

Some bluebird lovers report that their flock is only interested in active mealworms, although I haven't noticed the problem at my place. If your blues are fussy eaters, try this trick in cold weather, when live mealworms turn sluggish fast: Just put an inexpensive hand-warmer package under their dish. You can find them in any sporting goods department for about $1 apiece. The heat lasts for hours and keeps the worms wriggling.

Getting over the revulsion of handling mealworms doesn't take long. The first feeding is the toughest. Using a scooper instead of your hand helps a lot. Disposable plastic gloves, sold at pharmacies and other stores, can also be a help, psychologically speaking.

Once you manage to make it past that initial turnoff, the next feeding will be easier and the next even more so. Soon, handling larvae will

Gross? Sure. But when it comes to attracting songbirds, mealworms are pure gold.

Eats and Treats
High-Pro Boost for Babies

Kitten food and egg whites add extra protein and nutrients to this moist treat, making it ideal for nesting season—for both parents and for baby birds.

1 cup high-quality dry kitten food

1 cup warm water

2 hard-cooked egg whites, chopped

½ to 1 cup dried mealworms

1. Soak the kitten food in the warm water until it's soft. Stir occasionally to make sure all crunchy bits are moistened.

2. Combine all ingredients. Serve in a mealworm feeder.

become more routine than repulsive. When the first bluebird arrives at your mealworms, that exciting reward will help you overcome the rest of your very natural *"Ewww"* reaction. You'll be saying, "Where are those mealies? The feeder's empty!" The arrival of hungry songbirds will be your best incentive for overcoming your initial gross-out reaction. Time to fill the feeder!

Buying Mealworms

Raising mealworms at home is quite a commitment and not one I'm eager to take on. Besides, I'd probably become attached to my very own mealies, and I'd never have the heart to feed them to the birds.

Instead, I buy my dehydrated mealworms at bird supply stores and from various mail-order suppliers, such as those listed in the Resources section at the back of this book. Dried mealworms are nicely portable and are sold in sturdy plastic containers with lids, like those used at a supermarket olive bar. They'll keep for weeks in your refrigerator. Just remember to mark the container—no one in your family wants to be unpleasantly surprised when foraging for a late-night snack.

What about live mealworms? Well, that's where it gets a little trickier.

Mail-order mealworms are usually packed in a box with damp newspaper as bedding. They crawl into every crevice, and that's a *lot* of crevices. The larvae must be transferred to better digs, furnished with food, and stored in your refrigerator to slow down their movement and growth. (Don't worry, they barely move when they're cold.)

Since we don't want any escapees, use this method to get mealworms out of their box and safely into their new home:

1. First prepare a new mealie container: Using an awl, ice pick, or stout nail, poke about a dozen airholes about 2 inches apart into the lid of a plastic shoe-box-size storage box. Label the box.

2. Cover the box bottom with a 2-inch layer of wheat bran or cornmeal. Lay a few slices of raw potato on top to supply moisture.

3. Dump all the contents of the mealworm package into a large white plastic kitchen trash bag. (It will be easier to pour the mealworms out of this bag next, because the worms won't be able to cling to its sides.) Shake the box and whack it several times over the bag, until you're sure the box is empty.

4. Empty the bag into your new plastic box by pouring from one corner of the bag into the box. Mealworms and bedding will slide out easily. Put the lid on the box and store it in the fridge. Sift out the mealworms as needed; a slotted spoon makes this quick work.

FEEDING MEALWORMS

Nesting season in late spring through midsummer is the best time to begin offering mealworms at your feeder. Songbirds of all sorts are on the lookout for easy pickin's, what with all those hungry beaks to fill. A dish of "caterpillars," free for the taking, is hard to resist.

The birds also benefit from the nutrition in these natural foods. Even the dehydrated type are still packed with protein and vitamins, just like our foil pouches of freeze-dried camping food or the MRE (Meal, Ready to Eat) rations that soldiers carry.

You can keep offering dried or live mealworms in every season. In summer, fledglings newly on their own or still with their parents will find them familiar food. Fall migrants will appreciate the boost, and chickadees, wrens, titmice, and other year-round songbirds will eagerly eat them in winter.

Location, Location

It's not only songbirds that come seeking mealworms. You can expect to share your offering with nuthatches, woodpeckers, starlings, and jays, too. Many mealworm feeders are small glass dishes that come with attachments to mount them to a metal feeder pole or shepherd's crook. If you're serving dried mealies, you can simply nail an old plastic saucer to the top of a post for a quick and simple feeder. A small, stick-on plastic window feeder is another great choice for mealworms.

Fruit-Fly Feeder

Kinglets, wood warblers, and vireos often show little interest in insect feeder foods, but a swarm of real live insects is a bounty they can't pass up. To attract these small insectivorous songbirds, try setting up the following fruit-fly feeder in spring, summer, or fall, when the tiny insects won't freeze. In a week or so, you should have quite a colony of swarming fruit flies—just the thing to attract insect-eating songbirds. When the fruit flies peter out in a week or two (depending on the weather), just throw out the feeder.

Materials

Overripe bananas

Mesh onion or potato bag

Method

1. Strip sections of peel from a couple of the bananas, to hasten the arrival of fruit flies.

2. Fill the mesh bag with the bananas.

3. Hang the bag from a low branch of a shade tree in your backyard. Choose a tree that's a good distance from your door, so that no fruit flies sneak inside. Your songbirds will come after them. Some butterflies, moths, and beetles (perhaps including the striking red admiral butterfly and the big eyed elator beetle) also will be attracted to the rotting bananas and to the juice dripping onto the ground. They, in turn, will become a bonanza of bugs for bigger songbirds, including wrens, catbirds, robins, thrushes, and other friends.

Get to Know Your Songbirds
House Wren

A house wren carrying sticks into a bird-house doesn't guarantee that it'll host a family: Males win females by showing them how many good homesites they've found. The female then selects only her favorite one and finishes the nest-building there.

Happy little house wrens have a dark side: With their long, sharp beaks, they may puncture the eggs of other cavity nesters, such as blue-birds, chickadees, tree swallows, and prothonotary warblers. It's probably their attempt to eliminate competition for food from other birds raising families.

But not all house wrens engage in such dastardly behavior. So enjoy your little brown song-birds, and make sure you have plenty of feeder treats and natural food available to help stave off competitiveness among your nesters. Avoid pesticides, and welcome the bugs, er, wren food.

Perky house wrens are pure pleasure—unless you're another cavity-nesting bird.

When to see them: Spring through fall, across the upper two-thirds of the country; winter, across the southern states. Some individuals winter far outside their usual range.

What to feed them: One of the species that are learning to seek feeders, house wrens like suet and other soft foods, canned pet food and hamburger, and mealworms. Add small bits of chopped dried fruit, alone or in soft-food treats, to the menu.

Other ways to attract them: Put up a birdhouse for these cavity nesters. Provide a pedestal birdbath or other reliable water source. Build a brush pile to supply insects and spiders among sheltering cover. Plant broccoli and other cabbage-family plants to support a host of European cabbage white caterpillars, a favorite wren food. Avoid pesticides in the vegetable garden; instead, mount your wren house in it for natural pest control.

What they sound like: An incredible, exultant waterfall of notes, plus rattlesnake-like *Chirrs* of alarm.

What to watch for: Fearless guardians of their own nests, they will chase and strike at squirrels or snakes that get too close.

Mealie Feeders

Straight, slippery sides—they're the most important attribute of a feeder dish for serving live mealworms or waxworms. If the live worms can climb the slanted sides of other containers and escape, you can bet they will. With dried mealies or waxworms, there are no worries: Any shallow dish will do, or you can simply scatter the worms on a board, a railing, or in a tray feeder.

Bird supply stores offer an array of dishes, from the simplest glass straight-sided saucer to artistic styles in which the dish is held within a frame of copper or a pretty wooden feeder. If you use a metal pole to hold your collection of bird feeders, you can buy a mealworm feeder that clamps to the shaft. (However, your mealworm feeder could draw jays and starlings if it's hung in the same location as your other feeders; you'll have to choose the best location based on your expected visitors.)

Mealworm feeders are extra easy to make yourself, too. The plastic lid from a jar works perfectly, as do cat food cans or tuna cans.

It's not the feeder itself that matters most to songbirds. As long as they can get a grip on it and reach the mealies, they'll be fine. It's location that's most important.

Mount your feeder where the songbirds you want can see it clearly. If you're hosting a pair of bluebirds in your birdhouse, put the feeder nearby. If you want thrashers, place the feeder near the hedge where they hang out.

Out of the Sun

If your songbirds devour the larvae soon after you set them out—say, within about 20 minutes— you won't need to worry about weatherproofing

Limited Admission
WIDER THAN THE AVERAGE BLUEBIRD

With a grid of bars or wire mesh spaced at about 1½-inch openings, cage-style feeders are great for limiting the entrance of larger birds. No starlings, no mockingbirds . . . and no mountain bluebirds?! Eastern and western bluebirds are able to fit through a 1½-inch opening, but mountain bluebirds, a slightly larger species, often have trouble.

If you see your pretty bluebird sitting outside drooling over your mealworms, give him a break and bend a couple of the wires using your fingers, so there's at least one opening that's wide enough for him to enter. Don't get carried away with your own strength; a very slight adjustment is all you need.

The perfect fit is 1‎9⁄16 inches, just ⅟₁₆ inch wider than the size for other bluebird species. That little change will make all the difference for mountain bluebirds, and it will still block mockingbirds and starlings.

your feeder. But if your offering sits around for longer than a day or two, choose a feeder with a roof to protect the larvae from rain and sun. Live worms dry out fast on a hot day, baking to a crisp. Rain can drown them or cause roasted ones to spoil quickly and lose all their appeal to birds. Remove and dispose of the spoiled worms, and try again with a scanty serving.

OTHER INSECT FOODS

Insects are the newest thing on the backyard bird-feeding menu, and new products are showing up all the time. Look for suet blocks, plugs, or balls enriched with insect content; birds love them all. Mealworms are the most common ingredient in these specialty foods, but you may also find products made with houseflies, fruit

Eats and Treats
High-Calcium Treat

Offer this calcium-rich food during nesting season to replenish the mineral in mother birds' bodies that's been depleted by their egg laying. Purple martins enjoy this snack as much as bluebirds, catbirds, and other songbirds.

¼ cup water

Heatproof glass measuring cup

6 eggs

Shells of the 6 eggs

Cookie sheet

½ cup roasted mealworms

1. Preheat the oven to 300°F. Measure the water in the measuring cup.

2. Crack the eggs into the measuring cup with the water.

3. Rinse the eggshells and set them on a cookie sheet. Leave them in halves to crush them later. Bake for 15 minutes to kill germs.

4. Use a whisk or fork to rapidly scramble the eggs and water.

5. Microwave the measuring cup of eggs and water for about 5 minutes, until they look like moist scrambled eggs.

6. Crush the sterilized eggshells into fine bits.

7. Combine the eggs, eggshell bits, and mealworms, tossing gently to combine. Serve in an open tray feeder, caged feeder, or small, straight-sided mealworm dish. Scatter the treat on an open area of lawn for purple martins and tree swallows, who will swoop in to snatch a bite.

Mockingbird Mania
SAVE YOUR BUDGET WITH A BARRED CAGE

The northern mockingbird is more than happy to claim a mealworm feeder. Not only will the mocker eat all the mealies, it'll also drive away other songbirds that would like a taste—and it may extend its claim to your entire backyard. If a mockingbird discovers your mealworms, the only solution is to switch to a cage feeder—a small, straight-sided mealworm dish inside a wire cage that will prevent the big bird from entering.

flies, or crickets. One of these days, I fully expect that some enterprising bird food maker will cook up a recipe using grasshoppers, which seem like a handy source of bird-beloved protein. Come to think of it, there are an awful lot of grasshoppers in my Colorado garden. . . .

Shop at bird supply stores, farm supply stores, or online sources for soft "meal"-type insect foods, like "Nuts 'n' Bugs," which comes in a plastic pail so you can scoop out chunks to serve your birds (www.wildbirdsonline.com/food_nutsnbugs.html).

You also can make your own insect foods by mixing insect products into your soft-food recipes. A little bit o' bugs goes a long way toward enticing birds, so I use about an eighth of a cup to a quarter cup of insects (dried mealies, usually) per cup of melted suet. (I'll use only a tablespoon or two of bugs when I'm running low.) Adding the products to suet and other ingredients will help stretch the high-priced bugs, and birds that eat insects also eagerly eat the fat.

CHAPTER 11

Seeds and Nuts

Think of attracting birds, and the first thing that pops into our heads is "Birdseed!" Think again. For many songbirds, seeds are way down the list. For some, they're not even on the list at all.

Bluebirds rarely touch a seed, unless it's inside a berry. Orioles second the motion. Thrushes say "Nix!" to seeds, too. Wrens pass them by with nary a glance. Vireos, nope. Wood warblers? No way. Kinglets, no seeds. Robins, only when absolutely necessary (can you say "snowstorm"?). Catbirds and thrashers, a bit of cracked corn on occasion, but having to crack seeds—no thanks.

But do keep seeds on the menu, because many of our other favorite songbirds adore these little packages of nutrition. Rose-breasted grosbeaks can't resist safflower seeds. Finches of every description (and that includes a slew of species, from purple to house to Cassin's to the trio of goldfinch species) depend heavily on seeds—once they spot a tube feeder or sock of niger seed, they'll come flocking. Towhees, chickadees, and titmice love seeds, too, and so does every one of the dozens of species of native sparrows. And let's not forget some of our most

colorful songbirds: tanagers and buntings, who happily visit feeders to enjoy seeds.

In this chapter, we'll talk about the best seeds for songbirds. Then we'll broaden the menu with the addition of nuts, which are, after all, only

Cassin's and other finches will pick their favorite seeds out of a seed mix that's padded with oat grains or other fillers, leaving the rest behind or kicking it overboard.

Surprising Seed Eater
TREAT TANAGERS WITH WHITE PROSO MILLET

Most of the beautiful, bright-colored, neotropical migrants aren't tempted by seeds. One of the most brilliant exceptions: scarlet tanagers. These spectacular red-and-black songbirds happily settle themselves on the seed tray, cracking millet and other seeds right beside the sparrows. Bright red-and-yellow western tanagers are also beginning to sample seeds at feeders.

Want to see those vivid colors at your own feeder? Place it near a shade tree, with a tall shrub nearby, so that the flashy birds can use a stepping-stone approach when they drop down from the treetops.

Tanagers love fruit and insects, but the scarlet tanager and its kin visit feeders for seeds, too.

seeds: big, meaty, high-fat seeds that songbirds can't resist.

For the following birds, seeds are tops on the menu and the main attraction at our feeding stations:

Buntings, 4 species

Northern cardinal

Chickadees, 5 species

Doves, 3 species

Finches, 6 species

Grosbeaks, 5 species

Northern mockingbird

Native sparrows, which include about 30 species

Tanagers, scarlet and western: I'm betting the other 2 species (hepatic and summer) will eventually join them.

Titmice, 4 species

Towhees, 3 or more species

These categories include close to 60 different species of songbirds. Time to stock up on seeds!

YEAR-ROUND BUFFET

Many of the scores of songbirds that like seeds are year-round species. They're the chickadees, titmice, cardinals, finches, and other friends that keep us company through the dog days of summer, to the flaming colors of fall, into the gloomy days of winter, and right up until pussywillow time—when the migrants return. Then those loyal chickadees and song sparrows fade into the background as soon as the first oriole arrives. Oh! Color! Wonderful! Yep, we can be as fickle as our birds.

Those "ordinary" seed eaters are still around, though, for most of us, and they're still looking for seeds to supplement the seasonal bounty of insects.

Cheap Eats

When it comes to seed eaters, their tastes are simple: Two basic seeds, black oil sunflower and white proso millet, satisfy them all. Add a tube of niger seed for extra incentive. A scattering of cracked corn. A handful of nuts when we happen to think of it. Seed-eating birds are easy to please, for sure. And seed is super easy on our wallets.

- A 50-pound sack of millet costs less than $20 and can last for months.
- Sunflower seed costs about $15 for 50 pounds, if we watch for sales.
- Cracked corn is super cheap, although the price fluctuates from year to year. Five bucks' worth feeds a lot of birds.
- Niger is the only seed that carries a premium price, and even that is only about a dollar or two per pound and much less when we buy in bulk.

Seeds are a real deal. We can feed dozens, scores, even hundreds of birds for less per week than we spend on a few lattes at our favorite coffee shop.

Shine with Sunflower

Black oil sunflower seed is the undisputed champion at our feeders. No other seed offers so much bang for the buck to birds—and to us. The shells take just a second or two to split, and within them are big, meaty kernels packed with protein, fat, and vitamins. That's a giant-size payoff for very little work, as far as songbirds are concerned.

We get a big reward, too. A backyard full of happy sunflower-munching songbirds at very little effort or cost: just the few minutes it takes to fill a feeder and the few bucks for a long-lasting sack of seed. Nice!

Easy Eating

Hulled sunflower seeds, also called sunflower chips, cost more per pound than those with shells, but boy, do songbirds love them! Every seed eater under the sun is attracted by these meaty, oily bits, no matter what their usual preference in seeds.

See that list of seed lovers at the beginning of this chapter? Sprinkle some hulled sunflowers in your feeders, or set aside a feeder just for this treat, and you may attract every bird on the list, and then some. Many songbirds that don't eat seeds will happily gorge on hulled sunflower bits that need no cracking. Look for wrens, thrashers, catbirds, bluebirds, even robins and orioles to help themselves to a nutritious feast when you add sunflower chips to the feeder menu.

(continued on page 198)

Get to Know Your Songbirds
Song Sparrow

We can't talk about song sparrows without talking about Margaret Morse Nice. This remarkable woman wrote the book on them. Two books, actually: *Studies in the Life History of the Song Sparrow,* Volume I, in 1937, and Volume II, 6 years later.

And that was only her work on song sparrows. She also wrote dozens of articles and more books, nearly all of them about the birds she watched in her own backyard.

Nice was passionate about birds from the time she was a child. When she finally got around to writing her autobiography, *Research Is a Passion with Me: The Autobiography of a Bird Lover*, in 1979, she noted, "The most cherished Christmas present of my life came in 1895. Mabel Osgood Wright's *Bird-Craft*." That old book is on my own shelf, too, and has been since I was a kid, 150 years after Margaret got her copy.

Nice was way more meticulous than I am, though. She kept detailed notes on her observations throughout her long lifetime, so she was able to compare more than 60 years of data.

And she was a trailblazer. Only one other woman was in the graduate program at Clark University in Massachusetts where she got her master's degree in biology in 1915. But even more important, her attitude toward birds changed the direction of ornithology. While her contemporaries were out chasing species to add to their lists, training their binoculars on rare birds, she focused on the most ordinary species around, and she learned how they live, down to every last detail. Today, her bird studies are still classics in bird science.

Song sparrows were a favorite subject, because they were near at hand and easy to observe. There's probably one of these ordinary little brown birds singing in your backyard right now, or pecking at the spilled seeds under your feeder. They're year-round friends across a wide, sea-to-sea swath of the entire country; summer friends in the Far North; and winter pals in the South. And they adopted our backyards as homes long ago.

All song sparrows are brown with streaked,

When to see them: Year-round

What to feed them: White proso millet, seed mix

Other ways to attract them: Try a low birdbath to suit this ground-dweller's style. Plant groundcovers and shrubs to supply nest sites; this species mostly nests on the ground, building its nest against a plant or shrub for support.

What they sound like: Long, cheerful whistled song, with several single introductory notes followed by a series of whistled and trilled phrases

What to watch for: Song sparrows are early-season nesters, so be careful when you're cleaning up your garden in spring—there may be a thick-walled grassy nest tucked at the foot of perennials, shrubs, or ornamental grasses.

pale bellies, and most wear a noticeable dark blotch on their breasts that makes them easy to ID at a glance. But some are browner than others—the brown runs the gamut from deep liver brown to chestnut in the more than 20 subspecies—and some are streakier than their kin. The color variations can be so pronounced that the song sparrow looks like a totally different species. If you live in the Southwest, for instance, your "little brown birds" are probably light rusty red.

Many "serious" birders pay little attention to song sparrows, dismissing them at first glance.

Watch your common little songbird for a while, though, and you'll see that it's just as interesting as any other bird in our backyards—or on the other side of the world. Don't believe me? Read Margaret Morse Nice's book (it's out of print, but you can still find used copies; see the Resources section at the back of this book for details), and you'll never say "Oh, just a song sparrow" again.

Yep, that's a nice song sparrow in your yard. And in Mexico, there's one that's even "nicer"— the subspecies *Melospiza melodia niceae*, named in honor of Margaret.

The song sparrow hardly gets a second glance at the feeder, thanks to its understated color. But this little bird has a standout voice.

Circumstantial Evidence

Most, but not all, seed-eating songbirds flock to sunflower seeds. Some have a decided preference for millet and other small seeds, although they'll eagerly devour hulled sunflower chips.

Native sparrows—song, field, tree, white-throated, golden-crowned, and dozens of others—are small guys. They don't crack sunflower seeds, but head for millet instead. Small birds, small seeds: It makes perfect sense. It's logical to assume these little birds just can't handle the size of sunflower seeds. Guess again. It's not size that's a stopper for sparrows. I'm guessing it's more a matter of taste.

The following small songbirds have no problem handling sunflower seeds:

Chickadees and titmice. These little songbirds, with their slim bills, don't want millet. But they do crack through black sunflower seeds with ease.

Goldfinches, siskins, and every other finch. Small birds all, they eat sunflower seeds with gusto, as well as tiny niger seeds. Yet they scorn millet.

Buntings. Definitely on the small side, but they switch it up. Sunflower, millet, niger—it all goes down the hatch. The small birds/small seeds theory just doesn't hold.

On the flip side of the coin, take a look at those big tanagers and varied thrushes when they visit your feeder. Do they seek out the sunflower seeds? Nope. It's millet, cracked corn, or other small bits for them. Must be a matter of taste.

MAKE MILLET A MAINSTAY

White proso millet runs a close second to black oil sunflower seed at the feeder. These tiny round, tan seeds feed a wide range of seed-eating songbirds.

All seed-eating songbirds that stay close to the ground are huge fans of millet. That's a long list, including every native sparrow, plus towhees, doves, and the lovely deep blue-and-orange varied thrush. These are the birds that we often see foraging beneath our feeders, as well as in them, and millet is what they're after.

Some songbirds of higher habitat, including the brown thrasher, the scarlet tanager, the western tanager, and colorful buntings, are also millet munchers.

It's easy to keep our customers satisfied. A scoop of white proso millet in a feeder, another in a low tray, perhaps a scattering on the ground or on a flat rock, and millet eaters will soon fill the backyard.

Plain and Simple, Please

Proso millet is included in every basic birdseed mix. The amount varies depending on how much of other ingredients the manufacturers use. Some tend to go overboard on cheap fillers like cracked corn and skimp on the millet. Some go the other direction, adding extra millets to their mix, like rusty brown German millet or golden millet. When we see a mix like this, most of us find ourselves thinking, "Oh boy! Songbirds love regular old millet, so these must be even better! And besides, look at the price—this is an expensive mix, so it must be really good. That clinches the deal."

Uh, not so fast.

Mixes with a variety of millet types do often carry a higher price tag than those with plain old proso. With sunflower, niger, and perhaps a few canary grass seeds in the mix, they're usually marketed as premium finch food, and the price skyrockets. Many of these mixes are packaged by reputable seed sellers, who you think would know better than us what birds like. Maybe not.

Turns out it's the proso that goldfinches,

Fabulous painted and indigo buntings are a real treat. Keep them happy with white proso millet.

indigo buntings, and other songbirds go for in those fancy mixes, not the specialty millets. German millet, golden millet, and every other kind but proso usually get ignored or cleaned up only after the other seeds are gone.

I've been trying for 30 years to find a millet that birds like better than proso. No luck. I wish they'd tell me why, but my goldfinches and buntings aren't talking.

Flax for Finches

I'm a plant nut with all kinds of unusual varieties in my garden, but it's the old-fashioned annuals that seed-eating songbirds, like goldfinches, visit first. Check stores' seed racks—especially those 10-packs-for-a-dollar discount ones!—for packets of marigold, zinnia, bachelor's-buttons, and cosmos seeds. They're simple to grow, even if your thumb isn't naturally green.

Just scatter the seeds on a patch of bare ground in a sunny spot and sprinkle a handful of soil over the top. Keep it moist, and the seeds will sprout in days and bloom in about 2 months. And they'll keep going right into fall.

Another top choice for finches and other small-seed eaters is common blue flax (*Linum usitatissimum*), a lovely blue willowy-stemmed annual flower that's the source of flaxseed, linseed oil, and fiber for linen. Check the natural-food shelves or bulk bins at your grocery store for this seed; I pay less than $1 for a pound, which goes a long way in the garden. Toss the seed thickly onto bare soil, and in several weeks, you'll have a cloud of sky-blue flowers dancing on graceful, foot-high stems.

And there's a bonus: Let the dead stems stand over winter or pile them in an out-of-the-way corner of your yard, and the same songbirds that helped themselves to the seeds in fall, as well as others, will pull the fibrous stems apart for nesting material in spring.

Acres of flax are grown in France to make linen from the stems. A few plants are all you need to attract seed-eating songbirds.

Grow Quinoa

It's an ancient grain, pronounced "*keen*-wah," and birds love the seeds. One of the most beautiful varieties is 'Brightest Brilliant Rainbow'. The name is redundant, for sure, but it's not off base.

In late summer, the 4- to 6-foot-tall plants go from "What are those?" to "Wow!" That's when the big, nubby plumes brighten to a mouthwatering mix of pink, orange, red, light yellow, lime green, and creamy white seedheads, with a splash of rich burgundy for contrast.

Sow 'Brightest Brilliant Rainbow' quinoa in a thick stand along a fence to get the full effect, or plant the seeds at the back of your flower garden. The tall annuals offer good cover for songbirds, with a plenitude of seeds to sustain them through fall and winter. Come spring, your patch is likely to renew itself, when seeds overlooked by the birds sprout into a new stand for the coming year.

PAYING FOR CONVENIENCE

Birdseed mixes are a great idea. Buy a bag, fill the feeder, have happy birds.

Mixes cost more money per pound than the same ingredients bought separately, but the convenience can be worth its weight in gold. Unless the mix you buy causes aggravation instead. "Aggravation" is putting it mildly. More like steam coming out of my ears. I don't mind paying for convenience. But I do mind being ripped off.

It didn't take me long to realize that birdseed mixes can be a real waste of money. I got peeved every time I scraped out the uneaten milo, wheat, and oat grains from the bottom of the feeder,

Trick or Treat
The Beauty of Weeds

Lazy gardener? No—smart bird lover! Letting weeds stand among your garden plants, or even better, dedicating a corner of the yard to them, is a great way to bring in the songbirds. Buntings, native sparrows, cardinals, and every other seed-eating songbird depend heavily on weed seeds to fill their bellies in fall and winter. They seek them out at other seasons, too, whenever the seeds ripen.

A weed patch is perfect, because it offers undisturbed cover in every season, as well as seeds and a plethora of insects. Weeds move in fast on "disturbed" ground, such as building sites or vacant lots. You can simply stop mowing and wait for weeds to sprout, but for a faster crop, it's best to till the ground to bring weed seeds in the soil up to the light and give them the chance to grow. I keep the border of my weed patch mowed, so that my neighbors can see it's an intentional space. It's a great educational tool, as well as a great restaurant and sanctuary for the birds.

Brown-eyed Susan (*Rudbeckia triloba*), native asters, and *Verbena bonariensis* grow like, well, weeds; just scatter seed on bare soil, and let the patch take care of itself.

nies a pound. That was the day I stopped buying mixes, except for research purposes, and turned to making my own. That was also many years ago. Seed mixes have come a long way, and today the shelves are stocked with all sorts of good mixes. Unfortunately, those same shelves are still full of bad ones, too.

Buyer Beware

You can't always count on the price tag to distinguish a good seed mix from one that's a waste of money. But you can depend on the label or on your own eyes. Many mixes are chock-full of filler ingredients that take up space and add to the weight, but hold little or no interest to the feeder birds we want to attract.

Grains of oat and wheat are an outright waste of money. So are the dull red, round seeds called milo in most regions; only in the West is milo eagerly eaten by native sparrows, quail, and a few other birds. In most regions, these grains can attract birds we aren't fond of nurturing at our feeders. Blackbirds and grackles are big grain eaters, and when they get wind of the seeds, they may show up in hordes.

where they lay untouched among the shells of sunflower and millet. Still, I continued buying mixes, because way back when, it was the only source I could find for the millet my birds loved.

Eventually, I wised up and visited a feed mill, where I found I could buy millet in bulk for pen-

Trick or Treat
WPM

WPM stands for white proso millet, and it's the only kind of millet that strongly attracts songbirds, as well as other types of seed eaters. Ask for it by name or by initials at your bird supply store. And beware of "red proso millet," "tan proso millet," or any other moniker that doesn't say "white." They're alternative names for German millet, golden millet, and other types that have less appeal to birds.

If you live east of the Plains, avoid seed mixes with the round, reddish seeds called milo (or sorghum). Western sparrows, doves, and quail eagerly eat it; eastern birds let it lay.

Cracked corn, another common filler in seed mixes, is great for cardinals, brown thrashers, and some other songbirds. But it can also attract blackbirds and grackles.

To avoid attracting blackbirds or grackles to cracked corn, serve it in a domed feeder or window feeder instead of in a tray. It won't be as visible there to passing blackbirds, and they'll also be reluctant to approach these types of feeders. If you do use cracked corn in a tray or hopper feeder, be sparing with it and scatter it lightly, so its golden gleam doesn't catch the wrong eyes.

Weighing the Choices

It's not price, but proportion, that will make you and your songbirds happy with a seed mix. Proportion of seeds, that is. The ingredients are listed by proportion, according to weight, on the label of the bag.

Read the label or look at the product to make sure the seed mix you're considering is all that it's cracked up to be. Here's how to determine whether the mix is worth the money:

- Sunflower seeds and white proso millet should be right at the top of the list of ingredients.
- Other highly attractive seeds should be included, too. Look for safflower, niger, or sunflower chips—all top picks for songbirds.
- A small amount of cracked corn is fine, because some songbirds relish it.
- German millet and other millets aren't nearly as appealing as proso millet. Although finches may eventually eat them, they're not worth a premium price.
- Wheat and oats should be nowhere to be seen.
- Pass up the mix with milo unless you live west of the Great Plains. Milo's not always listed as milo on the ingredients label. You may also see "sorghum" or "kafir." Don't be fooled. They're nothing but milo under a different name.

Worth Their Weight in Gold

Sometimes, I just have to put my penny-pinching attitude aside—and my skepticism. When I saw the picture on a bag of seed mix a couple of years ago, my first thought was, "Yeah, right." The colorful drawing showed an extraordinary array of songbirds, all happily eating at the same tray. I'm thinking it was bluebirds, rose-breasted grosbeaks, indigo buntings, orioles, chickadees, goldfinches, and a scarlet tanager—a bright assortment of primary colors, with a charming chickadee thrown in for good measure.

Then I looked at the ingredient label. The mix included premium seeds like safflower, nuts, and sunflower chips, along with black oil sunflower and millet. But it also listed juniper berries, blueberries, cherries, and "bird nuggets" that gave it an extra boost of vitamins and minerals.

I was sold.

Though I still couldn't quite believe that picture on the label, I bought the mix and poured out about a quarter of the small bag into an open tray feeder the next morning. It happened to be May, and every bird in the picture was already in my backyard. But they were eating separately at à la carte feeders I'd stocked according to their tastes—a tube of niger seed, a wire cylinder of nuts, a cage of soft food, a peanut-butter-stuffed log, an oriole feeder, and my usual big tray of seeds.

The mix delivered. Within an hour, my feeder looked just like the picture and then some. Wrens joined in, too, and my pair of brown thrashers and a gray catbird, plus an assortment of house finches and purple finches. Not all of the birds visited at once, but they were all highly interested—enough to take a side seat and return when there was room at the table.

Specialty seed mixes and seed-and-fruit mixes cost more than basic seeds or a DIY recipe. But some of them really live up to their hype, and the convenience is worth its weight in gold (goldfinches, of course). Give them a try and see what your birds think.

Create Your Own Premium Mix

I still buy the basics in bulk, but I reserve another feeder for premium seed mixes—which aren't only seed. Those bags include dried fruits, berries, and nuts, too, and that's what makes them pay off. The premium mixes attract both seed eaters and non-seed eaters alike, and birds quickly learn which feeder holds the one-size-fits-all mix. It's the most popular spot in my backyard, with at least 10 species of songbirds checking out the offerings every day and even more during spring migration.

Sun in the Garden

Sunflowers (*Helianthus annuus*) increase in popularity every year, it seems, with new colors and shapes joining the crowd. They've even become popular florist flowers, often showing up in

Trick or Treat
You Have the Money, I Have the Time

Birdseed mixes can be a real drain on the birdseed budget. Most cost about $1.50 to $2 a pound. At that price, it's far more cost effective to make our own. Buy sunflower seeds and white proso millet à la carte and add your own niger, safflower, or other specialty seeds later.

Finches Are Fans

SEEDS ARE KEY FOR FINCHES BIG AND SMALL

The category of finches includes a bunch of songbirds that don't have the word "finch" in their names. Grosbeaks are finches. So are native sparrows. Buntings are part of the family, too, and so is the northern cardinal. Every single one of the finches is a seed eater, and nearly all of them are fine singers. That makes for a simple equation: Fill your feeders and your yard with seeds, and you'll fill it with singing finches.

Refill a "thistle sock" with amaranth or other unusual grains for seed-eating songbirds, such as this male lesser goldfinch.

tempting bouquets at the local flower shop or near the supermarket checkout.

Songbirds have been sunflower appreciators for thousands of years. These all-American plants grow wild from Missouri westward, sparking fields and roadsides with stretches of sunny yellow.

Sunflowers are so easy to grow that even a child can do it, so encourage yours to help plant a packet of seeds in your backyard. You'll find dozens of varieties on seed racks and in seed catalogs. Or simply let the feeder seeds your songbirds drop sprout where they will, and enjoy the serendipity of the sunny flowers popping up hither and thither.

Rich with History

Sunflowers were a staple among Native Americans, and several strains were developed by various tribes. Seeds have been found in ancient cliff dwellings and other shelters, as well as carefully handed down through the generations. More recently, plant breeders have been busy developing new varieties.

Native Americans harvested sunflower seeds from the wild form of the plant, a branching type with a slightly larger head at the top (the "mother") and lots of smaller heads (the "children") farther down the stalk. Centuries later, Mennonite farmers developed the single-stalked, huge-headed, biggest mother of them all: the 'Mammoth' variety.

Birds love them both, so the choice is up to you. I like the grace of the smaller, branching, wild type that you can buy from American Meadows in Vermont (americanmeadows.com). Or start your patch by snitching a seedhead from a wild plant in a vacant lot next time you visit Kansas or other states where sunflowers grow like weeds.

All sunflower varieties are welcomed by songbirds once those plump seeds ripen. I experiment with every sort that catches my eye, including just about every new variety that comes down the pike. But I save a special place for the time-honored ancient variety 'Tarahumara White'. I love to think about the people who grew it centuries ago and wonder: Who found that first plant with the white seeds? Its

Garden of Grains

Plant seeds of these unusual annual grains in a sunny spot to supply seeds for goldfinches, indigo buntings, cardinals, and other songbirds. Although these grains may sound exotic, they grow like weeds—which is how many of them started out, before humans adopted them.

To start your crop, you can buy a packet of seeds from catalogs such as those listed in the Resources section at the back of this book. Or plant the raw grain itself—buy it at a natural foods market or at supermarkets (Bob's Red Mill is one reliable brand).

You can let the plants stand for a self-serve "feeder," or harvest the seedheads to dry and offer later in a feeder or as a decorative spray.

GRAIN	COMMENTS
Quinoa (*Chenopodium quinoa*)	An ancient grain with gold-to-red seedheads jam-packed with round, tan seeds that many species of songbirds relish
Amaranth (*Amaranthus* spp.)	Related to pigweed, a common widespread weed, grain amaranth has feathery red plumes with zillions of teeny, nutritious seeds that are eagerly eaten by goldfinches, house finches, and other finches, as well as native sparrows and buntings.
Lamb's-quarters (*Chenopodium album*)	Erect, branching plants to 4 ft. tall with nubby green flowers and vast quantities of tiny seeds, sought by finches, buntings, native sparrows, and other songbirds
Buckwheat (*Fagopyrum esculentum*)	Sprawling plants with nectar-rich flowers and bountiful triangular seeds for finches, native sparrows, cardinals, grosbeaks, and doves
Safflower (*Carthamus tinctorius*)	Vivid orange (sometimes yellow) fluffy daisies on branching plants mature to produce the familiar white, hard-shelled seeds that cardinals and grosbeaks adore.

color adds variety to my birdseed mixes and may even be part of the reason why my seed feeder gets so much traffic.

SEED FEEDERS

The songbirds you see at a particular kind of feeder are there for two reasons: The food is what they like best, and the feeder style suits their eating habits.

If you can only have one feeder, make it a tray type. All songbirds will eventually use this feeder, even if they prefer other kinds. Be forewarned, though: Squirrels will happily claim the tray if they frequent your yard. If squirrels are more than occasional visitors, see Chapter 16 for tips on feeder choices that will deter them.

Songbirds don't need special feeders made just for them, when it comes to seeds. They'll quickly adopt an open tray, a roofed tray, a hopper feeder, or any feeder that they can perch on.

Tube feeders are great for many songbird species, because the birds recognize these feeders as a source of their favorite seeds. Add one to your repertoire, fill it with niger, and you'll quickly attract finches at any time of the year and buntings in spring and fall. Larger seed-eating songbirds, such as cardinals, use tube feeders, too, when they're filled with the sunflower seeds they crave. But birds that usually stay at ground level prefer a lower feeder.

To snag more songbirds, include more than one kind of feeder.

NUTS TO YOU

Seeds offer birds protein, fat, and some carbs. But nuts are even better—they're super high in fats and rich with protein. Because of that high fat content, nuts appeal to many songbirds that don't eat seeds, as well as to those that do.

Both peanuts, which are technically legumes, and tree nuts, like walnuts and pecans, are highly tempting to songbirds. Shelled nuts—those with the shells removed—are favored by soft-food eaters, because the nutmeats have no hard shells to crack. Chickadees, titmice, and other songbirds that are able to crack through seeds or whack into a nutshell also avidly eat nutmeats that already have their shells removed. Nuts are one of the most expensive items at our feeding stations, and birds will scarf up every bit of nuts that we put out. To help cater to your clientele, just provide nuts in a feeder that's tailored to their usual habits:

- Offer a chopped handful in small feeders or window feeders to bring in chickadees, titmice, and wrens.

- Scatter chopped nuts among the seed in a tray or hopper feeder for cardinals, grosbeaks, catbirds, and brown thrashers.

- Provide nuts with your raisins or seed-and-fruit mix in a low tray feeder for robins, cardinals, thrashers, varied thrushes, native sparrows, and doves.

- Fill a plastic-coated wire mesh feeder or steel mesh tube feeder with shelled whole nuts for agile small songbirds, including Carolina and Bewick's wrens, brown creepers, chickadees, and titmice, to peck away at.

- Mix chopped nuts into soft-food recipes for all birds who enjoy these treats, including orioles, tanagers, wrens, brown creepers, and many others.

- Sprinkle finely chopped nuts in a low feeder with seed, or right on the ground or on a large flat rock for native sparrows and doves.

Going to Pieces

To attract the widest variety of songbirds with nuts—and, just as important, to keep jays and other feeder greedies from carrying them all off—you'll need to take the nuts out of their shells and chop them.

Keep the pieces small, about the size of the peanuts in a jar of chunky peanut butter. That way, all songbirds will be able to eat them, and the nuts can be shared among more birds instead of being carried off by nuthatches and jays.

Booth or Table?

Choosing the right feeder is a matter of matching up the songbirds' eating habits with the seeds or mixes you feed them. Try these guidelines to decide which kind of seed feeders you want to add.

FEEDER TYPE	SEEDS TO PUT IN IT	SONGBIRDS ATTRACTED
Open or roofed tray	Sunflower seed; millet; seed mixes	All seed-eating species
Open or roofed tray	Seed-and-fruit mixes	All seed-eating species plus American robin, bluebirds, gray catbird, northern mockingbird, orioles, tanagers, thrashers, wrens, yellow-rumped warbler
Low open tray	Seed-and-fruit mixes; millet	American robin, bluebirds, doves, gray catbird, native sparrows, thrashers, towhees, varied thrush
Tube feeder	Niger	Buntings, finches
Tube feeder	Sunflower	Buntings, finches, northern cardinal
Tube feeder	Millet	Buntings
Window feeder	Sunflower	Chickadees, finches, northern cardinal, titmice
Window feeder	Seed-and-fruit mixes	Bluebirds, chickadees, finches, northern cardinal, titmice, wrens
Window feeder	Niger	Buntings, finches
Domed feeder	Sunflower	Chickadees, finches, titmice
Domed feeder	Seed-and-fruit mixes	Bluebirds, brown thrasher, chickadees, finches, gray catbird, northern cardinal, titmice, wrens

Best Buy

Peanuts are by far the least pricey nuts, and songbirds love 'em. Raw unsalted peanuts are best, because they're softer, but songbirds will also happily devour roasted nuts.

You can buy raw peanuts for about $2 a pound or less. Stock up at Christmastime, when many supermarkets offer raw Spanish peanuts for use in making peanut brittle. Although peanuts in the shell may be cheaper per pound, a big part of that weight will go to waste—the shells, which you'll have to remove to feed songbirds.

Tree nuts cost at least twice, and as much as four times, the price of peanuts. Buy shelled nuts, to save yourself the time and work of cracking them, and watch for sales. Holiday baking times are when stores usually put nuts on sale, so stock up then.

The Freshness Factor

Their high fat content can cause nuts to go rancid within a few weeks, and spoiled nuts have no appeal to songbirds. Be sure to check the expiration date on any nuts you buy, to make sure they're fresh from the get-go. Store your extra nuts in the freezer to keep them from going bad. They'll keep indefinitely in there.

EXPANDING THE MENU

The list of seeds that songbirds eat covers those of hundreds, probably even thousands, of plants. That sure makes our feeder offerings seem mighty paltry in comparison. Yet songbirds flock to our feeders, so they must have something going for them. A big part of it, of course, is convenience: Our buffets may not be as diverse, but they do fill a belly in a hurry, and our restaurant is always open.

Even though songbirds seem perfectly content with what I provide, I'm always looking for other seeds that will really tickle their fancy, especially those that I can grow and harvest myself, right in my backyard, or easily buy at a grocery store.

Flaxseed was a hit with my finches, although they seemed to prefer eating it from the plants rather than the feeder. No problem: The seeds they tossed out of the tray sprouted into pretty blue flowers that gave them more seeds to eat naturally.

Trick or Treat
I've Got a Crush on You

To break nuts down to size in a hurry, without having stray bits fly all over the counter and kitchen, simply put a handful in a zip-top freezer bag, squeeze out the air before sealing, and crush with a rolling pin. No muss, no fuss, and no cleanup! Freezer bags are best, because sharp bits of nutmeat can poke holes in lightweight sandwich bags.

If you want to be lazy like me and not even search for the rolling pin, just crush the bag of nuts under your foot. Stomping works great to break nuts to bits in a flash.

Birds don't care what the feeder looks like, as long as they can easily reach the food. If you enjoy feeding a crowd, lean a few branches against a simple raised board.

Let Us Grow Lettuce

Goldfinches like lettuce seeds even better than niger seed. How do I know? Because they forsake the feeder as soon as my lettuce crop goes to seed. I plant a patch of lettuce just for them, and I sprinkle the seeds among my flowers, too. No need to worry about the plants bolting when the weather warms—that's the whole point. The finches move in as soon as the seeds are ripe, clinging to the plants like little parrots as they pick off the tiny parachute seeds.

Super Safflower

It's about time for another big seed preference test, I'm thinking. The last major research, conducted by the National Science Foundation and Cornell Lab of Ornithology, was in 1993 to 1994—nearly 20 years ago, believe it or not.

The birdseed industry tried to conduct its own test beginning in 2005, called Project Wildbird, using citizen scientists. But the geographical sampling wasn't broad enough to produce definitive conclusions, beyond the fact that black oil sunflower, sunflower chips, niger, and white proso millet were by far the most favored seeds. And the seeds that were tested were limited to only 10 different types—four of them sunflower seeds (black, striped, fine chips, medium chips), plus white proso millet, red millet, niger, cracked corn, safflower, whole peanuts, and milo.

I'd love to see a huge, comprehensive test of all different kinds of seeds. Might turn out that lettuce is even better than niger for attracting finches, and farmers could try out a whole new crop.

In the meantime, it's experiment time at our own feeding stations, with whatever seeds we can get our hands on. Safflower's a great place to start. This seed is fairly new to bird feeding, and more and more birds are discovering its potential.

Cardinals were first to adopt the seeds, although it took several years before word spread throughout the species. In some backyards, cardinals may still ignore safflower in favor of sunflower seeds. Don't give up—they're learning. Rose-breasted grosbeaks were next to give them a go, and boy oh boy, did they find a new favorite. Other species have joined the crowd of safflower appreciators, too.

The white seeds can be very hard to crack—I almost broke a tooth trying it myself the first time, although once I got the knack, it didn't take so much jaw power. But small songbirds, including titmice and finches, manage to whack or crack them open with ease.

Eats and Treats
International Accent

This unusual seed mix includes foods that you can find at ethnic groceries, health food stores, and well-stocked supermarkets. Paprika and sesame seeds are high in Vitamin E, which helps nourish the plumage of songbirds.

1 cup dried chile peppers, with seeds, chopped

1 cup pepitas (pumpkin seeds), coarsely chopped

1 to 2 tablespoons peanut oil

¼ cup sesame seeds

¼ cup paprika

1. Combine the chile peppers, pepitas, and 1 tablespoon of the oil. Stir thoroughly until lightly coated with oil; if you need more oil, add another tablespoon.

2. Add the sesame seeds and paprika, and toss with a fork to combine. They will stick to the oil-coated ingredients.

3. Serve in small amounts, about ¼ cup, in a mealworm feeder, window feeder, or domed feeder. Leftovers will keep indefinitely in the fridge.

It's All Connected
LOOKING A LITTLE SEEDY?

When wild grasses go tawny at the end of summer and in early fall, it means their seeds are ready to eat. Native sparrows get the signal: It's time for fall migration. Those multitudes of small seeds on grasses and weeds along roadsides, in fields, and at the brushy edges of woods nourish them along the way and give them plenty to eat all winter.

To grow your own tawny grasses for songbirds, plant native prairie types, such as switchgrass (*Panicum virgatum*), for the best seed production. Or toss a handful of wheat seeds among your flowers. While birds shun wheat seed in the feeder where tastier alternatives are available, they'll forage for it on plants and on the ground.

That 1993 to 1994 study listed only five types of birds that ate safflower seeds. With the boom in bird feeding, I'd say it's way past time for an update.

Captive Audience

Foods for caged birds are a great way to glean some hints as to what wild songbirds might enjoy, so I often investigate what manufacturers put in their products.

"Higgins Snack Attack" line is a popular brand, and now I can see why. Here's what's in the brand's "Song Food," sold for caged canaries and finches: "Thistle, Lettuce, Oat Groats, Anise, Hemp, Canary Seed, Poppy, German Millet, Flax, Sesame, Whey, Soybean Concentrate, Casein, Lecithin, Fish Oil, Wheat Germ Oil, Sucrose, Lactose, Brewer's Yeast, Vitamin A Supplement, D_3 Supplement, B_1, B_2, B_6, B_{12}, Calcium Carbonate, Calcium, Pantothenate, D-Activated Animal Sterol (D_3), Vitamin E, Niacin, Folic Acid, Choline Chloride, Ascorbic Acid, Dicalcium Phosphate, Sodium Chloride, Calcium Phosphate, Zinc, Nickel, Magnesium, Manganese, Iron Sulphate, Cobalt Sulphate, Potassium Chloride, Ferrous Sulphate, Lysine, Tyrosine, Valine, Proline Glutamic Acid, Serine, Isoleucine, Tryptophan, Aspartic Acid, Alanine, Cysteine, Histidine, Glycine, Threonine, Methionine, Phenylalanine, Arginine, Natural Flavors, & FD&C Colors."

While there's no way we at home can match that batch of ingredients (I'm a little low on isoleucine around the house), we sure can experiment with some of the seeds that are mentioned. "Thistle," I'm hoping, means most likely niger. Hemp is illegal in most states (it's low-grade marijuana), although it's a common birdseed in England. Canary seed is nearly impossible to find for sale, except as, duh, part of caged-bird mixes for canaries. I already know that my songbirds don't like German millet or oat groats, although captive birds may indeed eat them, having nothing better in their dish.

That leaves lettuce, anise, poppy, flax, and sesame seeds, plus a laundry list of unpronounceables. Why not raid your garden-seed packets and your spice rack and give them a try?

CHAPTER 12

Treats from the Kitchen

My own tastes in food overlap quite a bit with those of songbirds, with one big difference: Ain't no way I'm eating bugs. Or earthworms. Snails either, not even if they're drenched in garlic butter and I've already polished off the whole bottle of that special pinot noir beside the plate. And *especially* not slugs.

Now that we've got that straightened out, let's see how the foods on our shelves and in our fridge do line up with the appetites of our songbirds. Our own menu includes plenty of items that are a close enough facsimile to natural bird foods or to store-bought products. In this chapter, you'll learn which kitchen foods songbirds like best and which work great as high-nutrition fillers in homemade recipes. You'll find many do-it-yourself suggestions for combining whatever's on your shelves or in your fridge into treats that songbirds enjoy.

PALATABLE DIFFERENCES

Research on birds' sense of taste is still in its infancy, but already we've learned some interesting stuff. Mainly, that birds don't experience taste like we do. We can taste sweetness, saltiness, bitterness, sourness, and umami, but birds may have only some of those taste receptors, it seems, and the sensitivity to those tastes varies, too.

Not only do birds taste things differently from us, they taste things differently from one another, too. Some, such as the wood thrush and gray-cheeked thrush, seem to have receptors for umami, so that they can zero in on the lipid-rich berries they need to fuel their fall migration. Some, such as the cedar waxwing, can sense sweetness. All seem unable to taste spicy-hot flavors; they'll gobble the most incendiary hot peppers without blinking an eye.

As for all the flavors that manufacturers use in our own foods, the best guess is that birds are oblivious to them. Parmesan-rosemary crackers or just plain saltines? To songbirds, they probably taste much the same.

Our Food, Their Way

Here's a quick rundown of some foods we humans eat and how songbirds respond to them.

Grain products. A big thumbs-up to everything and anything that started its life as a seed before it was milled, pressed, packaged, and put in our pantries. Songbirds will eagerly eat bread crumbs, stale donuts, leftover muffins, crushed cereal, and all other grain products—with one big "if." *If* they're mixed with fats, such as suet or peanut butter. That's the magic trick that turns grain products into the soft foods that attract many songbirds.

Meats, including canned meats and deli meats. There's limited appeal for raw or cooked beef, except for hamburger; chickadees are the best customers. Hamburger, however, and chopped deli meats or canned meats are small and tender enough and have a high enough fat content to be appreciated by orioles, tanagers, wrens, bluebirds, and other soft-food eaters. Interestingly, at my feeder, plain old sandwich baloney seems to attract more customers than sliced ham or other higher-priced deli meats.

Dairy products. Songbirds say no to milk and butter. But "You betcha!" to sour cream, cream cheese, and cheese, say the brown thrasher, gray catbird, American robin, and others.

Fats and oils. Yes, except for margarine and olive oil.

Fruits. Absolutely, especially for orioles, American robins, bluebirds, tanagers, wrens, rose-breasted grosbeaks, blue grosbeaks, black-headed grosbeaks, and thrushes.

Vegetables. Yes to corn and shelled peas; anything else, don't bother.

Canned goods. Canned fruit and canned corn can go on the menu. Other canned veggies, soups, beans, and everything else, forget it; they won't eat it.

Pizza. You bet your booties! Serve it by the slice.

OFF THE SHELF

The collections of cereals, crackers, cookies, and other dry foods in our cabinets are some of the most appealing kitchen goodies to songbirds. Stale foods are fine by birds, so don't worry about the "sell by" dates on those packages.

Served straight from the package, with no more preparation than to be crumbled into bite-size bits and scattered in a tray feeder, these foods attract seed-eating songbirds, including chickadees, cardinals, towhees, and native sparrows. Finches and buntings ignore them, though.

Mix the dry foods with fats and serve them in a wire cage or other suet-type feeder, and the list of customers lengthens dramatically. Fats are great for adding bulk and nutrition to soft-food recipes.

Salted or Salt-Free?

"Put salt on a bird's tail and you can catch it," goes the old saw. Well, maybe. If you're close enough to sprinkle those feathers, you may be able to make a quick grab for the birdie.

As for shaking salt into bird food, that's a matter that gets some folks up in arms. If excess salt is bad for us, any salt must be bad for birds, too, is the thinking. So maybe we should avoid feeding birds bacon, bacon grease, ham fat—anything that may have salt in it.

The issue's not quite so simple, though. Here's

Seed-eating songbirds, like this American tree sparrow picking through a packaged seed mix, will eagerly eat crumbled crackers and breakfast cereal, too.

some more info to consider before you make up your own mind.

We'd like some salt, please. Goldfinches, house finches, purple finches, grosbeaks, native sparrows, doves, and other songbirds flock to salt blocks to peck at the mineral. Natural salt deposits or "licks" along streams or in mountains are also a prime gathering place for wild birds.

Roadside salt. Many birds, including robins, pine grosbeaks, finches, sparrows, and other songbirds, gather along roads in winter to glean the rock salt that collects there after having been spread on the road to melt ice. That's not necessarily a good thing—the birds often die from collisions with vehicles, and birds that overindulge and then can't find water to balance the salt may

die from the effects. A Canadian study of bird deaths along salted roads in wintertime concluded that some may have ingested lethal amounts of salt, while other deaths may have been caused by "salt toxicosis," which caused the birds to be struck by vehicles.

Research is scarce. Although many websites online say "Salt is bad for wild birds," there's no proof to back it up. No studies have been done on how salt affects the health of wild birds.

Natural instincts can protect them. Songbirds are pretty smart about not eating foods that are bad for them. They won't touch moldy birdseed, for instance, or rancid suet. If you've experimented with feeder foods, you know that songbirds simply show no interest in some offerings. No sense forcing the issue; I just trust that most birds know what's good for them and what's not.

Salt-free and salted are both acceptable. Skip the salt when you make your own bird treats. It's not necessary. But there's no need to use only unsalted crackers or other unsalted processed foods. Offered occasionally, salted foods won't harm birds. Or at least, there's no reason or research to believe they will.

Serve seed scantily at open feeders, to avoid waste.

A hopper feeder keeps seed clean and dry.

Fresh water is a must. If you feed processed foods with salt, such as crackers or salted nuts, to your songbirds, make sure there's fresh water available, especially in winter and during summer droughts. The birds will balance their salt intake by flushing it through their systems with a good drink.

Salt can be an attraction. I offer coarse salt, all by itself or mixed among seeds, to my songbirds. That way, those who crave the mineral can peck it up, and those who don't can leave it alone.

Crackers and Cereal

Serve your songbirds the same types of cereals and crackers we should be eating ourselves: whole grain with minimal salt and sugar. No need to worry about fat content, because more is better when it comes to birds.

In times of need—uh oh, you ran out of birdseed and it's snowing—you can offer birds any dry product on your shelf. An occasional handout of sugary cereal or bright orange crackers won't harm them, or us, for that matter.

Songbirds will eat just about any cereal or cracker if it's crushed and added to a soft-food mix. Some birds, including robins and brown thrashers, will also eat the flakes, puffs, or other pieces just as they are, when you offer a handful in a low tray feeder.

Crackers, cereal, bread, and other grain foods turn into an unappetizing soggy mess when they get wet in your feeder. Head off the problem by using them in small quantities, unless you plan to mix them with suet, peanut butter, or other fats. Or serve grain products in a roofed feeder or window feeder that's protected from rain and snow.

Trick or Treat
Cheep! Cheap!

Breakfast cereals with fruit are often less expensive per pound than premium seed-and-fruit birdseed mixes. I mix them with sunflower, millet, and safflower seeds for a reasonable substitute that attracts cardinals, brown thrashers, catbirds, rose-breasted grosbeaks, and other songbirds. Choose a cereal that has tempting blueberries, cherries, or raisins in it and coarsely crush the flakes before mixing them with your seeds.

Bread

Feeding bread to birds has been a standby for decades, and it still works. Whole-grain products are healthier, but birds eagerly eat white bread, too.

Croutons and bread crumbs are fine additions to the feeder menu. Crush the croutons and use them and bread crumbs in soft-food recipes. Stale bread is fine, but don't use moldy bread; the birds won't eat it.

Let Them Eat Cake

Seems like if a food is bad for us, songbirds love it. That makes sense, since most of the foods we try to eat only occasionally—"try to," I said—are ultra high in fat or sugar or both. Those high-calorie foods pack on the weight. Bad for us, good for birds. Nearly all of their waking hours are spent trying to find as much food for fuel as they can.

The brown thrasher has a big appetite for kitchen leftovers—even cooked pasta.

Of course we don't want to stuff our songbirds with rich, sweet foods. But an occasional treat of cake crumbs or cookies should be just fine for them. Wrens, bluebirds, robins, catbirds, thrashers, chickadees, titmice, and other songbirds eagerly peck at cake crumbs or an entire piece of cake, as well as cookies served whole or crumbled. If those cookies have fruit, nuts, or peanut butter in them, they'll disappear even faster.

Junk Food Junkies

Fat is the foundation of many of our favorite snacks, from Twinkies to chips. That's just fine with birds. You'll want to use moderation when you offer highly processed junk food, though, because many of these foods are packed with chemicals and artificial colors, and we still don't know what effects those may have on songbirds.

Still, junk food is definitely popular with many songbirds. And it's fun to watch our feathered friends chow down on the same guilty pleasures we love to eat.

A Little Experimenting

Enticing songbirds to try new foods can take patience. Speed up the process by including a familiar food or two in any new mixes you serve. Mealworms are always a huge temptation. Whether or not songbirds are accustomed to your feeder, the birds will recognize the bugs. Raisins are popular at many feeding stations (but not all—some birds just haven't gotten the message yet), so you can give them a try, too. Serve a sample of the

---

Eats and Treats
Peanut Butter Roll-Up

This quick treat is a favorite of wrens, catbirds, brown thrashers, bluebirds, chickadees, and titmice. Orioles, tanagers, and robins may sample it, too.

1 slice bread, any kind

2 tablespoons peanut oil or melted lard

Chunky peanut butter

1. Spread the bread with a thick layer of peanut butter, about 1/4 inch thick.

2. Roll up the slice of bread like a jelly roll. Squeeze the roll gently with your hands to smush the bread and make it stick together securely.

3. Pour the oil or melted lard onto a dinner plate. Slowly roll the roll-up in it, so that the bread soaks up the fat.

4. Put the roll in a wire mesh nut feeder, or flatten it and serve it in a wire suet cage.

Fresh or Stale

SAVE THE SCRAPS FOR SONGBIRDS

Songbirds don't seem to mind foods that have lost their crispness. As long as they haven't gone rancid, birds will swallow stale foods as fast as they will fresh foods. Whenever you clean out your cupboards, store stale cereals, bread, crackers, or cake in a tightly lidded galvanized pail to use in bird foods later.

If it's winter, when songbirds can use an extra helping of food, just mix up a big batch of stale grain-based foods with peanut butter and suet (crushing or breaking the baked goods into smaller bits first, for easier eating).

new food among familiar foods that birds already eat: fruity treats at an oriole jelly feeder, for instance, or raisins in the tray that rose-breasted grosbeaks investigate.

Organic Bird Feeding?

Life in this modern world can be a tightrope act when it comes to chemicals. There's no doubt that farm and lawn chemicals have had detrimental effects on birds, in some cases causing direct die-offs.

Possible chemical residues in foods can be a cause for concern in our own menu, which is why so many folks are going organic. I haven't yet seen organic bird foods, but I have no doubt that some of us would be happy to buy them if they were available.

If you're worried about affecting the health of wild birds with chemicals in food, you'll have to skip processed foods of any kind, unless they're certified organic. That means you'll have to raise your own cows for suet. And grow your own birdseed, too, since those seeds are highly likely to contain traces of pesticides,

herbicides, and who knows what else. Raisins, ditto. Organic farming hasn't quite reached the bird industry yet.

That's why, when it comes to feeding my songbirds, I follow the same rule I employ for myself: "Everything in moderation." I don't feed my birds only bacon grease or Doritos every day, nor do I make processed foods the basis of my feeder menu. I do go through hundreds of pounds of store-bought seed every year. I do keep commercial suet available at all times. And I freely use nonorganic peanut butter, cornmeal, flour, and other ingredients in my bird food recipes.

Each one of us gets to decide where to draw the line for the health of our own backyard birds. Until 100-pound sacks of organic sunflower seeds and blocks of organic suet start showing up on store shelves, we can only hope that manufacturers are following good practices for safe bird food.

Super-Bowl Snacks

Don't forget the birds when you're setting out some goodies for football fans. Songbirds enjoy a taste of many of the same foods that we do—including junk food. An occasional serving won't harm the birds . . . or set them to tapping on your door to cadge another bag of chips, either.

Late winter (the Super Bowl's in February, for you nonsports fans) is a time when songbirds need extra fat to keep them warm during long, cold nights. So the timing is perfect. Try these variations on traditional Game Day snacks, and watch your feathered friends dig in.

Eats and Treats
Fruit Nuggets

When I had difficulty coaxing songbirds to try the fruit I put out for them, I decided to try my hand at making fake berries. Edible, of course, but made from other fruits instead of picked from the bush. Pomegranate juice gives these nuggets that red-berry glow.

1 jar pureed peach, pear, or plum baby food

1½ cups to 2½ cups whole wheat flour

A few drops of pomegranate juice

Cookie sheet

1. Preheat the oven to 250°F.

2. Mix the fruit puree, flour, and pomegranate juice to form a thick dough.

3. Roll a lump of dough between your palms to make a "snake," about ¼ to ⅓ inch in diameter.

4. Repeat with the remaining mixture, laying the "snakes" side by side on a cookie sheet. A little irregularity in size and shape is fine.

5. Slice the strips into bite-size nuggets, about ⅓ to ½ inch long.

Separate them gently with your fingers, so that they cover the cookie sheet.

6. Put the tray in the heated oven and turn the oven off. Keep the tray inside with the door closed (no peeking) for about an hour.

7. Remove the tray from the oven. The nuggets will still be flexible.

8. Cool and store them in a tightly lidded plastic food container.

Serve the fruity nuggets a few at a time in a tray feeder, mealworm dish, or any other feeder where songbirds eat. Mix them into bird-food doughs and other recipes, too. (For a recipe for homemade bird dough, see "Millionaire's Mix" in Chapter 8.)

You can serve the snacks along with your standard feeder items, or put messier snacks in a separate feeder.

Oh, some words of warning: Starlings are huge fans of all these foods, and squirrels, raccoons, and other wildlife may take a liking to them, too. So use a feeder that bars their entry if you have a hungry horde cruising your neighborhood. Or if you can't take one more minute of football, open the door and invite them in.

GREAT GRAINS

Oatmeal and cornmeal are ideal for adding bulk to soft-food recipes and helping stretch that precious fat. Their coarse texture allows fat to coat them well, creating the lumpy texture that songbirds seem to like. And they're packed with nutrition, too.

You can also use bread crumbs, crushed crackers or cereal, or flour, in any combination, to give your soft food more body. Crushed dry

Snack Foods That Birds Love

SNACK	HOW TO PREPARE	SONGBIRD FANS
Corn chips	Crush a handful of Fritos, Doritos, or other corn-based chips, mix in a bit of peanut butter, and serve in a tray or domed feeder.	Brown thrasher, chickadees, gray catbird, native sparrows, titmice, wrens
Chili	It's the meat that attracts birds, so scoop out some hamburger or chunks of beef, and put it on top of a thick slice of bread to soak up the meaty sauce. Serve in a tray feeder, a domed feeder, or a mealworm feeder.	American robin, brown thrashers, chickadees, gray catbird, northern mockingbird, wrens
Dip fixin's	Set a dollop of sour cream or cream cheese aside before you add the onion soup mix, and serve it plain in a mealworm feeder.	Brown creeper, Carolina wren, gray catbird, house wren, thrashers, yellow-rumped warbler
Deli meat	Dice a slice of ham, roast beef, chicken, salami, or whatever you have, and scatter the bits in a tray feeder, a domed feeder, or a bluebird feeder.	Bluebirds, Carolina wren, chickadees, gray catbird, house wren, northern mockingbird
Pizza	Impale a slice of leftover pizza on a stout nail hammered into a post.	Carolina wren, chickadees, titmice; also an entertaining way to serve starlings, who will scramble and flutter to snatch a bite

dog food works fine, too. I use my hands to combine the ingredients in a mixing bowl, but you can also use a sturdy wooden spoon to mush them together, as you would cookie dough.

Figure on about 2 to 3 cups of filler for every cup of fat you use in a recipe. Adjust as needed until you have a texture that works for your feeder. If you want to mold blocks or balls for a suet cage or tubular wire feeder, you'll need more fat than if you aim to serve the goodies in a tray or domed feeder where birds can pluck up the bits.

Flours

The fine particles of flour are too dry and dusty to interest songbirds. They're just plain hard to eat. And they quickly soak up moisture, turning into a gluey mess. Like us, robins, orioles, and other soft-food eaters prefer their flour mixed with fat or baked into pancakes, muffins, biscuits, or other breads and cakes.

Whole-grain flour is the most wholesome, because it contains all the nutrition of the seed. And any flavor of flour is fine with songbirds. It's fun to visit a well-stocked natural foods market to see what you can find. Try any of these possibilities, or a combination, in your soft-food recipes:

Buckwheat	Peasemeal flour
Corn, such as masa	(pea flour)
harina	Rye
Graham flour	White
Oat flour	Whole-wheat

And for extra temptation, search out these specialty flours made from high-appeal seeds or nuts:

Almond	Mesquite pod
Amaranth	Peanut
Chestnut	

Make a Meal of Meal

Coarsely ground flours are called meal, and if the particles are big enough, songbirds will eat them as is. Be sure to put meal into a roofed feeder, so it doesn't get wet, and serve it in small quantities of about a quarter cup. Except in winter, though. That's when a more ample spread of high-fat coarse cornmeal or almond meal is just what the doctor ordered for native sparrows, cardinals, and other small songbirds.

FROM THE FRIDGE, GARDEN, AND PANTRY

Leftovers are highly attractive to two species of songbirds: the northern mockingbird and starlings. Leftovers also attract jays, crows, grackles, and other omnivorous scavengers, such as raccoons and opossums. Squirrels and other rodents may also be attracted, as well as any straying dogs or cats.

Keeping that in mind, leftovers from the fridge are still a decent option for songbirds. The trick is to keep the servings small or to incorporate them in soft-food recipes. And make sure you use a feeder that limits the crowd to only desirable birds, instead of dumping leftovers on the ground or in a tray for a starling free-for-all.

Songbirds like their meals tidy, so skip anything with juicy liquids, sauce, or gravy, unless you mix it with pieces of bread or other moisture-absorbing foods.

The most important caveats to consider

when it comes to serving leftovers: Songbirds are dainty eaters with generally small appetites, and those that eat leftovers usually visit our yards in limited numbers.

Keep their serving size small—about a quarter cup. If your birds gobble it up, you can always add more. Otherwise, leftovers can easily attract undesirable birds or vermin.

Vegetable Bin

Corn. Peas. That's about it, as far as songbirds' vegetable preferences. These birds aren't vegetarians, and veggies have little appeal.

The seeds inside vegetables are another story. Pepper seeds, hot pepper seeds, squash seeds, melon and watermelon seeds (yes, those last two come from fruits, but as long as we're in the kitchen, I figured we'd toss 'em in here) are treats

Greasy pepperoni and cheese, plus crust—pizza is a fine meal for a chickadee. Slip it in a wire cage feeder if starlings are a problem.

for seed-eating songbirds, including cardinals and grosbeaks.

What's That White?

Songbirds are curious and quick to investigate anything that seems like a source of food. White foods in particular seem to attract their attention, at least in my backyard, so I often add a bit of chopped hard-cooked egg white or cottage cheese to new mixes, along with fruit or fat. You can simply scatter the egg white in a tray with the dried fruit, while cottage cheese is best incorporated in soft-food recipes.

Spuds Are Duds

There are a zillion ways to fix potatoes—mashed, boiled, baked, fried—and songbirds pretty much ignore them all. Seems potatoes just aren't very tempting to them, especially when more alluring foods are around.

Some folks report that their catbirds, Carolina wrens, or brown thrashers do eat potatoes, but I've had no luck. My main customers for cooked potatoes of any kind are, you guessed it, star-lings. My northern mockingbird enjoys them, too. Everybody else says nix to spuds.

Skip the Tomatoes

Very few songbirds show any interest in tomatoes. They'll avoid them, or in the case of pizza, say, they'll eat the parts of pizza that aren't tainted by tomatoes.

Cooked pasta is popular with brown thrashers, gray catbirds, mockingbirds, and some wrens, and robins may sample it, too. But if it's full of tomato sauce, they're likely to say no thanks, unless they can eat around the edges to find sauce-free noodles.

Meats and Cheese

No need to worry about having to share your T-bone with your birds—songbirds are way more interested in fat than in flesh. Chickadees will peck at raw meat, but the food mainly draws jays, crows, and other omnivorous non-songbirds.

Most songbirds prefer meat products that better suit their style: small pieces, especially

Supplement, Not Replacement
BIRDS BALANCE THEIR DIETS WITH NATURAL FOODS

No matter how tasty our offerings, birds still spend plenty of their waking hours seeking and eating natural foods. Watch your birds when they leave your feeder, and you'll see them following their instincts as they move through tree leaves, scour the mulch, or otherwise fulfill their natural diet.

Of course we want to offer nutritious feeder foods, but there's no need to worry about supplying every mineral and vitamin that birds need. If it's not at the feeder, they'll fill in the gaps with foods they find elsewhere.

Eats and Treats
Nut and Seed Medley

This mix appeals both to seed eaters, such as cardinals, buntings, tanagers, and finches, and to soft-food eaters, including bluebirds, wrens, catbirds, and robins.

1 cup raw peanuts, finely chopped

1 cup walnuts, finely chopped

½ cup hulled sunflower seeds

¼ shelled raw pumpkin seeds

¼ cup dried mealworms

Toss ingredients in a bowl. Serve the mix in small portions in a mealworm dish, a domed plastic feeder, or a tray feeder for larger birds.

---

when sliced into thin strips, perhaps because they resemble caterpillars.

Processed meats and hamburger are the top picks for songbirds, because they're soft bite-size foods that are dripping with fat. Canned fatty meat is a hit, too. Bluebirds, I've discovered, have a real appetite for Spam, and my brown thrasher enjoys sliced circles of Vienna sausage. Beef fat trimmings, which fall into the category of suet, are always popular. Chicken or turkey fat, not so much.

Bacon and Ham

Lard is often cut from fatback, the layer of adipose tissue (a.k.a. fat) between the skin and backbone of a pig. Although it's almost pure fat, it's one of the cuts used for making bacon, especially in other countries. The streaky strips we're accustomed to, sometimes called American bacon, are cut from pork belly rather than fatback.

House wrens, catbirds, and other fat-eating

songbirds eagerly eat raw bacon and ham fat. They'll take beakfuls of the cooled grease from cooking, too, and happily sample homemade treats made with the fats (see "Dripping with Fat").

Bacon and ham are cured meats that are salted or soaked in brine and usually smoked. These meats and their fat, especially of bacon, contain nitrosamines that are released into the grease during frying. Consumed often enough, nitrosamines can contribute to colon cancer and other cancers in humans. But there's no word as to how they affect birds, if at all.

Should you feed your songbirds these fats? It's a complicated question. I set them out when I have them on hand, and let the birds figure it out for themselves.

Dripping with Fat

Meat drippings from a pot roast or other cut of beef are welcomed by Carolina and Bewick's

(continued on page 228)

Get to Know Your Songbirds
Hermit Thrush

I was concentrating so hard on trying to spot a regal condor soaring across the sky that I hardly noticed the mousy brown songbird hopping on the ground near me in a campground in Los Padres National Forest, near Ojai, California.

A little smaller than a robin, the bird seemed to want to be my friend. As I walked through the nearly empty campground, it kept me company, staying a few hops ahead. When I paused to scan the sky for one of those huge, elusive birds of prey I'd come to see, it hopped up on a rock, tilted its head, and seemed to do the same.

That's when I noticed its tail-flicking tic. I knew the bird was some sort of a thrush, but I hadn't taken a break yet from my condor-hunting to figure out just which one. But that constant lowering, raising, lowering, raising of the thrush's tail was enough to turn my thoughts away from giant vultures.

I was brand-new to California birds back then, but another thrush I knew did the exact same thing with its tail—the hermit thrush of Pennsylvania, where up to that point, most of my bird-watching had taken place.

This couldn't be a hermit thrush, could it?

Let fall leaves decay in place under shrubs to boost earthworms and bring in a hermit thrush.

Not in exotic coastal California, where new (to me, anyway) species were around every corner?

My field guide was way back at my campsite, and without it I was at a loss. Thrushes look so similar that I still had trouble remembering which of my locals had reddish backs and olive tails and which had vice versa. And I hadn't studied western species at all.

While I was pondering, my brown friend moved back into the chaparral of scraggly leathery-leaved bushes under scrubby oaks. A minute later, he began to sing. Now I knew for sure who he was.

"Go to the piano," advised bird-music aficionado F. Schuyler Mathews in *The Book of Birds for Young People*, "and strike in succession the five black keys going upward from G flat and you have it." He was talking about the song of the hermit thrush.

Hermit thrushes are hermits, indeed—at least when it comes to singing. The male hides deep in the branches to sing.

Although these songbirds nest in secluded places, often on the ground near conifers, they're equally apt to venture into backyards that aren't too far from wild areas. They seem undisturbed by human activity, venturing right up to our houses to investigate beneath foundation shrubs or at feeders.

Even boisterous dogs hardly faze them. I'd often see a hermit exploring the leaf litter or flowerbeds for insects while my big shaggy galoot of a dog and I were sharing the same yard, playing fetch. At most, the thrush would do a quick tail flick before hopping out of the way.

When to see them: Hermit thrushes are unaffected by habitat destruction in Central and South America. They're the only brown thrush that winters in the United States and Mexico, so their population is in better shape than the wood thrush and other relatives. Their winter range covers nearly the entire southern third of the country and appears to be expanding, perhaps because of abundant food in bird-friendly backyards. In breeding season, these birds move north or upward into mountains. During migration, a hermit may show up anywhere.

What to feed them: Suet and other soft foods; moist pet food; pieces of bread; mealworms; small bits of dried fruit and berries; dried currants and raisins; halved fresh blueberries, cherries, grapes, and apples. Berries on the bush or tree are especially popular at migration time and in winter.

Other ways to attract them: Native hollies (*Ilex* spp.), both deciduous and evergreen, are practically guaranteed to attract migrating or wintering hermit thrushes. Let fall leaves lay; these birds forage in leaf litter by tossing leaves aside with their bills to expose insects and snag earthworms.

What they sound like: A haunting song, especially near dusk, consisting of a long, low introductory note, followed by very quick, high, silvery phrases. Translated into phonetic English, it sounds something like this, if you say it fast: *Ohh, holy holy; ahh, purity purity; eee, sweetly sweetly.*

What to watch for: Hermit thrushes hop across the ground like a robin or run in short bursts, stopping in between, like a killdeer. They take much of their insect food on the ground. Watch for the bird to hop a few feet, then stop suddenly, upright, and examine the ground without moving until it suddenly nabs its prey. See the similarity in hunting style to that of its robin cousin? In winter, a hermit thrush or two often will band together with kinglets, chickadees, tufted titmice, nuthatches, and brown creepers in a foraging flock.

wrens, brown thrashers, bluebirds, and other songbirds. You can let them cool and harden to white, then scoop the fat as is into a mealworm dish or other small feeder. Or you can mix the fatty drippings with bread crumbs, crushed cereal, cornmeal, or other foods. However you serve it, the fat from your Sunday roast is a fine treat for soft-food-eating songbirds. Chicken, turkey, or duck fat may also be accepted by your birds, though mine usually turn up their bills at it.

Scrambling for Scrambled Eggs

This bird treat has plenty of fat and protein to fuel a songster, and it also costs very little to make. What is it? Simple scrambled eggs. Chicken eggs are jam-packed with protein and vitamins, including a good amount of vitamin E, which is essential to breeding songbirds. The yolk also has a high fat content. You won't need to worry about your birds' cholesterol, because this is only an occasional treat.

Serve a couple of tablespoons of scrambled eggs in a domed plastic feeder or mealworm feeder, and you'll have fun watching house wrens, Carolina wrens, gray catbirds, and other songbirds sharing a sample of your breakfast.

A Song Is Rising

To get a "rise" out of your songbirds, try nutritional yeast as a "song-food" supplement to boost the vigor of singing male birds.

You can buy nutritional yeast by the jar in any

Fort Knox
GELATIN NOT AN AID TO GROWING FEATHERS— OR FINGERNAILS

When I was much vainer than I am now, I wanted long, strong fingernails, instead of my stubby ones that were always breaking. So I followed advertisements and my girlfriends' advice and for months drank plain Knox gelatin mixed with juice, so that I, too, could have lovely nails.

Gelatin is pure protein, and boosting protein seems like a great way to fuel the growth of fingernails—and bird feathers, too—which are both made of keratin, another protein.

There are a few problems with the gelatin method, though: First, the stuff goes throughout the body, not just directly to nails or feathers. Second, gelatin is an incomplete protein. And third, songbirds aren't interested in sitting down to a bowl of jiggly gelatin chunks.

So give your songbirds a better boost: Use other high-protein foods to make sure your feathered friends are well nourished when going through their molt.

In case you're wondering, I never did grow those long, elegant nails. I'd forgotten to factor in what my fingernails were doing: prying up rocks to see what was underneath, catching crayfish, digging out plants, and doing other such things that most girls' weren't.

And because gelatin is an incomplete protein, even if I'd taken in mass quantities for months, it wouldn't have done what the ads promised. Ah, the power of advertising . . . and vanity.

Eat, Drink, and Be Merry

natural foods store. It's rich in B vitamins that benefit overall health and improve the renewal rate of cells and metabolism. More energy for singing plus better feathers—sounds like the perfect supplement for songbirds! Next time you refill your tube feeder, simply stir a few tablespoons of the yeast in with the niger seed to give your singing finches a nutritional boost.

The yeast is high in protein, too, which will give your songbirds extra vitality. And its nutty, aged-cheese aroma seems to appeal to birds. I've seen them avidly pick up the grains of yeast from the ground beneath the feeder or from the seed-catching tray attached to its base.

Fruit Smoothies

Fruit juice and tree sap are favored by some special songbirds, although they usually have to resort to pecking into ripe fruit in summer or visiting sapsuckers' holes or broken, dripping twigs in late winter to get their sweet treat.

Here's a simple way to satisfy songbirds with a sweet tooth in late winter to early spring: Just scoop a couple of tablespoons of frozen fruit juice concentrate into a leak-proof feeder, such as a glass mealworm dish. Year-round songbirds such as house finches, yellow-rumped warblers, chick-

Strong, snazzy feathers, like those of this lark bunting, require good nutrition, just as our own fingernails do. Both are made of protein.

adees, and titmice may all partake, even when the juice is frozen. And since insects aren't yet out and about, you won't have to worry about protecting the sweet stuff from bees, wasps, or ants.

Open Sesame

Ounce for ounce, sesame seeds have more than twice the oil of soybeans. They're packed with antioxidants and Vitamin E, too, and they're

Trick or Treat
No Measuring Cup? No Worries

Cooking for birds isn't an exact science, so there's no need to worry if you're short on any of the ingredients for the recipes in this book. Just use your noggin, and substitute something similar in texture, moisture content, and food value. No bread crumbs? Crush some crackers. No suet? Reach for the vegetable shortening.

Eats and Treats
Hot Tamale

This treat is for you and your birds to share. Make a batch for dinner, and save one or two tamales for the birds. The recipe combines meat, fat, fruit, and a soft dough that songbirds can easily eat.

1 package trimmed corn husks (usually in the Mexican foods sections of supermarkets); you'll need about 12 husks, soaked in warm water for 1 hour

Paper towels

Filling

1 pound hamburger

1 cup raisins

1 tablespoon crushed red hot pepper flakes, with seeds

½ cup water

Tamale

⅔ cup lard

1 low-sodium beef bouillon cube, dissolved in ¾ cup boiling water

2 cups masa harina or cornmeal

1 teaspoon baking powder

1. Make the filling: Cook the hamburger until it's brown throughout, separating it into small pieces and mixing with the raisins, hot pepper flakes, and water. Set aside.

2. With a handheld mixer or a fork, beat the lard with a tablespoon of the broth until fluffy. Stir the masa harina and the baking powder into the lard mixture, while slowly adding the rest of the broth. This will form a spongy dough.

3. Remove the cornhusks from the water and set them on paper towels. Pat with a paper towel to soak up extra water; they should be very moist, but not dripping wet. Lay the husks in a row for filling, separated from each other to allow room to fold them later. Spread the dough over the cornhusks to about ¼-inch thickness. Spoon about 1 tablespoon of filling in the center of the dough. Working with one husk at a time, fold one side of the husk toward the center, and then the other to make a cylindrical bundle of dough and filling. Repeat the process until you've folded up all the cornhusks.

4. Set the tamales in a steamer (or a metal colander on top of simmering water) and steam for an hour.

Sweet fruit juice—whether it's in the whole fruit or in frozen concentrate—may be enough to keep a northern mockingbird from monopolizing your other feeders.

almost 25 percent protein. That's a lot of nutrition in a little seed.

Oh, and did I mention seed-eating songbirds are quick to snap up sesame? Add it to seed mixes for finches and native sparrows; incorporate it into soft foods for wrens, bluebirds, thrashers, and catbirds; sprinkle it on and in muffins for birds; and use your imagination to figure out other ways to offer it.

To avoid paying an exorbitant price for a small bottle of spice-rack seeds, buy sesame seed in bulk at natural food stores. Or try tahini, a paste made from ground sesame seeds. You can use it just like peanut butter: as a fat in bird food recipes; as a spread on bark or wooden feeder posts for chickadees, yellow-rumped warblers, and other suet eaters to peck at; or slathered on half a bagel for an instant mini-feeder hung or stuck on a nail.

Pet Food

Pet foods are popular with many songbirds. Dry foods are best, because they're not gooey and messy—songbirds like to eat neat. They can't clean their faces like cats can.

Try these serving suggestions:

- Crush dry dog or cat food and scatter among your seeds for native sparrows and juncos.

- Moisten dry pet food and serve small amounts in a domed feeder or window feeder to bluebirds, wrens, robins, and catbirds.

- Run out of mealworms? Serve a premium brand of canned meat dog food instead, finely chopped.

- Use a big, separate spread of about 2 cups of cheap dry pet food as a decoy feeder, to lure jays, starlings, and other greedy birds away from your songbird feeders.

CHAPTER 13

The Allure of Water

We see it everywhere we look. Well, once we start looking, that is. As soon as a good-size puddle forms after a rain, songbirds start sipping and splashing. Water holds an appeal that's nothing short of magic for attracting these birds.

It works the same way in our backyards. Goldfinches forsake a tube of niger seeds to take a drink and refresh their feathers. Robins visit the birdbath many times a day. All the other songbirds who happen by our backyards are likely to stop in and help themselves to the H_2O, too.

Songbirds will eventually find water, no matter what container it's in. I've seen house wrens leaning way in, tails teetering to the sky, to reach the water in a wheelbarrow I'd left outside in a rain, and a whole family of bluebirds lined up on the edge of a 2-foot-deep horse trough.

But just as with feeders, the way we offer water can make a big difference in who comes to drink, how many, and how often. In this chapter, we'll take a look at a variety of options for providing your songbirds with water for drinking and bathing. Where you put those water sources is

Fancy birdbath? Nope, forgotten Frisbee, which suits this Carolina wren just fine.

important, too, so we'll consider locations—locations that work best for the birds, while keeping our viewing pleasure in mind, too.

STILL WATERS

The simplest birdbath is a puddle. But it takes some doing to make a puddle where one doesn't naturally form—we have to stop the water from soaking deeper into the ground. Besides, most of us don't think of a big puddle as a desirable addition to our backyard landscaping. We're usually trying to figure out how to fix those places where water pools after a rain. Puddles and people usually aren't a good match—unless those people are kids or kids at heart, splashing joyfully in bare feet or rubber boots.

But *small* puddles, on or off the ground, are fine by birds. Small puddles, like the kind that are contained within a birdbath.

"Old School" Works Great

An oldie but goodie, the pedestal birdbath is a top choice for robins and other songbirds that have long been accustomed to visiting backyards.

With a pedestal birdbath, there's no learning curve. The birds recognize it on sight, just as they've learned to do with tube feeders, suet feeders, and nectar feeders. Robins, thrashers, finches, catbirds, and many others know that this thing means water.

That puts us a giant leap ahead in the game, since it usually takes a while—days, weeks, maybe even a month—for birds to make the connection between a new element in our backyards and its purpose. Songbirds play monkey-see, monkey-do, so the presence of a cardinal at our birdbath can cause a passing migrant to come see what all the splashing's about.

"Hey, move over! I was here first!" Great reason to have more than one birdbath.

Must-Haves

Concrete birdbaths fulfill every basic requirement when it comes to supplying water to songbirds.

Secure footing. Their rough surface and nonslip rim are as reassuring to them as our rubber bath mat in the shower is to us.

Good perching. The rim is a good width for small or larger songbird feet to grip.

The right depth. The basin is shallow enough for birds to feel safe, yet deep enough to splash with abandon.

Easy sipping. The water is easily accessible from the rim, for birds who arrive to get a drink, not take a bath.

Room to splash. The size of a birdbath basin "puddle" is ideal by the Goldilocks rule: not too big, not too small, but just right.

Add a pedestal birdbath to the backyard, and you can stop right there. You'll have plenty of birdbath visitors to enjoy.

- You'll see goldfinches and house finches at the water and in it, sometimes several at a time.
- Bright orioles will happily take to the water as soon as they return in spring.
- Catbird and brown thrasher couples may arrive side by side, or take turns when nesting is under way, to dip their beaks and tilt their heads for a deep drink before they step in to bathe. Their bold cousin, the northern mockingbird, will fly in with a flourish.
- Robins will splash with such exuberance, they're likely to leave an occasional feather floating on the water.
- Chickadees and titmice will make brief stops to snatch a sip of water. Dashing grosbeaks will show up to freshen their pretty feathers and quench their thirst.
- Cardinals and bluebirds will visit often, to drink or to ruffle their feathers in the water. So will starlings, who are mighty hard to despise when they're having so much fun in the bath.
- Active little wrens are likely to stop by the birdbath, too, often in pairs.

All great news to us songbird lovers. But there's somebody missing. Quite a few some-bodies, in fact. Native sparrows? Wood warblers? Vireos? Kinglets? Tanagers? Where is everybody?

Go Low

Sure, we can stop with a single pedestal birdbath. But if we go one simple step further and add another basin at a lower level, other songbirds will feel more comfortable.

Birds that live near the ground are much more likely to use a low-level basin than one that's perched on a waist-high pedestal. These birds include doves, towhees, and a long list of native sparrows.

Remember the must-haves when choosing a container for a low-level bath. An unglazed clay

Trick or Treat
Day In, Day Out

There's nothing like a good drink of water on a hot summer day. Or a cold winter day. Or a fine spring or fall day.

To songbirds, fresh water is just as much a destination year-round as the best-stocked feeder. They'll visit daily to drink and bathe, whether they're only passing through on migration or choosing to call our place home. Birds are adept at finding water in the wild, drinking from puddles or sipping dew when rain is scarce, but as with food, a reliable source of the wet stuff is a huge attraction. That's good news for us, because it's easy to make sure there's water ready and waiting.

plant saucer works well as a low-level bath. So does the basin from a pedestal type; they're sold separately, as replacements, at garden centers.

The Don'ts

Slippery basins, such as glazed pottery or smooth glass, will work for offering water to birds, but usually only for drinking. Songbirds are understandably wary of slick surfaces, and most will be reluctant to use a glazed or smooth glass bowl to bathe in. Add a brick or small paver to give the birds more stable footing.

Hanging birdbaths have a similar problem. Birds feel insecure when their bathtub swings in the breeze. Although some may become accustomed to the motion when they land on the rim or move about in the bath and learn that it won't give way, others are likely to be reluctant to use it.

Yet that may not necessarily be a bad thing. Hanging baths often deter starlings, jays, mockingbirds, and other weightier birds that you may want to discourage. But if you want more than the lightweight chickadees, wrens, and goldfinches, it'll be best to fasten that birdbath to a nonswinging support.

Ground-Level Birdbaths

When it comes to pleasing our own eyes, it's all about proportion. Try these quick tricks to make a ground-level birdbath look more attractive—to you, not to birds, since they don't care what their bathtub looks like.

- Place the basin on a supporting rock or concrete block or an upside-down plant pot to raise it about 6 to 8 inches off the ground.

- Choose a rock or block support that's wide enough to be proportionate to the bowl, but that doesn't extend beyond it.

- Level the ground so that the basin is level. A tilted basin catches the eye, and not in a good way.

These fine points may sound picky, but they can make the difference between an eye-appealing element and one that just doesn't look right. Boosting up the bath just a bit will give you a better view of your bathers, too.

PRIME PLACEMENT

Songbirds are vulnerable when they're in water or have wet feathers. The cover of plants is a must near the bath, so our friends can get to safety in a flash. But cover can also be a Catch-22 if there are cats in your neighborhood. Stalking felines can sneak up on the bathing beauties, using the same cover that draws birds to the bath.

Birds will happily use a birdbath that's placed as a focal point in the lawn, in a bed of low flowers, or at the center of an herb garden. But the shelter of a nearby shrub or small tree—one within about 15 to 20 feet, or closer—does a lot to increase the attraction of a birdbath. It'll also boost your own enjoyment as you watch your perching songbirds preen and fluff their feathers after they finish getting clean.

As for those prowling meowing predators, turn to Chapter 16, Plain Talk about Pests, where you'll find tricks for deterring cats.

Try a Bench Feeder

My newest "feeder" is a long wooden bench on my deck. I spread seed at one end and park a clay saucer of water at the other. This setup is mostly for my ease in restocking the seed and refilling the water in winter. In a minute or two, I can dump a coffee can of sunflower and niger seeds, fill the saucer to the brim with warm water from the teakettle I carried out, and scurry back inside.

Heather's "Almost Puddle"

"Whenever there's a bit of concrete left over from a project," says Colorado bird painter Heather Bartmann (www.heatherbartmann.com), "I have them [the workers] pour some on the ground to make a 'puddle.'"

Her finches, chipping sparrows, and other songbirds use their puddle bath constantly. "It's their favorite," she explains. "They love that rough surface."

If you're planning to have concrete poured for a patio or other yard project, you can do the same. No concrete mixer on the way? Just mix up a sack of some quick-set concrete or a similar product. Here's how to make your own puddle.

1. Scoop out a slight depression in the soil, about 2 feet in diameter, to make the mold for the concrete. No need to tamp down the soil; a rough surface will allow the bowl to have a more natural shape.

2. Pour the concrete into the depression, so that it spreads into a shallow bowl-shaped form.

3. Scrape out the center with a trowel while the concrete is still soft, smoothing the extra concrete toward the edges, to make a place for water.

4. After the concrete hardens in a day or two, fill the bath with water and get ready to watch the birds investigate their new puddle. The new gray color of the cement will mellow to an unobtrusive grayish brown as dirt collects on the rough surface and lichens eventually take hold. Your puddle will last for years.

As close to a natural puddle as it gets, this homemade birdbath draws birds year-round.

But it's also convenient for the goldfinches, Cassin's finches, pine siskins, and pine grosbeaks that stay for hours, cracking seeds. They often take a break between bites to sip from the saucer.

MAKING WAVES

A simple saucer of still water will attract thirsty birds, but to bring in the biggest variety of songbirds, add some motion to that liquid. It's not the movement that attracts them, but the sound. The music of moving water is magnetic to songbirds, especially to migrants such as vireos and wood warblers, who are seeking refreshment after a long night of flying.

Try a low-tech, inexpensive fountain to stir up some waves and add some droplets to your water source. Or go all out with a major project and add a recirculating naturalistic brook to your yard if you have the space, the money, and the time.

If you can find a tabletop fountain for less

Who wants to fool around with finicky contraptions in snow and cold? Free-for-all seed and a clay saucer of water satisfy the crowd, and fast.

than about $20, it'll be cheaper to adapt it for the birds than to buy a separate pump and create your own fountain from scratch. A small battery-operated, submersible recirculating fountain pump costs about $20 to $35; you'll find mail-order sources at the end of this book.

Mineral deposits from dissolved lime or calcium in the water can collect in the pump or spray nozzle of a fountain. To prevent the gunk, use distilled water in your small tabletop fountain. If minerals have already accumulated, soak the pump and fountain head overnight in vinegar or in water with a couple of denture-cleaning tablets to dissolve the deposits. Rinse thoroughly, reassemble, and fill with distilled water.

Small and Serene

Inexpensive indoor tabletop fountains are supposed to soothe our souls with the serene sound of trickling water, or so the advertising says. Me, I just find it jarring—water music belongs outside. (I'm one of the very few folks who isn't charmed by Frank Lloyd Wright's famous Fallingwater, the house built on top of a waterfall with a stream flowing right through the lower part of the home.)

Those $20 tabletop fountains (well, $10 to $15 on clearance; up to $50 in fancy catalogs) are popular gifts, and I was truly thrilled when I got one. I figured I could enjoy it outside, since it ran on batteries, not on electricity.

In May, when the weather warmed up to sitting-outside season, I set up my little fountain on the patio coffee table and flicked its switch. After listening to the water for a few minutes, I wandered off, serenely forgetting all about it. I was transplanting some flower or other when a flash of red feathers at the fountain caught my eye.

What Were They Thinking?

KEEP FOOD AND WATER SEPARATE

I stopped in my tracks when I recently came across a combination feeder/birdbath hung proudly in a bird supply store. It was a good-looking thing, with a feeder on top and a pretty blue water basin below it.

Great idea, was my initial thought—for a split second. Then I realized that, lovely as it was, I was looking at a maintenance nightmare.

Seeds and shells will foul a basin of water. And water gets seeds wet. Not a good combination in close proximity. I guess the manufacturer just never noticed all the shells and bird droppings beneath a bird feeder.

Unless you like cleaning chores, don't try to double up. Keep your life simpler by placing your birdbath away from feeders, or beside them, where the water will stay clean longer.

Cardinal? That would've been thrill enough, but this was a much rarer bird—a summer tanager! So far, none of these treetop dwellers had come to my feeders. The sound of water, though, had done the trick.

I took a seat well away to watch. Within half an hour, three wood warblers had visited, too—a gorgeous orange Blackburnian, a sweet bay-breasted, and a dashing black-and-yellow magnolia warbler. Visitors continued stopping by throughout migration. And in nesting season, the bowl of smooth river stones through which the water burbled was a daily stop for my backyard robins, catbirds, wrens, and orioles.

I did switch to rechargeable batteries, though. No sense disturbing my serenity by going broke replacing those double A's.

Bigger and Better

Ornamental outdoor fountains attract songbirds even better than the battery-operated cheapies

I'm fond of. The sound of moving water is louder, so it'll carry farther to catch the ear of more passing birds. And, of course, there's plenty of perching space around the rim of the big bowl.

That big bowl, though, can stop them from frolicking. Many fountains are too deep for songbirds to feel safe hopping into the water, so they'll only sip from the rim. Solve the problem by setting a paver or rock in the bowl to provide a shallow lower part of the pool for trepidatious songbirds.

Save Money with the Sun

The electricity required to power a recirculating pump for a fountain can add up to a fair chunk of change on your monthly bill. So go off the grid with a solar pump instead, if you can. Photovoltaic cells that collect the energy of the sun are rapidly being improved upon. They're getting way smaller, and while they can still cost a pretty penny, they're less expensive these days. Cost of power after installation = free!

You can find birdbaths with built-in solar-powered fountains, as well as small solar fountains that you can add to existing birdbaths. Look for them at bird supply stores, pond supply stores, home-and-hardware stores, online, and from mail-order sources, such as those listed in Resources at the back of this book.

Solar fountains are simple to add to a garden pool or even a birdbath. They're very reasonably priced, starting at about $20, and lots of fun for

Trick or Treat
Simplify, Simplify, Simplify

That advice from Henry David Thoreau, a bumper sticker favorite, always makes me laugh. Wouldn't just one "Simplify" be simpler? Nitpickiness aside, it's great advice when it comes to tabletop fountains. Simplify the setup for songbirds by removing the cutesy statues, artificial flowers, candle, or anything else that gets in the way of the water. Strip your little fountain down to the bowl of stones and the pump, and you're good to go.

Another simple, low-tech solution for providing running water is to set your sprinkler on a timer so that it turns on for an hour every day, if your water supply can afford it. Robins, orioles, cardinals, and other birds quickly learn the schedule, and will fly through the spray or settle underneath the shower to take their bath.

My kind of project: Yank the frou-frou stuff off a cheap tabletop fountain; have a tempting, trickling birdbath in minutes.

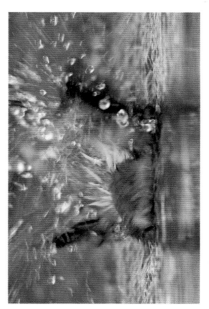

A solar cell powers the burbling fountain; be sure to choose a site in full sun.

Put your birdbath where you can see the action. This whirling dervish? Painted bunting.

you and the birds. Your pool will need to be in sunlight for the floating solar fountain to work, because the solar collector is built right into its "lily pad" base. Birdbath models feature a cord that runs from the diminutive fountain pump, which sits in the basin, to the solar collector, so you've got a little more room to play with—you can put the solar cell in a sunny spot and the birdbath in the shade, as far away as the cord will reach.

As long as the solar cell is in the sun, the pump will work. It's even fun to watch the spray fizzle out when a cloud moves across the sun, then spring back up when Old Sol returns. Some models of solar pumps include a storage battery, so that the water keeps spraying when the sun takes a break. If you can't find what you need, or if you want to convert an existing electric-powered fountain or waterfall to sun power, contact a local solar business. It may have just the right product, or may be able to make you a custom setup.

BIG PROJECT, BIG PAYOFF

Ready for a serious investment in songbirds? A naturalistic creek or waterfall can bring in scores of species, including all those hard-to-get songbirds that rarely visit backyards. For these birds, water is more tempting than any feeder treat. Not just any water, though—it's water that looks and sounds like the natural thing that brings hard-to-get tanagers, vireos, wood warblers, bluebirds, and others down from the trees or in from the brush. All other backyard songbirds will eagerly visit these features, too. Building your own backyard waterfall or stream may seem daunting, but if you have the patience and the energy to do the work, the payoff can be enormous.

If you already have a garden pool, or plan to add one, you can connect a small waterfall to it to

(continued on page 244)

Get to Know Your Songbirds

Painted Bunting

My mother kept caged birds when I was a kid—a couple of singing canaries in the kitchen, orange-and-black African weaver finches in the dining room, and a painted bunting on the sun porch.

Yes, a painted bunting.

I'm sure it was already illegal to sell these glorious North American birds as pets—they've been protected since 1918, with the passage of the federal Migratory Bird Treaty Act—but small pet shops seemed to disregard the law back then. Looking back, I'm also sure that the bunting had been caught in the wild, not raised by breeders. An adult male, the gorgeous bird was desperate at first to get out of his cage.

"He's very scared," my mom would warn friends and family. "Don't get close, or he might hurt himself bashing against the cage."

Planning a snowbird vacation? Keep an eye out for painted buntings wintering in Florida.

The bunting eventually calmed down, but he never stopped looking for an escape route. Unlike the canaries who were so tame they'd hop on your arm, this guy had to be fended away from the cage door whenever his food and water dishes were replaced.

It wasn't until 20 years later, when I was paging through my very first field guide, that I found out that that poor beautiful creature was actually a wild songbird. I was as stunned as if I'd just found out my mom's bird was a cardinal.

So was my mother. "Oh, the poor thing," she mourned, when I showed her the picture. "I wish I'd never bought him."

We lived in Pennsylvania then, which isn't in painted bunting range. Many years later, my mom traveled to Florida. It was wintertime, and her first report was an excited ramble about all of the flowers and plants she was seeing. "House-plants! They grow wild here!" she exclaimed.

Then came an even greater thrill. "Painted buntings! They're all over the place! And the females are *green!*"

"All over the place" may have been a slight exaggeration, but her excitement was real. And painted buntings are definitely way more plentiful in Florida than in Pennsylvania. It's their winter home.

Painted buntings have two distinct populations: Eastern birds breed along the southeastern Atlantic coast, and western birds breed in the south-central states. In winter, the birds head for southern Florida, Cuba, Mexico, and Central America.

While those of us north of the Mason-Dixon Line are tending winter chickadees, titmice, and a few lingering robins, folks in Florida are filling the feeder for painted buntings, as well as other wintering songbirds. Guess it's time to plan a winter vacation that's strictly for the birds!

As for my mother's caged painted bunting, I'm happy to report that the poor guy eventually succeeded at making a break for freedom. And I have to admit that I helped his cause. One day, I "forgot" to use one hand to guard against his escape while refilling his seeds and water. Oops! The bird made a beeline for an open unscreened window and disappeared in a flash. I like to think that maybe those birds my mom saw in Florida were some of his progeny.

When to see them: Spring through fall; year-round on wintering range in Florida and Texas

What to feed them: White proso millet is No. 1; niger and sunflower seed are also favored.

Other ways to attract them: Provide a birdbath; these birds love a vigorous splash.

What they sound like: Similar to the indigo bunting, this bird sings a series of phrases in a high, musical voice; it sounds something like these silly syllables: *Wee sittee, wippity, pickity, snickity.*

What to watch for: Females are often called greenies, because unlike adult males, they wear green feathers that blend in with the brush they nest in, instead of standing out. Immature males are greenies, too, until they finally switch to parrotlike colors in their second year.

increase its songbird-attracting potential. Look for a kit at your pond supply store or from online or mail-order sources (see the Resources section for sources of water devices).

Bathing Shelf

Garden pools are too deep for songbirds to safely bathe in, but you can fix the situation by installing a shelf along an inside edge to create a shallow bathing area. Use light-colored pavers, so the songbirds can see the extent of the safe area through the water.

If your pond is deeper than a few stacked pavers, first settle rocks along the edge under the water, then top with the pavers. Be sure the pavers are level and solidly balanced on the rocks, so they don't shift when a bird splashes.

Waterfall in a Box

If you're thinking about adding a waterfall or creek to your backyard, you may want to consider buying a kit. Kits contain detailed instructions and all the parts you need, except for rocks and plants. For about $900, you can buy a kit to make either a waterfall or a stream up to 8 feet long. For $1,250, your stream can be up to 13 feet long. Look for the kits at pond suppliers or from online or mail-order sources, such

Water is such a scarce resource in winter that thirsty songbirds often share the wealth.

The Polar Bear Club

FRESH WATER IN FRIGID WEATHER

I've never seen a Carolina wren, song sparrow, or robin dip a toe into my birdbath in winter, except to perch at the edge for a quick drink. Yet all of them are enthusiastic summertime bathers. Guess they just aren't interested in joining the avian equivalent of the Polar Bear Club, those intrepid people who take a (usually very fast) plunge on New Year's Day, no matter how frigid the weather.

Some songbirds, though—goldfinches and starlings, in particular—just seem to love splashing year-round. These birds may take a dip even in 10-degree weather, as long as the sun is shining so they can warm up afterward.

Make it easier for feathered "polar bears" by giving them a hot-water bottle, er, brick. Just heat a brick in your oven at about 250°F (or on your woodstove) until it's very warm but not finger-burning hot, and add it to the bath to help keep the water cozy.

Cold-Weather Welcome

Water, water, everywhere, and not a drop to drink—because in winter, natural water freezes solid. Songbirds are still thirsty, though, so they look for any source of liquid they can find: a dripping icicle, the runoff from melting snow, a puddle beside a salted road. Some even eat snow itself, if there's no liquid H_2O to be had.

A backyard source of ice-free water will attract a constant stream of customers in winter. Most will come for a few quick sips throughout the day, but others still seek their daily bath. Clean feathers are important for good insulation.

Birdbath Heaters

I procrastinated for years before finally taking the plunge and buying a birdbath heater. What a time-saver and what a great investment for the birds! These submersible contraptions keep a basin of water ice-free in frigid temperatures.

The initial price is fairly high, about $50, which is one reason I was reluctant to try one. Plus, there was no outdoor electrical outlet near my birdbath. So I had just kept refilling it with warm water, heating bricks, and using other make-do tricks instead. They'd worked just fine, at least for an hour or so, and I hadn't minded the extra effort.

Then I came across a submersible heater on clearance at the local farm store. Intended for chicken houses—hey, chickens are birds, too—it was marked down to only $10. I couldn't pass it up, even though I suspected the 150-watt heater would cost me a lot in electricity bills. Hooking it up to a less-than-subtle bright orange outdoor extension cord, I set the contraption in my birdbath. It did everything it promised! It kept the

as those listed in the Resources section at the back of this book.

basin ice-free for the next four months, even at 8 degrees below zero, and it only boosted my electricity bill by less than $10, even in the coldest weather.

If you buy a birdbath heater, make sure you get a model that has a built-in thermostat, or buy a thermostatic outlet to plug your device into. That way, the heater will shut off when the water doesn't need any further warming, keeping it at about 35 degrees, instead of turning your birdbath into a hot tub. The heater will only use electricity when it's running. Many models have an automatic shut-off feature if the birdbath doesn't have enough water in it.

Energy Matters

A 150-watt lightbulb costs about 3 cents an hour to use, if your power company charges 20 cents a kilowatt hour.

A 150-watt birdbath heater draws the same amount of power as that lightbulb when it's running. That's a hardly noticeable boost in your monthly bill—about $6, if you only run the heater for 8 hours a day. It costs even less if it's thermostatically controlled, so that it only runs when necessary.

Easy on the wallet, for sure. But these heaters are not exactly the most earth-friendly choice.

My flirtation with birdbath heaters took place before we knew about global warming, so I have to admit that my concern for the world we live in wasn't the reason I stopped using the heater after only one winter. Nope, I just didn't like the look of that extension cord, nor did I trust its safety. And I didn't want to move the birdbath, as I had the best view of it right where it was. So I went back to my old ways of keeping my birds supplied with water all winter—mainly, filling a

basin with warm water every morning, at what quickly became bath time.

Bath Time!

Songbirds quickly learn the routine at our bird feeders, and they'll do the same at a birdbath in winter. Simply set out the warm water at about the same time every day, and they'll quickly learn when to expect the opportunity for a good long drink or a refreshing bath.

You can reinforce the routine by calling "Bath time!" or whatever rallying cry you like, or by using a distinctive whistle when you bring the water outside. Just like a cat responding to the sound of a can opener, your birds will be ready and waiting.

In desert areas where the black-throated sparrow lives, a dripping faucet is a real find.

Trick or Treat
Simple and Safe Antifreeze

When the first honeybee of the season showed up on a dank, chilly, late winter day with no flowers in sight, I rushed to the kitchen and fixed the poor thing a drink: a small saucer of sugar water. The bee went away and the temperature kept sinking. By morning it was in the single digits. Yet the sugar water I'd left outside hadn't frozen.

It was a "Eureka!" moment. Maybe I finally had a simple solution to keeping a birdbath from freezing. Was sugar a natural antifreeze? How much was enough? And how could I safely use it?

Sticky feathers are bad news, so I used a straight-sided CorningWare custard cup. The cup was too small to tempt even a bath-loving goldfinch into trying it on for size, but heavy enough to support the finches that came to drink from it.

Two tablespoons of sugar, I learned, seems to be enough to keep 1 cup of water from freezing for about 4 hours in 20-degree temperatures. You'll have to experiment yourself to see how low in degrees you can go, because my trials ended early: Spring arrived.

Going Green

Reduce, reuse, recycle? That's the way I've lived my whole life, long before those three words became an environmental slogan.

Maybe I just like doing things the old way—or as some might say, the hard way—but I've always had a make-do attitude. Why buy it if you can figure out how to make it for practically nothing? Besides, I can spend all that money I save on gadgets and gizmos to buy the fanciest birdseed and best-built feeders and birdhouses on the market! That stuff I don't mind paying for.

Nowadays, there's an even more compelling reason to DIY than saving money or having fun with crafty projects: reducing our impact on the world around us. As I've taken steps to reduce the fossil fuels I was personally using and to live in a more earth-friendly way—reducing, reusing, and recycling, not to mention replacing incandescent lightbulbs with compact fluorescents—I've been glad to go back to my old low-tech ways of providing water for my birds in winter.

Running the equivalent of a 150-watt lightbulb around the clock, no matter how few dollars it costs, eventually does add up to making the world less livable for us. Not to mention the toll that strip mining, air pollution, and other behind-the-scenes effects of producing that cheap electricity may cost both us and our songbird friends.

Read on to learn some more tricks for keeping water available to your songbirds in winter—without a birdbath heater.

Anti-Freezing Tricks

Try the following tricks to warm your birds' water in winter:

Paint the container black. Switch to a black basin for winter water. The color absorbs the sun's heat, transferring it to the water inside the bowl.

Use thick crockery. A heavy crockery dog food bowl can help your bird water stay ice-free, because it retains solar heat. Find a chipped one at a garage sale and paint it black for better heat absorption.

Add a heated brick. As the heat dissipates, it'll warm the water.

Add insulation. Find two bowls or basins of similar shape but with about 1½ to 2 inches difference in diameter. Pack foam "peanuts" between the two bowls to insulate the water in the inner bowl. Not the prettiest birdbath, but it'll keep the water from freezing quite so fast.

Heaters and solar options aside, the easiest trick for offering fresh water in winter is to make it a limited offering. Provide a birdbath or basin of warm water for only an hour or so at a time, and you won't need to try to keep it from freezing. When ice forms on the water, bath time's over.

COME IN, PLEASE

Songbirds will visit a birdbath in the middle of nothing but lawn, just as they'll come to a feeder

Sandwiched between driveway and road, this small garden, anchored by a flowering crabapple and blue spruce, is an inviting oasis for songbirds.

that's sitting out in the great wide open. But they aren't comfortable there. They're anxious, so they'll generally only take a quick sip and be gone. Bathing is a big risk, because with wet feathers or when engaged in vigorously cleaning themselves, they're even more vulnerable than at a feeder. They're sitting ducks, so to speak, for hawks and other predators.

It's simple to make our friends feel more at home at our basin of water. Just put it near plants.

Safe Approach, Quick Getaway

Easy access, under cover, is the watchword when it comes to picking a place for our birdbaths. Think like a bird when you scan your yard: Where could you easily reach the bath, without exposing yourself to a high-flying hawk? How close is the escape route, if a cat should try to make a grab?

Think about which areas of your yard songbirds approach from when they're heading for a hearty drink:

- Songbirds who spend most of their time in the treetops, such as orioles and tanagers, prefer their bath near a tree.

- Shrubbery skulkers, such as the brown thrasher, gray catbird, and the yellow-breasted chat, like another shrub "stepping-stone" to land on when they leave the security of their twiggy homes.

- Indigo buntings, common yellowthroats, native sparrows, and other birds of the brush will visit more freely when the bath is near a bush or in a garden of tall perennial flowers that lend protection.

- Even robins, house wrens, and cardinals, which freely range about our yards, appreciate the protection of plants near their bathing place.

Wet birds look silly, but there's a serious side to bathing: vulnerability to predators.

How to make everyone happy and safe? Go for the middle ground: shrubs and a small tree. High-altitude birds can move down, step by step, to approach the bath; ground dwellers can move on up.

Think Big

A ground-hugging shrub isn't a good choice near a birdbath, because birds like a clear view of their surroundings. The taller the plant, the better they can see. Since not all songbirds will rise high into tree branches, here's where a good-size shrub, one that reaches about 4 to 5 feet tall, is the best choice.

Instead of planting a creeping juniper or a dwarf pink spirea near your bath, plant a bush of significant size, such as a butterfly bush (*Buddleia davidii*), a burning bush (*Euonymus* spp.), a lilac (*Syringa* spp.), or an old-fashioned mock orange (*Philadelphus coronarius*). Or try a small tree that has branches at about that height as well as higher ones. Plant a birch tree (*Betula* spp.), shad-blow (*Amelanchier arborea*, *A.* × *grandiflora*), haw-thorn (*Crataegus* spp.), flowering cherry (*Prunus* spp.), or dwarf fruit tree.

Serviceberry is a prime pick for songbirds. Not only will the branches of this small tree offer cover to birds at the birdbath, it's also an irresist-ible target for rose-breasted grosbeaks, blue gros-beaks, brown thrashers, and many other songbirds when its sweet blueberry-like berries ripen in summer. Serviceberry includes several native species, from low growers to shrubs to small trees, and all of them are heartily approved by birds. But for bath duty, go with the small-tree type, such as 'Autumn Brilliance', which will also reward you with glorious autumn foliage.

Toweling Off

The plants near your birdbath have another vital purpose, besides providing songbirds with a safe approach. Those inviting branches supply a safe place to perch after a bath. When an oriole or other songbird finishes splashing, it retreats to a nearby perch to put its feathers back in order. It shakes them out and then smoothes them down, combing its wings and tail feathers with its beak to align each one.

Good-size shrubs and small trees fill the bill here, too. Include a tall shrub with open branches, such as witch hazel (*Hamamelis* spp. and hybrids), beside your birdbath, so you'll have a better view of the birds as they towel off.

With its open form and widely spaced, thin branches, a pussywillow (*Salix* spp.) is perfect as an after-bath perch. Pussywillows do fine in aver-age garden soil, but they will gladly take extra water that comes their way—such as when you dump to refill the basin. The plant's form is ideal for both songbirds and songbird-watchers: The slim, easily graspable branches make for easy perching, and the plant's open habit creates a fine after-the-bath view for us.

Is There Really a Magic Fix?
NO SUBSTITUTE FOR THE SCRUB BRUSH

Chlorine shock treatment works like magic in a swimming pool to clear the water and kill the algae. But a big dose of chlorine can be a bird killer in birdbath water, so it's not marketed for them. Many manufacturers do sell "harmless" or "natural" tablets or other products that sup-posedly keep the water in birdbaths or fountains sparkling fresh.

I've tried a few types of these products, and none worked very well. Before you plunk down your money, read the reviews of such products on online gardening forums or on the product's page on www.amazon.com and other online sellers. Opinions are mixed, but most seem to give the products a grade of C at best. Few offer the glowing praise you might expect when you read the ads for these "magic" fixes.

Get to Know Your Songbirds

Red-Eyed Vireo

This songbird never seems to know when to stop talking. Its loud, insistent voice goes on and on and on, all day, every day, during the singing season. Surely that can't be why old-timers knew this guy as the preacher bird?

Unlike the robin or goldfinch, the red-eyed vireo isn't a bird that most folks know by name. Yet it's one of the most abundant songbirds in the United States. Although its population has declined like that of so many other songbirds, it's still common across the country.

Wherever you live, you're likely to hear this species in spring, when the birds return from tropical wintering grounds. And in the eastern half of the country, as well as a wide swath of the upper western half, you'll get to hear them go at it all during nesting season, too.

Vireos are birds of the treetops, usually camouflaged by leaves as they move quickly through the canopy looking for insects to snatch. But the emphatic voice of the red-eyed is a dead giveaway to its whereabouts. Next time you hear the preacher holding forth, grab your binocs and see if you can spot him slinking through or hovering at the leafy treetops.

Long-winded sermon? The "preacher bird" sings thousands of times a day.

When to see them: Spring and fall, all across the country; summer, throughout a large nesting region

What to feed them: Fruit, jelly, and mealworms are the best temptations at the feeder. This bird may also visit nectar feeders.

Other ways to attract them: Small fruits on the bush are popular in late summer and fall, especially elderberries, raspberries and blackberries, arrowwood viburnum (*Viburnum dentatum*), spicebush (*Lindera benzoin*), and flowering dogwood (*Cornus florida*). In the South, red-eyed vireos gather in numbers at the berries of southern magnolia (*Magnolia grandiflora*).

What they sound like: A loud, warbling song of chirrupy phrases that sounds something like "*Here I am, over here, vireo!*" repeated over and over.

What to watch for: Like all songbirds, this one has a specific niche for collecting food. It grabs caterpillars and other insects from the underside of tree leaves, usually near the tips of branches. Watch for this little bird to show off its hovering skills when grabbing a bite, whether it's in a tree, at berries, or at the feeder.

CLEAN AND FRESH

We can put off cleaning our feeders—birds will simply pick through the shells to find the good stuff—but deferring the maintenance at our birdbaths is a big no-no. Keep it filled, keep it clean, keep it fresh. Songbirds will quickly abandon a water source that's become fouled with droppings or slippery algae, and that can happen in just a couple of days.

Give your basin a quick swish every day and you won't have to worry about algae. A plastic kitchen scrubby puff, vegetable brush, or scrub brush works great for fast daily cleanup. Just swish the basin, dump, rinse, and refill—the whole operation takes less than five minutes.

Even with the best of intentions, our birdbaths often go a few days between cleanups. Algae grow fast in warm water and sunlight. Placing your birdbath in a shady spot in your backyard will slow that down by at least a couple of days. A couple of hours of morning sun is fine. The rays aren't as strong as later in the day, and the water is still chilly from the night before. But shield the water from the heat of the midday and afternoon sun, which can cause the water to go green in a hurry.

Straight to the Source

We're much more likely to keep our birdbaths clean and filled when the basin is conveniently near the garden hose. Here are some tricks I use to make it easy to do frequent cleanings:

- Buy a second hose of shorter length and a color that blends in with foliage (black is more discreet than green), and let it lie in place near the birdbath.

- Use a Y-connector at the faucet, so that both your birdbath hose and garden hose can be attached to the same tap.

- Spend a few dollars on a quick shut-off valve, and screw it onto the end of the hose before the nozzle, if you use one. That way, you can turn the water off and on without walking to the faucet.

- Investigate an "extension cord" for your faucet: a short section of heavy-duty hose connected to a portable faucet on a short metal pole (called a "hose bib," ranging from $12 to $30), which you stick in the ground near your birdbath.

Leaf Bathing

When I stepped outside one morning after a rain, I was surprised to hear a chickadee calling repeatedly from the lilac hedge. The little birds don't usually forage there—they stick to the trees or feeders—so I took a few steps closer to see what it was after. The black-capped guy (or gal—they look alike) was swinging from leaf to leaf, moving fast, but it wasn't foraging. Quickly it tugged at one leaf and another from below, so they'd spill their precious drops onto the bird's head and back. After every few leaves, it'd pause for a quick shake, endearingly ruffling its damp feathers.

Leaf bathing is one of the most charming habits of songbirds, especially small ones. It's exactly what it sounds like: The bird rubs itself against the leaves of trees and shrubs after a rain, collecting the water on its feathers. Then it puffs and shakes and flicks its wings to distribute the moisture, just as it does in a basin of water. The bird's pleasure in its bath is so apparent, it'll make you smile while watching it.

Look for your vireos, wood warblers, chickadees, and other small songbirds (and hummingbirds, too) delighting in leaf baths the morning after a rain or after an afternoon shower.

PART III

Songbird Sanctuary

CHAPTER 14

Home Is Where the Heart Is

Playing hard-to-get is a time-tested method of winning attention, and it works like a charm with the targeted heartthrob. Or so I hear, anyway.

I do know that it's mighty effective when *songbirds* play the hard-to-get game. It only makes us want them more. Oh, please, Mr. Bluebird, won't you come and have a treat? Look at these nice mealworms I got just for you! And you orioles, please don't just fly on by. Here, have a good juicy orange!

Food is a major motivation to get songbirds to drop in. But it's not the only one, so setting up a feeder doesn't always guarantee success. And besides, in spring, when orioles, tanagers, indigo buntings, and the other most-wanted migrant songbirds return, natural food is plentiful. Insects are popping out just as fast as the buds on the trees. The bounty keeps going into summer, with insects, seeds, and fruit everywhere right up to fall migration. There's not much incentive for songbirds to seek out feeders when wild food is abundant on every side.

What's a songbird lover to do? Why, fill our yard with all those sorts of temptations they simply won't be able to pass by. That means favorite feeder treats, fresh water, and most of all, the trees, shrubs, and other plants that make them feel at home by providing both natural food and protective cover. These plants are what this chapter is all about.

WAYFARING STRANGERS

Traveling cross-country can be challenging, and not only for migrating birds. I drive thousands of miles every year, and some stretches are just plain desolate.

Not as far as nature is concerned—there's always something interesting to see along the roadsides. But when it comes to sustenance and comfort, well, it doesn't take long for rest-stop vending machines to lose their charm, especially when the

Songbird Gardeners

Ever wonder why poison ivy, grapevines, and Virginia creeper keep popping up in your flower-beds? Songbirds do a great job of planting the berries they like best by dropping the seeds right in our yards.

In my yard, it's dogwoods, English ivy, hackberry trees, and poison ivy that crop up all over

roadside rest area has no shade trees and is subject to the glaring sun and prairie wind. Where can I get a good meal while sitting in a comfy chair? Or splash water on my dusty, sunburned face?

Those sorts of enticement for birds are exactly what we're aiming for with our bird-friendly backyards, especially at migration time: one-stop shopping for weary travelers.

Instant Oasis

Any kind of large tree works to attract songbirds—it's an instant oasis, offering cover from predators, insects to eat, and a place to rest. Most important, a big tree is highly visible from a distance, so migrating songbirds often flock to it. Select your own favorite kind to plant, or try one of the following types of large trees that have high bird appeal. All of them provide great cover, singing perches, nest sites, and extra incentive, too—plentiful food of various kinds in all seasons. These trees are great choices for a bird-friendly yard.

TREE	SONGBIRD FOOD IT PROVIDES
Black cherry (*Prunus serotina*)	Insects on foliage and bark; insects at flowers; nectar at flowers; bountiful bite-size fruit
Cottonwood (*Populus deltoides*)	Insects on foliage and bark; insects at catkins; seed fluff for nesting material; tiny seeds in fluff for food
Hackberry (*Celtis* spp.)	Insects on foliage; abundant bite-size fruit that persists into winter
Black locust (*Robinia pseudoacacia*)	Insects on foliage and bark; insects at flowers; nectar at flowers
Maple (*Acer* spp.)	Insects on foliage and bark; seeds in fall
Oak (*Quercus* spp.)	Insects on foliage and bark; myriad of tiny insects at pollen-laden catkins; oil-rich acorns
Pecan (*Carya illinoinensis*)	Insects on foliage and bark; countless tiny insects at pollen-laden catkins; oil-rich nuts with thin shells
Tuliptree (*Liriodendron tulipfera*)	Insects on foliage and bark; insects at flowers; nectar at flowers; seeds persist into winter

It's All Connected

CATKINS TELL TALES

Got an oak in your backyard? Look for migrating wood warblers in spring when the catkins lengthen and turn yellow with pollen. Those tree flowers attract zillions of tiny insects to their bounty of pollen, a perfect high-protein food. On the trail of the little buggers come waves of wood warblers, scooting along the boughs as they snatch insects en route.

the place, none of them planted by me. Some of those seedlings are fun to nurture along, but some are definitely not on my most-wanted list. Only the dogwoods get to stay in my yard, I'm sorry to tell the birds, even though the other plants are dear to the hearts of the bluebirds, thrushes, robins, and other songbird friends who planted them. I *am* happy the birds feel comfortable enough to hang out in my yard, even if I do have to don gloves a few times a year to get rid of the poison ivy they planted.

Most of us don't want our yards to go completely wild, even though our songbirds would be happier with it that way. We choose the berry-producing shrubs, trees, and vines that we like, too, whether it's a stately holly or a patch of blueberries.

You'll find suggestions for good berry plants throughout this book. Weave these trees, shrubs, and vines into your backyard to create homes for songbirds as well as a few weeks' worth of irresistible food for them.

To fit more plants into your yard without turning it into a total jungle, stack them in layers. Plant small trees beneath large ones, shrubs beneath small trees, and groundcovers or flowers as the lowest layer. Migrant songbirds will make

use of all of them. And the birds' visits will last longer, because there's more to explore.

Downsize Your Trees

Full-grown shade trees are a true treasure for attracting songbirds. Those millions of leaves hide zillions of insects, the absolute best temptation

Bird-loving gardeners in the East and Midwest can plant hackberry (*Celtis occidentalis*), a large tree with warty gray bark and plentiful bite-size berries. Bird lovers in the West plant desert hackberry (*C. pallida*), a shrub or small tree that grows to about 15 feet and produces equally appealing berries for birds. Here, a black-throated sparrow pauses to investigate.

for tanagers, vireos, and other birds of the tree-tops. Park your padded chaise lounge beneath the tree, and you'll hear their voices overhead while you gaze up at . . . leaves.

It's darn hard to see the actual birds in a big tree. All that foliage shields the singers from view. So I plant small trees by my sitting spot, too. Small trees that have something extra going for them, so they lure my favorite singers down from those high branches.

The plan begins with blossoms. Choose a flowering tree, and the insects those flowers attract will soon bring in the birds. Those blossoms will be followed by fruit or berries, another draw when the time is right.

The following adaptable small trees thrive in most regions:

Apple, any dwarf variety

Apricot, any dwarf variety

Sour (pie) cherry, such as 'Montmorency'

Sweet cherry, such as 'Bing'

Flowering crabapple (*Malus* cvs.)

Flowering dogwood (*Cornus florida*)

Callery pear (*Pyrus calleryana*)

Redbud (*Cercis canadensis*)

Serviceberry (*Amelanchier arborea*, the tree form)

And the Winner Is . . .

First, the nominees for best small tree for birds: On the left, flowering dogwood. On the right, serviceberry. These small trees run neck and neck when it comes to attracting songbirds, as well as looking good in our yards.

Both offer graceful form and vivid fall foliage, as well as flowers for insects and fruit that songbirds find irresistible. Both trees attract bluebirds, thrashers, robins, thrushes, rose-breasted grosbeaks, and a host of other songbirds to their

Planting for the Future
SONGBIRDS PLAY A BIG ROLE IN REFORESTING

Populations of many songbird species are declining across the United States, and that spells bad news on many levels. Every species is vital for keeping insect populations in balance. And those bird species that eat fruit, berries, and nuts are the "Future Farmers of America," planting all manner of trees, shrubs, and vines across the country.

The decline of neotropical migrants is particularly worrisome, because they're vital at both ends of their long journey. They hold down insects and replant forests and other fruiting plants in North, Central, and South America.

As songbird numbers sink, researchers are already beginning to notice differences in the plant communities of wild places in the tropical zones where these birds winter. Further studies are under way.

feast of berries. And I do mean attract: Birds make a beeline for these trees.

So who's the winner? Dogwood, hands down. No other backyard tree attracts such a huge variety of songbirds, although serviceberry comes close. Unfortunately, the disease called anthracnose, or dogwood blight, can affect the trees in some regions, disfiguring and even killing them, although the species does seem to be developing some resistance. If dogwood blight is a problem near your place, go with serviceberry instead, and you'll have a winner.

Dogwoods produce an incredibly generous crop of berries that keeps songbirds busy for weeks. Serviceberry, on the other hand, lives up to its other common name of Juneberry—the fruits are gone in a flash as soon as they ripen in June.

Why not plant both?

THE SONGBIRD SANCTUARY

I've spent a lot of time peering into backyards as I travel back and forth across America. Feeders, check. Shrubs, check. Ornamental trees or evergreens, check. Water, sometimes a check.

And yet, no birds. Or not many. Maybe a robin hopping about or finches clustered at a tube feeder. But certainly not the kind of diversity that makes me whip my head around from that yard to the wilder side of the road, where orioles, tanagers, vireos, wood warblers, and small birds galore are flitting about.

What gives? It's easy to see at a glance. While most of our yards include many of the elements that attract birds—food, shelter, water—there's an awful lot of open space.

The problem is the lawn.

Feeling Safe

The amount of space most of us give to our lawn is way bigger than the part that's filled with shrubs, trees, and other plants for songbird food and cover. Because we like to see those wide open spaces of grass, our plants are usually dotted around. A handful of foundation plants hugging the house, a lilac or flowering crabapple in the front yard, not much of anything in the side yard, and maybe a hedge of arborvitae or a shade tree out back.

Yet most of the songbird species we want to attract are birds of the forest, treetops, or brush. Big stretches of cover and safe "corridors" of plantings to travel along are what makes them feel at home.

We don't want to give up our play space or turn our yards into natural woods, even if we could convince the neighborhood to let us get

This is the sort of yard that attracts songbirds: perches aplenty, inviting cover, and the promise of insects in hedge and trees.

Get to Know Your Songbirds

Brown Thrasher

It never fails. At least once a year, I stumble upon a songbird I'm not expecting. Last summer, it happened when I was picking raspberries from the little patch by the garage. Just as I reached my hand into a particularly tricky space between the thorny branches, a big rusty bird came rocketing out. The briar scratches on my wrist have pretty much disappeared, I'm happy to say, but the encounter was a lasting lesson: Be prepared for a brown thrasher in brambles.

Of course, I'd learned that same lesson the year before. And the year before that. Maybe it will eventually stick, but I doubt it. When raspberries are ripe, my mind is entirely on the yummy fruit, not on feathered friends who may be sharing my crop.

Big as he is—and these birds are *big*, almost a foot long, from stem to stern—the brown thrasher can easily escape our notice.

When to see them: Spring through fall; year-round in wintering range in the Southeast. Some individuals linger throughout winter far north of their usual cold-weather range.

What to feed them: Suet and other soft foods; canned or moistened dry dog food; fresh or dried blueberries, grapes, raisins, and other dried fruit; mealworms

Other ways to attract them: Provide a high or low birdbath near good cover. Create a brush pile of loosely piled branches for a foraging place. Plant small fruit trees and berries, including serviceberry (*Amelanchier arborea*), elderberry, mulberry, and strawberries, for natural food. Grow a grapevine, a native honeysuckle (*Lonicera* spp.), or an autumn-flowering clematis (*Clematis paniculata*) on an arbor. Start a hedge or a raspberry patch, and group your shrubs together. Let fall leaves nestle around shrubs and under hedges to boost the population of insects and other critters that thrashers seek.

What they sound like: One of the most talented songbirds, with a long, loud song consisting of short phrases, each repeated twice.

What to watch for: Scan the tops of backyard trees and shrubs for the distinctive silhouette of a singing thrasher; the bird holds forth from a conspicuous perch, with tail held straight down. When they're not singing, brown thrashers often forage among dead leaves and mulch under hedges and shrubs.

away with it. Most of us don't have thousands of dollars to spend on landscapers or designers, either.

What can we do to solve this dilemma? Why, DIY, of course, one small but powerful change at a time.

Start at the Edges

The boundaries of our backyards are the perfect places to start revamping our landscapes for the birds. They're the ideal places to start adding cover, because it won't interfere with the lawn.

Not much, at least. No matter how small our yards are, we can deepen the edge by several feet, or dedicate a corner to songbird cover, without the reduction of the lawn being very noticeable to our own eyes. Improving the edges or creating a bird corner in our yards is easy, and we can do it little by little.

- There's no need to get stressed over figuring out a design. Straight line, sorta straight line, straight on the lawn's outside edge, curvy on the inside edge: All perfect!

Safe Haven
AND KEEP OUT!

A hodgepodge of orange cosmos, red zinnias, and other flowers, this no-care patch will attract songbirds year-round. Buntings, common yellowthroats, native sparrows, and other privacy-loving birds will appreciate its cover and lack of human disturbance while they forage for insects, butterflies, and later, seeds.

Fill in any gaps in your boundary-line planting with sunflowers and a jumbled patch of easy, fast-growing annuals that thrive on neglect. Cosmos (*Cosmos* spp.), spiderflower (*Cleome hassleriana*), tall marigolds (*Tagetes* spp.), and bachelor's-buttons (*Centaurea cyanus*) make a pretty no-care garden; sow the seeds thickly so the plants knit together. Even easier: Plant a bag of birdseed mix along the edge of your yard.

Songbirds love their seeds and the insects these plants attract, as well as the welcome cover. Don't worry about any weeds that sneak in; they're simply more food and cover for the birds. The only hard part about this planting will be fighting down the urge to visit it daily. Stay away instead, so songbirds get used to feeling safe there.

- Nor do we have to scour plant encyclopedias trying to decide just what we need. A big planting of pretty much anything will attract songbirds—and a good-size corner or the entire boundary of our backyard is a big planting. Use a mix of plants, not all the same kind, for heightened appeal.

- If you already have a boundary planting, make it wider. Plant more shrubs and small trees in front of what's already there.

- If you have very few plants along the edges of your yard, start by bolstering what you have by adding others to create groups of shrubs

and small trees instead of a skinny single-file planting of individual specimens.

- If you have no plants along your boundary line, start with a fast-growing hedgerow of mixed inexpensive shrubs, such as elderberries, roses (*Rosa* spp.), privet (*Ligustrum* spp.), and burning bush (*Euonymus* spp.)—good songbird plants, all.

Moving Out

Here's another solution to the problem of too much lawn, and it won't cost you a penny. It will give you a workout, though, because we're moving bushes.

Greenery snuggled up against the house is a nice idea, but not for birds. The house and its foundation plantings are nothing but an unwelcoming island in all that lawn. Many songbirds are reluctant to approach a house, even if there are shrubs along the foundation, and even if some of those shrubs are great bird plants, like hollies or native viburnum bushes.

So let's free up our foundation plants. Move them out into groups near other elements in the yard, where lawn won't be missed: by our patio, near our feeding station, beside the birdbath, behind the garden bench.

Before you dig in, though, be aware that this will be a good physical workout. If your budget allows, you can also buy new shrubs to create bird habitat in your lawn, instead of moving the foundation plants. It's not an instant job, but the work is well worth it. By moving the shrubs out into our yards, we create "stepping-stones" for birds. The groups of shrubs will allow songbirds to safely travel about our lawn, instead of being limited to our lonely shade trees. And the shrubs will

Songbirds often "plant" their own favorite trees and shrubs in a hedge—by dropping seeds of berries they've eaten. Chokecherry (*Prunus virginiana*) is one of the most common small trees that spring up thanks to birds. Here it finds room to grow in a dense mixed hedge of evergreen junipers (*Juniperus* spp.), poplars (*Populus* spp.), and other fast growers.

Safe Haven

THROUGH THICK AND THIN

A single row of shrubs along the edge of your yard is a good start. But their attraction to songbirds will multiply exponentially when you vary the depth of the planting front to back along the row. Create wider areas of cover here and there, by adding more shrubs in front of the row of singletons.

Aim for a rounded curve in those thicker areas. Just two or three additional shrubs or trees will do the trick. Most shrubs get about 4 to 5 feet wide, so your curve will create a good-size area of cover.

Skip about 15 to 20 feet of row, and then plant another wide area. Songbirds will use the skinnier parts of the row as travel corridors between the wider oases that are ideal for nesting and resting.

be a destination in themselves, because they'll host insects and probably produce flowers, seeds, or berries of some kind.

We've also made our own house look better, if all we started with was a house with close shrubs and a wide sweep of bare lawn. Instead of an isolated island, it's now a softer focal point, thanks to those groups of shrubs in the yard that carry the viewer's eye out and away. It's a much more graceful design that we'll appreciate as much as the songbirds.

And there's one more thing: Now we can get to know our former foundation shrubs better, instead of barely giving them a glance. Plants deserve to be appreciated.

Transplanting Established Shrubs

I'm no Hercules; I'm just your average creaky-kneed, weak-backed, soon-to-be-senior-discount gardener. Yet I still manage to move major bushes and even small trees without having to take to my recliner for a week afterward. If your shrubs have been in the ground for less than three years, their roots are probably not much bigger than the pot you bought them in. They'll be easy to lever out with a shovel.

It takes brains, not brawn, for moving bigger shrubs or those that have been in the soil for years. Call in a helper if you can't manage the job yourself. Ten or 20 bucks to a teenager with a strong back will benefit both of you! Here are some tricks I've learned for making the operation easier:

- Move shrubs when they're dormant, after the leaves drop in fall, or in early spring when the soil thaws. This way, the shrubs don't have to try to nourish their leaves after their roots have been disturbed and most likely slightly damaged. You give them time to recover.

- Dig the new hole for the shrub before you start working on transplanting it. Fill the hole with

(continued on page 266)

Get to Know Your Songbirds

Grosbeaks

A snowy, freezing-mist kind of day—mid-May in the high Rockies—and great weather for holing up inside, baking cookies, playing chess, and watching birds at the feeder. No matter what the weather, birds were coming back fast and furious from their winter homes in Central or South America as mid- to late May brought the last big wave of migration.

Dozens of gray-headed juncos had come in the day before, foraging on the ground beneath the feeder to glean every seed I'd missed in the uh-oh-bears-are-out cleanup.

Lack of musical talent is easy to forgive in the gorgeous evening grosbeak, who sticks with a high, clear whistle or rattling trill. His cousins, the pine, blue, rose-breasted, and black-headed grosbeaks, may not be as drop-dead gorgeous, but they are lovely, and so are their sweet, warbling voices.

When we woke to snow and cold, I'd filled the feeder again, in hopes that the hungry juncos would eat every bit before a bruin sniffed it out.

Turned out that the entertaining juncos were just the opening act. Because then I spotted a flash of yellow-and-white against the dark pines, heading for the feeder. "Oh, cool, evening grosbeaks!"

Looking like giant goldfinches, the flock of six or so birds, mostly males, took over the feeder without resistance.

Recognizing futility when they saw it, the juncos wisely retreated to nibbling oatmeal cookies and cracking seeds on the ground, staying away from the grosbeaks.

Soon came an even bigger surprise. "Oh, wow, an orange one!" A black-headed grosbeak male in full breeding plumage, that is.

"They come up this high? I had no idea," I said to the friend I was staying with. I'd only known these birds in the Pacific Northwest, where they sought out creeks and lowlands and left the high mountains to others.

What a sight, watching the glorious orange-and-black bird settle down to crack seeds beside his big-beaked yellow cousins. Eating machines, all of them.

"Two kinds at once, cool!" I said. "Hey, where are the pine grosbeaks?" We'd had a few pairs of these lovely birds, male rosy red, female golden green, keeping us company this winter, but I hadn't seen them that day. "Wish we could have a grosbeak trifecta."

"They were here this morning. Guess they're taking a break right now," my friend replied, cracking open the field guide to the grosbeak section. "Sibley says rose-breasted here, too, in migration."

"Oh, and blue grosbeaks, maybe?"

"Lower elevations. But you never know."

Nope, you never know. That's what makes migration time so much fun.

Even birds that don't nest anywhere near where you live may stop in for a bite to eat or a drink of water while on their long journey from South or Central America back to their breeding grounds.

A quinfecta of grosbeaks? Maybe. Meanwhile, we've got plenty of other friends to welcome home. That's the joy of migration time. Every day brings the possibility of new birds at the feeder or in the backyard. What fun!

When to see them: Evening grosbeaks, anytime, depending on where you live; black-headed, pine, and rose-breasted grosbeaks, spring through fall

What to feed them: Safflower, sunflower, and hulled sunflower seed; several grosbeak species are developing a taste for jelly and soft foods.

Other ways to attract them: A birdbath or saucer of water is popular year-round. Plant a shadblow or serviceberry tree (*Amelanchier arborea, A. × grandiflora*), sweet cherry or sour cherry tree, or a mulberry tree for fruit. Tulip tree seeds (*Liriodendron tulipifera*) attract evening grosbeaks in winter.

What they sound like: Except for the evening grosbeak, who isn't much of a singer, all grosbeaks have sweet, warbling voices.

What to watch for: Watch those fascinating, super strong, humongous hinged beaks at work as these birds plow through seeds without pausing.

Better than a feather in this snowman's cap—an impromptu feeder on his head to attract cardinals and other songbirds.

water, let it drain, and fill it again. By the time you bring the shrub to its new spot, the soil will be moist, which will help roots grow faster.

• Water the shrub thoroughly to soften the ground where it's been growing. With a sharp spade, slice vertically down into the soil all around the base of the shrub, to the depth of the blade.

• Do it again, slicing deeper this time, and angling the blade inward.

• Firmly tug a sturdy branch to gauge which areas of the roots still need shovel work. Slice away at those sections until they pull free.

• If you run into a stubborn root, use your hands to clear the soil around it and figure out which way it's heading. Then give it a firm pull in the opposite direction; it most likely will pull free.

• Bundle the roots in an old sheet or tarp to move the plant. Keeping as many fine roots in the soil as possible will help the shrub recover quickly.

Mix 'Em Up

To increase your backyard's appeal to songbirds, use a variety of shrubs and small trees. You'll find suggestions in Chapter 9, Fruits, Berries, and Sweets, and elsewhere throughout this book.

A hedge of arborvitae (*Thuja* spp.), one of the least tempting plants to songbirds because of its dearth of flowers and fruit, will barely rate a second glance from birds. But if we switch it up by replacing some of those arbs—one here, one there—with shrub dogwoods (gray dogwood, *Cornus racemosa*; silky dogwood, *C. amomum*; and Cornelian cherry dogwood, *C. mas*, are all excellent bird plants), dwarf fruit trees, shrub roses, or whatever you like best, we can give a great big boost to songbird potential.

WINTER FRIENDS ARE EASY

Attracting birds that spend winter with us couldn't be simpler. It's feeders that do the trick. Birds are opportunists, and natural food can be mighty hard to come by in winter, especially in snowy regions.

An empty stomach is great motivation for checking out a feeder, so attracting winter songbirds is a cinch: Set up a feeder and they will come. Hang a cage of suet, you'll get chickadees. Fill a tray with seeds, and cardinals and native sparrows will arrive.

Some of our winter regulars are songbirds, for sure, even though they won't be singing during the off season. But all of them are accustomed to looking toward feeders for goodies, and they quickly become regulars. That loyalty pays off in spring, when some of our winter songbird friends include our yards as part of their nesting territory. If we're not honored with a nest, our birds

Miss the Flight?

WATCH FOR STRAGGLERS AT THE FEEDER

I couldn't believe my eyes when a Baltimore oriole showed up near Christmastime to stuff his bill at the suet feeder in my yard. After all, my feeder was in Indiana, not in South Florida, the Caribbean, or Central America, where this species typically spends winter.

Seems to be a sign of changing times: A few songbirds that usually fly far to the south are hanging around longer in fall, after the rest of their kind have migrated. A few are even lingering into winter. Are they confused, or simply the first wave of opportunists taking advantage of our reliably stocked feeders? There's no way to know. But their possible presence is another argument for making sure we have the soft foods, fruits, and mealworms they crave, as well as the kind of habitat that lets them know they're safe in our yard.

will at least come back to fill their bellies or splash their feathers in between taking care of their kids elsewhere.

Who's Still Here?

These songbirds are winter friends across much of our country.

American goldfinch	Song sparrow
American robin	Titmice
Chickadees	White-crowned
Doves	sparrow
House finch	White-throated
Juncos	sparrow
Northern cardinal	

Some songbirds migrate only as far as the southeast quarter of the country. If you're speaking with a Southern drawl, you may be enjoying these birds in winter:

American robin	Chipping sparrow
Bluebirds	Gray catbird
Brown thrasher	House wren
Carolina wren	

Changing Habits

Several species of songbirds are becoming more common winter visitors to feeders, and the trend shows no signs of stopping. Some, such as our pal the American robin, are simply learning that feeders mean food. Instead of retreating to wild areas for winter, as they usually do, they're hanging out in our backyards, or at least coming by to fill their bellies.

Other birds, such as brown thrashers, are beginning to winter outside their usual range, perhaps because of the helping hand we offer with our feeders.

These birds are all soft-food eaters, not seed eaters. So keep the suet and fat-based treats a-coming. They'll love a helping of mealworms, too. Look for these birds at your winter feeders:

American robin	Gray catbird
Bluebirds	House wren
Brown thrasher	Yellow-rumped
Carolina wren	warbler

SPRING ARRIVALS

Sorry, winter pals, but spring migrants are the songbirds we seem to want most—the bright orioles, tanagers, rose-breasted grosbeaks, and other beauties, as well as the sweet-voiced but quiet-colored thrushes and other singing friends. I figure there's a number of reasons we look forward to their arrival.

A special treat. Spring migrant species aren't as common as our year-round friends. There simply aren't as many individuals of each species. Seeing one of these birds is like spotting a genuine diamond ring in a bubblegum dispenser.

Absence makes the heart grow fonder. Seeing the first rose-breasted grosbeak at the feeder warms our hearts as much as bumping into a long-lost friend on the street. How nice to see you again!

A welcome splash of color. Migrants include the most vividly colored songbirds—colors we haven't seen all winter. Blue grosbeaks and buntings, orange orioles and black-headed grosbeaks, yellow warblers, green vireos—it's a whole rainbow of birds coming through. Most of them are in full breeding plumage, or growing it fast, and their colors are a real treat for winter-dulled eyes.

Wonderful voices. Migrant songbirds include the most highly accomplished singers, those with complex, lengthy songs and beautiful vocal tones. From fluting wood thrushes to soaring orioles, their voices add a whole new delight to spring. And they're already singing when they stop by to visit.

A Point of Pride

Surely none of us would be so crass as to brag about the special birds we've seen, would we?

You better believe we would! The competition may seem casual among backyard bird-watchers,

It's All Connected
SPRING GREEN IS TANAGER TIME

Look and listen for scarlet tanagers and summer tanagers about the time that oaks and maples get their leaves. The birds usually arrive when the leaves are nearly full-size but still have that young spring-green color.

Those tender leaves are an inviting target for insects, which emerge in big numbers to nibble the succulent greenery or to stalk each other. Watch a tanager in a tree, and you'll see it busily picking off insects as it slinks through the foliage, peering at the underside of the leaves to make sure it doesn't miss any tasty bugs.

but it's definitely a serious part of the fun, so we may as well embrace it.

Who's hosting the first indigo bunting? Who had an orchard oriole at their orange feeder? Who snapped a photo of a Blackburnian warbler at their birdbath? If it's you, go right ahead and claim your bragging rights—you deserve them!

When a migrant songbird comes to your yard—whether it's in your flowering crabapple tree, at your fountain, or investigating your bird food—it means you're doing things right. Attracting these birds isn't like attracting a flock of, say, common English sparrows, and you deserve that pat on the back, even if it's self-applied. Congratulations!

Now, let's get more birds to brag about.

The Window of Opportunity

With migrant songbirds, the biggest window of opportunity is in spring, not winter. Spring is when the birds are moving through on migration, and a little later, choosing their nesting territories. These birds are finding plenty of natural food—insects emerging along with the leaves and early flowers—and many of them haven't yet become accustomed to recognizing feeders as another source of abundant food. So it takes a little extra incentive to tempt them into visiting—or staying.

A Special Sight

The reason we see fewer neotropical migrants, or see them less frequently than our year-round feeder regulars, is because there just aren't that many of them. Oh, there are plenty of species—it's the number of individuals in those species that's pretty paltry.

In recent years, the populations of many songbirds have been declining because of habitat destruction, the effects of pesticides, and climate

Lucky enough to own acres? Retire the lawn mower and add a few young trees to make songbirds feel comfortable—they can fly from one tree to another to reach the inviting yard beyond the field, where feeders and bath await.

change. Count yourself lucky to enjoy these special birds. The sighting of a scarlet tanager—or any kind of tanager, for that matter—will always be a red-letter day. Unfortunately, there just aren't very many of them.

PLEASE DO NOT DISTURB

To make birds of the brush, such as common yellowthroats, yellow warblers, thrashers, and towhees, feel at home in your yard, all you have to do is go wild. Dedicate a discreet corner—over there by the garage? in the far corner of the fence?—to wilderness, and you'll greatly improve its appeal to songbirds that seek privacy.

As Greta Garbo said when public attention became too much for her, "I vant to be left alone." Many songbird species share her attitude. While they don't hesitate to visit our feeders or scour our shrubs, they prefer an area that's all theirs, without intrusions.

Safe Haven
SOLOMON'S SEAL

Understated in their brown plumage, the supremely sweet-voiced brown thrushes blend right in on the forest floor. If you're lucky, they may drop by your shady backyard—if they spy the blue-black berries of Solomon's seal (*Polygonatum* spp.).

Check a native plant nursery or catalog, such as those listed in the Resources at the back of this book, for common Solomon's seal (*P. biflorum*), giant Solomon's seal (*P. biflorum* var. *commutatum*), southwestern McKittrick's Solomon's seal (*P. cobrense*), and other species. Thrushes love them all, as well as false Solomon's seal (*Maianthemum racemosum*). These easy-to-grow perennial wildflowers, most reaching about knee-high, will slowly spread, adding to the cover in your yard as well as providing tempting fall berries.

A crop of deep blue berries on the golden-leaved clump of Solomon's seal (*Polygonatum biflorum*) at center tempt fall thrushes to this shady garden.

The Good Side of Invasives

Some plants that were introduced into America—many of them by our own USDA—have been way too successful. Blame it on the birds: The berries of the multiflora rose, Russian olive, Tatarian honeysuckle, English ivy, and Japanese honeysuckle are prime food sources, and the seeds are spread like wildfire by the birds.

Bluebirds, robins, cardinals, thrashers, catbirds, and a host of other frugivorous songbirds don't call it a problem. They seek out the small fruits of these plants all winter, and many use the plants for nesting come spring.

Many of these invasive plants are actively being eradicated, but some of them are probably here to stay. If you happen to have Japanese honeysuckle or a multiflora rose in your backyard, you might consider embracing it rather than removing it. We don't want the weed police knocking at our doors, but we do want the songbirds that these invasive species attract.

Yes, songbirds will spread the seeds, but these two plants are already integrated in the wild landscape. Personally, I'm on the songbirds' side: A generous food source is welcome, no matter where it comes from. Especially since many of our own activities—like destroying habitat to put in houses—have also done so much harm to native plants.

THE NEXT MULTIFLORA ROSE

Not too long ago, 'Bradford' Callery pears (*Pyrus calleryana*) were planted along the streets of just about every city. Fast-growing and beautiful, they bloomed with abandon and carpeted sidewalks and parked cars with a lovely snow of white fallen petals in spring. In fall and winter, the trees fed many a songbird, as flocks of robins, bluebirds, and others sought their small fruits on migration or to get through winter.

Then the trouble started. First, it was structural problems: The trees had a habit of splitting and keeling over beginning at about 20 years of age. Next, another drawback became evident: The zillions of seeds dropped by birds were sprouting into an invasive species in some areas.

As far as the songbirds are concerned, the spread of 'Bradford' pears is not a problem—to them, it's more fruits for the taking. To people who worry about invasive species, getting control of the 'Bradford' is beginning to feel like locking the barn door after the horse has escaped.

Will 'Bradford' join the multiflora rose, Japanese honeysuckle, and Tatarian honeysuckle as the next great escape artist? Time will tell.

Private Places

Planting a hedge is another quick way to create privacy for our songbirds. Put away the pruning shears and let the shrubs grow naturally. That way, you don't disturb the birds by fiddling with the bushes, running noisy pruning shears or spending an hour or more snipping away. And your plants will provide more cover, perching places, and nest sites when you allow them to reach their full potential.

A brush pile is another simple trick for creating undisturbed habitat. Just pile fallen limbs, woody plant clippings—even thorny ones—and small branches into a mound to attract Carolina, Bewick's, and house wrens. These perky birds will forage over, under, and in between the sticks, plucking out spiders and insects.

RELAX AND ENJOY

I think of listening to songbirds as meditation of the best kind. When I sit down with the intention of doing nothing but listening to the birds for a while, my cares and woes simply fall away.

Take the time to attend a songbird concert as often as you can. An early morning in spring is the best time, when birds are singing their hearts out to greet the day, and the busyness of our own everyday lives isn't making demands on us yet. But anytime is a fine time, as long as birds are singing.

Even 10 minutes of listening will put you in a wonderfully relaxed state of mind. I like to close my eyes, so that the music really sinks in without visual distractions. Often, I find that half an hour or more has slipped away before I know it.

A private nook is an ideal place to take in the concert. Just nestle an outdoor chair among your plants and birds. Or create a simple arbor with a grapevine that will quickly cover it for a sense of seclusion—and attract birds with insects and fruit. Settle your garden bench near your bird-bath or other water, to delight in the songbirds that will soon flutter down. Or place your garden bench or patio settee at the end of a path and surround it with shrubs and a small tree or two for perching songsters, to make an inviting cul-de-sac for their concert.

Summer Slowdown

When birdsong begins to dwindle in the heat of summer, it's not because the singers are enjoying a siesta in the shade. It's because nesting season is coming to an end. Once the last batch of babies is out of the nest, the hormones that fueled breeding season simmer down fast. Songbirds move into the next phase of their lives, molting their feathers, and for some, preparing for a long journey. All are still eating, but since they're no longer feeding nestlings, the bird traffic in our backyard and at our feeders may dwindle.

As birds disperse from their relatively small nesting territories, we may spot new visitors in our backyards. And as soon as songbirds begin bulking up for the flight south, it's boom time again at our berries and feeders.

Treetop or Ground Dweller?
LIVING FLOWERS IN TREETOPS, DEAD LEAVES ON GROUND

Birds of the treetops are usually bright-colored. Birds that live on or near the ground usually wear much quieter clothes.

Watch the songbirds in your backyard, at the birdbath, and at your feeding station to see for yourself. Vivid orioles, tanagers, and grosbeaks will head for the trees when they've finished their sip or snack. Native sparrows, towhees, catbirds, and thrashers sneak back into or under the bushes.

Welcome Home!

Room for improvement in your yard? Always! Try these easy ways to create the welcoming habitat that draws in songbirds every season of the year.

EXISTING ELEMENT	COMMENT	HOW TO IMPROVE	INCREASED APPEAL
Apartment; no yard	Ack!	Got a balcony? Grow vines in containers; add a shepherd's crook to hang a feeder or bath. Use stick-on window feeders.	Chickadees, goldfinches, northern cardinal, titmice
Beloved lawn	Valuable to robins, but not much else	Add a perimeter planting of mixed shrubs and small trees to provide cover and natural food while still keeping that sweep of green. If you can bear to break it up, add groups of shrubs or trees as "stepping-stones" within the lawn.	American robin, black-headed grosbeak, blue grosbeak, buntings, common yellowthroat, gray catbird, native sparrows, northern cardinal, rose-breasted grosbeak, thrashers, thrushes, yellow warbler
City yard	Many songbirds prefer to live near wilder places.	Focus your efforts on spring migration, when songbirds can stop anywhere. A generous buffet and trees, which are easily visible from the air, tempt them into sticking around, or at least returning to visit in other seasons.	All songbirds
Mature shade tree	Already a magnet for treetop song-birds, such as tanagers and orioles, because of plentiful insects; birds may not leave the tree to investi-gate feeders	Add a small flowering tree nearby, to tempt birds to lower levels—including your feeders. Sweet or sour cherries, serviceberries (*Amelanchier* spp.), and dogwoods (*Cornus* spp.) of any kind—shrubby or tree-type—are irresistible.	Grosbeaks, orioles, tanagers, vireos, warblers

(continued)

EXISTING ELEMENT	COMMENT	HOW TO IMPROVE	INCREASED APPEAL
Neat and tidy flower garden	Looks great, but not to songbird eyes, which prefer a knitted-together jumble that offers cover, instead of plants separated by bare spaces where the birds are highly visible	Add self-sowing annuals, such as cosmos (*Cosmos* spp.) and bachelor's-buttons (*Centaurea cyanus*), among taller perennials that spread by roots or seed, such as bee balm (*Monarda* spp.), perennial sunflowers (*Helianthus* spp.), and purple cone-flower (*Echinacea purpurea*).	American goldfinch and other finches, buntings, chickadees, doves, juncos, native sparrows, titmice, towhees, vireos, wood warblers, and wrens
Neatly trimmed hedge	Has bird appeal, but maintenance may disturb nesting	Plan your hedge's "haircut" for non-nesting season—trim in early spring, then let it alone until late summer.	American robin, chipping sparrow, golden-crowned sparrow, gray catbird, northern cardinal, song sparrow, and thrashers
Pet dog	Dogs can scare off songbirds, especially ground-feeding native sparrows.	Keep your dog indoors during prime songbird-feeding times in early morning and late afternoon. As for cats—they belong in the house, or outside only with close supervision.	All songbirds
Play areas and pathways	Too much human activity for songbirds to settle down	Create an undisturbed area away from such activity. Plant a group of dense shrubs—burning bush (*Euonymus alatus*), lilacs (*Syringa vulgaris*), and privet (*Ligustrum* spp.) grow fast and thick. Add seeds, insects, and cover with a casual garden of low-maintenance flowers, such as black-eyed Susans (*Rudbeckia* spp.), and ornamental grasses.	American robin, chickadees, northern cardinal, thrashers, titmice, warblers, and wrens

EXISTING ELEMENT	COMMENT	HOW TO IMPROVE	INCREASED APPEAL
Small yard	No room to add large trees or big gardens	Get creative, and "grow up" with your greenery: Add vines on trellises and against the house or over the porch; stack plants in layers by planting ground covers and ferns under shrubs, with the shrubs under small trees. Fill containers with seed-rich flowers, such as blue anise hyssop (*Agastache foeniculum*). Grow a holly (*Ilex* spp.) in a large pot on your patio.	American robin, bluebirds, chickadees, finches of all types, native sparrows, titmice, towhees, vireos, and wrens
Solid wood privacy fence	No food or cover; a barrier to ground-level birds, such as native sparrows	Plant easy-care, fast-growing vines to cover the fence with greenery to transform it into a travel corridor. Bird-approved choices include American bittersweet (*Celastrus scandens*), grape (*Vitis* spp.), Virginia creeper (*Parthenocissus quinquefolia*), and red- or orange-flowered honeysuckle (*Lonicera sempervirens; L. ciliosa;* and hybrids). Nail a wren house or robin shelf to the fence, among the vines. Set a birdbath among ferns at the foot of the fence.	American robin, chickadees, gray catbird, northern cardinal, thrashers, vireos, wood warblers, and wrens
Squirrels	Songbird nestlings are a favorite food; depredations at feeders can leave the budget reeling.	Invest in squirrel-deterring feeders.	All songbirds

CHAPTER 15

Building Boom

Hey, they like us! They really like us! That's the warm and fuzzy feeling we get when a pair of songbirds decides to make its home in our backyard.

Nesting pairs are the ultimate accolade. Not only do we feel honored by their presence, but even better, we get to enjoy watching our songster friends raise their family.

In this chapter, we'll talk about how to attract nesting songbirds to our backyards.

Talk about connection. While we may not be able to recognize "our" cardinal when he's cracking sunflowers at the feeder, we know that pair of redbirds working on a nest in the privet is ours, beyond a doubt. So are the robins in that mud-plastered nest in the crabapple tree, the house finches in our hanging basket, the song sparrow in the strawberry patch, and every other songbird that chooses to call our place home.

What fun it is to watch the birds carry sticks, pluck dead grass, select just the right dead leaves, and collect other furnishings for their nests. We see a lot of the parents once their eggs hatch, too, because their every waking moment will be spent gathering food—often at our feeders.

And just wait'll the fledglings leave the nest.

We're as joyful and as full of ownership as if *we* had done all the hard work of feeding those mouths every 5 minutes ourselves.

"Oh, look! It's my baby robin!"

It sure is.

COURTSHIP SEASON

"First comes love, then comes marriage, then comes (fill in name) with a baby carriage," we sang as we jumped rope on the playground of Rosemont Elementary School.

That's the way of the birds and bees. Except that in the case of songbirds, "love" isn't exactly what I'd imagined back in my jump-rope days.

Behind the Music

By listening to your backyard songbirds, you can tell exactly what's going on in their lives. Even when you still haven't managed to find the location of a single nest.

If your Baltimore oriole, say, is singing up a storm, he probably hasn't found a partner yet. Male birds pour forth their best songs when they're trying to snag a female. Unmated males sing more than those who already have partners. When your oriole's singing drops off, it's because he's moved on to a new stage of family life. As soon as egg laying begins, the males save their energy. They sing less, maybe because they're mighty busy finding food or perhaps they don't want to attract predators.

If your oriole suddenly starts singing a lot again, it means something's happened and nesting has to start over. The nest may have failed because of a windstorm or predator. The female may have died. Or maybe it's simply time to raise another brood. The male shifts back into high gear again, singing his heart out as if he were starting courtship from scratch.

On the Alert

Once songbirds begin working on their nests so that the female can lay her eggs, you'll notice that the male no longer moves around their territory so much, nor sings from one perch after another. As soon as his partner becomes focused on her home, he stays mighty close, even if he doesn't help with the actual construction.

A smart guy, he knows that this is the critical

A pair of American robins may raise two or three broods a year, and every one of those goofy babies makes our hearts melt.

period when other males may try to win her favor—or when she may decide to test other partners herself. From the start of nest building until egg laying is complete, the male guards his mate, sticking close to her side to fend off advances. The term ornithologists use is *mate guarding,* and it's when fights with competitors are most

Snug as a Bug
KEEP OUT THE CHILL WITH WOOD

Bluebirds, chickadees, and titmice are early nesters with an advantage: They raise their families in holes in trees or posts or they nest in birdhouses. The wood offers protection from the elements, keeping the birds from getting wet or snow-covered. And it provides a layer of insulation from the cold. Inside, the nestlings can snuggle up under Mama's warm breast and wings to stay warm and cozy.

intense. There's a lot at stake. The male partner wants his genes in every one of those eggs. Of course, since he's not exactly toeing the straight-and-narrow himself, he may still slip away to try to mate with other nearby females.

You'll hear a lot of squawking and see a lot of feathers flying during this period as males defend their mates. And you'll hear the male doing most of his singing from a perch nearby the nest, where he can keep close guard.

Watch, too, for a posture called *head-forward,* which is the most intense sign of aggression in songbirds. The male lowers his back and tilts his head upward, as if ready to suddenly fly up and peck the offender—and he will, if the other bird doesn't back off.

Birds Behaving Badly

For years, I watched my mom's pair of cardinals—the ones that nested in the same red climbing 'Blaze' rose every spring. Although they seemed to be the perfect match, something didn't quite jibe. Other male cardinals would try to sneak into the proclaimed nesting territory, setting off raucous and sometimes vicious fights. If the pair was mated for life, I wondered, then why didn't other males leave the couple alone?

What was even more of a mystery was that sometimes the male of the pair seemed to be flirting, shall we say, with the female next door.

The Baltimore orioles were even worse. Mass attacks, with two or three male orioles leading the charge, were the norm, it seemed. And hey, didn't I even see the female oriole giving a come-hither look to the male oriole down the hill, who already had his own mate?

Sorry, but it's true. The marriage vow of forsaking all others is pretty much a myth in songbird land, except when it comes to caring for their families.

Lasting Bonds

Despite all this flitting about among partners, romance isn't totally dead in the songbird world. It turns out that some species do indeed mate for life.

Even though they may have their little flings, they keep the same primary partner, the one with whom they've formed a pair bond, and apparently stick together happily ever after. But there's still very little scientific proof, since discerning one individual from another isn't easy. Several studies of house finches, beginning with W. H. Bergtold in 1913 and as recently as Philip Hooge's work in 1990 for the University of California, and Kevin McGraw and Geoffrey Hill's study published in 2004, concluded that the same individuals often nest together in successive years.

Keep in mind, we're not talking golden anniversary here, or even silver. A paper anniversary—that's one year—is more like it.

Although birds in captivity may live a dozen or even a score of years, their life spans are usually much shorter in the wild. When a bird has to deal with the daily dangers of its outdoor existence, a natural life span may be only a year or two, maybe 5 years if the bird is really lucky. Cats, hawks, cars, blizzards, you name it—all manner of fatalities can befall a songbird or its partner.

What's the newly widowed bird to do?

You guessed it: Sing to find a mate, if male. Or select another singer, if female.

HIGH TIME FOR A HOME

Nesting season begins early for our year-round songbirds, such as chickadees, cardinals, and song sparrows. The singing that signals the start kicks off in late winter, and in about 6 weeks or so, the female may be sitting on eggs. Bluebirds are early nesters, too, in areas where they stick around all winter.

Early nesters take a risk by starting their families so soon. The weather is still cold, and snow can blow in unexpectedly. For these songbirds, our feeders are a real lifeline. A cold snap can send all the insects into hiding, leaving bluebirds with a short supply. An ice storm can make it impossible for chickadees and titmice to find enough sustenance for themselves, let alone their families. In the South, where brown thrashers, gray catbirds, and wrens live year-round, they,

too, get an early jump on the season. By February, they may be making nests in southern comfort.

If at First You Don't Succeed . . .

A nest attempt can fail for all sorts of reasons. Predators take a heavy toll. Storms blow down the fragile constructions or even topple the tree the nest is in. Cowbirds shove out the original eggs and lay their own. A mate may meet its fate.

What to do? Get busy! "Try, try again" is the motto for nesting songbirds, and they'll keep plugging away. Widowed birds find another partner, damaged nests are replaced, new eggs laid, and on they go.

These black-capped chickadees are almost ready to go, about 17 days after hatching.

Weather Warning
FAST FIX FOR DROPPING TEMPS

High-fat foods are important any time of the year, but they can be an absolute lifesaver for early nesting songbirds. When a cold spell or an early spring storm is predicted, don't skimp on the suet, peanut butter, soft foods, and nuts—hand them out freely, so the calories can keep the birds warm.

Timer Reminder

As soon as you hear the first songs of your chickadees and titmice, add "Put up birdhouses" to your to-do list. These early singers are cavity nesters, and the start of singing means they'll soon be shopping for real estate to raise their families. Put up a nest box of a size that suits them, and they just may take you up on it. Now's the time to mount bluebird houses, too, if you're lucky enough to have these beauties in your neighborhood. Remove old nests from existing boxes and sponge out the interior with a 10 percent bleach-to-water solution to kill any lingering mites that could infest the new nests.

Mount your nest boxes a good distance from any of your birdfeeders. Predators looking for leftover food at night or trying to get at the suet might be all too willing to settle for baby birds instead.

Ready, Set, Go

In deserts, birds have to be ready and able to breed whenever their chance arises. When rain comes, food is plentiful; when insects are scarce in the dry times, the birds' nestlings may not survive. That's why the hormones of some desert species work differently from those of birds from gentler climes, and their singing habits differ, too.

Zebra finches, a popular research subject for scientists, live in the punishing Australian desert. The males get an early dose of testosterone when breeding season nears, which readies the vocal control region of their brains. The hormone doesn't yet spur them into action, but merely gets them ready, so the birds can start singing as soon as conditions are right—when rain and bugs arrive. That's when another hormone, androgen, kicks in, and breeding season starts off with a song.

The hormones for birds in less harsh habitats work differently. An early dose of testosterone isn't needed, because the change in season almost always guarantees an abundance of plant and insect food. Instead, androgen rules the roost, being released in response to the shifts in day and night length, and that sets the birds to singing.

No Time to Lose

Migrant songbirds have one thing on their minds when they get to where they're going in spring: breeding time. For weeks, they've been on the road, hurrying to get home, and now that big time is near.

(continued on page 284)

Homebodies

Many songbirds have already adapted to the backyard life of suburbia, small towns, and even cities. Here's a look at the birds that may nest in our yards, even if we're not near woods or other wild areas. The songbirds are arranged from easiest to most challenging to attract.

SONGBIRD	YOUR CHANCES OF ATTRACTING A NESTING PAIR	POPULATION	HABITAT NEEDS FOR NESTING
Robins, cardinals	Almost a given	Both extremely numerous, with plenty of birds to go around	Even if your place is nothing but lawn with a single shrub, you have a decent chance of attracting a nesting pair.
Song sparrow	More than likely	Abundant	These low-level birds need places to hide themselves and their on-the-ground nests. A garden, a hedge, or a weedy spot is all you need.
Chipping sparrow	More than likely	Abundant	Not a super singer with its simple trilling song, but welcome as a backyard friend. Often nests in foundation shrubs or small trees right near the house.
House wren	Maybe	Fewer in number than song sparrows	Insect-filled gardens and a bird-house give you the best chance.
Thrashers, gray catbird	Maybe	There are fewer individuals of these species, so consider yourself honored if one chooses your place.	They're more particular about habitat, both at feeders and for nesting areas. These skulkers need a good-size stretch of shrubs or hedge before they'll hang the "Home Sweet Home" sign.
Carolina wren and its western counterpart, the Bewick's wren	Maybe	Populations rise and fall from year to year.	Insect-rich brush piles, gardens, shrubs, and nest boxes (or a back-yard shed they can call home) give these singers what they need.

SONGBIRD	YOUR CHANCES OF ATTRACTING A NESTING PAIR	POPULATION	HABITAT NEEDS FOR NESTING
Orioles	Maybe	Sorry, not even one per backyard. These birds used to be much more common, but have dropped in numbers.	Trees, trees, beautiful trees—that's what it takes to attract a nesting pair of orioles. Not a forest, though; a single shade tree. For western orioles, often an oak, willow, or palm can be enough to catch their eye.
Rose-breasted grosbeak	Maybe, maybe not	Dropping in numbers	Limited nesting range; within it, a backyard with mixed shrubs and trees and a hedge may coax them home.
Common yellowthroat	Possible	Common among wood warblers, but widely dispersed	Weedy, grassy fields, meadows and edges, dotted with shrubs, are their nesting pick, so if you can imitate that, they may come. Some individuals are adapting to perennial gardens, too.
Yellow warbler	Probable if your yard includes a body of water	One of the most common wood warblers, but not numerous	If you've got a pond, you've got a great chance of getting nesting yellow warblers in the willows at its edge. Just a garden pool? It might work if you plant to make the surroundings natural-looking.
Bluebirds, thrushes, tanagers, buntings, most wood warblers, most vireos, most native sparrows	Depends on the naturalistic habitat that your yard offers	Many are declining in number; all are picky about habitat	These songbirds visit backyards on migration or in winter when they need food. But for nesting, most of them head for wild places. If your home isn't near these places, you're likely to be out of luck—but you can always hope.

For a week or two, the males, who arrive first, go through the preliminaries. Singing and fighting, they stake out the best nesting territory they can find. Then all they have to do is keep singing to proclaim and reinforce their boundaries, and wait for the girls to arrive.

Courtship moves swiftly for migrants. These songbirds don't have any time to waste, because that return trip is only 10 to 12 weeks away. Many songbirds pair up within a few days after the females arrive. Ain't no time to lose.

THE PERFECT PLACE

I was driving around looking at real estate with an agent when I fell in love with the perfect place—one that featured a great old garden with 50-year-old shrubs, a fine view but plenty of privacy, and a diner within easy walking distance.

Not so different from the features that songbirds look for when choosing a home. And just

No time to waste—a Bullock's oriole has to cram in establishing a territory, finding a partner, building a nest, raising a family, and fattening himself up before migration—all in just 12 weeks.

like us, nesting birds have distinct preferences when it comes to choosing a site. Some like the high-rise life of the treetops. Others are happy in a wide range of middle ground. And some songbirds prefer to keep their home down low, on or near the ground. As a general rule of thumb—but with plenty of exceptions—songbirds usually nest at about the same levels at which they forage.

Check the "Homebodies" table on page 282 to see which birds are most likely to nest at your place.

Birds of the Trees

Trees are a favored homesite for the tanagers, orioles, and other songbirds that spend most of their time above the ground. If you have to crane your neck to spot a songbird, it's a pretty safe bet that you'll have to crane your neck to spot its nest, too.

Wood warblers and vireos don't hold to this rule, though. Even though these small songbirds are usually moving through treetops when we spot them during their spring migration, that's not necessarily where they nest. Turns out that wood warblers nest at various heights, depending on their species. Their homesites range from close to the ground, to brush and shrubs, to trees.

But you'd never guess the right level by watching wood warblers on spring migration, because trees are where wood warblers usually feed when they're traveling through. That's where most of the food is at this time of year. In springtime, trees are loaded with blossoms, catkins, pollen, and thus insects—a practically continuous feast all the way along the warblers' migration route.

Moving from treetop to treetop may also be a shortcut for these traveling birds, which put a lot of miles under their little wings. Most of the approximately 50 species in North America head for the Far North and into Canada to breed, but several species do stay southward and may possibly nest in our backyards.

Birds of the Bush

From rhododendrons along rushing mountain streams, to willows at quiet ponds, to tall grasses in meadows, to lilacs in our own backyards, shrubby homesites and weedy brush beckon many species of songbirds.

It's mostly small birds, including buntings, goldfinches, some wood warblers, song and chipping sparrows, and the common yellowthroat, who prefer this level of homesite. A few notable exceptions include the large, svelte brown thrasher and its western cousins; the equally long-tailed northern mockingbird; and the somewhat more petite gray catbird. Cardinals and grosbeaks are fond of mid-level homes, too, although small trees may grab their attention as nest sites as well.

Upstairs, Downstairs

The American robin freely ranges about from the highest of the high (the tippy-tops of large trees), to the lowest of the low (our lawns), and everywhere in between. Its nest may be in any of those places, from 80 feet high in a tulip poplar to 3 feet off the ground in a rosebush—to right on our porch, on a nest shelf, or in the wreath on our door.

Robins don't nest on the ground, though. That location is reserved for many species of native sparrows, including the common and widespread streaky-brown song sparrow, our little friend with the dark spot on its breast. As we know from seeing these birds scratching under our feeders, native sparrows prefer to forage and

A Cape May warbler may stop for a bite to eat or a dip in the pool during spring or fall migration, but it nests in the spruce forests of the Far North.

The American goldfinch often builds its soft nest in a fork of goldenrod or other sturdy plants of the fields it frequents.

Courtship to Kids: A 12-Week Time Line

It's an incredibly hectic schedule and a nail-biter: Will the bird couple have enough time to raise its family and get ready for their return trip? Just barely. Here's the schedule for a hypothetical pair of migrant Bullock's orioles, raising its family in the Great Plains. Let's see how their timing works.

ACTIVITY	TIME IT TAKES
Male arriving from spring migration	Mid- to late May for Midwest birds; we'll say May 20.
Female arriving from spring migration	May 26
Forming a pair bond	It takes only a few days to a week for many migrant songbirds to pair off once the females return.
Nest building	In about a week (sometimes two for complicated constructions, such as oriole nests), the nest is finished, for many species.
Egg laying	Egg laying usually begins as soon as the home is built. Many songbirds lay an egg a day until their clutch is complete. That's another several days ticking by, since the Bullock's oriole usually lays four to five eggs.
Incubating eggs	10 days is about the average time a female sits on her eggs; Bullock's orioles usually incubate for 11 days.
Caring for nestlings	14 days of stuffing those babies' beaks, for most songbirds
Fledging nestlings	Fledglings are still fed by their parents for several days after leaving the nest.
Teaching fledglings	Young birds follow their parents around for another several days, still begging for food but learning to take care of themselves.
Preparing to leave for fall migration	And it's time to get ready to travel! The birds take a deep breath and start bulking up for the long trip south.

COUNTDOWN TO DEPARTURE
Departure is in early September; we'll say September 10 for this pair we're following. That's a stay of only 12 weeks on their nesting ground.
We're down to 11 weeks now.
10 weeks
8 weeks
7 weeks and 2 days
5 weeks and 5 days
3 weeks and 5 days
3 weeks
2½ weeks
Only a couple of weeks to rebuild the fat reserves that were depleted by the busy nesting season. No wonder so many songbirds show up at our feeders in fall migration!

live near the ground. Towhees also like the low life. Doves, on the other hand, forage almost exclusively on the ground but take to the trees to build their flimsy platform of sticks.

The moral of this story? Be sure to include plants of varying heights in your yard, so songbirds can take their pick.

A HOLE IN THE WALL

Even the cutest birdhouse on the block won't entice the vast majority of songbirds into calling it home. Most of our songbird friends build their nests in trees, bushes, and on the ground, not in natural cavities in trees or wooden posts, and not in birdhouses, either.

About 80 species of American birds do nest in natural cavities and birdhouses, though—but hang on. Don't go running for that hammer and saw just yet. Of those 80 or species, only a handful are songbirds. They include:

Bluebirds	Titmice
Chickadees	Wrens
Prothonotary warbler	

Yep, I bet I can guess what you're thinking. Even though there aren't many songbird species that want a hole in the wall, the ones that do nest in birdhouses are some of our most beloved backyard friends. Let's get hammering!

Shopping for Nest Boxes

If my backyard was half an acre or bigger, I'd probably overcome my well-founded fear of power tools and make my own birdhouses. I'd want a bluebird trail, a couple of wren houses, of course some chickadee McMansions, a titmouse hostel . . . maybe I could squeeze a dozen nest boxes into my space.

But since I only have a regular small-town yard (no, that dream house never came through, in case you're wondering; someone else beat me to it), I bought my three boxes instead. It doesn't pay to scrimp when you're buying birdhouses. Well-made nest boxes may seem expensive for a few pieces of wood: They run about $25 for a bluebird box. But they last for years. My chickadee house is at least 10 years old and it's still going strong.

If you're the handy type, you can make your own boxes instead, of course. Many books, including previous ones of mine, as well as websites, will guide you through the process.

Reputable nest box manufacturers, like those listed in the Resources section near the back of this book, make sure their labels list all the info we need to be successful bird landlords. Check the label to be sure each box will fit the songbirds you intend it to house, and mount it at the height it recommends.

Bluebirds of Happiness

The conventional wisdom for mounting bluebird boxes is to put them at a height of about 4 to 5 feet from the ground, to discourage predators. I'm not sure how that height became the norm, but bluebirds accept it instantly.

Only trouble is, house sparrows like it, too. And if any of these aggressive nonnative birds are in your neighborhood, they'll quickly drive the bluebirds out of house and home so they can claim it for themselves.

It's not easy to block house sparrows (also known as English sparrows) from a bluebird box. They seem to quickly outwit every trick in the book. To discourage house sparrows, try mounting your bluebird box way up high on a tree, instead of on a sparrow-level post. In the wild, bluebirds often nest in natural holes that may be 20 feet or more above the ground. So haul out that ladder, and set up your high-rise house.

Sometimes it's best just to give up on housing bluebirds, and put your energy into feeding them instead. It may be such a relief to stop being frustrated by house sparrows that you can then find that the bluebirds at your feeder truly bring you happiness.

Protection Is Paramount

It's a wonder that any bird nests survive, what with all the predators on the prowl for their residents. To help your little bird families stay safe,

Our own comings and goings deter wild predators, which may be why the American robin often nests on or near our houses.

Watch the Sun Rise
ENTRANCE HOLE TO THE EAST, PLEASE

Mount your nest boxes facing east, if you can. The morning sun is welcome after a chilly night. An eastward opening will also protect the nestlings inside the house from the full brunt of the mid-day sun, as well as from the intense rays in the afternoon when the sun begins to sink.

use cylindrical predator guards on your nest boxes, fasten sheet metal collars around your posts, and try other tricks from Chapter 16, Plain Talk about Pests.

Tattletale Genetics

We can see with our own eyes birds behaving badly, but anecdotal evidence isn't enough for scientists. It took genetics to really spell out what's going on.

Research into the sexual behavior of birds began in earnest in the mid-1990s, when genetics entered the scene, and is still going strong. Thanks to studies of DNA of eggs and birds, as well as scientific observations "in the field" that quantify nesting data and bird interactions, we now know that straying from a partner seems to be par for the course in songbirds.

"True sexual fidelity is hard to find," wrote science journalist Virginia Morell in a 1998 *Science* magazine article, "A New Look at Monogamy." But that's not such a bad thing, at least in an evolutionary sense. Offspring of mixed parentage may be stronger, bigger, more colorful, smarter, or in other ways a new-and-improved version of their parents. Bringing in a variety of genes benefits birds by giving them a better chance at future adaptations, too. And with the world changing as fast as it is, due to climate change and other big factors, adaptation can help songbirds survive.

Hedging Her Bets

Mothers want the best for their babies, and female songbirds are no different. If a female is unable to pair with a top-notch male and has to settle for a lesser guy—maybe she was a latecomer on migration or not as experienced as her female competitors—she may engage in "extra-pair couplings," often with bigger, stronger, healthier males, so that her eggs will carry some of their superior genetic material.

Not all species have been studied, so we can't say that all songbird females are flagrant flirts. But a DNA study of house finch nestlings proved that better than 8 percent of the offspring were sired by males other than Dad. Opportunity may play a part in this behavior, too: House finches whose nests were close to those of others had higher numbers of "illegitimate" babies.

"D-I-V-O-R-C-E"

It shouldn't surprise us that songbirds and people behave a lot alike—after all, we're animals, too. Biology rules behavior, and no matter how sophisticated or rational we may think we are,

(continued on page 292)

Get to Know Your Songbirds
Finches

"**D**o you hear the finches?" I asked a friend who stopped by for coffee one morning.

"I hear *something,*" she said with a laugh. "It sounds like a jungle out there."

The chirping, tweeting commotion was so loud that we could hear the birds from inside the house with the windows shut. The high, sweet songs of a hundred or more goldfinches were going constantly, joined by a dozen or so reddish house finches in full voice.

Finches are relatives of the singing canaries kept in cages in the 1950s as popular pets because of their sweet songs. Most wild finches have mellifluous voices that are a delight to listen to, especially in late winter when they first begin performing.

But a few finches' songs aren't exactly music to our ears. The raucous jungle effect in my backyard that day wasn't because of the goldfinches and their strawberry-colored cousins. Scores of small, streaky brown finches known as pine sis-

At first glance, a pine siskin can easily be mistaken for a female house finch, a species it often joins at the feeder or birdbath.

kins had been hanging around with their relatives for weeks, and now they were singing, too.

"Singing" is a matter of opinion. Pine siskin songs are melodic, but they're interspersed with what sounds more like fingernails scratching a blackboard—a rising, repeated *Zheeeet* that goes up the scale. Put a hundred of them together—or even 20—and you've got a cacophony that sounds like monkeys chattering along the Amazon.

Pine siskins may not be what most of us would consider songbirds, but since they're early birds, I welcome them, especially because they're almost always accompanied by their more-melodious finch relatives—American goldfinches, lesser goldfinches, Laurence's goldfinches, house finches, purple finches, or Cassin's finches.

Finches like to flock in close company from fall through spring, until they're ready to split up and go their separate ways at nesting season. All during winter, they pal around together, often in flocks of mixed species, arriving daily at our feeding stations for niger seed and other goodies. As spring approaches, the flocks grow bigger and bigger, collecting migrants that are passing through, like a magnet picking up iron filings.

If you have large trees in your yard, you've probably noticed that these little birds gather in a staging area in a tree before they alight at your feeder and between snacking sessions. Once the singing season starts, they'll fill the branches and whistle away for hours.

They'll retreat fast to that perching place when they fly up en masse in a panic, too. And panic they do, sometimes for discernible reasons (say, when a jay comes shrieking in), and sometimes for what seems like no reason at all, except that one bird took off in a hurry and the rest followed.

If you have no trees near your feeding area, it's easy to fake it: Just put up a nearby perch that will accommodate a good part of the gang. You'll get more traffic at your feeder, because the birds won't have to fly so far to find a place to regroup. And, whether or not you have trees in your yard, a faux perch near your feeders will give you a fine view of your singing finches—including those screechy siskins, whose accents of yellow plumage and incredibly tiny but sharp bills are best appreciated up close.

When to see them: American goldfinch and house finch, year-round; purple finch, Cassin's finch, lesser goldfinch, Laurence's goldfinch, pine siskin, fall through early spring, except in breeding range.

What to feed them: Niger, black sunflower, and hulled sunflower seeds, "finch mix"; some species are learning to enjoy safflower seed.

Other ways to attract them: Water is a guaranteed draw for all finches. When a flock arrives, refill the birdbath daily.

What they sound like: High, sweet, warbling voices; siskins, similar melody but mixed with rising screechy notes.

What to watch for: When a male and female finch arrive at the feeder as a pair, breeding season has begun. Watch for the male to tenderly feed choice bits of birdseed to his partner.

we're subject to the same elemental urges as those with feathers or fur. "Go forth and multiply"—that's not only the Bible, that's our evolutionary genes calling the shots.

I get a kick out of human terms used to describe other animals. Like "divorce," which means nearly the same thing in songbird terms as it does to us. Studying the mountain bluebird, researchers such as Dr. L. Scott Johnson of Towson University in Maryland concluded that a bonded pair may "divorce" should the female's adultery become known or even suspected. The pair argues, they may physically clash, and soon they separate, going on to find other mates.

Divided Loyalty

Watch the birds in your own backyard, and you'll see all sorts of less than lovey-dovey behavior in action. Sure, the male bird may sing sweetly to his female partner, and yes, the happy couple stays close while the family is getting under way.

But even though a male may be sweetly singing to his partner one minute, he's likely to be off gallivanting with the girl next door the next—or vice versa. Early morning seems to be prime time for females with a roving eye to visit the boy next door, even when his mate is sitting on their eggs.

Stepping Outside the Bounds

Biologists call these flings EPCs, or *extra-pair couplings*. They're the norm for so many species of songbirds, as well as other animals, that there's even a form of monogamy to describe them. In *social monogamy*, a pair bond is formed with the partners dedicated to each other in the necessities of daily life, but the partnership also allows for some "fooling around," shall we say, on the side.

As if this weren't enough to destroy the happily-ever-after myth, there's even worse news about songbird pairings. Romance? Forget it. Mate stealing, forcible mating, and what sure looks like other violence also take place on a regular basis in many bird species. David Barash and Judith Lipton, in their book *The Myth of Monogamy—Fidelity and Infidelity in Animals and People,* noted that "Males are sometimes aggressive in seeking EPCs, verging on rape, as in the case of indigo buntings."

Won't They Be Surprised?
RECYCLE FORMER BIRD HOMES

When a friend chain-sawed into an aspen tree that had keeled over, I spotted a good-size hole in one firewood log—a nest site from years past.

Cavity-nesting birds often use the same home year after year. Since the chain saw had cut far enough above and below the hole to leave it intact, all I had to do was screw a sturdy eye hook into the top of the log for hanging. Reusing, recycling, and a lot easier than making a nest box from scratch. Wonder if the same bird pair will find their old home?

Make a "Moat"

No alligators needed for these "moats"—just barriers that will make a predator pause. Snakes, cats, 'coons, and other nest raiders are leery of the sound and feel of crackly cellophane and rough chicken wire under their scales, paws, or feet. Their anxiety at stepping on your birdhouse "moat" may be enough to encourage them to hunt elsewhere.

Materials

Roll of cellophane in an earth-toned or green color (available at craft stores for a few dollars a roll)

Strip of 36-inch wide chicken wire, about 10 feet long

Method

1. Crumple cellophane into a strip about 8 to 10 inches wide.

2. Lay it in a circle around the bottom of your birdhouse post, about 4 feet from the post.

3. Top the cellophane with the strip of chicken wire, bending it as needed to make a flat "moat" around the post.

You can hide your cellophane moat with plants, but be sure to use low growers that stay at about 6 inches or less. Taller plants may allow predators to leap onto the post, avoiding the moat.

Still, despite all this extramarital behavior, the pair bond holds strong. Well, mostly.

Researchers have also discovered that, just as in the human world, it's the female's—rather than the male's—suspected infidelity that may be cause for a breakup. Female songbirds can be pretty sneaky about sneaking around, but when a male mountain bluebird thinks his partner is hiding such behavior, he may abandon her and take up with someone new. Barash and Lipton observed the reality involved: "It is probably no coincidence that mountain bluebird males attacked their mates after they had been deceived as to their fidelity; among this species, there is typically a reservoir of available, unmated females."

Lifelong Partners

Are your bluebirds back in their nest box this year? If you're like me, you probably take it for granted that those lovely creatures are the same pair returning year after year, right on schedule, to delight your family with their presence.

Or perhaps your thrashers return to the same part of your hedge each year to build their nest, or your song sparrows to your strawberry patch. Is it the same pair? It's hard to tell, because individual birds sure look alike.

Tagging or DNA testing the birds could give us the answer, but researchers seem to be slow to head down this path. Only one or two recent studies have focused on what scientists call the "longevity of the pair bond." Maybe it's because studies of songbird infidelity are, well, sexier.

They look lovey-dovey, but this mountain bluebird pair near Estes Park, Colorado, may seek flings on the side. The many nest boxes in the area increase the opportunity, which could lead the couple to "divorce."

SNEAK PEEK

I'm just as tempted as anybody to get a close look at nesting birds. I'd love to see what those eggs and those fuzzy-headed babies look like. But getting too close to the nest can have disastrous effects. Our lingering presence may alert predators to the nest's location. And once they know where it is, those songbirds don't stand a chance.

Besides, nesting birds need their privacy. Approaching their home will alarm and agitate them, because for all they know, we might have bad intentions.

"I'm Warning You!"

Songbirds can be so secretive when building their nests that we may never even know they're there until the trees or shrubs go bare in fall. A warning *Chip*, though, is often a dead giveaway that there's a songbird nest nearby. An alarmed bird will usually come out into the open somewhat to get a better look at the threat. Pay attention to these signals and watch the bird's behavior. If it goes back into the foliage, it likely has a nest in there.

To try to get a look at the nest, use your binoculars instead. If it's too well hidden to see, you'll at least get to enjoy watching the parents carrying food to their young.

Super Sleuth

Want to track down your nesting songbirds? Look for these 10 clues and you might be on to something.

1. A bird carrying nesting materials or tugging at twine in your garden

2. Parent birds carrying away eggshells

3. Parent bird carrying away a white fecal sac of nestling droppings to tidy the nest

4. Songbirds suddenly getting sneaky

5. Repeated trips to the same spot in shrubbery or trees, especially after eating soft foods at the feeder

6. The sounds of nestlings

7. Joining forces to harass a predator

8. Warning notes when you or your pets get too close

9. Cowbirds showing interest in a particular area

10. Singing

SUPPORTING CAST

It was a particularly nasty evening, blowing and raining, when I pulled into a campground in Nevada and hurried to get my little tent set up.

As usual, I couldn't find the tent stakes, which were buried somewhere in the miscellaneous clutter that filled my car. No problem, I figured: My body would weigh down the tent just fine.

I wasn't counting on that late-night pit stop, though. When I got back to the campsite, the tent lay yards away, collapsed against the sagebrush that had snagged it. This time, I dug out the stakes and tied it down tight, before I fluffed up my sleeping bag and settled in again.

A songbird can't just set its nest on a branch, like I tried to set my tent on the ground. Whether its little home is on the ground or in the branches, it needs to be well anchored so it doesn't blow away. That's where the nest materials in our backyards come in handy. They're the supporting cast, as well as the soft lining, and songbirds will flock to them.

Stealth Fighter
SNEAKY TRICKS WIN A MATE

One fine May morning, I watched a duel between two male Baltimore orioles, one of whom had already won the affection of a female and the other who was still without a partner. The bonded pair had already consummated their union, but egg laying hadn't yet begun, and the loner was still trying desperately to woo the female away.

"Woo" isn't quite the word for it. A competing male's attempts are more like an attack of pillaging Huns than a whisper of sweet nothings. What the second male wanted to do was drive out the first so he could lay claim to the bride—by force if necessary.

While the two males were diving and swooping around and around, a third male saw his chance. He flew in, pursued the female, and mated with her while her partner and her other suitor were otherwise occupied.

The Natural Way

Every species of songbird has its preferred materials for building its home, but nearly all birds are quick to accept an easy handout. Orioles, robins, vireos, titmice, and many others will eagerly take us up on an offering of nesting materials in a basket or wire suet cage, or draped on bushes and lawn.

But remember, songbirds usually collect natural materials for their nests, and that's where our garden plants can play an important part in attracting these homemakers.

Going Down

Throw pillows and bed pillows packed with down, down and feathers, or feathers are almost giveaways at thrift shops and garage sales, often sold for $1 or less. Down vests, coats, and comforters can be bargains, too.

No need to get picky about stains or saggy spots—inside these items is enough fluff to supply your songbirds with nesting material for years to come. The stuffing is prized by nest-building chickadees, titmice, wrens, finches, and a host of other songbirds in search of a soft lining.

Nest Materials from the Garden

I've seen songbirds pulling fibers or collecting beakfuls of fluff from these plants in my backyard. Keep your eye out for your own birds at work, and I'm sure you'll be able to add other plants to the list.

A cactus wren gathers grass to make a soft lining for its nest in a prickly cholla cactus.

A-Tisket, A-Tasket
HANG A BASKET OF NEST MATERIALS

A basket makes a fine container for a self-serve selection of nest materials for songbirds. Fill the basket loosely with cosmetic cotton balls, strips of cloth, natural unspun wool, Spanish moss, string, yarn, twine, and any other fluff or fibers you can find.

Do add feathers, too. But don't offer dryer lint: The tiny bits of fiber get sticky and matted when damp.

String Tricks

A LOOSE KNOT KEEPS ORIOLES IN VIEW

Orioles are adept at undoing loose knots and even some pretty tight ones, too, when they spy a string for their nests. To give yourself a longer chance to view these gorgeous creatures in your yard, knot or twist pieces of string, instead of simply draping them, onto the twigs of your trees or onto your trellis, so you can watch the orioles deftly untying their prizes.

Fibers for Attaching and Weaving Nests

Butterfly weed (*Asclepias tuberosa*)

Dogbane (*Apocynum androsaemifolium*)

Flax (*Linum* spp.), both annual and perennial

Indian hemp (*Apocynum cannabinum*)

Hollyhock (*Alcea rosea*)

Mallows (*Malva* spp.)

Milkweeds (*Asclepias* spp.)

Yuccas (*Yucca* spp.)

Fluff for a Soft Lining

Clematis seedheads (*Clematis* spp.)

Cottonwood and poplar catkins (*Populus* spp.)

Ferns (*Osmunda* spp. and others)

Fleabane daisies (*Erigeron* spp.)

Milkweeds (*Asclepias* spp.)

Oak catkins (*Quercus* spp.)

Pussywillows (*Salix* spp.)

Nature's Glue

Ever walk into a spiderweb? It's tricky to peel those tightly plastered strands off our faces and clothes, because they stick so well to us and to each other.

A trap for insects and for us unwary types, spider silk is an ideal natural glue for the following songbirds to use in their nests:

- Vireos, wood warblers, and other small songbirds that fashion delicate hanging nests depend on sticky spider silk to suspend their homes from twiggy supports.

- Tiny ruby-crowned and golden-crowned kinglets use spider egg cases and silk to glue their circlet nests in place and keep the fine materials together.

- Orioles incorporate spider silk in their complicated weavings.

- American goldfinches and lesser goldfinches use spider silk to attach their nests.

- Indigo, lazuli, and painted buntings use spider silk to secure and wrap their nests and to strengthen their rims.

Any sort of spider silk is fair game to songbirds. Classic webs, big and small; webs made into sheets or funnels; single strands; and silken spider egg cases are all sought and snatched for their nests.

A British cousin of our chickadees, the blue tit collects hair for its nest, just as our black-capped, Carolina, mountain, and other chick-a-dee-dees do.

Speaking of Tents

Once we gain an appreciation for how insects and birds are connected, it's hard to think of any bugs as pests: They're bird attractors, instead.

Even tent caterpillars have their fans. Lazuli buntings take full advantage of tent caterpillar nests, collecting the silken webbing for their own houses. The female bunting, who does the construction duties, often returns over and over to the same tent caterpillar hideout until her nest is finished. Another reason not to spray those pesky 'pillars: The caterpillars themselves make fine food for wood warblers, orioles, and other songbirds.

Tied Down

Long blades of dead grass are the usual "tent stakes" for many species of native sparrows and buntings. These small birds nab and weave the grass tie-downs around neighboring rooted plants to securely hold their nests in place.

To give them a ready building supply—and enjoy watching them visit your backyard "Home Depot"—plant a clump of miscanthus ornamental grass (*Miscanthus* 'Morning Light' is a pretty one). The dead blades are long, strong, and flexible, and my backyard birds snatch them up in nesting season. Fine grasses, such as ornamental blue fescue (*Festuca glauca*), are also in high demand. Chipping sparrows, song sparrows, juncos, and many other songbirds use the thin, flexible, dried blades to make the delicate inner part of their nests.

You're also likely to see songbirds collecting tan blades of dead grass in places where the lawn mower hasn't reached—along fences, in meadow gardens, or anywhere else they can find the prized material. Miscanthus and other ornamental grass clumps always include some dead leaf blades at their base, even during growing season, so songbirds will find a ready supply. Be

To everything, there is a purpose: Tent caterpillars are food for orioles and other songbirds, and their silk is bird nest material.

The Dark Side of Squirrels
SONGBIRD NESTS SPELL A FINE MEAL

Squirrels can be real pests at the feeding station—or personable charmers, depending on how we think of them—but there's no denying that they have a dark side when it comes to bird nests. Songbird eggs and young hatchlings are simply another fine meal to these sharp-toothed rodents.

A ready source of winter food from us can encourage the climbing, leaping bushytails into making their own nests in or near our yards. That's something to think about when we stick another ear of corn on the squirrel feeder. For more on squirrels, see Chapter 16, "Plain Talk about Pests."

sure to let some long, dead stragglers remain when you give the plants their crew cuts in late winter.

GROWING UP

Back in the old days, until just after World War I, it was easy to tell at a glance who was a boy and who was a man: Boys wore short pants. Graduating from knee-length knickerbockers to trousers was a big day in a boy's life. It meant he was now one of the grownups.

Clothes make the man, even in the bird kingdom—or at least make it easy to see who's reached breeding age. It's not short pants but the color of feathers that tells us at a glance which bird's an adult and which hasn't quite reached dating age yet. A young bird's first suit of feathers can vary a lot from its adult outfit, in many bird species.

First year birds are youngsters that were hatched last summer and haven't reached their full adult plumage yet. The timing of their molt,

(continued on page 302)

Fluffy seedheads of ornamental grasses, especially miscanthus (*Miscanthus*) and pampas grass (*Cortaderia*), may be woven into bird nests, like this one abandoned by a song sparrow. Looks like the seedheads made a soft substitute for the feathers that usually serve to line the nest.

Feather "Flowers" Wreath

It's fun to watch songbirds sort through nesting materials to find just the right pieces, and this wreath will keep them busy at that all season long. The "flowers" are made from down and feathers; the "leaves" are linen and burlap; tendrils come from an unraveled sweater. The cost of this wreath? About $2, if you recycle your own clothes or shop garage sales.

Materials

Loosely woven, natural tan or white cotton sweater

Large scissors

Natural burlap, about 1 yard

Old clothing item of pure linen

Plastic mesh onion bag

Old down or feather throw pillow

Twist ties

White chicken or duck feathers, generous handful for a 12-inch wreath; more for larger wreath (available at craft stores)

Packed-straw wreath form, 12 inches to 24 inches in diameter

Floral picks for attaching materials to wreath

Method

1. Cut any ribbing off the bottom of the sweater.

2. Cut a 3- to 4-inch-wide strip from the bottom of the sweater. Slice off the seams, so you're left with two strips of knit yarn; cut them into 6-inch lengths.

3. Find a loose end of a strip and pull gently while it unravels. (Some knits will unravel from either side; some only unravel in one direction, so you may need to do some experimenting.) Unravel about 3 inches of the strip. Make several of these.

4. Cut leaf shapes, each about 6 to 8 inches long, from the burlap and from the linen clothing item. Don't include any seams in the leaves; we want them to unravel. Set aside.

5. Cut 6- to 8-inch squares of plastic mesh from the onion bag. Take a

handful of feather/down stuffing from the throw pillow, squeeze it tightly, and quickly wrap it in a square of mesh before it drifts all over the place. Fasten the little bundle with a twist tie.

6. Attach the leaves in groups of three all around the wreath, using the floral picks.

7. Attach the mesh bags of down and small feathers here and there around the wreath with floral picks; these are the flower centers.

8. Poke the curled chicken or duck feathers into the mesh bags to make petals.

9. Attach the strips of partly unraveled sweater yarn with floral picks, tucking the knitted ends under leaves.

10. Hang the wreath on a wooden fence or post. Secure it at top and bottom, so it stays in place when songbirds tug at the materials.

as well as its extent, can vary from one species to another. So some birders narrow down their descriptions even further, using the term *first winter* birds to describe youngsters in their first cold season—when they're still wearing the avian equivalent of short pants.

Many first-winter male birds look a lot more like their mom than their dad. We have to look extra close to figure out who's who, especially when the migrants return in spring and young birds still haven't switched into their adult suits.

Fool-'Em Plumage

I used to wonder why I saw so many olive-green female scarlet tanagers during fall migration, but only rarely a bright red male. Eventually, I

Just to Confuse Us

Who's still wearing short pants? Which one's a he and which one's a she? Use these clues to figure out the age and sex of your songbirds when they aren't in full regalia.

SONGBIRD	STAGE OF LIFE	PLUMAGE DIFFERENCE
Buntings: Indigo and lazuli	Adult males, nonbreeding season, and first-year males	Blotchy blue and brown
Finch: House and purple	First-winter males	Many lack any rosy red at all.
Grosbeaks: Black-headed, blue, and rose-breasted	First-winter males	Look similar to females but with a wash of adult color
Oriole: Hooded	Adult males, nonbreeding season	Yellow-orange instead of rich orange
Orioles: Most species	First-year males	Resemble females
Sparrows, native: White-crowned, white-throated, and many others	First-winter birds	Adult males and females look alike in these species, but first-winter birds don't have the distinctive head coloring of adults.
Tanagers	First-winter males	Look like females; by the time they return in spring, they're sporting some red on their heads and chests.
Tanagers: Scarlet and western	Adult males, nonbreeding season	Similar to females, but with black wings
Wood warblers	Adult males, nonbreeding season, and first-winter males	Look like females, with subtle differences

Speckled Bellies
THRUSH FAMILY TIES ARE SHOWN BY SPOTS

A strongly spotted breast is the hallmark of the wood thrush and some of its cousins in the Thrush family. But not all adult thrush species sport the markings or are named "thrush." The American robin is a thrush, as are our beautiful bluebirds. The varied thrush has no freckles, and the veery has faint streaks instead.

In nesting season, though, it's simple to tell which young birds are kissing cousins in the same family. All young thrushes, including robins and bluebirds, wear spots on their breasts.

realized I *was* looking at males—they had simply changed into their off-season outfits, which look a lot like the females'. The key detail I finally noticed? Males retain the black color of their wings.

First-year birds can be tricky to recognize, too, before they don their grownup plumage. When I used to see white-crowned sparrows with a dingy head stripe instead of a bright one, I figured they were females. Less showy, made sense. Wrong again—adult male and female white-crowneds look alike. I was looking at young birds.

CHAPTER 16

Plain Talk about Pests

It's a sickening moment when we discover that a nest of baby robins or a bluebird box has been destroyed during the night by a predator. Oh, no, the poor babies! Are the parents okay? What got 'em, anyhow? Probably one of those doggone raccoons, I'll bet.

Worse yet is when we eventually realize that we could've done something to keep our birds safe. Could've attached a predator guard at the nest box entrance. Kept a cat indoors instead of letting it out to prowl at night. Installed a metal guard blocking the 'coon's climb up the birdhouse post.

And what about the hawk that takes a keen interest in our bird feeder? The first day it shows up, we're mesmerized and even proud ("Guess what's at my feeder? A Cooper's hawk!"). Until it nabs its first chickadee or mourning dove, that is. Then we remember, oh right, hawks eat other birds.

The list goes on, with possible dangers on every side—on the ground, in the bushes, in the air, 24/7.

Not all pests are dangerous to songbirds in a life-or-death way, but they are all deterrents to our efforts to attract and host songbirds. Every one of the less-than-welcome critters we'll talk about in this chapter can cause songbirds to desert our feeders—or be reluctant to come to them in the first place. Keeping away pests in our backyards is only fair to the songbirds we've coaxed into being there. It pays off for us, too, because songbirds that feel safe spend more time with us.

PEST BIRDS

Everyday feeder frustrations aren't always a matter of life or death. Starlings, for instance, can be irritating enough to make us want to pull our hair out. They can cause our songbirds to look for easier places to eat or less stressful spots to nest. Starlings may cost us extra money, too, because they gobble up so much food. But they aren't going to directly harm our songbird friends.

Other common pest birds can, indeed, directly harm songbirds and their families. Often, there's not much we can do to prevent the situation, because predation is a natural part of nature, and songbirds are near the bottom of the totem pole in the eat-or-be-eaten world. But we can try a number of tricks to minimize the pests in our own yards. We owe it to our singing friends.

FOOD WORTH FIGHTING FOR

My friend's dogs know the limits: If food hits the floor, it's fair game. Anything else, they can only wait and drool and gaze with soulful yearning eyes, hoping the humans will give in and share.

The first sighting of a sharp-shinned hawk (or similar Cooper's) in the backyard is a thrill. Then we realize . . . this guy's here to eat our birds!

A piece of pizza on the coffee table is almost more than they can bear, but they know it's "Paws off."

Good thing, because if I had to keep pushing the dogs away from my plate when I was trying to enjoy my food, I'd soon give up, especially if they bared their teeth at me to show they meant business. I'm not going to fight for my meal (well, unless anyone tries to snag my last french fry).

And songbirds act the same way.

When pest birds or squirrels claim a feeder, it's the songbirds that give up first. Only the northern mockingbird gets feisty about staking a claim. Bluebirds, wrens, robins, cardinals, chickadees, and all the others simply say, "Go ahead, if you want it that badly," and fly off to find food elsewhere.

That's not to say that songbirds are angels when it comes to feeder behavior. Competition is natural there. Finches, grosbeaks, cardinals, and others that feed in groups can get mighty irritable, jabbing at neighbors that get a little too close. A brown thrasher busy at the mealworm feeder doesn't take kindly to the house wren that tries to horn in.

In nearly all cases, the challenged songbird quickly yields to the more aggressive one.

Too Much of a Good Thing

My own feeding setup is "Come one, come all," or so I like to believe. Yet there are still times when I'm ready to run outside, yelling "Shoo! Shoo!" like a . . . well, like a person who gets really aggravated at feeder greedies.

When a flock of grackles—several hundred strong—stops in while passing through on early spring migration, dollar signs flash in my head as I watch them plow through the cracked corn, the

Predators from Both Perspectives

It's easier to relate to how songbirds feel about predators and other pests when we translate their experiences into those in our own lives.

SONGBIRD PESTS AND PREDATORS	WHAT THEY'D BE LIKE FOR US	SONGBIRDS' SOLUTION
A cat in the backyard	Would you invite your friends to dinner and let a mountain lion stalk the dining room?	Forsake the feeder or berries until the cat is gone.
Night-roaming raccoons, opossums, snakes, or cats in nesting season	Would you let your kids spend the night in sleeping bags in a swamp infested with hungry alligators?	Choose the most protected nest site possible, sleep with one eye open, and defend the family to the death.
Hawks	Would you enjoy a picnic under a construction crane swinging a grand piano, attached by garden twine, back and forth overhead?	Stay hidden, stay alert; desert the feeder and maybe the entire backyard if the trouble continues.
Owls	Would you sleep outdoors on the lawn if you knew a pterodactyl's talons could strike at any moment?	Roost and nest deep in twiggy shrubs, evergreens, and dense trees, where branches and possibly thorns may prevent a nocturnal attack.
Starlings	Would you stay at a bistro when 20 busloads of hungry travelers arrive and hurry in?	Try to grab a bite at the edge of the crowd, or abandon the feeder.

sunflower seed, the seed mix, and anything else they can get their beaks into.

Everybody has their own list of birds they'd rather not see at their feeders. But one species is a standout: starlings.

Starlings

If starlings were as few and far between as, say, western tanagers, we'd all be wanting them. They're just as fascinating as any other bird, and their complicated warbling song is lovely to listen to. Plus, when you really look at a starling, you'll see the bird is beautiful. Squat and plump, sure, but decorated with little stars in fall and winter, and glistening purple and green in spring and summer.

Starlings aren't native to North America. Their full name, according to the American Ornithologists' Union, is European starling, and Europe is where they hail from. Every starling we see in

(continued on page 310)

Get to Know Your Songbirds
Northern Mockingbird

The big, long-tailed mockingbird, one of the mimic thrushes, is famed for its serenades after dark. The bird takes a perch way up high, all the better to let its song be heard, I suppose, and sings just as full-throated as during the day.

Before the days of cable TV, a metal television antenna on the roof of a house was a highly favored singing spot. Now that those artifacts are mostly gone, the mockingbird often makes do with a chimney—or a satellite dish.

Did I say "famed" for its serenades? Although mockers have been praised in story and song, the word is more like "notorious" to anyone whose rooftop is chosen by one of these highly vocal birds. The concert is almost impossible to sleep through, because the loud song keeps changing. Rhythm, pitch, phrasing—it's start and stop and veer in another direction. For hours.

The mockingbird is just doing what mockingbirds do: imitating. It's a fascinating performance to listen to, because it's a mini-course in birdsong all coming from one bird. With almost perfect inflection, the mocker can run through the trademark songs of a dozen different species or more.

The virtuoso does the same thing in his daytime singing, too. And, like a hip-hop DJ sampling records, he often adds snatches of other sounds to the mix, from frog and insect calls to human sounds, including the same whistle you use to call your dog, the squeal of your water faucet or that gate hinge that needs a drop of oil, and the ringtone of your cell phone.

If you're lucky enough to have a mockingbird in residence during the summer singing season, be sure to listen closely to that repertoire before you slam the window and pull the covers over your head. It's remarkable. One

With personality to spare, the bold mockingbird inspires strong feelings. "Love 'm!" "Hate 'm!" He's just being a mockingbird.

mockingbird appreciator on Long Island says her bird's repertoire mimics as many as eight creatures and goes something like this: cardinal-cardinal/titmouse–song sparrow/wren–house finch/redwing blackbird–lawnmower–cat.

Its amazing song also varies depending on where the mockingbird lives. The bird imitates the sounds it hears, so a mocker in Massachusetts sings a far different set than the same species in Mississippi.

Mockingbirds have other less than endearing habits, too. They're thugs at the feeder, chasing away every other bird that tries to approach, so they can have all the goodies to themselves.

A lone mocker—and these birds are loners, except in breeding season—can easily guard an entire backyard against all comers, including cats.

You can remove the bird food for a while, in hopes that the mocker will move elsewhere. But I love these clever, courageous birds, so I take a different tack.

I add more feeders and get even more generous with the handouts. After all, even a mocker can't be in two places at once, and he soon starts to feel silly himself, it seems, doing nothing but dashing hither and yon. Eventually the bird narrows its claim to just one or two favorite feeders, and my other birds can eat in peace. Mostly. Once in a while, the mocker just can't help charging at the other customers. They soon settle back in to eat.

A mocker in residence may be bad news for us sleepers and our feeder guests, but it's great news for nesting songbirds. Snakes are one of the worst predators of bird nests, and to a mocker, the slithery creatures are a sworn enemy. Like a snake charmer, the bird dances in front of a snake on the ground, flashing its white wing patches, perhaps to dazzle and confuse the reptile. Then it attacks without warning, pecking ferociously.

I've even seen mockingbirds "dance" in front of a poisonous copperhead snake. The mocker kept a respectful distance, but made enough of a fuss to drive the serpent away. I've also seen one courageous bird do a prolonged battle with an inflatable plastic snake I'd put in my garden as a joke. Day after day, the poor bird wore himself to a frazzle trying to make the super-size faux snake slither away.

When to see them: Year-round

What to feed them: Suet and other soft foods; white proso millet; fresh and dried fruits and berries

Other ways to attract them: Keep a pedestal or ground-level birdbath fresh and filled. Plant thorny shrub roses, such as *Rosa rugosa*, for nesting. Add a grape (*Vitis* spp.) arbor for fruit and nesting.

What they sound like: The king of mimics, with a long and varied repertoire of other bird songs and calls interspersed with notes of its own. Songs vary by region, because the mocker imitates birds and other sounds (avian, animal, human, and even mechanical) he hears around him.

What to watch for: Aggressive and territorial at the feeder, the mockingbird is also one of the chief policemen of songbirds. A fearless fighter, he'll chase away snakes, squirrels, chipmunks, and even cats. Watch your head if there's a nest nearby.

America is descended from the original hundred birds that were released in New York back in 1890 and 1891. In only about 120 years, those 100 birds exploded into an American population now estimated at a jaw-dropping 200 million starlings flocking across the country.

And we think a bunch of 20 in our backyard is bad news? Guess we should count our blessings.

Starlings have hearty appetites, but they also have found a niche that in my mind helps make up for the food they gobble at our feeders: They eat a huge number of beetle grubs in our lawns, waddling about and stabbing with their long bills to reach their prey. The good news: A huge number of those grubs are Japanese beetles-to-be.

Studies of tasting ability have shown that starlings, unlike many songbirds, can discern salt, some sugars, astringent tannin, and tart citric acid. Perhaps that's because these birds eat such a varied diet. From stray french fries to fruit to insects to birdseed to grains, starlings eat just about anything they can manage to get down their throats. In California, they even drink the nectar

A generous spread of cheap food elsewhere may distract house sparrows and starlings from feeder treats meant for other birds.

All by Myself
"DOCILE" GROSBEAKS GET GREEDY

The lovely, docile pine grosbeaks I watch all winter can be vicious when it comes to food. The prime place of contention is a lantern-shaped hopper feeder that has limited perching room around its octagonal tray. Luckily, the hopper blocks the birds on its far side from view. Unless their view of each other is blocked by the central hopper, the grosbeaks don't eat companionably. Even a bonded pair, which usually sticks together, can have a bad day when the female decides she wants the whole place to herself.

Chink the Cracks

BLOCK STARLINGS FROM SHARING YOUR HOUSE

Starling nests are often just as unwelcome as a horde of the birds at the feeder. These adaptable birds are cavity nesters, and they manage to find any crack or loose board in house siding or soffits. Before you know it, the house is decorated with splashes of "whitewash," and there's a loud bunch of babies hollering in your wall.

Nesting season starts early, so get out there in late winter and start looking for possible access holes. Patch any cracks or holes you find; starlings are adept at wiggling under a loose shingle, and they can fit through a 1½- to 2-inch diameter opening. For a quick fix for soffit cracks, consider using expanding insulating foam; it hardens fast to fill the space and keep starlings from slipping in.

from the brilliant orange-red blossoms of coral trees (*Erythrina* spp.) planted along the streets.

While starlings may have their idiosyncrasies and faults, nest robbing isn't one of them. Although these birds will happily gobble meat scraps, cooked eggs, or meaty pet food, they don't seek out songbird nests as a food source.

A Little Too Crowded

The sheer numbers in a flock of starlings or grackles can be such intimidating competition to songbirds that it causes them to give up on a feeder or even an entire backyard, if the intrusion is frequent enough. Although the birds in the flock aren't aggressive, their very presence crowds feeders and foraging areas on the ground, causing other birds to back off.

Starlings don't usually hang out at a feeder all day. When the flock departs, grab your chance and set out your special treats for your other birds—the cup of mealworms, the homemade foods, the nut spread. Serve only a small quan-

tity, so it gets consumed before the starlings come back.

Mass Consumption

A block of suet can disappear in a day when a half-dozen starlings turn their attention to it. A peanut-butter log feeder might be emptied in a single feeding frenzy, a dish of mealworms decimated in minutes.

"Feeder hogs!" many folks say scornfully, as they watch the starlings attack the soft foods they most enjoy. Big eaters, yes, but starlings are no greedier than other birds. They eat fast and furious, because they've learned to take advantage of food when it's available.

Goldfinches often sit at our tube feeder all day long, nibbling at tiny niger seeds. Are they gluttons? We hardly notice all the seeds they consume, because each little bird eats only an ounce or so of seeds each day—the amount that's just right for its small body.

Starling appetites are way more noticeable,

(continued on page 314)

No Admittance

The type of feeder you choose can make a big difference in which birds it attracts. Pest birds will generally avoid feeders that are difficult to get a grip on, favoring easier opportunities. You'll find many models of feeders that permit only smaller birds to reach the food. Here are the basic versions; choose whichever kind or kinds you like best.

DETERRENT FEEDER	FOODS	SONGBIRDS THAT CAN ACCESS IT	PEST BIRDS DETERRED
A feeder within a cage of metal bars or a wire grid	Seed, fruit, suet or soft foods, mealworms	Buntings, chickadees, creepers, finches, kinglets, titmice, vireos, wood warblers, wrens. Possibly bluebirds, gray catbird, northern cardinal, orioles, tanagers. Plus black-headed, blue, and rose-breasted grosbeaks, depending on the spacing of the bars or grid.	Blackbirds, grackles, starlings. House sparrows may use it, however.
Weighted hopper feeder, in which the food supply is shut off when a large bird lands on the perching bar	Seed, seed-and-fruit mixes	Buntings, chickadees, finches, kinglets, titmice, vireos, wood warblers, wrens. Possibly bluebirds, gray catbird, northern cardinal, orioles, tanagers. Plus black-headed, blue, and rose-breasted grosbeaks, depending on the sensitivity of the mechanism.	Blackbirds, grackles, most starlings. House sparrows may use it, however. Clever starlings may figure out how to outwit it by clinging to the feeder itself to grab a bite.
Small plastic window feeder	Seed, soft foods, mealworms	Buntings, chickadees, finches, kinglets, titmice, vireos, wood warblers, wrens	Blackbirds, grackles, and starlings are generally reluctant to approach a window. House sparrows may adapt.

DETERRENT FEEDER	FOODS	SONGBIRDS THAT CAN ACCESS IT	PEST BIRDS DETERRED
Domed feeder	Seed, soft foods, mealworms	The distance between the dome and the dish is what limits access; adjust it to exclude large birds, and it'll still attract buntings, chickadees, finches, kinglets, titmice, vireos, wood warblers, wrens	Blackbirds, grackles, starlings. House sparrows may use it, unless you lower the dome even further (which will block buntings and finches, as well).
Upside-down suet feeder, with suet held horizontally beneath a roof	Suet	Brown creepers, chickadees, titmice, wrens, yellow-rumped warbler	Blackbirds, grackles, house sparrows. Unfortunately, starlings may quickly learn how to outwit this feeder.
Tube feeder made from plastic for niger seed or from metal with holes for larger seeds	Niger, millet, sunflower, safflower, finch seed mixes; no nuts or hulled sunflower seed	Buntings, chickadees, finches, northern cardinal, plus black-headed, blue, and rose-breasted grosbeaks, titmice	Small seeds aren't usually enticing enough for blackbirds, grackles, or starlings to bother with, although the feeder may still interest house sparrows.
Bluebird feeder made of an enclosed box with entrance hole	Suet, soft foods, nuts, mealworms, and other premium songbird foods	Bluebirds, chickadees, titmice, wrens	Blackbirds, grackles, starlings. House sparrows may learn how to use it.
Nectar feeder	Sugar water	Orioles, tanagers, wood warblers	Of no interest to blackbirds, grackles, house sparrows, starlings

for sure, and their eating habits aren't exactly restrained. They stab and swallow chunks of soft foods that cost a pretty penny. They gobble with gusto, noisily fighting with each other over the food. They're big birds, so they eat more food. But they're no more gluttons than goldfinches are.

If starlings, blackbirds, grackles, evening grosbeaks, or house sparrows showed up singly or only a few at a time, we'd probably welcome them at our feeders. We'd never notice the birds consuming a large amount of food for their large size, or at least we wouldn't feel resentful, because we'd prize seeing the birds.

But as for the cumulative effect of a whole flock of big birds—well, let's try some tricks for keeping them from eating us out of house and home.

Discouraging Crowds of Pest Birds

We've got three possible options for keeping flocks of pest birds from the feeders we want to reserve for songbirds and other desirable birds. Try these methods to deter starlings, red-winged and other blackbirds, grackles, and house sparrows from eating all the songbirds' goodies:

- Block them by using caged feeders and other models that they can't access.
- Divert their attention by putting out a tempting spread of food for them elsewhere, as far away from songbird feeders and soft-food feeders as you can manage.
- Change the menu at seed feeders to foods they can't easily eat or aren't interested in.

I use all three tricks, since these birds can be a real plague in my small town, which borders the farm fields where enormous flocks numbering in the tens of thousands range about in winter.

Draw 'Em Away with a Decoy Feeder
Starlings, blackbirds, and grackles enjoy nothing better than a generous spread of food. Luckily, some of their top favorites are dirt cheap.

Trick or Treat
Anti-Starling Safflower

Rose-breasted grosbeaks, cardinals, chickadees, and many other songbirds have recently taken to safflower seeds in a big way. These white, pointed seeds have tough shells to crack, and starlings don't have the bills that can do the job. If you're plagued by starlings, switch to safflower seed instead of sunflower and seed mix. The pest birds will soon go elsewhere to find something to eat.

As for the claims that squirrels don't eat safflower, don't believe it. Like songbirds, they, too, are quickly learning that the meaty white seeds are worth investigating.

House sparrows, too, may be diverted from songbird feeders by an offering of decoy grains. Try these menu items to lure pests away from your other feeders.

- Cracked corn is a powerful enough decoy all by itself for blackbirds, grackles, and house sparrows. If starlings are your problem, add kitchen leftovers, because corn alone won't hold their attention for long.

- Chicken scratch or other poultry feed, usually based on ground wheat or corn; just pennies a pound at a feed mill or farm store

- Dry dog or cat food, served as is if it's in small pieces, or moistened if in larger chunks

- Stale bread, bagels, hot-dog buns

- Old muffins, cake, and other baked goods

- Crackers or cereal

- Leftover pasta, mac-and-cheese, pizza, sandwiches, or whatever scraps you may have

- Ham bones and fat

- Halved apples or oranges that are past their prime

To avoid attracting rodents, feed only as much as the birds can clean up in a single day. I put the feast right on the ground, so the flock has plenty of room to argue over the best pieces; you can also offer the banquet in a low tray feeder.

"Exclude" or "Discourage"?

Read the label descriptions on feeders to make sure you're getting ones that are most likely to keep out pest birds. An upside-down suet feeder or tube feeder, for instance, may "discourage" starlings or house sparrows, but it won't stop them entirely—only until they figure out how to use it. A caged feeder, however, will definitely exclude starlings.

Scare Tactics

Sometimes the simplest solutions are the most effective. Try scaring away the flock of starlings, blackbirds, or grackles by bursting out the door, yelling, clapping, banging pans, or charging at them whenever they settle down in your backyard. After a few rounds of such inhospitable treatment, they just might take the hint and move on.

This trick works best before the pest birds discover what's delicious in your feeders. Once these birds know there are goodies available, they're likely to be more determined. Dash outdoors as soon as you see the first flock.

NEST PREDATORS

Adding plant cover to our yards and near our feeders gives songbirds a fighting chance against hawks and helps them out if a cat comes prowling.

A hawk's attack is straightforward, but some of the creatures that prey on our songbird friends are way sneakier. Let's start with a trio of pests that we may not even recognize as problems: squirrels, chipmunks, and cowbirds. All three are wolves in sheep's clothing, as far as nesting birds are concerned.

Squirrels and Chipmunks

Aw, what a cute little chipmunk! A charmer for sure, and most of us are thrilled when the little striped guy ventures to the feeder or patio for a handful of nuts or seeds.

But the songbirds in our yard have a different opinion. To them, the adorable chipmunk is a big threat. Like his larger cousins, the squirrels, Chippy has a big appetite for bird eggs and helpless nestlings—as well as the ability to climb to bird nests or sniff out ground-nesting towhees, thrushes, and native sparrows.

Most anti-squirrel methods focus on the fact that these rodents can gobble up birdseed in nothing flat. But there's an even bigger reason for not encouraging squirrels into our backyards—they're nest destroyers.

The frenzied alarm calls of songbirds in our backyards are often due to squirrels. Luckily, a squirrel isn't too difficult for determined parent birds to drive off. But each foray takes a toll on the watchful parents. And if two or more squirrels join forces, one can dart in and snatch an egg or baby while the bird defenders are occupied with the other.

Squirrels and chipmunks are, of course, only a natural part of the balance of nature. Songbirds lay a good-size clutch of eggs, because very few of the nestlings make it to adulthood. And the birds will re-nest if their first batch is totally destroyed.

Squirrels may be cute at the feeder, but they're natural predators of songbird nests.

Still, this is a dilemma that each of us will have to decide for ourselves. Do we enjoy the squirrels' antics at the corncob wheel or peanut box, knowing that these creatures may decimate the bird nests in the neighborhood? Or do we put up a "Squirrels Keep Out" sign and invest in feeders they can't access, in hopes that they'll look for food elsewhere? Weigh these factors before you decide:

- Like songbirds and all other animals, squirrels choose a homesite that offers abundant food for their young. A free handout of corn, sunflower seed, or what-have-you may tempt them into building a big leafy nest in your backyard tree or gnawing their way into a nearby birdhouse.

- All squirrels and chipmunks dine on bird eggs, but red squirrels may have the most voracious appetite for these prized morsels, as well as for nestlings. If you're hosting red squirrels, think twice before nurturing their furry family.

- Squirrels are less of a problem in a large yard (of about a quarter-acre or more) with many trees and shrubs, simply because there's a lot more area to cover when prowling for nests. In this case, a squirrel feeder with plenty of ready food may be more alluring than a treasure hunt with no guaranteed payoff.

- Many species of squirrels breed early, and their youngsters are usually out and about, beginning to forage on their own, by the time songbirds are nesting. This means more predator pressure for our singing friends, but again, a generous handout of squirrel food may deter the squirrel youngsters from their quest.

- Predator guards on the poles or trees on which nest boxes are mounted have little effect, because squirrels will quickly figure out an alternate route. Predator guards on the box itself, though, which prevent squirrels from reaching inside, are definitely helpful. These metal or plastic tubes attach to the outside of the nest-box opening, so that squirrels can't reach their claws inside. You'll find nest guards at bird supply stores or at online sources such as those listed in the Resources section at the back of this book.

Cowbirds

Songbirds face yet another serious pest: brown-headed and bronzed cowbirds that lay their eggs in other birds' nests so those hapless adoptive parents have to raise them. Every size of songbird is targeted by these parasites, from large cardinals to tiny wood warblers. And any nest is fair game, even those built in birdhouses. I've seen tiny black-capped chickadees doing their best to keep a squawking cowbird fledgling satisfied.

Out of the hundreds of North American birds, only a scant handful have learned to recognize cowbird eggs and shove them overboard. The rest raise them with as much care and attention as if the big eggs and hatchlings were their own.

The brown-headed cowbird shows up in spring, usually about goldfinch time, making a beeline for our feeders. Males go through elaborate posturing "dances" to attract the grayish females, and they're fascinating to watch.

Opening the Door

Cowbirds don't usually venture deep into the woods to parasitize songbird nests. They stay fairly close to the woods' edge or zero in on birds of more open spaces.

Our backyards are ideal habitat for cowbirds,

Even birdhouses won't stop a parasitizing cowbird, if it can squeeze inside to lay its egg in another bird's nest. Can you spot the one from the dastardly cowbird? The eastern bluebird parents can't.

and many backyard songbirds already deal with their depredations. Regrettably, we're making more opportunities for these parasitic birds all the time. As we add roads and clear patches of forest to build houses or other buildings, we create great cowbird habitat. Not a good thing for the wood thrushes, wood warblers, and other forest birds that choose nesting sites near the edge of that now-fragmented forest—or in our backyard.

Cross Your Fingers

That's about all we can do when it comes to cowbirds. These nest parasites and their eggs are protected by federal law, for starters, even if we were inclined to take drastic measures.

As for possible deterrents, there aren't any surefire solutions, other than to stop feeding birds in springtime—which is exactly when the most beautiful tanagers, orioles, buntings, rose-breasted grosbeaks, and other migrant songbirds are showing up at our feeders.

These measures may help reduce the problem:

- Switch to feeding only suet, soft foods, nectar, and fruits in spring. Without the seeds they seek, cowbirds may go elsewhere.

- Use exclusionary feeders that bar larger birds from seeds, nuts, and similar foods, and don't feed crackers or other grain products on open tray feeders in spring.

Don't bet on the results, though. Even if cowbirds find no food at your place and go elsewhere, they won't go far. And come egg-laying time for female cowbirds, the nests in our backyards are still likely to be on their hit lists.

This Steller's jay couldn't eat just one—he carried off every Dorito to stash, while other birds enjoyed their seeds in peace.

Jays, Grackles, and Blackbirds

It's not only big numbers that cause a problem. A mere couple of jays can be an aggravation, too. Can't they leave just a few of those precious nuts for the Carolina wren instead of gobbling up every one like a vacuum cleaner?

Nope. They can't. Jays will eat their favorite foods if they're available, and they'll carry every bit away to cache if their bellies are already full. I don't mind that aspect of their behavior, because I get a kick out of these beautiful, feisty birds. And I know they provide a real service to other birds, by alerting them to predators and by playing a major role in driving away dangers.

On the other hand, other birds' eggs and nestlings are among the favored foods of jays, just as they are of yellow-headed blackbirds, grackles, crows, and other large omnivorous birds.

Luckily, unlike squirrels or raccoons that help themselves to the entire contents of a nest, these birds usually snatch just one egg or nestling. Although they may make return trips, their chances of getting the whole brood are lessened, because the parent birds have another opportunity to drive them away.

SCAT!

Cats are ranked right near the top as one of the worst dangers to songbirds, with staggering estimates of millions of birds killed every year. Since we really have no idea how many cats prowl backyards, woods, and fields, it's impossible to pinpoint the number of birds killed by them. All we know is that it's a lot. A whole lot.

I've yet to meet a cat that won't kill a songbird if the opportunity presents itself. And when we make our yards appealing to birds, that opportu-

Cat Myths Debunked

Even if your kitty is the cutest, gentlest creature on earth, you need to be aware of its genetic predisposition to kill birds. Here's what I've heard from cat owners, and here's the truth.

CAT OWNER'S ARGUMENT	MY BOTTOM LINE
"My cat doesn't kill birds."	Yes, it does. Unless it's on a leash or in a cage, a cat is a natural-born killer.
"I only put Kitty outside at night."	That's when birds are sleeping and most vulnerable in their nests. They can be destroyed in a flash—nestlings and parent alike.
"My cat is declawed."	It can still pounce and bite.
"I don't let my cat out in nesting season."	Birds are around year-round.
"My feeder's so high, my cat can't reach it."	What about those sparrows, juncos, and other birds on the ground?
"I'm willing to lose a few birds; it's too inconvenient to keep my cat inside."	Now you're telling the truth.

nity presents itself every day, all day. The only solution? Keep our cats indoors.

Anti-Cat Measures

Even if we're the most responsible of pet owners, keeping our own complaining cats indoors, other felines may still show up in our backyards. They're drawn by the birds at the feeders, in the garden, and on the ground.

Asking a neighbor to keep their cat at home is a touchy subject, so I usually skirt the issue and simply chase the cat away, whoever it belongs to. Hard for a neighbor to complain, when their cat shouldn't be in my backyard to begin with.

I've never used a live trap to nab stray cats, but I have scared them off by temporarily "trapping" the cat inside my yard. A fence around the whole place would be ideal, but I've made do with just a piece of relatively inexpensive 48-inch-high wire fence. Here's how you can do it, too:

- If a cat starts patrolling your yard regularly, scare it off by running at it, hollering, clapping, banging cooking pots, throwing water, or using a "super soaker" type squirt gun.

- Watch which way the cat exits. Most cats use the same exit route every time.

- Repeat the scare-it-off routine for several visits, then block its exit with the wire fencing. The fence doesn't need to be attached to a lot of fence posts to serve its purpose; one anchor on each end will do the trick.

- Next time you scare off the cat, it'll run head-long into the fence. Keep charging the cat, getting closer. Panic time! That kitty knows you mean business, and that experience of being trapped against the fence is often enough of a scare to keep the feline from coming back for a long time.

OTHER BIRD EATERS AND NEST DESTROYERS

Songbirds are pretty low on the eat-or-be-eaten totem pole, and nestlings and eggs are even lower. A host of wild creatures patrols our backyards looking for a meal—and they don't stop at the feeder. Raccoons, opossums, skunks, rats, weasels, owls, and snakes all include songbird eggs and nestlings in their diets and some eat adult birds, too.

We can't outwit these predators, but we can give our songbirds safe shelter, should they choose to make use of it. Include a number of spiny, thorny, prickly shrubs and trees in your backyard, which help deter climbing bird eaters.

Evergreen hollies (*Ilex* spp.), honey locust trees (*Gleditsia triacanthos),* dense shrub roses and climbing roses (*Rosa* spp.), barberries (*Berberis* spp.), junipers (*Juniperus* spp.), and other spiky sorts are popular places for sleeping and nesting songbirds. Their natural thorny barricade is tricky to penetrate by predators on the prowl.

To discourage predators and to keep raccoons and opossums from eating your suet and other feeder foods, use feeders that they can't climb to or access. Tube feeders, caged feeders, and bluebird feeders will discourage these opportunists from plowing through your seeds or pulling down your suet. Which is not to say they won't try: I've had 'coons remove what I thought were securely attached caged feeders and carry them off to try to eat the suet and soft food inside.

Deer and bears are much more difficult to deal with. If deer are a problem, raise your feeder out of their reach—their reach when standing on hind legs, that is. Or set up a deer-feeding area as a decoy with corn, apples, and other foods they love.

If bears frequent your area, remove your feeders and clean up all spilled seed. It's simply too risky to feed birds in bear country, especially in spring, when the bruins come out of hibernation and natural food is still scarce.

To discourage snakes from slithering up into

Get Baffled
A SLIPPERY SLOPE FOR PREDATORS

It takes only a few minutes to wrap a sheet of metal around the pole or install a baffle collar, either homemade or storebought, below the house. They're well worth the investment—about $25 for a sturdy, long-lasting baffle that's easy to clip to a metal pole.

a shrub or tree, pile the thorny clippings from roses and other shrubs in a wide circle around the trunk. The slitherers may reconsider before trying to cross.

An Ounce of Prevention

There's a lovely home surrounded by several acres on the Oregon coast, along a narrow road that leads to a state park. The yard is part natural and part landscaped, filled with beautiful flowers and trees. It should be a beautiful place, but there's something wrong with the picture: a tall fence topped by shining coils of razor wire runs around the whole property.

Now I'm all in favor of privacy, but the message that fence sends is a little different than "Please do not disturb." I'm sure those folks have their reasons, and I don't know their story, but what that fence says to me is "We live in fear." The fence also reminds me that staying safe is the top priority for every animal, including us.

Birds on the nest—and in the nest—are especially vulnerable. To keep nest-box birds safe, add a birdhouse guard at its entrance hole before you mount the box. These inexpensive, rigid plastic or metal tubes extend a few inches from the entrance to prevent squirrels, raccoons, cats, and other pests from finagling a hand inside to reach the birdies. Songbirds quickly learn to enter through the guards and can raise their families in safety. You'll find nest guards at bird supply stores or at the online sources listed in Resources at the back of this book.

RODENTS

Seed attracts rodents, there's no doubt about it. To avoid the problem entirely, you can try feeding only "no waste" type seed mixes, in which every bit is edible by your songbirds. Of course, the birds will still spill the bits of seed, so you'll have to feed only the amount that birds can clean up in a single day.

That's not the way most of us feed birds, which is why most of us have to deal with chipmunks, mice, or other small rodents at some point. I generally let nature take its course—in the form of owls. Screech owls and other owls often include feeding stations on their nighttime rounds, precisely because of those tasty little rodents.

Can't . . . quite . . . reach. . . . Not with an extension tube at the entrance, you can't, you doggone raccoon! Go find supper somewhere else.

And here we have a double-edged sword: Those same owls aren't above snatching a sleeping bird for supper. Still, rodent control may be worth the trade-off, since poison bait and snap traps can't be used at a feeder—they'd kill birds.

If rats show up at your feeder, it's time to clean up seed and remove the feeders for a few weeks until they move on. A harsh measure, to be sure, but way better than having rats come into your house. And that's often their next step, as they move closer to your food supply.

STINGING SWEET-EATERS

Ants, wasps, yellow jackets, hornets—insects love sweet fruit, jelly, and nectar. And unfortunately, most of the biggest fans have a wicked bite or sting.

You can protect nectar feeders with bee guards and ant moats to pretty much eliminate the problem. But when it comes to that all-too-attractive jelly sitting right out in the open, there's no way to bar the door.

To reduce your chances of getting stung, keep your jelly and fruit feeders well away from sitting spots and walkways. For even more insurance, switch to a seasonal schedule when feeding jelly.

Late spring is the best time to offer this super-sweet treat. That's when the songbirds who love jelly are moving through on migration, and insects aren't yet present in big numbers.

I remove my jelly feeder before highly aggressive yellow jackets and bald-faced hornets find it in late summer—and find it they will. Although I miss watching the birds scoop up their jelly, it's best to play it safe.

Honeybees feed peaceably on drips at a nectar feeder, but the yellow jacket at top is a meanie who drives away all competitors—including people who walk nearby.

For Further Reading

For all sorts of fascinating information about every bit of bird life, from plumage to eating habits to nesting materials to calls and songs:

Bent, Arthur Cleveland, ed. *Life Histories of North American Birds.* Many volumes; various publication dates over about a 20-year period. Many are out of print but can still be found in used bookshops and online; try www.abebooks.com or www.amazon.com.

Birds of North America Online. Cornell University. http://www.bna.birds.cornell.edu. This extensive website requires a paid subscription; you can try a sample page before you buy. For a lighter version, try Cornell's free site, All About Birds, at http://www.birds.cornell.edu/.

Roth, Sally. *The Backyard Bird Lover's Field Guide.* Emmaus, PA: Rodale, 2007.

Roth, Sally. *Backyard Bird Secrets for Every Season.* Emmaus, PA: Rodale, 2009.

For a deeper look at the scientific matters mentioned in this book:

Bennett, Andrew, Innes Cuthill, Julian Partridge, and Klaus Lunau. "Ultraviolet Plumage Colors Predict Mate Preferences in Starlings." *Proceedings of the National Academy of Sciences of the United States of America* 94, no. 16 (1997): 8618–21.

Bergtold, W.H. "A Study of the House Finch." *The Auk* 30, no. 1 (Jan. 1913): 40–73.

Bermúdez-Cuamatzin, Eira, Alejandro A. Ríos-Chelén, Diego Gil, and Constantino Macías Garcia. "Experimental Evidence for Real-Time Song Frequency Shift in Response to Urban Noise in a Passerine Bird." *Biology Letters* 7, no. 1 (Feb. 23, 2011): 36–38.

Cezilly, Frank, and Ruedi G. Nager. "Comparative Evidence for a Positive Association between Divorce and Extra-Pair Paternity in Birds." *Proceedings of the Royal Society B: Biological Sciences* 262, no. 1363 (Oct. 1995): 7–12.

Del Rio, Carlos Martínez. *Sugar Preferences in Birds: Physiological and Ecological Correlates.* Gainesville, FL: University of Florida, 1990.

Dhuique-Mayer, Claudie, Anne-Laure Fanciullino, Cecile Dubois, and Patrick Ollitrault. "Effect of Genotype and Environment on Citrus Juice Carotenoid Content." *Journal of Agricultural and Food Chemistry* 57, no. 19 (Oct. 2009): 9160–68.

Hooge, Philip. "Maintenance of Pair-Bonds in the House Finch." *The Condor* 92, no. 4 (1990): 1066–67.

Hoye, Bethany, and William Buttemer. "Inexplicable Inefficiency of Avian Molt? Insights from an Opportunistically Breeding Arid-Zone Species, *Lichenostomus penicillatus.*" *PLoS ONE* 6, no. 2 (2011): e16230.

Huang, Ya-Chun, and Neal A. Hessler. "Social Modulation during Songbird Courtship Potentiates Midbrain Dopaminergic Neurons." *PLoS ONE* 3, no. 10 (2008): e3281.

Luther, David, and Luis Baptista. "Urban Noise and the Cultural Evolution of Bird Songs." *Proceedings of the Royal Society B: Biological Sciences* 277, no. 1680 (Feb. 7, 2010): 469–73.

MacDougall, Amy, and Robert Montgomerie. "Assortative Mating by Carotenoid-Based Plumage Colour: A Quality Indicator in American Goldfinches, *Carduelis Tristis*." *Naturwissenschaften* 90, no. 10 (2003): 464–67.

McGraw, Kevin J., and Geoffrey E. Hill. "Male Attentiveness, Seasonal Timing of Breeding and Long-Term Pair Bonding in the House Finch (*Carpodacus Mexicanus*)." *Behaviour* 141, no. 1 (Jan. 2004): 1–14.

Mennill, Daniel J. "Female Black-Capped Chickadees Eavesdrop on Male Song Contests to Make Extra-Pair Mating Decisions." *Science* 296, no. 5569 (May 3, 2002): 873.

Mennill, Daniel J., Stéphanie M. Doucet, Robert Montgomerie, and Laurene M. Ratcliffe. "Achromatic Color Variation in Black-Capped Chickadees, *Poecile Atricapilla*: Black and White Signals of Sex and Rank." *Behavioral Ecology and Sociobiology* 53, no. 6 (2002): 350–57.

Meyer, Gretchen, and Mark Witmer. "Influence of Seed Processing by Frugivorous Birds on Germination Success of Three North American Shrubs." *The American Midland Naturalist* 140 (1998): 129–39.

Morell, Virginia. "Evolution of Sex: A New Look at Monogamy." *Science* 281, no. 5385 (Sept. 25, 1998): 1982–83.

Reichard, Ulrich, and Christine Boesch, eds. *Monogamy: Mating Strategies and Partnerships in Birds, Humans, and Other Mammals.* Cambridge: Cambridge University Press, 2003.

Reid, J. M., Peter Arcese, Alice L. E. V. Cassidy, Sara M. Hiebert, James N. M. Smith, Philip K. Stoddard, Amy B. Marr, and Lukas F. Keller. "Fitness Correlates of Song Repertoire Size in Free-Living Song Sparrows (*Melospiza Melodia*)." *The American Naturalist* 165, no. 3 (2005): 299–310.

Society for the Diffusion of Useful Knowledge. *The Penny Cyclopædia of the Society for the Diffusion of Useful Knowledge.* London: Charles Knight, 1842.

Wilkie, Susan E., Peter M. A. M. Vissers, Debipriya Das, Willem J. DeGrip, James K. Bowmaker, and David M. Hunt. "The Molecular Basis for UV Vision in Birds: Spectral Characteristics, cDNA Sequence and Retinal Localization of the UV-Sensitive Visual Pigment of the Budgerigar (*Melopsittacus Undulatus*)." *Biochemical Journal* 330 (1998): 541–47.

Resources

BIRD FEEDERS, BIRD FOOD, AND BIRDHOUSES

All of the seeds and soft foods mentioned in this book are widely available at discount stores, farm stores, and bird supply stores. You'll find a selection of feeders at these places, too, along with some birdbaths, including classic concrete or pottery pedestal models, and usually some birdhouses, too. Ask about anti-pest models, if problem animals like bear, deer, squirrels, or other critters are scarfing down your birdseed.

If you can't find what you're looking for locally, or if you just want to explore the wide world of bird supplies, check out online and mail-order sources. Here's a small sampling of the many suppliers for backyard birds:

Hurley-Byrd
462 Williams Cross Way
Fairmont, West Virginia 26554
877-363-0199
www.hurleybyrd.com

You'll find only feeders at this source; no foods, houses, or baths. But what feeders they are—their beautiful, simple lines and natural wood make them the standout among all of the fussy, fancy, too-small feeders on the market. Crafted out of clear-grade western cedar, they're built to last. You'll find a variety of sizes and styles, all designed for the way birds like to eat. And you can even buy your deer a feeder of their own at this source, which makes heavy-duty feeders and troughs for larger wild friends.

Duncraft
102 Fisherville Rd.
Concord, NH 03303
888-879-5095
www.Duncraft.com

An extensive selection of foods, including mealworms; many feeders and poles; well-made birdhouses; nest guards; birdbaths and misters. Duncraft sells one of the best birdbaths I've ever used—a naturalistic faux-rocky pool that warblers, tanagers, thrushes, and other forest birds take to as if were the real thing. You'll find many anti-pest feeders in their catalog, too.

BestNest
4750 Lake Forest Dr., Ste 132
Cincinnati, OH 45242
877-562-1818 or 513-232-4225
www.Bestnest.com

Lots of bird foods, feeders (including anti-pest styles), houses, nest guards, and birdbaths, plus ladybug houses, arbors, and other fun additions to your bird-friendly backyard. Best Nest has a big selection of appealing "human style" birdhouses—you'll find everything from a Nantucket Cape Cod to a cozy cottage. I prefer the uncluttered look of unadorned nest boxes, but these would make pretty yard accents, even if they don't get any tenants.

Bird-House-Bath.com (online only)
www.bird-house-bath.com

All kinds of foods, plus an unbelievable selection of artsy feeders and birdbaths to drool over, as well as the usual types. I fell in love with the sculptured pair of cupped hands that proffer a handful of seed, but at more than $300 . . . well, that's a whole lotta birdseed.

Insect Foods

Oregon Feeder Insects
Office: 208-642-8190
Toll free voice: 877-314-4411
Toll free fax: 877-642-8190
www.oregonfeederinsects.com

This small company began in 1984 with its first product, the Oregon Suet Block. The suet is blended with insects (particularly house flies, raised for the purpose), and it's irresistible to wrens, catbirds, thrashers, bluebirds, brown creepers, and many other birds. Other varieties of suet are available, too, as well as "Bug'Mmms," a bagged mix of seed enriched with insects. You may also be able to find the Oregon Suet Block at pet stores; it's popular with cage birds, too.

Duncraft
102 Fisherville Rd.
Concord, NH
888-879-5095
www.Duncraft.com

One of the first bird suppliers to introduce mealworm feeding to America (it was already a hit in England), Duncraft is a great source for well-packaged mail-order mealworms, waxworms, and other larvae and insect foods. You can buy them dead or alive, in small or large quantities, and you'll find a very good selection of feeders for them, too. If you're a newbie at feeding mealworms, you'll find the staff friendly and helpful.

HOT PEPPER-TREATED SEED

Ask your bird supply store for treated seed, or check online sources, such as:

Cole's Wild Bird Products Co.
P.O. Box 2227
Kennesaw, GA 30156
877-426-8882
www.coleswildbird.com

The "Hot Meats" line includes hulled sunflower seeds; suet blocks; and a cardinal blend with safflower. The company also sells bottled "Flaming Squirrel Seed Sauce" so you can treat your own bird foods. You'll find other premium seed mixes and foods on the site, too.

Squirrel Free, Inc.
255 Great Arrow Ave.
Buffalo, New York, 14207
888-636-1477
www.hotbirdseed.com

This wholesale company experiments with treated seed, and sells their products through retailers. Visit their website to learn about the research that's gone into the products, and to find a list of retailers in your area.

BIRDBATHS, FOUNTAINS, AND MISTERS

Many of the previously mentioned sources for bird foods and supplies also carry birdbaths, fountains, misters, and other water devices. You can also check these suppliers for your backyard water needs:

Hayneedle.com
9394 West Dodge Rd. Ste. 300
Omaha, NE 68114
800-216-2616
Contact_us@hayneedle.com
www.birdbaths.com
866-579-5182

Many styles of birdbaths and other ways to offer water to your birds, including baths with a built-in solar fountain.

Gardener's Supply Company
128 Intervale Rd.
Burlington VT 05401
888-833-1412
www.gardeners.com

If you want more bugs, butterflies, and birds, and a chemical-free yard, this company offers a wide range of garden tools and supplies, birdbaths, and other temptations, from practical to pretty. More garden hoses and nozzles than you ever knew existed, plus a good selection of baths and solar fountains.

CRAFTS AND PROJECTS

I find great inspiration for bird projects at just about any store I enter, which is why I try to keep from entering stores—too many crafty ideas to add to the "Someday I'll try this" list!

Dollar stores, discount stores, craft shops: All of them have items that can be adapted to use as feeders, birdbaths, nest guards, you name it. And then there are yard sales, my favorite source for cheap finds I can include in projects.

Some items can be tricky to track down, though, so I also shop online for specific needs. Here are a few sources for items I used in various projects in this book; you'll find other suppliers by searching online for the item you need.

Strong Magnets

Force Field
2606 West Vine Dr.
Fort Collins, CO 80521
888-727-3327
www.wondermagnet.com

Great selection of very strong magnets in all sorts of shapes and sizes at reasonable prices, from a small family-owned company. Ideal for attaching bird feeders to your window, or just plain fun to play with or give as gifts.

Applied Magnets
1111 Summit Avenue Suite #8
Plano, TX 75074
800-379-6818
www.magnet4less.com

Another good source for strong magnets of all varieties.

Suction Cups

Can't find extra-strong suction cups at your local discount store? Here's the industrial version, held in place practically forever via a vacuum handle.

ANVER Corp.
36 Parmenter Rd.
Hudson, MA 01749
800-654-3500
www.anver.com/document/vacuum%20
    handcups/hndcup-manual.htm

No direct sales on the website, but you can search for a dealer near you.

BIRDSONG RESOURCES

Parabolic Microphone

This isn't a low-budget item, so you'll want to do your own research if you're planning to invest in this item. These websites are a good place to start getting educated; you'll find others with a Net search.

Markertek Video Supply
http://www.markertek.com/Audio-
    Equipment/Microphones/Parabolic-
    Microphones/JonyJib/JONYSHOT.
    xhtml
1 Tower Drive
PO Box 397
Saugerties, New York (USA) 12477
800-522-2025

Telinga Microphones
http://www.telinga.com/
Pl. 129 Botarbo
S-748 96 Tobo
Sweden
Tel: int+46 295 310 01
Fax: int+46 295 310 01
e-mail telinga@bahnhof.se

Birdsong Identification Recordings

Many sources sell CDs of bird songs; you can even get an app for your smartphone, so you can carry it with you when you're in the yard or out exploring. Start by looking for the recordings in bird supply stores, or search online. You'll also find the recordings on www.amazon.com.

Birdwatching.com
http://www.birdwatching.com/cds/index.html
Online only

An extensive selection of bird song recordings, including the Stokes and Petersen audio CDs, as well as others. You'll find other great nature recordings here, too, including frogs and toads.

BOOKS

All books mentioned in the preceding chapters are widely available at bookstores or online. For out-of-print books, including Margaret Morse Nice's *Studies in the Life History of the Song Sparrow,* Volume I and Volume II, check www.abebooks.com or www.amazon.com for used copies.

WATER FEATURES

Check your local big box store or home supply store to find waterfalls, pond kits, and other elements for your bird-friendly yard. These online sources will give you an idea of what's available; you can also order the products through them.

Home Depot
http://www.homedepot.com/buy/outdoors/outdoor-living/wfk16-waterfall-weir-kit-6126.html

Berkey Supply Inc.
http://www.berkeysupply.com/vanishing-waterfall-kits-backyard-waterfall-kits.html
15500 Woodinville-Redmond Road
Woodinville, WA 98072
Building C-100
800-959-8353
Email: support@berkeysupply.com

Amazon
http://www.amazon.com

Many companies retail their water features through Amazon.

MOTION-ACTIVATED CAT CHASER

To find a device that hooks up to your hose to deter cats and other trespassers with a sudden blast of water, or ultrasonic devices that repel them with sound, check bird supply stores, well-stocked garden centers, mail-order sources such as those listed above, or suppliers such as these:

Biocontrol Network
5116 Williamsburg Rd
Brentwood, TN 37027
800-441-2847
www.biconet.com

SafePetProducts.com
KMP Products LLC
1060 Zygmunt Circle
Westmont, IL 60559
888-977-7387

http://www.safepetproducts.com

PLANTING FOR BIRDS

Native Plants

It's much easier to find native plants these days than it once was. Start by asking your local nursery for native junipers, native oaks, native shrubs such as spicebush or arrowwood, or whatever natives you're looking for. If you have a nursery that specializes in native plants in your area, check it out. Ask for whatever it is you want; if it's not in stock, the owners may be able to acquire it. And just asking for a plant creates a demand that savvy nursery owners will pay attention to.

Independently owned nurseries are the best bet. Native plants—the same plants that are common as dirt in wild places—are often hard to find at garden centers. When I do manage to find a few, they're often priced higher than common ornamentals, probably because there's a smaller demand for them. But even the garden centers of big-box stores are beginning to stock some native species—and the more often native plants are requested by their customers, the more likely that stock will increase.

Another good place to find natives is at plant sales. I keep an eye on my newspaper in spring, looking for plant sales by garden clubs, plant conservation groups, native plant societies, and other organizations that may have interesting native plants for sale—usually at bargain prices.

The Internet has been a boon for finding mail-order sources for unusual plants. Not so long ago, only a handful of nurseries specialized in native plants; today, there are scores of them, in every area of the country. Just do a search for "native plant nursery [your state]" and see what turns up.

To find out what kind of experiences others have had with the company you're considering buying from, you can read the reviews by actual customers on the website "Garden Watchdog," http://davesgarden.com/gwd/. This site provides a great service, acting as a sort of Better Business Bureau for mail-order gardeners.

If you can't find natives nearby, check mail-order or online sources, such as these:

All Native Garden Center
300 Center Rd.
Fort Myers, FL 33907
239-939-9663
www.nolawn.com

Fabulous plants with tropical flair, and natives that can take the heat and dry spells. More than 200 native Florida species of plants, many of them superb for songbirds and hummingbirds. No mail-order services currently, but worth the drive; the staff includes two National Wildlife Federation Backyard Wildlife Habitat Stewards, so you'll find plenty of information just for the asking.

Blake Nursery
316 Otter Creek Road
Big Timber, MT 59011
406-932-4195
www.blakenursery.com

Specializes in plants for western gardens, including a terrific selection of hardy Montana natives that will thrive elsewhere in the West, too—or give that western touch to an eastern garden.

Digging Dog Nursery
P.O. Box 471
Albion, CA 95410
707-937-1130
www.diggingdog.com

Get ready to fall in love—this catalog has so many unusual plants that songbirds adore, you can fill your yard *and* your neighbor's with great finds. You'll also discover other interesting perennials, including native plants for hummingbirds. Specializes in plants for the Southwest, but many of these beauties will thrive elsewhere, too.

Forestfarm
990 Tetherow Rd.
Williams, OR 97544
541-846-7269
www.forestfarm.com

Plant addicts, beware: One look at this chunky, jam-packed catalog and you'll be hooked. An unbelievably vast selection of thousands of plants, including natives from across America. Lots of favorite plants in my gardens have come from Forestfarm over the years, and I've been thrilled every time with their superior size and vigor.

Hamilton Native Outpost
16786 Brown Road
Elk Creek, MO 65464
417-967-2190
www.hamiltonseed.com

Seeds and plants for native grasses, prairie flowers, native shrubs and trees, and other great finds.

High Country Gardens
2902 Rufina St.
Santa Fe, NM 87507
800-925-9387
www.highcountrygardens.com

Want a nice low water bill? Explore the fabulous drought-tolerant perennials and shrubs in this enticing catalog. Many natives, including a huge variety of penstemons for hummingbirds, plus many other bird-beloved perennials, native grasses, and shrubs.

Las Pilitas Nursery
8331 Nelson Way
Escondido, CA 92026
760-749-5930
www.laspilitas.com

Discover wildflowers, shrubs, and trees for Southern California, many of them natives. This company emphasizes gardening for butterflies, birds, hummingbirds, and other wildlife, and you'll turn up all kinds of must-have plants. If you can't visit either of the two locations in person, you can browse and order online.

Prairie Nursery
P. O. Box 306
Westfield, WI 53964
800-476-9453
www.prairienursery.com

Prairie plants are tough and adaptable, and this company has supplied many of those in my gardens. Reasonable prices and a super informative catalog chock-full of beautiful grasses, coneflowers, perennial sunflowers, and other wildflowers.

Raintree Nursery
391 Butts Rd.
Morton, WA 98356
800-391-8892
www.raintreenursery.com

Terrific fruit trees and bushes for people—and birds! It's a treat to open a well-packed box from this company and find big, healthy, high-quality plants rarin' to go. You'll discover all of the usual fruits and berries, plus a great selection of varieties that are hard to find elsewhere, such as mulberries and native fruits.

Tripple Brook Farm
37 Middle Road
Southampton, MA 01073
413-527-4626
www.tripplebrookfarm.com

Hundreds of fabulous plants—I need a bigger yard!—including native viburnums and many, many other natives.

Woodlanders, Inc.
1128 Colleton Ave.
Aiken, SC 29801
803-648-7522
www.woodlanders.net

One of the older native plant specialists (since 1979), Woodlanders offers mouth-watering natives for the Southeast. Call for a catalog; no online shopping—yet.

FLOWERS AND GRAINS FOR BIRD GARDENS

Planting a few handfuls of birdseed from your feeder is the simple way to start a birdseed garden. But lots of other plants supply excellent seeds for birds. You can find seeds for zinnias, cosmos, and other bird favorites on local seed racks. Or you can discover the wider world of bird seeds in mail-order catalogs and websites. Look for grains in catalogs, as well as seeds for annual flowers that birds like. If you have a big yard, check out prices for seeds in bulk. Here are just a few of my favorites; you'll find dozens of others online.

Abundant Life Seeds
P.O. Box 279
Cottage Grove, OR 97424
541-767-9606
http://www.abundantlifeseeds.com/

Abundant Life Seed Foundation is famed for its collection of all-organic heritage seeds from around the world, many of them painstakingly gathered from gardeners who shared their own personal stock. Unfortunately, a devastating fire hit the warehouse in Port Townsend, WA, a few years ago. To help out this worthy cause, Territorial Seed of OR has taken over the mail-order catalog, so you can still find that wonderful selection of grains, grasses, sunflowers, Indian corn, flowers, and all the other treasures for which Abundant Life is known. Enjoy and support a good cause—the seeds that link us to gardeners of generations before.

American Meadows
223 Avenue D, Ste. 30
Williston, VT 05495
877-309-7333
www.americanmeadows.com

One of the very few companies that sells all-native mixes of wildflowers, instead of fattening the mix with inexpensive "filler" seeds. Also stocks many common annual flowers and wildflowers, plus regional mixes, both in small quantities and in bulk. Extremely reasonable prices—how about a pound of blue bachelor's-button seeds (*Centaurea cyanus*) for less than $12?

Native Seeds/SEARCH
3061 N. Campbell Ave.
Tucson, AZ 85719
520-622-5561
www.nativeseeds.org

This fantastic small company offers a catalog of about 350 types of seeds, every single one of them suitable for farming in arid lands, and many of them great for birds in any garden. From grasses to grains to sunflowers, these seeds will make birds drool. All are heritage types, handed down through the generations, including Native American varieties of corn and sunflowers, not to mention amaranth, millet, and others

that are perfect for a birdseed garden—or a loaf of bread. Simply reading the catalog is an education.

Pinetree Garden Seeds
P.O. Box 300
New Gloucester, ME 04260
207-926-3400
www.superseeds.com

The first company I ever bought mail-order seeds from, and still going strong decades later. This family company offers a huge selection of interesting annual flowers at reasonable prices. You'll also discover a great collection of sunflower varieties at prices cheap enough to try them all, plus graceful millets, wheat, corn, and other grains for birds.

Territorial Seed
P.O. Box 158
Cottage Grove, OR 97424
800-626-0866
http://www.territorialseed.com

You'll find a mix of interesting vegetables and bird-beloved annuals in this delectable catalog, including an unbelievable array of sunflowers. Look for grains and corn, too, including Native American varieties.

Wildseed Farms
425 Wildflower Hills
P.O. Box 3000
Fredericksburg, TX 78624
800-848-0078
www.wildseedfarms.com

A good source for fast-growing annual flowers with seeds that birds adore. Look for cosmos, zinnias, and many other bird faves, in packets or in bulk. You'll find low-priced wildflower mixes, too, but they're not entirely native. Personally, I don't mind red Flanders poppies (*Papaver rhoeas*) adding some zing to my flower beds, but if you prefer natives-only, you can make your own mix by buying seeds of individual plants.

Photo Credits

© Scott Sinklier/AGStockUSA/Alamy: page 202
© Roberta Olenick/All Canada Photos/Alamy: page 137
© Tim Zurowski/All Canada Photos/Alamy: pages 197, 290
© John Anderson/Alamy: page 276
© Linda Freshwaters Arndt/Alamy: pages 68, 217 (bottom), 249
© De Meester Johan/Arterra Picture Library/Alamy: page 304
© Mary Liz Austin/Alamy: page 254
© Krys Bailey/Alamy: page 316
© Barnes Custom Services/Alamy: page 185
© Vicki Beaver/Alamy: page 158
© Birdpix/Alamy: page 298 (top)
© Daub/Blickwinkel/Alamy: page 199 (bottom)
© Rick & Nora Bowers/Alamy: pages 37, 169, 251, 257
© Gay Bumgarner/Alamy: page 261
© John Cancalosi/Alamy: pages 109, 296
© Bruce Coleman Inc./Alamy: page 285 (bottom)
© Wendy Conway/Alamy: page 170
© Gary Carter/Corbis Premium RF/Alamy: page 49
© Derek Croucher/Alamy: page 58
© John Van Decker/Alamy: pages 163, 216 (top), 231
© Adam Jones/Danita Delimont/Alamy: page 24
© Marvin Dembinsky Photo Associates/Alamy: pages 101, 112
© Daniel Dempster Photography/Alamy: pages 16, 72, 317
© Andreas Von Einsiedel/Alamy: page 66
© Ensign Images/Alamy: page 264
© John T. Fowler/Alamy: page 288
© Ross Frid/Alamy: page 114
© Dwayne Fuller/Alamy: page 93
© Tim Gainey/Alamy: page 310
© Richard Mittleman/Gon2Foto/Alamy: page 308
© Holmes Garden Photos/Alamy: page 14
© Martin Hughes-Jones/Alamy: page 201
© iWebbtravel/Alamy: page 102
© Don Johnston/Alamy: page 156
© Andrea Jones Images/Alamy: page 125
© Doreen Kennedy/Alamy: page 134
© Linda Kennedy/Alamy: page 299
© Pat Kerrigan/Alamy: page 180
© B. LaRue/Alamy: page 234
© William Leaman/Alamy: pages 57 (top), 60, 71 (bottom), 86, 98, 99, 100, 111 (top, bottom), 129, 131, 150, 199 (top), 204, 216 (bottom), 229, 242, 260, 285 (top), 294, 298 (bottom)
© Cristina Lichti/Alamy: page 146
© Dave McAleavy Images/Alamy: page 74
© Charles Melton/Alamy: page 90
© Heather Angel/Natural Visions/Alamy: page 321
© Rolf Nussbaumer Photography/Alamy: page 172
© Bill Draker/Rolf Nussbaumer Photography/Alamy: page 89
© Heeb Christian/Prisma Bildagentur AG/Alamy: page 126 (bottom)

© Steve Round/Alamy: page 188
© Greg Ryan/Alamy: page 270
© Robert Shantz/Alamy: pages 108, 193
© Stone Nature Photography/Alamy: page 61
© Michael Stubblefield/Alamy: pages 62, 95 (left), 161, 194
© David Stuckel/Alamy: page 141
© Aidan Tompkins/Alamy: page 123
© Tom Uhlman/Alamy: pages 5, 209, 266
© Genevieve Vallee/Alamy: pages 64, 168
© Christopher Vernon-Parry/Alamy: page 139
© Cal Vornberger/Alamy: page 95 (right)
© Jennifer Weinberg/Alamy: page 2
© Jerry Whaley/Alamy: page 118
© Elizabeth Whiting & Associates/Alamy: page 232
© Wildlife Gmbh/Alamy: page 124
© Wildscape/Alamy: page 46
© Michael Habicht/Animals Animals: page 122
© Matt Bartmann: pages 7, 36, 148, 212, 223, 237, 238, 248, 269, 318
© Richard Cohen/Echo Valley: page 241 (top)
© Eyewire: page 26
© Shane Hutchinson: page 262
© Photodisc: page 106
© John W. Bova/Photo Researchers, Inc.: page 215
© Jim Zipp/Photo Researchers, Inc.: page 138
© Lee Leckey/Rodale Images: page 192
© Mitch Mandel/Rodale Images: page 217 (top)
© Sally Roth: pages 240 (left, right), 259, 301, 322
© G. Bailey/Vireo: page 80
© Spike Baker/Vireo: page 284
© G. Bartley/Vireo: pages 71 (top), 75
© R. & N. Bowers/Vireo: page 12
© R. Crossley/Vireo: pages 51, 56
© R. Curtis/Vireo: pages 18 (bottom), 35, 140
© R. & S. Day/Vireo: pages 126 (top), 178
© S. Fried/Vireo: pages 22, 147, 246
© D. Huntington/Vireo: page 27
© S. J. Lang/Vireo: page 120
© G. Lasley/Vireo: pages 34, 69, 241 (bottom)
© G. McElroy/Vireo: page 18 (top)
© J. McKean/Vireo: page 244
© A. Morris/Vireo: page 278
© C. Nadeau/Vireo: page 280
© Laure Neish/Vireo: pages 43, 115
© S. & S. Rucker/Vireo: pages 179, 233
© B. Schorre/Vireo: page 39
© J. Schumacher/Vireo: pages viii, 23, 226
© H. P. Smith, Jr./Vireo: pages 182, 306
© T. Vezo/Vireo: page 8
© Doug Wechsler/Vireo: page 57 (bottom)

Index

Boldface page numbers indicate photographs or illustrations. Underscored references indicate boxed text, charts, and graphs.